BETWEEN CATASTROPHE
AND REVOLUTION

BETWEEN CATASTROPHE AND REVOLUTION

ESSAYS IN HONOR OF MIKE DAVIS

Edited by
DANIEL BERTRAND MONK
and MICHAEL SORKIN

OR Books
New York · London

© 2021 Daniel Bertrand Monk and Michael Sorkin
Published in association with Terreform/UR, with support from the Graham Foundation.

Published by OR Books, New York and London
Visit our website at www.orbooks.com

All rights information: rights@orbooks.com

All rights reserved. No part of this book may be reproduced or transmitted in any form or by any means, electronic or mechanical, including photocopy, recording, or any information storage retrieval system, without permission in writing from the publisher, except brief passages for review purposes.

First printing 2021

Cataloging-in-Publication data is available from the Library of Congress.
A catalog record for this book is available from the British Library.

Typeset by Lapiz Digital Services. Printed by BookMobile, USA, and CPI, UK.

paperback ISBN 978-1-68219-277-1 • ebook ISBN 978-1-68219-279-5

For Joan...

*and for the millions of others
who have lost loved ones
to the "Monster at our Door."*

CONTENTS

Preface: "How About Just Plain 'Catastrophe and Revolution'?"   1
    Daniel Bertrand Monk

Introduction: A Dialectic of Catastrophe and Revolution   5
    Daniel Bertrand Monk

A Sorrowful Storm: Between Penitence and Anthropolitics
in the Anthropocene   11
    Mauro J. Caraccioli

Planetary Events, Climate Catastrophes, and the Limits
of the Human Sciences   29
    William E. Connolly and Jairus Grove

A Late Neoliberal Holocaust   55
    Don Mitchell

Settler Colonial Urbanism: From Waawiyaataanong to Detroit
at Little Caesars Arena   79
    Andrew Herscher

Steel Bloom: Lineages and Landmarks of Borderland Violence   97
    Ana Muñiz

Where Did the Future Go? Notes on the Fantasies and Strategies
of the Hyper-Right from the United States to Brazil   121
    Bruno Carvalho

Eruptions of Rage   147
    Mustafa Dikeç

A Theory of the Middle East: Oil for Insecurity, Permanent War,
and the Political Economy of Late Imperial America   161
    Jacob Mundy

Maximalist Elites and the Ecological Burden of Southern History   191
    Christian Parenti

Aviation, Hijackings, and the Eclipse of the "American Century" in the Middle East   223
    Waleed Hazbun

Lineages of Infrastructural Power: Los Angeles as a Logistical Nightmare   249
    Charmaine Chua

Death Cults of East Anglia   269
    China Miéville

The Calculus of Climate Change   287
    Andrew Ross

Gated Ecologies   307
    Rob Wallace, Kenichi Okamoto, and Alex Liebman

Othering the Mall   321
    Michael Sorkin

Contributors   349

PREFACE

"How About Just Plain 'Catastrophe and Revolution'?"[1]

Daniel Bertrand Monk

This collection of essays is the first to aggregate and, in some sense, document the afterlife of the kind of global ecological history that Mike Davis has developed in the course of his own efforts to analyze the relation between an urbanizing humanity and the Anthropocene. Most of its authors came to intellectual maturity in a time when Davis's arguments were already "out there," and served as inspiration for the further labor of others. Each of the works assembled here already assumes prima facie what Davis fought to reintroduce into debates about the historical trajectory of humanity under a neoliberal order: that one must recognize the affirmative character of given definitions of what is "realistic" in order to lay claim to what is "necessary."[2]

The collection begins with the reconsiderations of time and of history that are prefigured in Mike Davis's methodology of excavating "futures past." In the contributions of William Connolly and Jairus Grove and of Mauro Caraccioli, we are presented with a rich conversation on how a commonplace "sociogenic" periodization of history has precluded our ability to incorporate the fact of catastrophe into our temporal frameworks of understanding; and then, to link the Anthropocene with a "penitent ecology." The editors' introduction, moreover, situates Mike Davis's historical vision within a dialectic of catastrophism that cannot be accommodated into normative historiographic trajectories: this is a vision that refuses vulgar models of political transcendence as vigorously as it rejects narratives of resignation, however much it is confused for championing one or the other of these poles.

All contributions assembled here catalog/document the political career of the epistemic failures just introduced. Each essay is a contribution to what Davis—in wry fashion—once referred to as the field of "disaster studies," and each author has also developed the historiography of disaster far beyond what Mike Davis himself could have imagined. Where Davis's *Prisoners of the American Dream* documented the American working class's identification with the counterrevolution being waged against it, Don Mitchell, Andrew Herscher, and Ana Muñiz respectively reveal the next steps of the ensuing "slow holocaust" that has followed. Mitchell anticipates the attention that white people would finally give to the normalized killing of African-American men following the murder of George Floyd in 2020 by documenting how a longstanding police practice of engaging in the extrajudicial eradication of the indigent and racialized poor has been a political project hiding in plain sight for a long time. Herscher, in turn, shows how established Marxist narratives concerning the status of the urban underclass under disaster capitalism are actually inadequate to analyzing the conditions now facing the residents of Detroit, where the paradigm of settler colonialism better explains a condition in which the same racialized poor are "replaced rather than exploited." In a reversal of the story outlined in Davis's *Magical Urbanism*, Ana Muñiz shows how the children of the same Latinx generation responsible for reviving deindustrializing American cities with their casual labor now cement their *own* class position by policing migrants and the informal proletariat along the southern border, in the shadow of Donald Trump's "beautiful" wall.

It is all worse than we think. As a number of essays in this volume show, our disaster imaginary is rendered inadequate by the extent to which the neoliberal order actually feeds on given concepts of resistance to it, or of its sublation. In Brazil, as Bruno Carvalho shows, the very visions of urban modernity that once served to characterize it as the progressive country of the future—a utopia of racial coexistence in particular—now feed the fantasies of the Bolsonarist "hyper-right." With such shifts in consciousness, contemporary mass protests can no longer be understood as moments of revolutionary potential or fleeting hegemony, but are instances of an established "politics of rage," argues Mustafa Dikeç. In such a context, even geopolitical conflict can be a function of market logic. In the Middle East, Jacob Mundy suggests, America's efforts to ensure its hegemony have engendered "a new system of *oil for insecurity* premised on *permanent war* in the region."

In the time since Davis deciphered LA's morphology by reviewing the "contradictory impact of economic globalization" on urban and regional infrastructures, those contradictions have been normalized into oblivion or routinely acknowledged as a form of their disavowal. This is because those impacts are either mentioned on the way to forgetting them or amortized under "necessary evil" arguments that identify the private sector with the public good. In a sense, this was always the case, argues Christian Parenti, as he reframes the entire ecological history of the American South as a "soil-mining" project that effectively *depended* on an infrastructure of "underdevelopment," the social costs of which were externalized onto the enslaved and then the racialized poor. This logic of underdevelopment was, and remains, generalizable as a feature of empire, suggests Waleed Hazbun: twentieth-century infrastructures of "aeromobility" introduced by the US in the Middle East advanced a global extractive network in which logistical connections began to supersede the sites connected; in this way, political regression was naturalized as technocratic advancement. This figure/ground reversal between cities and "supply chain capitalism" is now complete, argues Charmaine Chua, as she lays out how the transformations of the port of Los Angeles (and regional transport arteries) now mark the city as an adjunct to a global logistics sector that "manages the circulation of goods, materials, and information" at a global scale.

The Los Angeles we have learned to associate with Davis's *City of Quartz* is already implicated in the making of a contemporary *Planet of Slums*, as capitalist mega-urbanization is accelerating toward—and is a primary cause of—the unfolding climate catastrophe. And yet, these transformations are also repeatedly assimilated as features of the status quo. Identifying climate change with "hyper-objects" that are sublime in both their scale and abstraction, China Miéville movingly reveals global warming's exteriority to any language we might deploy to describe it. Indeed, Miéville shows us how the gap between knowledge and understanding is left wide open, precisely *in the way* that we now talk about the heat itself. This does not mean that the same hyper-object may not be monetized, however. As Andrew Ross shows us, climate change is itself now treated as an extensive market opportunity by global risk insurance conglomerates and predatory lenders hedging against any rescue of the planet. In other words, capitalism continues to feed on the same alienation of Nature that it will "rationally" advance until we reach system collapse. In what amounts to a rebuttal to the instrumental reasoning of the catastrophic risk arbitrageurs themselves, Rob Wallace, Kenichi Okamoto, and Alex Liebman seek to model this alienation-cum-catastrophe in quantitative terms, referring to it as a "gated ecology" by means of which the agents of disaster capitalism segregate themselves conceptually from the planet against which they are betting.

This collection emerged out of a conversation between two friends about the profound importance of a third; a volume of essays in honor of Mike Davis seemed both necessary and overdue, Michael Sorkin and Daniel Bertrand Monk agreed. So did the contributors, who enthusiastically encouraged the editors to proceed with the project, regardless of the obstacles. In the course of its making, some of the collection's authors fell ill with COVID-19. Michael Sorkin died of the disease in March 2020, a day after shooting his coeditor an email exhorting him to finish the book. Sorkin's essay is, aptly, the last in this collection. In it he documents how, inscribed in the form of the National Mall in Washington, is the history of the United States' failure to realize the universals its founding documents invoke; at the same time, Sorkin shows us, those failures unconsciously serve to sustain the same regulative ideals. A vision of and a demand for an emancipated existence is sedimented in the built record of our inability to realize it.

The editors and authors of this work gratefully acknowledge the generosity shown by the Graham Foundation for the Arts and the Colgate University Research Council in bringing this project to fruition. Equally, they would like to recognize the important contributions of Cecilia Fagel and Deen Sharp of Terreform in the making of this volume. Marieke Krijnen was this project's soul, pure and simple. We are also deeply indebted to Colin Robinson for his gallantry and kindness at a crucial moment in the collection's history. Finally, this book exists because of the selflessness of Susanna Hecht and Anthony Fontenot. It would not have seen the light of day without the sacrifices they made on its behalf.

Endnotes

1. Michael Sorkin to Daniel Bertrand Monk, March 21, 2020. This was the last communication from Michael.
2. "Mike Davis on the Global Crisis: 'This Moment Is Not a Tunnel with a Bright Light at the End,'" *Salon*, July 9, 2020, https://www.salon.com/2020/07/09/mike-davis-on-the-global-crisis-this-moment-is-not-a-tunnel-with-a-bright-light-at-the-end/.

INTRODUCTION

A Dialectic of Catastrophe and Revolution

Daniel Bertrand Monk

> It's difficult you see
> To give up baby
> These summer scumholes
> This goddamned starving life.[1]
>
> —David Bowie

The jacket blurbs of any of Mike Davis's ten monographs present the reader with the image of an activist, former meatcutter, and truck driver who only happens to have won a MacArthur genius award and written some stuff about impending ecological and social doom. And yet, the man that *The Nation* has described as the "master of disaster prose" is clearly more than that.[2] The disruptions he has caused in the process of examining our shared *imagination* of disaster actually point to a rigorous and coherent intellectual project that is too easily misrepresented or overlooked. Even sympathetic evaluators seem unable to resist making statements like "judgement day is every day with Mike Davis."[3] His work is "overlooked" even as it is ubiquitously cited in the sense that Davis's systematic destruction of our collective destruction imaginary is part of an intellectual trajectory that can only be defined by what it negates.

BETWEEN CATASTROPHE AND REVOLUTION

Both the trajectory and its logic may be briefly sketched as a prosopography and intellectual history at once. Like those of Angela Davis, Stokely Carmichael, and many of his contemporaries, Mike Davis's politics were honed by his experiences in the oppositional mass actions of the sixties where, a decade before it hardened into a "City of Quartz," Los Angeles served as the capital of an "age of revolt."[4] Unlike many of his counterparts, however, Davis did not reject what he saw as a bourgeois, imperialist, racist, homophobic, and sexist postwar US culture only to then embrace and submit to the Soviets' "actually existing socialism," or any other variants of political or religious authority. Rather, in the experience of collective action itself, Davis encountered a "spirit of utopia" that he would later recognize in the revolutionary disruptions of the Paris Commune, the anarcho-syndicalist enclaves of fin-de-siècle Catalonia, Red Vienna, and California's Llano del Rio. To cite Ernst Bloch (one of Davis's philosophical influences): all of these "summon what is not," in the same sense that the younger Beethoven scandalously and without much cause declared himself to be a genius as part of the process of becoming one.[5] These are "traces," in Bloch's terms, of a potential future that interrupts the present and renders time into something indistinguishable from catastrophe—that is, indistinguishable from an interruption of the eternal sameness sedimented in our notions of progress.

This is not a naïve political theology of hope, however. A fateful encounter with the British New Left during a period of extended residence in England and Ireland (when Davis joined Verso and the *New Left Review*) coincided with—or influenced—a turn to political economy. And, with that, a consideration of the structural impediments to invoking a new proletarian mass politics and its consciousness. At the same time, Davis would reject the teleological gradualism of the New Left, and more particularly the model of historical transformation it fashioned out of suspect exceptionalist doxa concerning the emergence of a British working class in the absence of violent/open class struggle. More than this, by denying a place to the catastrophic interruptions of Nature in visions of history that were otherwise entirely anthropogenic in their orientation, it is clear that in the mind of Mike Davis, his contemporaries' arguments concerning the evolutionary path to proletarian hegemony actually *thwarted* both the time and the necessity of revolutionary possibility itself.

Davis's entire oeuvre rehearses a dialectic of catastrophe and revolution—that is, of an apocalyptic Nature that will not be subordinated to normative

INTRODUCTION

periodizations that would instrumentalize it as an adjunct to human history, but that, in the course of that refusal, potentiates both the consciousness and possibility of a revolutionary time. This accounts for the contrarieties animating Davis's early works, in which the problem of collective action—the failures of labor to gain political hegemony in the US—are examined instead as *triumphs* of collective action, and indeed of class war, waged by "postreformist" interests against both the racialized and indigenized poor in North America and the targets of American imperialism abroad. In *Prisoners of the American Dream* (1986) and *City of Quartz* (1990), the "sunbelt Bolshevism" of homeowners' associations in California's suburbs and neoliberal boosters in LA pointed to the need for insurgent alliances among members of a global precariat. A commodified Nature and naturalized political economy alike are referenced in these volumes, but chiefly in order to focus on their effects on the production of a grotesque urbanism.

This dialectic of catastrophe and revolution approaches self-conscious expression in *The Ecology of Fear* (1998), where a "natural" revolution—in the form of capitalism's encroachments on the Western landscape—meets a revolutionary environment in the form of firestorms that, in turn, reveal Angelinos' anxieties about an alienated Nature to be synonymous with dread of an imagined "incendiary other." (This is how the volume makes a sound case for "letting Malibu burn," for example: as the naturalized "view corridors" of the real estate industry reveal themselves to have always been the fire corridors of an ignored ecology, the return of a repressed Nature is then acknowledged and displaced onto the indigenized poor, who are in turn disproportionately sacrificed to the blaze . . .) The demographic authors of what Davis termed "a magical urbanism" to describe the Latinx remaking of the American metropolis in this way become the denizens of his *Dead Cities* (2002) instead.

In Davis's so-called disaster narratives, each inversion of received history necessarily points to the next. The tragic fires and bedraggled mountain lions of *Ecology of Fear* are synecdoches for a history that has denatured ecological processes of the planet as a whole, just as the forms of land speculation outlined in the book stand in for a mode of production to which we have given quasi-ecological status, along with the hierarchies attending its social Darwinist assumptions. In *Late Victorian Holocausts* (2001) and *Planet of Slums*, Davis abandons these metonyms so that the level of analysis is

7

finally systemic and planetary in scale. In *Late Victorian Holocausts*, global climate patterns and the economy of "long waves" are synchronized with one another via permanent and anticipatory forms of counterrevolution practiced by Great Britain's viceroys in India, Lord Lytton and Lord Curzon. They have an agentic origin. As Davis puts it, the New Imperialism becomes "the third gear of this catastrophic history."[6] The policies that made, displaced, and then killed the precariat of the Global South are not incidental to the confluence of economies and ecologies or an attendant "development gap," but the result of a politics knowingly advanced on utilitarian grounds. The reasons Lord Lytton allowed Indians to starve to death while their grain was exported elsewhere, return or persist in the IMF and the World Bank's expressions of concern about "dependency syndrome" a century later, when the structural adjustment policies they implemented were, in part, responsible for generating the largest single migration in human history and the ensuing creation of a *Planet of Slums* (2006).[7]

To recognize that the majority of the world's urban population is forced to seek shelter under a brutal regime of privatized squatting—on pavements in Mumbai, rooftops in Cairo, or cliffside shanties in Rio de Janeiro—is to invite speculation about the relation between a "surplus humanity" warehoused in this manner and the forms of agency or imagination that might alter the ecological fate of the planet as a whole.[8] (This is because the urbanization of humanity, as Davis reminds us, is the single most important cause of global warming.) In *Old Gods, New Enigmas* (2018), Davis takes up the same problem of subaltern agency raised by the "late capitalist triage of humanity" he documented in *Planet of Slums* and explicitly links it to the climate crisis, asking: "Who will build the Ark?" Splitting his response into what appear, at first, to be opposed "pessimistic" and "optimistic" imaginaries/scenarios, in actuality Davis advances a *single* dialectic of catastrophism that seems to recuperate the concept of revolutionary time as a logical/historical necessity. This is how: in the universalization of designations like "the Anthropocene," contemporary humanity both acknowledges the climate catastrophe it is making and simultaneously domesticates it in the [as the] *catastrophism* of various "'post-natural' ontologies."[9] In this way, a sober assessment of the possibility of catastrophic time—that is, of sudden intrusions of the future into the present—is abandoned in favor of a species of historical periodization that

INTRODUCTION

is indistinct from resignation. When we abandon ourselves in this fashion to a teleology of disaster, ideology mistakes itself for gritty realism. And, in the face of such a turn, the act of summoning "what is not" becomes simultaneously pragmatic and revolutionary: "either we fight for 'impossible' solutions to the increasingly entangled crisis of urban poverty and climate change, or become ourselves complicit in ... [the ongoing] triage of humanity."[10]

The global ecological history that Davis inaugurated in the oeuvre outlined here has always refused dogmatic closure in favor of an urgent program of action and thought premised on the negation of the neoliberal order's given alternatives. This is why it has enjoyed a viral career across a series of disciplines ranging from urban studies to history, geography, political science, and more. It is also why Davis's work has become a crucial referent for the production of new knowledges by a generation of scholars, artists, and activists represented in the pages of this volume. Beyond their willingness to delve into the catastrophes of the present that hide by not hiding in plain sight, what binds the studies assembled here to one another and to the work of Mike Davis is an appeal to "what is not" in the relentless critique of what *is*.

Endnotes

1. David Bowie, "Thru These Architect's Eyes," *Outside* (Arista/BMG, 1995).
2. Jane Holtz Kay, "Apocalypse Now?," *The Nation*, December 17, 2002, https://www.thenation.com/article/archive/apocalypse-now/.
3. Kay, "Apocalypse Now?
4. Mike Davis and Jon Wiener, *Set the Night on Fire: L.A. in the Sixties* (London: Verso, 2020), 3.
5. Ernst Bloch, *The Spirit of Utopia* (Stanford, CA: Stanford University Press, 2000), 3; Theodor W. Adorno, Shierry Weber Nicholsen, and Paul A. Kottman, "Ernst Bloch's Spuren: On the Revised Edition of 1959," in *Notes to Literature*, ed. Rolf Tiedemann (Columbia University Press, 2019), 204–5.
6. Mike Davis, *Late Victorian Holocausts* (London: Verso, 2002), 13.
7. Mike Davis, *Planet of Slums* (New York: Verso, 2006), 151–73. It bears stating that, although Davis acknowledges that the founders of contemporary political ecology, Nancy Watts and Michael Peluso, were important influences in the writing of *Late Victorian Holocausts*, a significant part of that work was completed after Davis joined the Faculty of History at SUNY Stony Brook. Encounters with a remarkable cadre of radical historians there—some whom were already developing historiographic arguments for what we now call "global history"—are also a part of this work's origin, as were the conversations Davis held with scientists at Columbia's Lamont-Doherty Earth Observatory, with whom he met to review the complexities of historical weather patterns. The origins of Davis's global environment history are multiple.
8. Davis, *Planet of Slums*, 176.
9. Mike Davis, *Old Gods, New Enigmas: Marx's Lost Theory* (London: Verso Books, 2018), xxi–xxii.
10. Davis, *Old Gods, New Enigmas*, 221.

A SORROWFUL STORM

Between Penitence and Anthropolitics in the Anthropocene

Mauro J. Caraccioli

Of the many lenses critical social theorists have developed to understand the present era, ruination is not usually one that comes to mind. There are several books, studies, and research collectives interested in how the catastrophic can serve as a potential site from where future forms of human life—if not just theories of the future—can emerge.[1] Mass extinctions, collapsed ecosystems, drought, and displacement are all mainstays of contemporary scholarship and media examining the effects of global climate change. Yet as the urbanization, automation, and large-scale dispossession that characterize our era of late capitalism expand, the crosshairs of ruination now seem to point at human activity itself. Indeed, proponents of the emergence of an "Anthropocene" have increasingly moved away from the mere epistemic dimensions of this concept toward what our present ecological condition means for the future of humanity itself. The human species today possesses a world-historical character that is no longer geared toward its own liberation. Rather, humanity now aims at a form of ecological domination that far surpasses the long-enduring optimism of a technological or providential fix to the problems posed by extraction, waste, and extinction.[2]

In this chapter, I turn to the distinct existential anxiety surrounding our contemporary ecological crisis. Specifically, I examine the social positioning of critics at the fringes of the so-called climate wars, as they offer contending narratives about humanity's future (or lack thereof) in the face of a dying planet. I am particularly concerned with articulating the growing sense of human penitence cultivated by voices who believe that we are on the brink of an ecological catastrophe. Though arguably a response to the innovation enthusiasts found in conventional sustainability narratives, ecological penitence has become a pervasive ethos among a growing number of climate change affirmers. It is also indicative of several political challenges. Most salient is the seemingly reactionary threat of wholesale class erasure, where rich and poor alike are allegedly judged equally in front of a grand, cosmic mea culpa. Though this verdict may seem reassuring to some, who think that money and class conflict no longer matter in the grand arc of the planet's demise, my goal is to show how a smothered class conflict remains latent within the eco-penitential vision.

I begin by examining the rise of what conventional media outlets have described as the "conceivable future," a normative shorthand for "painful ethical questions that previous generations did not have to confront."[3] Among the dilemmas present generations encounter is the legitimacy of having children, which is itself a stand-in for a spectrum of reproductive concerns over a future environmental collapse. I situate this crisis of fecundity within what I call the political economy of climate terror: a distinct form of rhetorical coping deployed by scholars, activists, and media figures alike in their dire assessments of the modern human condition. Juxtaposing evangelical and journalistic depictions of climate change's wars to come, I focus on what it is about climate catastrophe that downplays the power of mass politics while simultaneously exonerating capitalism as if it were a kind of ghost that cannot be exorcised. I conclude with a call for a kind of reflexivity that mediates the use of climate narratives with a critical analysis of collective reckoning that eschews solitude.

By addressing idealistic expressions of climate penance, my aim is to undo the distinction between two kinds of historical narratives: those that make contrition the centerpiece of their analysis and those that frame global political liberation as the goal of all human action. In this sense, I maintain that ecological penitence is but one side of the same coin of historicist reasoning: whether by death or deliverance, human salvation remains rooted in human agency. Instead of lamenting the challenges of climate change, critics and activists should reframe our collective futures as a reckoning over where our political imaginaries have failed. Doing so allows us to conceive of collective action as a necessary expression of climate change narratives, rather than as a response to them. Such forms of critical social thought may then help us to more confidently and imaginatively take on the multiple ends of the world, particularly as we currently know it.

The Guilt of a Conceivable Future

Environmentalists are no strangers to existential dilemmas. The very notions of conservation, preservation, sustainability, resilience, and a plethora of other watchwords are inherently about the limits of any ecosystem to endure human presence and (more often than not) exploitation. Yet much of the ethos behind "green" movements and ideologies has also been about human ingenuity in the face of crisis. Though critics may historically regard environmentalists as luddites, a significant strain of environmental activism in the Global North is rampantly optimistic about technology's capacity to solve specific ecological problems, as long as there are resources and the political will to do so.[4] Indeed, the dividing line between those who consider themselves environmentalists and those who do not is quite often ideological, rather than technological, based as it is on whether one believes that the so-called "free market" should drive innovation and change or whether some variant of the state should. Hence, contrary to depictions in popular media, the charge of apocalyptic reasoning only *partly* applies to environmentalists.

There is, however, a broader ethos that modern environmentalists in the Global North have been guilty of: the need for penance as a result of the human exploitation of nature. The concept of ecological penitence itself has multiple origins. Be it a Socratic veneration of the "things under the earth and the heavenly things";[5] the accounts of early explorers of the New World as they documented the beliefs and practices of indigenous people;[6] or the Christian modification of naturalism as a form of bringing about the Kingdom of God on earth, Western conceptions of humanity's place on the planet are rife with overtones of cosmic awe. In his celebrated *Traces on the Rhodian Shore*, for example, Clarence Glacken documents the longstanding influence of monastic orders on such pious interpretations of nature. The domesticating activities of the "heroes of penitence and purity," as one observer described them, combined a "zeal for conversion with readiness to make those changes in the natural environment which were required for the performance of heavenly tasks on earth."[7] That many of these later monastic orders held millenarian conceptions of the coming end of the world only added to the urgency of finding a balance between human activity and natural life.

As industrialization drew greater numbers of people away from the countryside into the cities, the penitential character of ecological advocacy gave way to more familiar vocabularies of economic and social justice.[8] Campaigns for fair wages and working conditions sought to relieve the plight of individuals and families, even if industry increasingly decimated nature. Some variants of socialist thinking went as far as to espouse fealty to the planet's inner workings. Peter Kropotkin famously called for the "functional integration" of town and countryside that would bring about the opportunity of experiencing rural life to skilled industrial laborers as well as put farmlands to work toward what Kropotkin called "the unification of farmer and mechanic within one person."[9] Nearly all early expressions of eco-socialism, however, suffer from a techno-optimistic ethos that made "history" a more valuable target to win than planetary homeostasis.[10] Nature was, at the end, a subject of and subjected to human progress.

Yet as climate skepticism today has become the weapon of corporate interests, environmentalist groups have begun to question this purported subservience. Recent media coverage has homed in on a growing trend among green-minded activists: the limits of a conceivable future. While "population bombs" and the "limits to growth" have been mainstays of environmental thinking for decades, popular debate over these never reached much of a global crescendo. Central to the growing narrative of the conceivable future is the idea that climate change—and more specifically, the scientific consensus around its inevitable and dramatic effects on the earth—warrants a reevaluation of humanity's basic proclivity for procreation. The movement broadly encompasses so-called "breeders" and "nonbreeders" alike, as the negative effects of climate change do not discriminate between those who desire to have children and those who do not. There is more nuance to the conceivable future movement, however, than merely a position in favor of or against having children. Various iterations of the population control mantra have emerged from (and been incorporated by) reproductive justice initiatives aiming to clarify various political and economic dimensions of the climate crisis.

A SORROWFUL STORM

In order to study the debilitating sense of guilt and dispossession that pervades much of the conceivable future platform, I want to first acknowledge the spectrum of positions within these narratives and show how they contribute to a form of so-called ecological penitence. According to Meghan Kallman and Josefine Ferorelli, cofounders of *Conceivable Future* (the eponymous research and advocacy network founded in Providence, Rhode Island, in 2015), the greatest challenge that climate change raises for people is not merely the impact generated by having children but rather the psychological effects of the guilt associated with such decisions. These concerns span a gamut of issues emerging from the paradoxes of contemporary capitalism: healthcare, affordable housing, childcare, environmental waste, and education. Added to these are fears of a child facing an ecological disaster on one's own, leading to families wanting to have more than one child. Naturally, the more idealist aspirations of changing the world's fate by raising more selfless people also continue to play a motivating role. As Kallman and Ferorelli put it in a 2018 story about their work in the *New York Times*: "These stories tell you that the thing that's broken is bigger than us.... The fact that people are seriously considering not having children because of climate change is all the reason you need to make the demands."[11]

Testimonies on the *Conceivable Future* forum include immediate and long-term concerns. These range from a woman posting about her atmospheric carbon legacy (in the United States) for every child she has (about 9,441 metric tons across a "genetic lifetime" according to one source, or 58.6 tons a year[12]) to the psychological effects of having to negotiate reproductive aspirations in an age where the costs of having a child are dwarfed by the price of other mainstays in modern society, such as a mortgage or a college degree. That having to choose between housing, education, or procreation has been increasingly normalized is no accident. Having children is only the most recent quandary in a wave of social transformations that have upended what scholars typically assumed about distinct pillars of modern social life in the West. It also coincides with the broad demobilization of trade unions and collective bargaining gains in advanced industrialized economies over the last forty years.[13]

Make no mistake: it is mostly middle-class individuals who are making the cost-benefit analysis of having children. The most affluent in these societies have in fact moved reproductive capacity away from the realm of aspiration toward a realm of more apocalyptic considerations of survivalist or interplanetary colonization.[14] The poor, to their credit and dismay, muddle through the puzzle of procreation as best they can, without access to contraception or adequate childcare. Therefore, buried behind the political advocacy of groups such as *Conceivable Future* are deep-rooted concerns over a kind of reproductive hierarchy being promoted across industrialized economies, not just the planet's carrying capacity.

The Political Economy of Climate Terror

The negative connotations of any ideology of population control are inherent to the claims themselves. That is to say, reining in human reproduction is always beholden to a governing ethos that aims to privilege social circumstances over natural proclivities. Only the most radical couch their calls for reproductive restraint around solely aesthetic or nativist claims. In the twentieth century alone, figures such as Rachel Carson, Garret Hardin, Paul and Anne Ehrlich, Donella Meadows, and Elinor Ostrom have all been linked in one form or another to extremist visions of antinatality when making their calls to slow down human growth on the planet.[15] Some have been more explicit than others about outright constriction, be it forced sterilization or state-led policing; others have used social and economic "priorities" to mask a more eugenicist resolve.[16] These polemics continue today, even though the same forces of capital that have historically relied on an expanding population to renew the ranks of workers and dispossessed are now calling for greater reproductive responsibility from the far more dynamic, yet still indentured middle classes. Call it neoliberal or neocapitalist, the outcome remains one of exploiting the material sensibilities of groups with the power to collectively organize against the unraveling of state regulation and widespread social safety nets in order to further the entrenchment of an individualist ethics that benefits the most well-off. And as Marxists have long shown, a division of labor in material production naturalizes the division between the governing values of an era, thus exacerbating class and political conflict.

Today's version of the "baby wars" differs from previous iterations in that it assents to the traditional concerns of capital: growth, advancement, innovation, and "fiscal" responsibility by way of reproductive responsibility. The alleged realism of not wanting more human beings on this planet to consume resources the way some do today completely ignores questions of material conditions and how conspicuous consumption is left unquestioned. The sentiment is not wrong: adding another person (let alone millions of others) to a hyperconsumerist landscape certainly increases the burden on our planet's ecosystems. But to draw attention to and blame the consequences of population growth on individuals, all while our global economic system incrementally ravages resources and people alike, is downright complacent. Most of the media coverage on changing attitudes toward reproduction resembles the same neoliberal arguments, stating that inequality and poverty are matters of "individual" responsibility. That the apocalyptic burden of a dying planet has been offset to aspiring professionals and couples is not the most worrisome factor here. Rather, the debilitating consequence of these narratives is the internalization of capitalism as an extension of human nature, which is (as so many critical social theorists have warned) the worst and most pernicious naturalization of an inherently greedy, imperialistic, and self-aggrandizing economic order.

As Kallman has argued elsewhere, scholars and activists *should* turn to the voices of those affected by climate change to make a case for global transformation. In her view, traction can emerge by directly telling people's stories, for: "The idea of testimony is that your truth and these lived experiences have more ability to move political structures than all the charts and numbers in the world."[17] Yet what Kallman and others downplay, perhaps inadvertently, is that the individuals that their work bears witness to are not born into social vacuums. Indeed, the lived experiences of climate change are only a stepping-stone to institutional transformation; necessary still is the recognition that the world's seemingly timeless order has never been solid, and is quickly melting into more than just air. More specifically, social circumstances in capitalist societies have a dramatic effect on how human beings conceive of their abilities, potential, rights, aspirations and, ultimately, of the source of their struggles. Climate change shows how these circumstances are unsustainable to an extreme, but also entails the entrenchment of capitalist interests against all facts. You can see some of these paradoxical conditions at work when the same media stories advocating for curtailed reproductive norms also employ penitential discourses as a way of goading other countries or individuals to follow suit.

BETWEEN CATASTROPHE AND REVOLUTION

As one recently published story in the *Independent* showcased, quoting Florence Blondel, director of a London-based charity organization called *Population Matters*: "You can't ignore the UK, because you also have migration here; people come here with their children. You need to be successful here in order to take the message to developing countries, otherwise people would just be suspicious. The UK needs to be an example."[18] These and other, similar accounts thus lead to the question: is the guilt over a conceivable future really about population?

In a photo essay published on August 1, 2018, the *New York Times* ran a story by Nathaniel Rich about the decade in which American scientists allegedly arrived at the realization of climate change's grave threats and attempted (unsuccessfully) to address these.[19] Titled "Losing Earth: The Decade We Almost Stopped Climate Change," the intervention is a massive investigative account of the motivations, exchanges, and commitments of a group of US climate scientists between 1979 to 1989, a period the author describes as "the decisive decade when humankind first came to a broad understanding of the causes and dangers of climate change."[20] Specifically designed for viewing on the web, the essay is flanked by aerial photographs of broken-up ice floes, burned-out neighborhoods, and sand-covered streets in a nondescript city. In disaster-movie fashion, each photograph is interspersed with fragments of an ominous warning: "Thirty years ago, we had a chance to save the planet. The science of climate change was settled. The world was ready to act. Almost nothing stood in our way—except ourselves."

These warnings are suggestive of both the contents of the piece and their implications, one presumes, for the places depicted in the photographs. Rich's essay has sparked a flurry of editorials, articles, and online fora in response. Within a few weeks of its publication, there was even a brief bidding war for the television rights to the article, with Apple Inc. successfully outbidding at least six other television producers for the rights to dramatize the story.[21] The article describes more than just the individual motivations and collective obstacles behind the seeming political impasse of the climate wars. Rich's narrative in fact spends more time tracing the source of planetary inaction away from the conventional "bogeymen" of fossil-fuel executives, lobbyists, spin-artists, and corrupt scientists. Rather, as he puts it, the focus should be on how in a certain opportune moment, "Almost nothing stood in our way—nothing except ourselves." That Rich actually uses his narrative to delve into musings on "human nature" and the redemptive value of suffering only confirms what critics have long suspected: it is easier to blame climate change on a cosmic flaw, an enduring original sin, than on calculated gain:

> We are capable of good works, altruism and wisdom, and a growing number of people have devoted their lives to helping civilization avoid the worst. We have a solution in hand: carbon taxes, increased investment in renewable and nuclear energy and decarbonization technology.. . . We can trust the technology and the economics. It's harder to trust human nature. Keeping the planet to two degrees of warming, let alone 1.5 degrees, would require transformative action. It will take more than good works and voluntary commitments; it will take a revolution. But in order to become a revolutionary, you need first to suffer.[22]

While the journalistic value of Rich's narrative should not be dismissed, his is an account of loss and regret over a collective diffusion of responsibility. It is important to point out here that such narratives, even when they support collective action and change, serve the function of dramatizing humanity's plight as a cycle of moral judgment. Revolutionary penitence is still a narrative of atonement, a kind of reflexivity that lays the blame for political deadlock, if not collusion, on a bogeyman or invading army that never materializes. More troubling about these kinds of penitential reflexivity, however, is how they perpetuate themselves as discourses of moderation in the face of an increasingly impotent and unstable status quo. Therefore, the goal of Rich's tryst with the origins of climate complacency seems to be less about generating a new springboard for action than about establishing a clearer basis for remorse.

Such collective fears of the coming deluge make opportune bedfellows in the marriage between modern broadcasting and climate capitalism. In the recent words of David Wallace-Wells of *New York Magazine*, the "transformation of the planet and the degradation may be the biggest and most important story of our time, indeed of all time, but on television, at least, it has nevertheless proven, so far, a 'palpable ratings killer.' All of which raises a very dispiriting possibility, considering the scale of the climate crisis: Has the end of the world as we know it become, already, old news?"[23] Wallace-Wells is quite familiar with how moralistic accounts of climate collapse produce a collective failure to take action and are reproduced by popular media. In July 2017, he published a similar narrative analysis, entitled "The Uninhabitable Earth," which generated a massive response from readers, experts, and journalists alike.[24] Though some criticism of the piece focused on the empirical research and evidence that Wallace-Wells deployed to make his case (which an annotated edition published shortly thereafter addressed), the core concern was the article's explicit alarmism. Why has the end of the world become old news? Is it truly as simple as a "ratings" phenomenon? Surely climate collapse is no less urgent once syndicated television networks change their coverage?

One answer, I am willing to venture, lies in the disconnected and dispersed ways in which coverage of climate catastrophes shies away from "blaming" anyone in particular. By relying on television's pastoral, near-clerical capacity to enthrall attentive (but increasingly restless) audiences in visions of spectacular suffering, penitential angst around the climate crisis reinforces a kind of separation between public and private. Failures in climate mitigation are rendered as products of bad government planning; failures to produce effective state planning are attributed to unreliable human impulses. It is easier to blame technology or policy processes than those who manipulate or stymie the tools of political action. The moral of the story is that human beings cannot save themselves because the problem transcends our mundane capacities; only something *more-than-human* can save us. In the meantime, the most affluent operate outside these constraints. As Emily Atkin recently put it, then, to "connect the dots" of global climate disasters means moving away from supernatural explanations for our collective moral failings, but also from treating it as a "niche issue" that only happens in contained spaces.[25]

Blaming God—or even ourselves—for our global path of destruction is to shy away from scrutinizing the worldly collusion and complicity that keep the most powerful free from responsibility and collective judgment. Ecopenitence in our times thus becomes more like a caricature of Catholic indulgences: the poor suffer their sins at full cost, while the rich can pay them off. Never mind that the brunt of the climate crisis is, and has always been, felt more acutely by the poor. Their precarity is naturalized by appeals to human fallibility and greed, instead of used as an impulse for action through calls for occupation, strikes, divestments, boycotts, and outright violence. These strategies are far from perfect or contradictory in their particulars; some of us may even feel they are downright deplorable. Nevertheless, they remain the most effective means through which those dispossessed of political power can exercise an agency that is not limited by technocracy or access to divine grace. They are politics in the face of doom.[26]

Though the most blatant illustrations of this tension between penitence and anthropolitics venture on the ridiculous, they are nevertheless examples of the tenacity of the eco-penitential ethos. In recent years, for example, American televangelists have altered their already specious defense of a so-called "prosperity gospel" to now include a focus on "end-of-times" commercial capitalism. None stand out more than disgraced televangelist Jim Bakker, who has attempted to capitalize on climate collapse by promoting what he calls "emergency food buckets" among other survivalist sundries. Bakker is but one of a wider selection of false prophets of the contemporary condition that peddle millenarian redemption alongside snake-oil hucksterism.[27] Although dystopian visions of the future have always existed in the industrialized Global North—particularly following crises of multiple sorts—climate change has upped the moral stakes of this genre to a now feverish pitch. Climate catastrophe today generates visions of disaster for the poor and rich alike; yet it also fuels renewed aspirations to escapism by the affluent, explicitly based on a fear of those who are most vulnerable—as a threat to their interests and a cautionary tale of what they could become in a post-apocalyptic landscape. Most troubling about the persistence of such narratives in the face of climate disaster is their numbing effect on the collective receptivity to (let alone desire for) social, political, and cultural transformation. Worse still is what these positions of privilege willingly forgive.[28]

Today's tabloid terror surrounding climate collapse more often resembles a collective group hug over the abyss than any genuine rite of remorse, repentance, or even retribution. Indeed, climate terror aims at something more than disempowering collective action against the whimsical, near-fantastical desires of the rich and mighty.[29] The terror of facing the end of the world—both literally and as we know it—most ably destroys the vestiges of critical thought that should lead us to ask "who benefits?" from the state of our world as it is. Climate terror in this sense is no different in its effects from what catastrophic terrorism in the wake of September 11, 2001, achieved: an anxious population beholden to the dictates of corporate media and its managerial political class. What is different in climate terror is the intention. Instead of propping up the security state, discourses of planetary collapse prop up market mechanisms that claim some facets of commercial life are nonnegotiable, even when the world itself is at stake.

Iconoclastic Reflexivity in the Face of Ecological Disaster

The questions facing environmentalists—and perhaps all human beings—in the contemporary Anthropocene are stark. That they present a kind of double bind in the conventional wisdom of theories of sustainability is fairly evident. More than this, however, they challenge critical social theorists and activists to reverse historical action's time horizon from one of "future generations" to one of interrogating our present state of atonement for the alleged sins of "past" acts. As Glacken points out, "One does not easily isolate ideas for study out of that mass of facts, lore, musings, and speculations which we call the thought of an age or of a cultural tradition; one literally tears and wrenches them out. There is nothing disembodied about them, and the cut is not clean. They are living parts of complex wholes; they are given prominence by the attention of the student."[30] The echoes of Karl Marx's own conceptualization of being "radical" are not accidental here. To grasp the root of the present climate crisis is to grasp the ambition, conspiracy, and *disenchantment of nature* that humanity has cultivated, where at last humanity has replaced nature with itself.[31]

In his latest book, *Old Gods, New Enigmas*, Mike Davis captures this need for critical reflexivity in more iconoclastic terms. Similarly positioning his "apocalyptic self" against his more idealistic aspirations, Davis makes a call to "start thinking like Noah," where "a new Ark will have to be constructed out of the materials that desperate humanity finds at hand in insurgent communities, pirate technologies, bootlegged media, rebel science, and forgotten utopias."[32] What this means in light of contemporary efforts to anticipate or survive the coming deluge is to get *in the way* of the storm, not avoid it. For activists in the Global North and South alike, that lesson is clear: no one but they will come save their communities. But what does it mean for critical social thought and those of us who wish to straddle the line between thought and action? To channel Davis, again, "only a return to explicitly utopian thinking can clarify the minimal conditions for the preservation of human solidarity in the face of convergent planetary crises."[33] At the broadest level, human solidarity here means confronting the evacuation of class conflict from our political ecosystem without illusions. That riots, strikes, and clashes will emerge from the continued contradictions of neoliberal iconography is a given; these are not instances to lament or attributes of our personal failings, but rather opportunities to embrace.

The rise of eco-penitence presents critical social theorists with the possibility to examine the pervasive and smuggled moralism of contemporary global capital while at the same time assessing the extent to which fragmented forms of political action can be made whole or collective again. As an ideology, it is both an expression of the contemporary diffusion of ecological responsibility and a shibboleth in the larger Oppression Olympics of who has it worse: the stunted middle and professional classes or the working, starving, and undeserving poor. However, as Davis puts it, to "raise our imaginations to the challenge of the Anthropocene" is a form of political utopianism that rejects millenarian and penitential aspirations. We can ask for forgiveness in our own time, but when the fates of so many are at stake, penitence is not just a luxury too expensive to entertain—it risks becoming "complicit in a de facto triage of humanity."[34] Though climate terror and the resulting eco-penitential gospel may seem paralyzing, perhaps the best antidote to their political poison is reflecting on what aspirations will be left after the end. God and humanity alike know that an apocalypse does not come about quickly, so while the scientists claim there is no time left, the critic must recognize the little time we need.

I would like to end here where I began and reflect on the meaning of anthropolitics in a time of climate change. As Peter Pels has described, anthropolitics is a framework that considers the "practical relationship between ethnographer and people described."[35] While rooted in practices of colonial exploration, the term is also relevant for what I see as the responsibility of critical social theory in the Anthropocene, a self-proclaimed age that reflects both the apex and the consequences of humanity's hubris concerning the defining categories of nature. Short of merely critiquing Anthropocene thinking as yet another view from the commanding heights of political and intellectual power, my aim has been to unpack the limits of this term in the face of competing normative trends, practices, and ideals. As a truism wrapped in the language of scientific consensus, the Anthropocene has brought together disparate worldviews and interests to face off in a cosmic negotiation over the future of the planet. But let us not be shy about it: the confrontation is a great deal more about the future of humanity than about the earth itself.

This is not a deal-breaker by any means, as all people should be concerned about the coming threats to social life that will only enhance the ecological harm that human beings have caused each other in the past millennium. It seems more than opportunistic to lay the blame for this violence on something outside of our purview, particularly when the changes that caused the contemporary climate crisis have invariably led to financial benefits for the few. To that end, the Anthropocene—and all its emergent discourses, disputes, and divisions—is the ideal icon against which critical social theory should struggle: not for the sake of merely condemning its findings, but rather to neutralize its multifaceted evasions of social, economic, and political conflict. This, in my mind, is what it means to conceive of iconoclastic reflexivity as a form of anthropolitics: interrogating the practicality of Anthropocene discourses and what they does to and for people in late capitalism.

In more than one way, Mike Davis's work across the years has worked toward a similar goal in linking the failed imaginaries that lead to environmental catastrophe to the "broader civilizational crisis of capitalism."[36] In this essay, Davis has led me to a space where the moral narratives that pervade policy and intellectual trends alike become reflections of our class commitments. That these material interests are often veiled, if not outright suppressed, is part of the same set of strategies that naturalize inequity for the benefit of a few over the many. How does eco-penitence fit in this matrix? As I have shown above, penitential impulses are the underside of historicist teleology: they make the well-off feel better about their gains from, if not complicity in, wholesale planetary dispossession. We should challenge these impulses with vim and unapologetic social transparency, leaving our expressions of sorrow for after the storm.

Endnotes

1   An entire subset of feminist, decolonial, and anthropological literature revolves around what Anna Tsing describes as "[confronting] the condition of trouble without end." Anna Lowenhaupt Tsing, *The Mushroom at the End of the World: On the Possibility of Life in Capitalist Ruins* (Princeton, NJ: Princeton University Press, 2015), 2. Other exemplary

titles in this vein include: Carolyn Merchant, *The Death of Nature: Women, Ecology, and the Scientific Revolution* (New York: HarperCollins, 1993); Mike Davis, *Planet of Slums* (New York: Verso 2006); Ann Laura Stoler, *Duress: Imperial Durabilities in Our Times* (Durham, NC: Duke University Press, 2016); and Donna Haraway, *Staying with the Trouble: Making Kin in the Chthulucene* (Durham, NC: Duke University Press, 2016).

2   Histories of ecological domination have centered on the human capacity for subduing and domesticating nature. Indeed, much of those same histories have homed in on the radical transformation of what "nature" actually means. Though some scholars have linked this question to the early modern and Enlightenment origins of the human need to control nature, few of these studies have attempted to examine what "human" nature itself is in the contemporary social and theoretical landscape. See Katharine Park and Lorraine Daston, *Wonders and the Order of Nature: 1150–1750* (Cambridge, MA: Zone Books, 1998); Bill McKibben, *Enough: Staying Human in an Engineered Age* (New York: Times Books, 2003); and Paul Wapner, *Living Through the End of Nature: The Future of American Environmentalism* (Cambridge, MA: MIT Press, 2010).

3   Maggie Astor, "No Children Because of Climate Change? Some People Are Considering It," *New York Times*, February 5, 2018, https://www.nytimes.com/2018/02/05/climate/climate-change-children.html.

4   See Paul Hawken, Amory Lovins, and L. Hunter Lovins, *Natural Capitalism: Creating the Next Industrial Revolution* (Boston: Little, Brown and Co., 1999); Janine M. Benyus, *Biomimicry: Innovation Inspired by Nature* (New York: Harper Perennial, 2002); Lester Brown, *Plan B 4.0: Mobilizing to Save Civilization* (New York: W.W. Norton & Company, 2009); William McDonough and Michael Braungart, *The Upcycle: Beyond Sustainability—Designing for Abundance* (New York: North Point Press, 2013).

5   Plato, "Apology of Socrates," in *Four Texts on Socrates*, rev. ed., trans. and ed. Thomas West and Grace Starry West (Ithaca, NY: Cornell University Press, 1998), 66.

6   See Mauro J. Caraccioli, "A Problem From Hell: Natural History, Empire, and the Devil in the New World," *Contemporary Political Theory* 17, no. 4 (2018): 437–58.

7   Clarence J. Glacken, *Traces on the Rhodian Shore: Nature and Culture in Western Thought from Ancient Times to the End of the Eighteenth Century* (Berkeley: University of California Press, 1967), 311.

8   See David Pepper, *Eco-Socialism: From Deep Ecology to Social Justice* (London: Routledge, 1993). More recently, see Sally Weintrobe, ed., *Engaging with Climate Change: Psychoanalytic and Interdisciplinary Perspectives* (New York: Routledge, 2012).

9   See Peter Kropotkin, *Fields, Factories and Workshops Tomorrow* (London: George Allen and Unwin, 1974), 156–58. See also Ya'acov Oved, "The Future Society According to Kropotkin," *Cahiers du monde russe et soviétique* 33, nos. 2–3 (1992): 303–20.

10 Recall here Murray Bookchin's critique of statist solutions, even Marxist ones, to social strife. For Bookchin, "[t]he objective history of the social structure becomes internalized as a subjective history of the psychic structure. Heinous as my view may be to modern Freudians, it is not the discipline of work but the discipline of rule that demands the repression of internal nature. This repression then extends outward to external nature as a mere object of rule and later of exploitation." See Murray Bookchin, *The Ecology of Freedom: The Emergence and Dissolution of Hierarchy* (Palo Alto, CA: Cheshire Books, 1982), 8.

11 Astor, "No Children Because of Climate Change?"

12 See Paul A. Murtaugh and Michael G. Schlax, "Reproduction and Carbon Legacies of Individuals," *Global Environmental Change* 19 (2009): 14–20.

13 See Connor Kilpatrick, "It's Okay to Have Children," *Jacobin*, August 22, 2018, https://jacobinmag.com/2018/08/its-okay-to-have-children.

14 See Douglas Rushkoff, "How Tech's Richest Plan to Save Themselves after the Apocalypse," *Guardian*, July 24, 2018, https://www.theguardian.com/technology/2018/jul/23/tech-industry-wealth-futurism-transhumanism-singularity.

15 Each of these classics has at one point or another been accused of running against the ethos of growth and "progress" informing industrialized societies. See Rachel Carson,

Silent Spring (New York: Houghton Mifflin, 1962); Garrett Hardin, "The Tragedy of the Commons," *Science* 162, no. 3859 (1968): 1243–48; Paul H. Ehrlich and Anne Ehrlich, *The Population Bomb* (New York: Ballantine Books, 1968); Donella H. Meadows et al., *The Limits to Growth* (Washington, DC: Potomac Associates, 1972); Elinor Ostrom, *Governing the Commons: The Evolution of Institutions for Collective Action* (Cambridge: Cambridge University Press, 1990).

16 Garret Hardin, for instance, notoriously called for a "lifeboat" approach towards humanitarian aid, judging unqualified assistance to the most precarious as "[diminishing] the quality of life for those who remain, and for subsequent generations." See Garret Hardin, "Lifeboat Ethics: The Case Against Helping the Poor," *Psychology Today* (September 1974): 800–812, http://www.garretthardinsociety.org/articles/art_lifeboat_ethics_case_against_helping_poor.html.

17 Linda Yang, "Our Planet Is So Fucked That Some Women Are Choosing to Not Have Kids," *Broadly, Vice Magazine*, December 14, 2016, https://www.vice.com/en_us/article/59mb5d/our-planet-is-so-fucked-that-some-women-are-choosing-to-not-have-kids.

18 Jessica Brown, "Why Climate Activists Can't Agree if We Should Be Having Fewer Children," *The Independent*, August 4, 2018, https://www.independent.co.uk/environment/children-carbon-footprint-environment-climate-change-adoption-birth-pregnancy-a8469886.html.

19 Nathaniel Rich, "Losing Earth: The Decade We Almost Stopped Climate Change," *New York Times*, August 1, 2018, https://www.nytimes.com/interactive/2018/08/01/magazine/climate-change-losing-earth.html.

20 Rich, "Losing Earth."

21 See Brooks Barnes, "Apple Buys Rights to Series Based on New York Times Climate Change Article," *New York Times*, August 21, 2018, https://www.nytimes.com/2018/08/21/business/media/apple-new-york-times-climate-change.html.

22 Rich, "Losing Earth."

23 David Wallace-Wells, "How Did the End of the World Become Old News?" *New York Magazine*, July 26, 2018, http://nymag.com/daily/intelligencer/2018/07/climate-change-wildfires-heatwave-media-old-news-end-of-the-world.html.

24 See David Wallace-Wells, "The Uninhabitable Earth," *New York Magazine*, July 10, 2017, http://nymag.com/daily/intelligencer/2017/07/climate-change-earth-too-hot-for-humans-annotated.html.

25 Emily Atkin, "The Media's Failure to Connect the Dots on Climate Change," *New Republic*, July 25, 2018, https://newrepublic.com/article/150124/medias-failure-connect-dots-climate-change.

26 Consider, as an illustration, the popular National Geographic reality television show "Doomsday Preppers," which rehashes several of the abovementioned tropes around the cultural politics of the end of the world. Airing between 2011 and 2014, the program showcased the outlandish fears, hoarding, and pessimism about the human capacity to stave off collective disaster that inform a marginal but growing portion of the American population. Many of these depictions, as expected, were denounced by the charmed circle of American intelligentsia (most notably the *New York Times*), and yet the show also boasted of being National Geographic Channel's "most watched series." See Chuck Raasch, "For 'Preppers,' Every Day Could Be Doomsday," *USA Today*, November 12, 2012, https://www.usatoday.com/story/news/nation/2012/11/12/for-preppers-every-day-could-be-doomsday/1701151/.

27 Justin Caffier, "I Tried to Live Off Jim Bakker's Disgusting Apocalypse Food," *Vice*, June 4, 2018, https://www.vice.com/en_us/article/ywx39j/this-infamous-televangelist-is-selling-disgusting-food-for-the-apocalypse-jim-bakker.

28 As Cara Daggett's recent work on "climate fascism" has shown, "[c]limate denial obviously serves fossil-fueled capitalist interests. However, coal and oil do more than ensure profit and fuel consumption-heavy lifestyles. If people cling so tenaciously to

fossil fuels, even to the point of embarking upon authoritarianism, it is because fossil fuels also secure cultural meaning and political subjectivities." See Cara Daggett, "Petro-masculinity: Fossil Fuels and Authoritarian Desire," *Millennium* 47, no. 1 (2018): 27.

29 See Maya Kosoff, "Peter Thiel Wants to Inject Himself With Young People's Blood," *Vanity Fair*, August 1, 2016, https://www.vanityfair.com/news/2016/08/peter-thiel-wants-to-inject-himself-with-young-peoples-blood.
30 Glacken, *Traces on the Rhodian Shore*, viii.
31 See Karl Marx, "Contribution to the Critique of Hegel's *Philosophy of Right*: Introduction," in *The Marx-Engels Reader*, ed. Robert C. Tucker (New York: W.W. Norton & Company, 1978), 60.
32 Mike Davis, *Old Gods, New Enigmas: Marx's Lost Theory* (New York: Verso, 2018), 202.
33 Davis, *Old Gods, New Enigmas*, 221.
34 Davis, *Old Gods, New Enigmas*, 221.
35 Peter Pels, *Colonial Subjects: Essays in the Practical History of Anthropology* (Ann Arbor: University of Michigan Press, 2000), 35.
36 Davis, *Old Gods, New Enigmas*, xxi.

PLANETARY EVENTS, CLIMATE CATASTROPHES, AND THE LIMITS OF THE HUMAN SCIENCES

William E. Connolly and Jairus Grove

* A much shorter version of this essay was published by the two authors as "Extinction Events and the Social Sciences" in *The Contemporary Condition*, July 2014, http://contemporarycondition.blogspot.com/2014/07/extinction-events-and-human-sciences.html.

In this chapter, we hope to show how a perennial indifference to the nonhuman world—from geological forces to nonhuman hominids to wolves and hawks—limited the explanatory and emancipatory potential of Western political thought. We argue that greater attention to the often chaotic as well as creative agencies well beyond the human estate are necessary now more than ever as we seek to confront our most current ecological catastrophe. Otherwise, we argue, the hubris of the same narrow humanism is likely to impede contemporary efforts for social and ecological justice as much as the lack of political and ethical thinking impedes the technocratic and elitist proposals for planetary survival by hyperindustrial and scientific means. Rather than a specific solution to the Anthropocene, what the chapter offers is a possible way out of the cul-de-sac of the science–social science divide that limits how we research, think, and act in an age of planetary politics. In the first section, we detail how we understand the limits of Western political thought's reliance on solely human explanations as sufficient reasons for historical change. We call this sociocentrism and see its myopic vision of historical explanation and change as endemic across ideological and theoretical divides. In the second half of the chapter, we explore four recent ecological historians—Jason Moore, Kyle Harper, Sam White, and Mike Davis—who we think have, in different ways, attempted to take nonhuman forces seriously as agents of historical change.

The Planetary Deafness of Classic Social Science

Mill, Marx, Weber, Mannheim, Durkheim, Hayek, Keynes, Berlin, Wittgenstein, C. Wright Mills, Hannah Arendt, Jon Elster, Joseph Schumpeter, John Rawls, Jürgen Habermas, Michel Foucault, Judith Shklar, Charles Taylor, Leo Strauss, George Kateb... The canonical list could be extended. These are justly famous, Euro-American, mostly male philosophical, social, economic, and political theorists writing predominantly in the nineteenth and twentieth centuries. They disagree with each other about several notable things. Those are the debates people love to pursue. Marx and Hayek, for example, disagree profoundly on the contours and trajectory of capitalism. Arendt and Rawls diverge on the sources and possibilities of political activism. Taylor and Foucault diverge on the role that transcendence plays in ethical life.

Some of this diverse crew even began to approach interpenetrations between planetary and social systems. Marx attended to entanglements between natural resources and social relations of production. Weber worried that capitalism would persist until the last ton of coal had been mined and burned. Habermas noted the possibility of "climate heating" in a 1980 book on capitalism, but did not pursue the lead.[1] Karl Polanyi—prescient about themes to be pursued here without in fact pursuing them himself—contended that no economic or social theory can be complete because the regimes in question are profoundly entangled with nonhuman processes such as climate change, war, a revolution, or a new technology, none of which are predictable within the terms of a socially self-contained theory.[2] But none thought carefully about the periodic volatility of *planetary* processes—with degrees of autonomy of their own—in relation to the contours of social life.

Even as new voices of postcolonial, Indigenous, and feminist theory such as those of Sylvia Wynter, Dipesh Chakrabarty, Stacy Alaimo, Catherine Malabou, and Kyle Whyte are moving away from the humanist provincialism that often dominates the academy, many in the academy still remain committed to a version of humanism at odds with appreciating nonhuman systems. Let us stick with the canonical figures for now: whether they define humans to be so exceptional that everything else fades into "nature," or construe nature to form the background, natural context, resource base, or staging ground of human action, or silently fold providential assumptions into natural trajectories, or treat humans as actual or potential masters of nature, or combine several of these views into a synthetic picture, they tend to think of most nonhuman configurations on their own as set in long, slow, cyclical time. There is a subterranean sense among many in the human sciences, even those who reject creationism, that the "chaotic earth" refers to a primordial past. The formative processes of upheaval that set the world in motion are thought to have congealed and cooled by the age of man. The natural world was for these thinkers either a necessary resource to be used or at best a garden to be tended. That diversities such as asteroid bombardments, ocean currents, symbiogenesis, plate tectonics, and the manufacture of the molecule CO_2 by early plants into free oxygen are subsumed under this capacious word "nature" is revealing. It discloses how the often accepted masters overlook or underplay a set of diverse planetary processes highly relevant to human social life and the cultural lives of other species.

Such canonical debates, then, conceal as much as they reveal. They conceal a set of affinities between the contestants, claimants, and beneficiaries. Affinities rather than identities, for some of the figures do make inroads into the zones we are investigating, but in doing so most downplay the volatilities and self-organizing capacities of a series of nonhuman processes that are critical to any insightful political ecology. Affinities, too, rather than radical differences: because while several worried about ecology and the environment in noble ways, none came to terms sufficiently with how a host of micro and macro nonhuman forces and agencies intersect profoundly with human processes and periodically go through deep changes that become imbricated with social life. That catastrophic regional droughts or on average colder winters, earthquakes, or astronomical events could have changed the course of colonialism or religious development exceeds the imaginations and analytic capabilities of thinkers that built the European social sciences. To understand change at local and global scales requires accepting that both human and numerous nonhuman processes form societies and break them.

BETWEEN CATASTROPHE AND REVOLUTION

The dominant tendency among social scientists today is still to construe "nature" as changing slowly unless and until "culture" becomes entangled with it. Much of the popular discourse about the Anthropocene, for instance, stakes the global state of emergency—its "unprecedented character"—on the grandeur of human ingenuity. The same call to emergency from this perspective ends all too frequently in proposals for large-scale industrial solutions to ecological destruction that are often indistinguishable from the cause.[3] Similarly, an intellectual cocoon is woven around cultural theory, with a small opening torn out by those who reduce recent planetary changes exclusively to the effects of capitalism. The recent idea of the Capitalocene is an advance, but it does not go far enough in coming to terms with nonhuman forces, agencies, and amplifiers that precede capital formation and recoil back on capitalist states as they wreak havoc on several regions. The danger in what is certainly a move in the right direction is a renewed sympathy for a modernist Prometheanism with a new mode of production. Marx's vision to set loose the productivity of labor could invite as much chaos as its capitalist predecessors, given the often delicate balance of nonhuman feedback loops between water, carbon, nonhuman species, and weather and ocean patterns. Not to mention the ways the interruptions of these feedbacks can accelerate human catastrophes such as wars. More work has to be done to prevent the critique of capitalism from recapitulating the sociocentrism that emboldens human hubris and selective political perception in equal parts.

Two versions of this sociocentrism were perhaps understandable until as late as the middle of the twentieth century: the first held that all of society and culture are to be explained by other social and cultural factors alone; the second holds that capitalism has become a geological force, but it tends to assume that planetary processes moved on a long, slow timeline until capitalism intervened. One source of the cultural lag is the only now eroding consensus among scientists on the stability of the planet: as Elizabeth Kolbert, Michael Benton, and Peter Brennan review in *The Sixth Extinction*, *When Life Nearly Died*, and *The Ends of the World* respectively, even eminent geologists and evolutionary biologists pushed a version of planetary gradualism for a long time. Echoing Kant's postulates about a human progressive history without radical breaks, Charles Lyell and Charles Darwin found no sharp punctuations in geology, climate, or biological evolution and neither did the most influential

PLANETARY EVENTS, CLIMATE CATASTROPHES

of their successive generations of followers. A certain tacit neo-Kantianism among geologists and evolutionary biologists reaches deep into the twentieth century. Even as Darwinian thinking came to displace theological providence from scientific thought, a kind of providential humanism was quick to fill the teleological void. Humans had exited the trails of nature thanks to technology and the earth was thought to no longer possess its once creative character, at least not on the timescale of modern human civilization. Geological and evolutionary changes were thought to be so gradual as to be imperceptible to the lives of individuals or even generations.

When Luis Alvarez and Stephen J. Gould challenged nineteenth- and twentieth-century gradualist views as late as the 1980s, the theory of "punctuated equilibrium" was at first ridiculed by many earth scientists. Early punctuationists such as Alvarez and Gould contended that evolution can proceed gradually and then turn, rapidly, due to a major, often exogenous, planetary event. If that theory turned out to be true, evolutionary biologists would have to attend to periodic geological change, astrophysical events, changes in the ocean conveyor, the changing sources, pace, and range of human migrations, modes of travel, and climate processes to study their own field. At the same time, anthropologists are having to reconsider many of the timelines and views of development that accounted for the Americas. The fact that multiple arrivals and routes to the Americas stretch back millennia earlier than previously accepted and the discovery of North and South American cities of comparable size to European counterparts all came to question the gradualism of geological and human change.[4] In particular, climate data correlated with ruins show the significance of climate patterns in the rise and fall of ancient civilizations as well as the effects of those ancient civilizations on climate patterns.[5] To account for the tangled web of geological, climatological, and human technological and urban change, siloed scholars across the natural sciences would have to become transdisciplinary. That alone was enough to cause consternation in academic departments.

The first punctuationist claim, advanced in 1980, was that dinosaurs had been wiped out suddenly sixty-six million years ago in the aftermath of a massive asteroid hitting Mexico. They later added a monstrous volcano in India to the mix, perhaps itself triggered by that monster asteroid. The impact, the global dusting, and the ensuing climate change destroyed these primeval masters, who had dominated the earth for millions of years, in a short time. That set off a new, slow turn in evolution that now favored mammals and other species. As late as the mid-1990s, an eco-friendly colleague strongly advised one of us to drop Gould from the list of people to engage because "the pros" in evolutionary biology found him lacking credibility. Today, of course, the asteroid/volcano event is supported by strong evidence, and its effect on evolution is now widely accepted. Sometimes, things change rapidly in both the world and theory. The scope and speed of planetary punctuations are pertinent retroactively and prospectively, whether they are widely accepted or not.

Extinction Events and Planetary Processes

Scientists are now confident that there have been several extinction events, the most devastating of which—when life itself came close to being extinguished—occurred about 250 million years ago. Only 50 million years later, 80 percent of the earth's species succumbed to extinction, with the rate and pace varying on sea and land. Why? That debate continues. Was it another asteroid? Few now seem to think so. Did it involve a series of huge methane bursts from the sea, fouling the atmosphere and changing the climate? Perhaps. Several other major evolutionary turning points are now under investigation as well, punctuated by a large number of "minor" events. One major extinction started around 450 million years ago, another around 200 million years ago, and, clearly, another is rapidly underway now. The most recent one is primarily triggered by collective and unintended human activity, in which modern modes of travel inadvertently carry bacteria, fungi, and other species into new environments, accelerating capitalist modes of carbon extraction contribute to rapid climate change, wider regional processes of deforestation contribute to the process, and the expanding global population breaks up former species migration routes. Welcome to the Anthropocene. A human event but not a solely human event.

What difference would it make to that diverse group of canonical thinkers listed at the beginning of this essay if each had been impressed, at least on this score, with Cuvier's catastrophism over Darwin's gradualism?[6] What if they had accepted evolution (against Cuvier) and stood Darwinian gradualism on its head (with Cuvier)? What then? Would Marx be quite so enamored with the explosive productivity of labor set free from alienation?

PLANETARY EVENTS, CLIMATE CATASTROPHES

Certainly, these thinkers would take the radical contingency of human and nonhuman relationality more seriously. Just consider Fredrick Engels's 1876 text, "The Part Played by Labor in the Transition from Ape to Man." Engels's account of human evolution put humans and their "singular" capacity for toolmaking and labor as the cause of their superiority. Instead, Engels might have seen the transition from prehuman hominids to modern humans as a collaborative effort with plants incipient with the possibilities for cultivation or emphasized the capacity of wolves to enter into complex social relations with early humans for mutually beneficial hunting and protection practices.[7] What would Engels think about his theory of human evolution now if he was told of the interbreeding and cooperation among Homo sapiens, Neanderthals, and Denisovans, much less the artistic and cultural habits of these nonhuman hominids?[8] Certainly, his story would less strongly feature the human dominance of nature and instead consider the complexity of tools and labor with more attention and care to the ecology that was so much more than a mere condition of possibility. The making of the human age is a multispecies story. A vision of natural history cum human history with participants from more species and less human heroism may have oriented Engels and Marx toward being more perceptive and more circumspect about the limits of labor and exclusive humanism in their visions of egalitarianism. Would Marxism's often tragic privileging of industrialization over agricultural and nomadic forms of life have taken place?

Well, they and we might have become alert much sooner to how a host of nonhuman processes—including glacier flows, plant evolution, hurricanes, tectonic plates, ocean currents, volcanoes, fungal transmissions, asteroids, bacterial flows, animal evolutionary patterns, and multispecies communities—polygenesis rather than monocausal origin stories with exclusive trajectories of human development—made the planet we now inhabit. These other forces, players, and relations follow rocky trajectories of their own and periodically become imbricated with human processes of production, travel, faith, politics, investment, art, production, migration, exploitation, consumption, and war but are not reducible to them. They might have folded a sense of how interacting force fields set on different timescales and capacities of agency can enable, interrupt, turn, and reshape our own cultural trajectories of being and becoming and vice versa, since many of these nonhuman forces also embody cultural capacities; just think of the importance of wolves becoming dogs in the story of human change.[9] Not only the mind/body dualism but the culture/nature dichotomy would be up for renegotiation. The twentieth-century thinkers might also have come to terms earlier with how capitalist and communist states profoundly affect climate, acidify oceans, and change the circulation of radioactivity through meltdowns and nuclear testing, therefore serving as prime movers of extinction events. After all, the hypothesis of planet warming through human action was available as early as 1879. Therefore, we argue that a commitment to gradualism and exclusive humanism was caused by more than just a lack of scientific data. Sociocentrism, as a worldview, constrained the critical thinking and political vision of the thinkers caught within it, such that evidence to the contrary received little attention until it was screaming in our faces.

Otherwise, had social and scientific thought been more affectable by the subtle signals of mounting nonhuman and geological forces for change, thinkers might also have begun to explore how the hotly contested cultural ideals of atomic individualism, national unity, racial superiority as speciesism, productive collectivism, market rationalism, providential theism, capitalist mastery, human exceptionalism, and organic holism may each reflect, in different ways, evasion from multiple planetary involvements in sociocultural life forms. Each ideal, in its current form, tends to project a distinctive future of smooth possibility in cultural relations with nonhuman processes, rather than to prepare us to cope with modes of change and unruliness arriving from multiple sites, which are often well beyond the capabilities of human institutions to deal with. It is difficult to imagine that thinkers engaged with the catastrophic tendencies of the world would continue to advance quaint ideas about market self-rationality or argue that ecological concerns were secondary to *real* politics. Realism itself would take a turn.

They might even have explored how the cultural hesitancy to accept the reality of a world set on multiple interacting tiers of temporality expresses a series of theistic and atheistic, conservative, revolutionary, and liberal demands that the world be ours for the taking. They might have challenged those secular/spiritual divisions in the human sciences. Certainly, Nietzsche proposed such a course of action some time ago; in large part, we argue, because of his attentiveness to limits of the human and the capriciousness of the cosmos.

PLANETARY EVENTS, CLIMATE CATASTROPHES

Are not all dominant modes of explanation, sociocentrism, the hegemony of capitalism, humanist exceptionalism, and the major ideals contending against capitalism interrupted by planetary challenges to the story of planetary gradualism? Certainly we believe that confidence in these modes of explanation would be significantly diminished, opening a space for contestation that would not immediately be rejected out of hand as heresy or *mere* speculation.

Should theorists and social scientists today, then, drop the crew listed at the top of this section? No—several of their insights remain. But we should not lionize them too much either or understand them simply in their "cultural contexts." (The "we" is invitational.) We need to draw some insights from them. But we also need to read them against themselves, with one eye on their complementary assumptions, demands, and affinities across the differences that divide and the other on the predicament they have helped bestow on us. We may also read them in the company of "minor" European thinkers who, though not perfectly prescient either, waged war against the dominant strains of Enlightenment thought contesting the existential spiritualities clinging to them. Think, for instance, of Sophocles, Lucretius, Thoreau, Nietzsche, James, Du Bois, the later Merleau-Ponty, Val Plumwood, Guattari, Kafka, Rachel Carson, Bateson, Gould, Terrence Deacon, Whitehead, and Werner Herzog. Finally, we need to explore with new eyes and ears modes of interspecies perspectivism coming from outside Europe. We also need to think further about what would happen if thinkers from outside of Europe were added to these lists who come from traditions that always took seriously the deep time of human and ecological change. In Australia, the Aboriginal and oldest civilizational account of fire that exists includes the hawk's use of fire in hunting as part of the story about how humans came to tame fire.[10] North American Indigenous scholars such as Kyle Whyte draw on much older scientific records of climate change, stretching back before European contact, and represent an intellectual tradition in thinking about catastrophe and adaptation for which the Anthropocene is just one of many times that humans have faced apocalyptic change.[11] To consider these other intellectual traditions means not just disrupting our narrow vision of geology with more data but also being open to other sources of data. Star maps painted by hand ten thousand years ago and oral traditions have vastly more fidelity than Wikipedia despite being transmitted through the analog technology of narrative.[12]

Again, without a doubt, Marx's theory of alienation reveals things about capitalist hegemony, the burdens of factory work, and the character of the commodity form. But we need to add to that list yet other modes of alienation not emphasized in the theory, such as alienation from human mortality, from limits posed by interspecies entanglements, and from the shaky place of the human estate in the cosmos. These latter modes of spiritual alienation can also surge into the intercoded domains of production, consumption, investment, voting, and rule as well as the violence of settler colonialism and intensified modes of primitive accumulation through dispossession, which come at the cost of Indigenous forms of life.[13] More of us need to explore how to transcend some modes of alienation as we ponder how to *transfigure* others (such as mortality and the shaky place of the human estate in the world) to help us *affirm* a world of intersecting temporalities of heterogeneous sorts that is much more than our staging ground. These are spiritual issues of today that infiltrate production, consumption, investment, voting, social explanation, and the construction of social ideals. Certainly, we might think twice before wagering a century and a half of industrial expansion and development in the hope of creating the true conditions for a *true* revolutionary class. We need both to confront the different contributions of different social forms to the sixth extinction and to affirm the shaky place of the human estate on the planet as one of its constitutive conditions of being.

What of Kant's postulate/reliance on "nature's secret plan" for the self-organizing, moral maturation of humanity?[14] Despite contemporary philosophy and liberal thinking claiming to be postmetaphysical, have cosmopolitans and neo-Kantian's really rid themselves of faith in providence, or at least in a world predisposed to human mastery? We do not think so. Even as those on the academic Left resist irrational climate deniers, many have not moved far from earlier views of a human-centric world. Like their fellow travelers, the neo-Arendtians, they bristle at the idea of a world not *for* humans or susceptible to *their* authority. Or worse yet, the possibility that *we* have never been entirely human to begin with, an assertion widely held to amount to species sedition. It seems, in an age in which thoughtless human globetrotting has spread fungus imperiling the existence of amphibians, we may want to take a break before we declare ourselves global citizens. Certainly, it should humble our sense of uniqueness among living things and maybe even inspire a little creaturely solidarity.

PLANETARY EVENTS, CLIMATE CATASTROPHES

Today, perhaps more of us need to experience plants and other actants through the eyes of Jane Bennett, capitalism through those of Gilles Deleuze and Eugene Holland, the frontier zones of late modern capitalism through the lens of Anna Tsing's mushrooms, the shifting affective tones of human perception through the skin of Brian Massumi, species evolution through the sensibilities of Elizabeth Grosz, Lynn Margulis, and Terrence Deacon, the pertinence of Sophocles and tragic possibility for today through the work of Bonnie Honig and Steven Johnston, the issue of sovereignty through the thought of Mike Shapiro and James Der Derian, the pursuit of theopoetic pluralism through the work of Catherine Keller and at times even Pope Francis, the event of the Anthropocene through the experience of Bruno Latour and Tim Morton, creative Bangladeshi ecological practices through the eyes of Naveeda Khan, the waxing and waning of Indian spiritualities through those of Bhrigu Singh, the thinking of forests through the work of Eduardo Kohn, the breakup of Antarctica through the images of Werner Herzog, and the relation between extinction events and existential politics through the research of Elizabeth Kolbert, Michael Benton, and artists like J.G. Ballard.

As The Dark Mountain environmental collective recently put it, maybe we should try to "paint a picture of homo sapiens which a being from another world or, better, a being from our own—a blue whale, an albatross, a mountain hare—might recognize as something approaching a truth."[15] This seems to us what is at stake in a revaluation of the presumed master thinkers. To take seriously the world at large is to think and feel alongside whales, trees, hurricanes, asteroids, the fleeting presence of iridescent frogs, minor human thinkers, human thinkers older than the rarefied concepts of philosophy and science, diverse ways and forms of life; all the while not losing sight of the human estate we struggle to hold on to amid the uneven sources of the Anthropocene—concentrated mostly in old capitalist states—and its uneven effects, focused often on southern African regions, southern Asia, Pacific islands, South America, and the Arctic.

Pathways beyond Sociocentrism

There is a set of recent historians and social scientists who are paving new pathways in the human sciences. Let us, briefly, focus on a few, charting the ways they speak to each other and to the Anthropocene in an effort to see where else our thinking could go if we were to loosen our grip on the explanatory power of the human-centered natural and social sciences.

To begin, we are inspired by the way Jason Moore presses internal ecological reform on the Marxist tradition.[16] Most pertinently, perhaps, he has shown how late modern capitalism has moved through exploiting labor and colonies (which continues) to agribusiness production of a series of "cheap natures" that preserve its patterns of growth and expansion. High-tech crops, for instance, simultaneously increase the profits of agribusiness, provide food for expanding populations, deplete soils, pollute the atmosphere with toxic emissions, and prepare capitalism for new crises. These shifts to a discount nature support capitalist expansion and threaten its future, as the future its institutions are designed to build becomes increasingly at odds with the natural and cultural possibilities of continuing the course, much less addresses the historical injustices of uneven distribution and the all too often racially determined possibilities for thriving. Though Moore does not say so, the binds created by the gaps between capitalist institutional demands and the world it ravages are amplifying support for neo-fascist movements in several Western countries. These movements are built around the insistence to pursue old patterns under highly unfavorable conditions, often under the guise of being anti-globalization and anticorporatist.[17] It is a cautionary tale to those who too narrowly pursue a critique of capitalism without attention to the anthropocentric limits of Marxist thought that so many Left populists find themselves among right-wing and neo-fascist movements. However, against this limited critique, Moore also challenges the mind/body and nature/culture dualisms that have haunted several traditions in Western social science. We think Moore would agree with us that the old slogan "socialism or barbarism" still seems a quite apt response to the sadism of our neoliberal times. However, we wonder if from the perspective of earth systems the demand goes far enough. We think socialism is a necessary but insufficient political project to address our political-ecological catastrophe.

This is where we diverge from Moore, even while taking on board the positive themes he advances. First, we are not confident that he has come to terms sufficiently with the periodic volatility of planetary forces of several types, both before and during the advent of capitalism. Second, we are hesitant for that reason about his choice of the term "Capitalocene" to cover the period of climate change from 1610 to the present day. Yes, capitalism is distinct (but not unique) in creating climate *triggers* that come back to plague it and other drivers of global and geographic transformation. These triggers activate a series of planetary amplifiers that can then exceed the initial effect of the triggers. Therefore, reversal of these triggers—capitalism—will not necessarily reverse the self-amplifying climate turbulence that has been set loose. The complexity of the earth system and its history complicates our basic assumptions about causality as much as it displaces our lingering belief in providence. More about that soon. Third, we wonder whether it is still appropriate today to project a vague ideal of communism as the best response to capitalism, partly because of the very volatility of planetary processes and the ways they impinge on multiple modes of social organization, and partly because communism too is tethered to the pursuit of consumption abundance and industrial modernism.

While we have already alluded to periods of deep planetary change before the advent of capitalism (and communism), let us underline our reservations about the sufficiency of the term "Capitalocene" through a review of very recent work by Kyle Harper. This is because he, like Moore, pursues promising work in history today that breaks with the traditions of sociocentrism; unlike the latter, however, Harper shows how rapid planetary changes with variable degrees of autonomy of their own interacted with human regimes well before the advent of capitalism.

According to Harper, in his *The Fate of Rome*, the "Roman Climate Optimum" persisted from about 200 BCE to about 150 CE.[18] It was a warm period with ample rainfall, one of several long blips in the "Holocene" that contribute to its reputation as a long period uniformly favorable to the advance of agriculture and population growth. Some other notable "blips" are the Medieval Climate Warming and the Little Ice Age. The Roman Climate Optimum was thus suitable for lavish crops, rapid population growth, and the takeoff of imperial expansion. Complex modes of governance, extensive trade, and dominance of the Mediterranean basin were consolidated during this period.

The "Antique Little Ice Age"—a very recently discovered and named event—started later and coalesced with devastating plagues induced by the importation of black rats and fleas from the East during the expansion of trade, which further weakened the empire. Such animal and climate incursions, of course, mean that a purely sociocentric approach to the decline of Rome cannot suffice. The participants themselves had little idea of the sources of the plague and climate change that wreaked such devastations. They often sought the sources elsewhere, in the wrath of God or the anger of the gods; whichever orientation to transcendence was favored during this period of rocky, theological diversity. Indeed, the rapid growth of Christianity in Rome loosely correlates with the dates of the pestilence, perhaps in part because Christianity could blame the widespread suffering on the weakness of the pagan gods, the just desert of Romans (a Second Coming was promised), and the capacity of an omnipotent god to cure the two intercoded phenomena. Christianity could also promise everlasting life beyond the plagued earth in ways that appealed to many constituencies overwhelmed by suffering.

Invading "Huns" from drought-saturated zones to the East pressed the Goths to increase their pressure on the Roman state as well. The point is that the Romans did not quite know what was happening, which suggests that sociocentrism is insufficient to explain either those events or the later emergence and trajectory of the Anthropocene.

But how did the Antique Little Ice Age acquire new momentum in 536 CE and surge until around 545, creating cold years that outstripped the later Little Ice Age that reached its own peak in the seventeenth century? Recent geological, ice-core, and tree-ring evidence suggests that the Antique Ice Age was started by a massive volcano in 536 CE, releasing massive amounts of sulfur into the stratosphere. This shift was bolstered by a cyclical "sun dimming" already underway and, soon thereafter, by another huge tropical volcano that finished it off. The great plague—which has been recorded by earlier historians of Rome—correlated with these events. One connecting link *may* be the ways in which the cold era damaged the abodes of black rats and encouraged infected fleas to feed on human flesh more actively. Volcanoes, cold winters, erratic summers, black rats, fleas: heterogeneous forces and agencies intersecting in many ways with other, more socially centered activities. Should this, then, be called the "Romanocene"? If so, would that, by its very title, play down too much the multiple intersections between heterogeneous agencies, forces, and drives in producing the fate of Rome?

This triple whammy did not itself "cause" the collapse of Rome—or, better, its devolution into a more decentralized, medieval era. Harper is not a geological determinist. Rather, "these harsh years quietly added stress to an imperial order already stressed."[19] Harper folds volcanic, sun dimming, climate, and plague events into cultural forces previously introduced to explain the fate of Rome. Planetary/cultural imbrications are seldom reducible to singular causes or even to an ensemble of efficient causes in which external pressures do not enter.

Once the Antique Little Ice Age and plagues were triggered, they encountered a variety of human and nonhuman amplifiers that helped the entire machine to accelerate and further weaken Rome. For example, the climate pressure on crops encouraged further deforestation to add new soil for cultivation, perhaps raising the temperature slightly and increasing drought tendencies. Those powerful processes intersected with a series of other contingencies, such as overextension of the empire, military adventurism, trade routes that drew rats and fleas with them, the destruction of Roman republicanism, the rise of Christian dogmatism, nomadic invasions, and internal corruption.

One thing to emphasize today, perhaps, is how earlier accounts of the rise and fall of Rome did not stress the role of the Climate Optimum or the Antique Little Ice Age in their stories. Some Roman chroniclers themselves had complained about changes in climate, but modern historians apparently did not emphasize these happenings, perhaps because they were unaware of a previous history of periodic rather rapid and deep changes. These historians unconsciously lived off the remains of the nineteenth- and twentieth-century sciences of geology, climatology, and paleontology, themselves stuck in the grooves of planetary "gradualism" or "uniformitarianism." Another thing to emphasize is that Rome itself had less effect on the planetary conditions that helped do it in (except for those trade routes) than capitalism has had on its own conditions of being. A third thing to highlight, however, is that both regimes found themselves caught in a series of rocky imbrications between human and nonhuman forces extending beyond their capacities of control.

Our third and final review of recent, promising work responds to Sam White's *A Cold Welcome* (2017) and Mike Davis's *Late Victorian Holocausts* (2001/2017) as well as Davis's earlier work on political ecology, *Ecology of Fear* (1998/1991). In these books, we get the beginnings of what a social science could look like that was equally attentive to the nonhuman forces of earth systems and the human forces of power politics that are amplified by changes in the climate system and at times alter those climate systems.

Sam White's *A Cold Welcome* inspires us to rethink the role we often assume protocapitalist drivers and Western technological superiority played in the colonization of the Americas. White's account of the seventeenth century is vastly different from those accounts we often inherit from the triumphant descriptions of automatic settlement and rapid expansion throughout North America. Instead, White describes lethal winters, failed colonies, frequent trips back to Europe to beg for supplies, and precarious dependence on Indigenous peoples to squeeze out the barest means of survival.

White's careful and dismal recounting of early settlements along the Atlantic seaboard and the Southwest shows just how much the weather determined the patterns of colonialism. Instead of technological dominance in war or agriculture, European settlers were prone to disease, cannibalism, and political extremism. White notes that witch hunts were most widespread during "the most miserable years—particularly the coldest summers—of the Little Ice Age."[20] Where Europeans did gain an advantage over Amerindians, this was also because the extreme weather had disrupted life too quickly for native inhabitants to adapt. The rapid onset of the Little Ice Age disrupted populations of animals they relied on for hunting as well as agricultural capabilities. Even in places like New Mexico, where the Pueblo people had developed significant food storage technology that allowed them to survive multiple winters, they were unable to accommodate erratic changes in rain patterns and seasonal extremes.[21] Chaotic weather disrupted the whole North American continent and resulted in desperate and often unsuccessful survival strategies for settlers and Indigenous peoples alike.

Rather than a story of rational economic interests pursued by technologically superior Europeans or perfectly adapted Indigenous peoples ready to welcome and feed unlucky European refugees, White gives us a history of "accidents, contingencies, and above all misfortunes of weather."[22] Without the dramatic climate instability of the late sixteenth century and early seventeenth century, "the whole geography and chronology of colonization would have unfolded differently."[23] That European settlers ultimately succeeded in settling North America often obscures the contingencies by which European powers succeeded, where they succeeded, and how close they were to total failure.

PLANETARY EVENTS, CLIMATE CATASTROPHES

At the very least, many of the convenient narratives about the superiority of European technology or political structure in explaining and often excusing colonialism seem difficult to sustain once the colonial project is placed in the context of historical climate change. Instead, after the introduction of climate history, it is clear that timing was everything, both in the slow beginning of settlement and in its eventual success. When one considers the work of Simon Lewis and Mark Maslin (2018) as well as others—who have persuasively connected the Little Ice Age to the reforestation of the Americas that resulted from the disease-induced apocalypse of European arrival—then the story of Western global expansion looks more and more like violent and catastrophic luck rather than a success because of superior skill or providence.[24]

Missed Encounters with an Untimely Book

Unlike the last three books, which have come out quite recently, Davis's work is two decades old. In 1998, when Mike Davis published *The Ecology of Fear*, most theorists were not yet talking about the Anthropocene. Even anthropogenic climate change, while broadly accepted by many on the Left, was only a bullet point on a long list of calamities to be addressed. Very few, if any, in political science thought about earth systems playing a significant role in human affairs. Jared Diamond's *Guns, Germs and Steel* and Manuel DeLanda's *A Thousand Years of Non-Linear History* had only come out a few months prior to Davis's book, and they were not yet at the forefront of the intellectual landscape of political thought. Davis's book *City of Quartz*, and later works such as *Planet of Slums*, had a more immediate impact on those of us studying global politics and the contemporary landscapes of control and urbanization.[25] While speculative at best, it seems likely that these books resonated more with the economic and statist accounts of political changes, which academics were more comfortable considering. To put it another way, these books made sense in a way that the analysis of El Niño simply did not. However, looking back, *Ecology of Fear* has proven to be as prophetic intellectually as it has been politically and environmentally.

In *Ecology of Fear*, Davis introduces us to the colliding and differential earth cycles that created El Niño as well as earthquakes and fire cycles that continue to disrupt political and social life in California. He folds what he calls the "geo-agency" of these systems into a "neo-catastrophist" approach, drawing from Stephen Jay Gould, Ilya Prigogine, and complexity research at the Santa Fe Institute.[26]

Unlike Diamond and even DeLanda, Davis took the risk of dragging geology, climatology, and oceanography into the world of contemporary politics and economics rather than relegating natural history to the deep time of the distant past. For Davis, California and even Los Angeles can be explored as highly contingent phenomena connected to earthquakes, floods, wildfires, and most importantly the turbulent feedback loops between these different systems.

Many historians and political analysts in the early twenty-first century still basically follow the "uniformitarianism" or "gradualism" of the nineteenth-century earth scientists—believing that nature is separate from the human world or changes so gradually as to be nearly irrelevant for sociopolitical questions—but during the period Davis was researching and writing this book, that was even more the case.[27] Making reference to the chance "benignity" of the late Holocene, Davis writes: "Los Angeles has been capitalized on sheer gambler's luck." A decade before Naomi Klein's *Shock Doctrine*, Davis explored how "natural" disasters were used by politicians to "leverage votes in Southern California and provide cover for market interventions in 1934, 1938, and 1994."[28] These arguments appear less radical in 2019. This is in large part because the contingent existence of LA posited by Davis has now become common sense, as we are witnessing the city's luck running out.[29]

Well before we sought to be aficionados of complexity theory, Davis writes: "Aficionados of complexity theory will marvel at the 'non-linear resonances' of unnatural disaster and social breakdown as Southern California's golden age is superseded forever by a chaotic new world of strange attractors."[30] *Ecology of Fear* presents us with a new vocabulary for thinking about causality and linearity that, while limited to one state in Davis's initial analysis, shows us a way forward for a political ecology of history.

Two years later, Davis pushed this political ecology well beyond Los Angeles, the state of California, and the historical boundaries of the twentieth century. *Late Victorian Holocausts* scales up the geological and historical perspective of *Ecology of Fear* to give an account of how the Third World was made. Unlike in *Ecology of Fear*, little ambiguity or contingency remains in the description of the natural systems such that they could challenge the hubris of human authority. Instead, the climate system and a chance shift in the turbulent El Niño-Southern Oscillation (ENSO) is capitalized by the great powers of Europe, an imperial enterprise that killed millions upon millions of people in what now is called the Global South. Between these two books there is, we think, a tension. On one side, *Ecology of Fear* tugs on the creative and unpredictable currents of nonhuman systems; on the other, *Late Victorian Holocausts* tugs on visions of human mastery of people and terrain through a power politics in which ecological change is merely an opportunity rather than a "geo-agency."

In the remainder of this chapter, we push further into the opening created by *Ecology of Fear* in which "small changes in driving variables or inputs—magnified by feedbacks—can produce disproportionate, or even discontinuous outcomes . . . the landscape incorporates a decisive quotient of surprise: it packs an eco-punch seldom easy to predict simply by extrapolating from existing trends."[31] The goal is to extend Davis's "quotient of surprise" to take on the species provincialism which has so thoroughly stunted the ability of liberal and even leftist theory to address planetary challenges we currently confront. We argue that this is a crucial moment in political history to meditate longer on the nonhuman systems that interpenetrate human institutions as new cataclysms unfold. Our hope is that such a meditation, taking inspiration from Davis, can provide tactics to redress the continuing resistance within the social sciences to incorporate volatile, intersecting ecosystems into social dynamics and to show how these social dynamics ricochet back and forth between eco-processes and the human domains we more comfortably understand; the exterior driving into the inside and the inside becoming geological.

Taking an eco-historical approach to colonization well before the publication of Sam White's book, Davis provides a historical puzzle piece in the ecological contingency of European hegemony and the making of the Third World that takes place almost two hundred years after White's account of its beginnings. The consolidation and intensification of colonial control during the late nineteenth century was essential for the resources and labor that made European economic development and hyperindustrialization possible.

However, the states of disorder and dependency that characterize the dominant histories of the colonial period did not happen by sheer European ingenuity or technological superiority, much less by the incompetence of the colonized. Instead, according to Davis, the ENSO explains a great deal about the massive disease outbreaks and famines that ravaged China and India during the Victorian era, sabotaging efforts at self-rule or successful colonial rebellion. However, even more than White, Davis establishes the *political* ecology of this ecological turbulence. According to Davis, unlike earlier periods of comparable drought in China and India, the climate instability caused death tolls in the tens of millions precisely because the infrastructure for redistributing stored food had been destroyed by imperial conquest and subsequent colonization. Davis draws connections between Victorian antipoverty work laws being enforced in India and the loss of redistributive capabilities used to respond to sudden changes in rain cycles in earlier historical periods.[32]

At the same time, Davis notes that European powers capitalized on periods of vulnerability and tumult to solidify trade routes and political control to accelerate the rate at which food and resources could be extracted from nations debilitated by famines. The consumption of resources by European metropoles further accelerated the lethality of agricultural instability. Droughts, combined with unprecedented amounts of European capital being invested into railroads defended by increasingly lethal weapons such as Gatling guns, created a perfect storm for the consolidation of a dominant Europe, an emerging United States, and a dependent Third World.[33]

So, while the whole planet experienced changes and instability in the climate, the ability to respond to those changes was heavily dependent on the advantages of capital and technology created by the previous periods of imperial expansion. What is significant about Davis's account of what he calls the "Late Victorian Holocausts" is how earth systems, even when global, create regionally and historically different outcomes. For Europe and the US, the earth systems ushered in a new period of imperial domination. For Indigenous peoples in the Americas and peoples in Asia and Africa, intensified vulnerability meant the acceleration of European dominance and control as a new ecological and then political-ecological form of order.

Davis's compelling account of the chancy and unpredictable nature and geography of the climate system combined with the significance of historical injustice and relations of power is an important warning against the often too easy characterization of climate change as a *global* crisis. While the importance of nonhuman forces such as rain patterns and ocean currents is brought to the forefront of our attention, so too are the ways some human populations, nation-states, and political movements are primed to capitalize on these periods of instability.

The complex retelling of conquest and colonialism by White and Davis should give us pause when considering how climate change has recently been posed as a kind of challenge to colonial and postcolonial studies. Dipesh Chakrabarty, most explicitly, has suggested a new kind of universal historical subject as a necessity to overcome all too particularistic tendencies of postcolonial approaches. He describes the need for a kind of negative universal subject based on enlightenment reason and united not by a commonality in character but by a shared experience of global catastrophe. Confronting the impending doom of climate change as *global* climate change inspires Chakrabarty to distance himself from particularistic histories of modernity and colonialism. For Chakrabarty, a renewal of reason in the face of particularity is necessary for confronting the challenges of our new global age.

There is no doubt that the "hermeneutics of skepticism," which animated much of critical and postcolonial scholarship in the 1970s, 1980s, and 1990s, seems unhelpful for incorporating advanced climate modeling into our analysis of history. The science wars that dominated the humanities and social sciences resulted, in many cases, in the dismissal of scientific research as a hegemonic discourse in the service of imperial interests and modernist consolidations of power and privilege. The critique of science is less appealing now that we are under assault by alternative facts and fake news. Contra the image of science as a technique of power, climate science is more appealing to those of us already favorably disposed toward a world of complexity and nonhuman forces. However, what we learn from Sam White's analysis of the first century of American settler colonialism and Davis's account of the nineteenth-century making of the Third World suggests that the complexities of climate change and history go well beyond China and India's claims in climate negotiations to a common but differentiated responsibility.

At the same moment that Chakrabarty's advice to avoid the provincial trap of the "hermeneutics of suspicion"—characteristic of some postcolonial studies—is compelling, the equally provincial trap of a new humanity is no less dangerous. Just as the problem of Eurocentrism obscures the role of

European conquest in the making of an industrial planet, so too does the rush to a new, "negative universal history" risk generalizing the consequences of the climate catastrophe. *A Cold Welcome* read alongside Davis's *Late Victorian Holocausts* shows just how regionalized and localized the consequences of climate change can be. Furthermore, Davis's analysis of how the Victorian era's colonial project in India and China stripped local populations of their capacity to adapt and respond to the famines of the late nineteenth century returns us to the very particularistic histories that Chakrabarty seems potentially too eager to demote in favor of a new form of species thinking.

For political, technical, and geographic reasons, mitigating and adapting to sea level rise, droughts, emergent diseases, migration crises, extreme weather events, and species extinction will be uneven in ways all too reminiscent of the geographies and histories of the Global South that defined the last four centuries.

Which dangers seem most significant and what political responses seem "feasible" or "realistic" in the face of rising temperatures also follow patterns of geographic privilege. According to the Intergovernmental Panel on Climate Change's (IPCC) most recent warning, the window for holding warming to 1.5°C closes in twelve years. After that, constraining natural feedbacks will be overwhelmed and global food production will become highly unstable, among other essential capacities. While North American and European populations will certainly be affected, the solution set for these countries is much more likely to resemble an assemblage of draconian immigration policies, selective climate engineering, and market-based solutions for accommodating food shortages. Whereas countries without the extreme elasticity of luxury and surplus capital to metabolize for adaptation are likely to see widespread famines, panicked migrations, and even war.

These differences in lethality and disruption are—like the Little Ice Age experienced in the Americas and the mass famines of the late nineteenth century—a complex encounter between human history, geography, and unpredictable nonhuman systems. Nations in Asia and South Asia as well as the Pacific and other areas in the tropical zone are more dependent on seasonal rains as well as coastal fisheries than North America or Europe. These are climatic differences, based on ocean currents and seasonal extremes related to where nations are located on the planet, *and* these differences exist because of precarious subsistence strategies and food insecurity, amplified by the effects of colonial and postcolonial globalization.

Neither the causes nor the consequences of climate change can be subsumed fully under bad luck or a kind of geographic curse. Instead, differences in geography act as a kind of amplifying feedback for the brute force of geopolitics and settlement. One can already see this particularistic history repeating itself in the solutions to climate change being discussed. Geoengineering or climate engineering is gaining more and more traction among highly industrialized states, despite the ominous warnings that artificially cooling the planet will slow ocean currents and rain cycles, accelerating drought in tropical zones. To add insult to injury, the most popular scheme for cooling the planet uses sulfur dioxide to alter the color of clouds in an effort to reflect sunlight. An accepted consequence of this strategy is extreme ocean acidification and the potential destruction of all or most coral reefs and coastal fisheries. *Successful* geoengineering requires an uneven sacrifice that is again territorialized along the same lines of conquest and colonialism that defined the seventeenth- and nineteenth-century climate catastrophes. Likewise, in Europe and the US it will be those populations made precarious by their racialized and economically marginalized histories that will bear the violence of *adaptation*.

It is not surprising that geoengineering is now seen by many as the only possible solution at a time when the political will for real climate mitigation is lacking in the very countries that are in the best position to adapt to warming and benefit from artificial climate cooling. So, while White's and Davis's insightful analyses of climate and histories do support Chakrabarty's timely insistence that we "rise above" our "disciplinary prejudices," it is not as clear that we are at the limits of history or the precipice of a new humanity.[34] Geoengineering, genetic manipulation of plants and animals, and garrison state strategies to prevent migration all suggest—contra to Chakrabarty—that the rich and the privileged do have lifeboats as well as strategically beneficial geographies from which to deploy them.[35]

There is nothing like a "shared catastrophe that we have all fallen into."[36] Instead, we must consider fully the limits of species thinking for understanding the contemporary predicament in addition to the limits of the human as a category for understanding political action and global-scale changes.

BETWEEN CATASTROPHE AND REVOLUTION

Certainly, everyone on the planet will be affected by the impending climate catastrophe but—like the disease epidemics and climate turbulence that accelerated the depopulation of the Americas in the sixteenth and seventeenth centuries and the regionwide famines that solidified European control of East Asia, South Asia, Africa, and the Americas—differences in power, politics, geography, and capital will matter once again.

To what extent these differences will determine an outcome in the final instance is uncertain, as the creative character of earth systems will react and respond beyond the human capacity for control. If there is to be something like a new global coalition to justly avoid the worst outcomes that climate change has to offer, it will have to be built explicitly in response to and against the violent neo-fascism and neocolonialism of the New Right that champions America First and a narrow interpretation of European civilization, rather than from a position of a new universality.[37] We need a resonance machine as wide-ranging as the abstract machine of European capitalism but with the care and concern for and full participation by those peoples and species that have been the most marginalized. A cross-national and cross-species general strike,[38] inspired by the differential injustice of the past five hundred years, rather than a false equality based on the current catastrophe, seems necessary to respond in kind to the crisis we face.

Endnotes

1   Jürgen Habermas, *Legitimation Crisis*, trans. Thomas McCarthy (Boston: Beacon Press, 1975).
2   See Karl Polanyi, *The Great Transformation* (Boston: Beacon Press, 1975).
3   More and more momentum is being built for large-scale geoengineering by a confluence of tech entrepreneurs and climate scientists who share a dismal view of politics and democracy. One such group, calling themselves Ecomodernists, have proposed formalizing a divorce between humans and nature in pursuit of a purely synthetic human existence. See Jairus Victor Grove, *Savage Ecology: War and Geopolitics at the End of the World* (Durham, NC: Duke University Press, 2019 192–97.
4   The discovery of Cahokia in Southern Illinois and the growing archeological evidence of advanced cities and road systems throughout pre-Columbian South America are evidence of several boom-bust eras before European contact. Similarly, DNA evidence suggests earlier Polynesian contact with South America than previously believed. Annalee Newitz provides a helpful summary and analysis here: https://arstechnica.com/science/2016/12/theres-a-1000-year-old-lost-city-beneath-the-st-louis-suburbs/.
5   The significance of pre-Columbian agriculture practice for global temperatures has been thoroughly reviewed by Simon Lewis and Mark Maslin in *The Human Planet: How We Created the Anthropocene* (New Haven, CT: Yale University Press, 2018).
6   We refer here to only one aspect of Cuvier. Unfortunately, both Cuvier and Darwin supported Caucasian and regional entitlements to the rest of the world, although in different ways. Cuvier believed there was a hierarchy among eternal species, with each species

being eternal unless and until a catastrophe hits. Caucasians were superior to other races. Some species died out through exogenous catastrophes. Darwin, in *The Descent of Man* (New York: Prometheus Books, 1998), modified his earlier theory of survival of the fittest to include sexual and aesthetic factors. But he continued to place Caucasians at the top of a gradual, evolutionary tree. Benton provides a fascinating view of these debates and affinities. See Michael Benton, *When Life Nearly Died: The Greatest Mass Extinction of All Time* (London: Thames & Hudson, 2005).

7   Friedrich Engels, "The Part Played by Labor in the Transition from Ape to Man," 1934 [1876], https://www.marxists.org/archive/marx/works/1876/part-played-labour/.
8   Neanderthal cave paintings date back at least sixty-five thousand years, which challenges many of the presumptions about the uniqueness of Homo sapiens. See Emma Marris, "Neanderthal Artists Made Oldest-Known Cave Paintings," *Nature*, February 22, 2018, https://doi.org/10.1038/d41586-018-02357-8.
9   For current research on the coevolution of wolves and humans, see Raymond John Pierotti and Brandy R. Fogg, *The First Domestication: How Wolves and Humans Coevolved* (New Haven, CT: Yale University Press, 2017).
10 Mark Bonta et al., "Intentional Fire-Spreading by 'Firehawk' Raptors in Northern Australia," *Journal of Ethnobiology* 37, no. 4 (December 2017): 700–718.
11 Kyle P. Whyte, "Indigenous Science (Fiction) for the Anthropocene: Ancestral Dystopias and Fantasies of Climate Change Crises," *Environment and Planning E: Nature and Space* 1, no. 1–2 (March 2018): 224–42.
12 For a compelling account of how Aboriginal science "queers" the hegemony of Western science, particularly in terms of astronomy, see Stephen Muecke, "Wolfe Creek Meteorite Crater," *Ctrl-Z: New Media Philosophy*, no. 7 (2017), http://www.ctrl-z.net.au/articles/issue-7/muecke-wolfe-creek-meteorite-crater/.
13 For a critique of the linear historical narrative that often sees primitive accumulation as an artifact of the past rather than as an essential component of contemporary capitalist violence, see Glen Coulthard, "The Colonialism of the Present," *Jacobin*, January 2015, https://www.jacobinmag.com/2015/01/indigenous-left-glen-coulthard-interview/.
14 Immanuel Kant, "Idea for a Universal History with a Cosmopolitan Purpose," In *Kant*, Cambridge Texts in the History of Political Thought, 2nd ed., ed. H. S. Reiss (Cambridge: Cambridge University Press, 1991), 41–53.
15 Dark Mountain Project, "The Manifesto," *Dark Mountain Project*, 2009, https://dark-mountain.net/about/manifesto/.
16 Jason Moore, *Capitalism in the Web of Life: Ecology and the Accumulation of Capital* (New York: Verso, 2015).
17 For a book that explores this bind and the fascist temptations it creates, see William E. Connolly, *Aspirational Fascism: The Struggle for Multifaceted Democracy under Trumpism* (Minneapolis: University of Minnesota Press, 2017).
18 Kyle Harper, *The Fate of Rome* (Princeton, NJ: Princeton University Press, 2017).
19 Harper, *Fate of Rome*, 254.
20 Sam White, *A Cold Welcome: The Little Ice Age and Europe's Encounter with North America* (Cambridge, MA: Harvard University Press, 2017), 128.
21 White, *A Cold Welcome*, 157.
22 White, *A Cold Welcome*, 250.
23 White, *A Cold Welcome*, 251.
24 Lewis and Maslin, *Human Planet*.
25 Just comparing the sales rank of the three books on Amazon.com shows that *Planet of Slums* and *City of Quartz* are each ten times more successful in terms of sales than *Ecology of Fear*.
26 Mike Davis, *Ecology of Fear: Los Angeles and the Imagination of Disaster* (New York: Vintage Books, 1998), 20.
27 Davis, *Ecology of Fear*, 15.
28 Davis, *Ecology of Fear*, 38.

29 Davis, *Ecology of Fear*, 39.
30 Davis, *Ecology of Fear*, 54.
31 Davis, *Ecology of Fear*, 19.
32 Mike Davis, *Late Victorian Holocausts: El Niño Famines and the Making of the Third World* (New York: Verso, 2017), 304.
33 Davis, *Late Victorian Holocausts*, 127.
34 Dipesh Chakrabarty, "The Climate of History: Four Theses," *Critical Inquiry* 35, no. 2 (January 2009): 215.
35 Chakrabarty, "Climate of History," 221.
36 Chakrabarty, "Climate of History," 218.
37 For a more detailed account of neo-fascist movements, see Connolly, *Aspirational Fascism*.
38 For a more detailed account of the general strike imagined here, see Chapter 5, "The Politics of Swarming and the General Strike," in William Connolly, *Facing the Planetary: Entangled Humanism and the Politics of Swarming* (Durham, NC: Duke University Press, 2017), 121-150.

A LATE NEOLIBERAL HOLOCAUST

Don Mitchell

Charly Keunang was pretty well known (if not by his real name) on the streets of Los Angeles's Skid Row, home to the largest concentration of homeless people in the world. Everyone called him "Africa" (or occasionally "Cameroon") and he had claimed a fairly regular spot on a sidewalk to set up his tent every night. Like others living on the street, Africa could set up his tent because he was protected—if that is not exactly the wrong word—by a 2006 court order that restrained the Los Angeles Police Department (LAPD) from enforcing the city's anticamping ordinance if not enough shelter beds were available. Enforcing the terms of the order, cops would cruise the streets and walk the sidewalks of Skid Row before six every morning and order people sleeping outside to wake up, pack up their tents and cardboard boxes, and get a move on. They could not return until after nine in the evening.[1]

The cops were typically neither subtle nor patient. For the court order came at the height of Los Angeles Police Chief William Bratton's reign. He had been hired in 2002 to replicate the zero-tolerance, quality-of-life, broken-windows policing he had pioneered between 1994 and 1996 as Mayor Rudolph Giuliani's chief of police in New York. Called the "Safer Streets Initiative" in Los Angeles, the hallmark of Bratton's style of "quality-of-life" policing is the aggressive, insistent policing—harassment is not too harsh a term—of homeless people's everyday actions (sleeping, making a livelihood, hanging out with friends, crossing the street, sitting on public benches, eating, finding somewhere to piss or crap), even if this is sometimes leavened with a bit of compassionate tough love and is often most effective when paired with the simultaneous deployment of "good cops" (who befriend and assist the homeless, who look out for their safety, who notice when they seem to have disappeared). Just how aggressive the Safer Streets Initiative was can been seen in the fact that over a period of four months at the end of 2006 (the year the court order was entered) and the beginning of 2007, police arrested (not just cited, but arrested) more than five thousand people on Skid Row.[2] The area—officially designated a "homeless containment zone" by the police—is huge, encompassing fifty square blocks and hosting a homeless population of around ten thousand (there are between fifty-five to sixty thousand homeless people in Los Angeles County, of which only 25 percent are sheltered). This means that around one in every two homeless people were arrested during those four months alone.

Indeed, by 2013 (after the end of Bratton's tenure, but under continuing Safer Streets–like policing), some 14 percent of all arrests made in the city were of homeless people. A 2009 survey found that 89.3 percent of Skid Row residents had been stopped and questioned by the police at some point, and 82.8 percent had been arrested. Fully half the respondents reported being physically or verbally abused by the cops during their arrest or citation. Most were arrested for minor offenses like sleeping on the sidewalk (before the court order), jaywalking, or littering. Another survey the next year showed that more than 50 percent of respondents had been arrested over the previous year and as a result had lost their jobs, access to shelter, or other services. In 2014, Los Angeles spent $100 million from its general fund on homelessness. $87 million of this went to the police.[3]

On Sunday, March 1, 2015, LAPD officers made their early morning rounds as usual. Mr. Keunang, like many, pretty much ignored the order to pack up and leave. Later on, around noon, four cops arrived at Mr. Keunang's tent. They had been summoned by a fellow resident with whom he had been having a dispute. One of the officers was well known on the Skid Row streets and by Charly Keunang, who knew him by name. Officer Francisco Martinez was reputed on the streets to be a violent cop, a "hard-ass bitch cop," a "Napoleon cop," in the words of a couple of residents.[4] Video surveillance, body cameras, and bystander recordings show Mr. Keunang repeatedly pleading with Martinez to "Let me express myself." Martinez responded by saying, "We're going to do things my way," and threatening several times to Taser him. Fed up, Mr. Keunang crawled back into his tent—the one that should have long since been packed away—and this seemed to have set the cops off. They ordered him out. As he emerged, Officer Martinez Tasered him, twice. Mr. Keunang whirled and spun, likely reacting to the voltage coursing through his body. Another cop, Joshua Volosgis, punched him "in the facial area," as Officer Volosgis later told police investigators, and the two fell to the ground, entangled. Officer Volosgis yelled that Mr. Keunang had grabbed his gun (he had not; the gun remained holstered throughout), and a third officer Tasered Mr. Keunang all over again. Seconds later, the cops opened fire, peppering Mr. Keunang's body with six bullets—two shot at point-blank range—and killing him instantly. Almost as fast, the police got to work vilifying Mr. Keunang, letting it be known in the press that he was in the United States illegally and was a convicted bank robber, as if either status justified his execution.[5]

It is tempting to see the killing of Charly "Africa" Keunang as just an isolated incident of aggressive policing gone overboard, or as just another example of what seems to be an ongoing war by the cops against black people—the war that has given rise to the #BlackLivesMatter movement. But while the latter (but not the former) is undoubtedly true and deeply important, it also risks missing the larger pattern into which Mr. Keunang's death fits.[6] For we are in the midst of what needs to be understood as a slow, diffuse, largely unspectacular holocaust (deaths like Mr. Keunang's are extraordinary only in the attention they garner; most do not garner any). Holocausts are "destruction or slaughter on a mass scale."[7] They do not need to be organized in the same way that the Nazi slaughter of Jews during the Second World War was organized; but they are systematic. They are *internal* to the logic of the social systems that give rise to them, as Mike Davis showed in his dissection of the "Late Victorian Holocausts": the repeated famines on the Indian subcontinent as it was colonized and incorporated into the global system of liberal capitalism.[8] Mr. Keunang's death, at once extraordinary and mundane,[9] is a clear representation of the new, slow, holocaust we are living through—a late neoliberal holocaust.[10]

The internal logic of Mr. Charly Keunang's death—its preordination within the conjuncture we call neoliberalism—has a deep history and a grim future, as well as a significant meaning: his very existence, I will argue, was both a necessary product of how capitalist circulation and accumulation proceed at this historical moment *and* a threat to these dynamics. As such, he, like so many others, had to be neutralized. That is what was so mundane about his death. What was extraordinary, still, was that he was murdered. The normal mode of neutralization is to simply let people die, to let lives be destroyed, to let the holocaust do its work. Though this is a holocaust coming to full flower in late neoliberal capitalism, we will see that it is one that has its roots in a different moment—a moment right at the peak of Keynesian social-welfare capitalism. Moreover, its paradigmatic figures are not homeless—and therefore putatively surplus—people like Charly Keunang but "guest" (and therefore putatively necessary) workers like the braceros, brought to the United States from Mexico to pick crops between the start of the Second World War and the middle of the 1960s.

Dead Labor: Or, We Are All Braceros Now

It is by now fairly well accepted that psychological illnesses "adapt themselves to a culture's preoccupations and fears," as journalist Rachel Aviv wrote in an investigative report on immigrant children in Sweden falling into comas (or coma-like conditions) as that country tightened its immigration and refugee policies in 2015 and began deporting asylum seekers, sometimes quite arbitrarily.[11] It is also well understood that diseases shape themselves in relation to the political-economic and social structures within which they develop—as has been made so readily apparent by the Covid-19 pandemic—and in turn reshape society. And it is hardly controversial that many diseases are socially and economically entrenched and even promoted (asthma, various allergies, certain cancers—those diseases that we know are fully intertwined with the environments within which we live and which can only be minimized or eliminated by changing the environment, rather than the patient).[12] Finally, no one disputes that there are culturally specific "ways of death"—from how we prepare to die to funerary rites. But (outside of war and capital punishment, and of course the gun epidemic in the United States) what about how people die—or rather are made to die, are *killed*—in the course of ordinary, everyday life?

In the two years between 1955 and 1957, perhaps as many as twenty braceros—Mexican agricultural "guest workers"—mysteriously died in their sleep in California. According to the California Department of Public Health's Dr. Irma West, "the patterns in nearly all the cases was identical." In the words of a news report on Dr. West's findings, they "went to work during the day with no complaint of illness. They ate heartily at the end of the day and went to bed. During the night they had violent nightmares and then they died." No obvious cause of death was found in most cases, even after autopsies. Dr. West told a conference of coroners that similar deaths had occurred among Filipino farmworkers in the Philippines and Hawaii, where workers called them "dream deaths" and attributed them to "voodoo" (in West's words). Eventually, Dr. West eliminated voodoo as the cause, discounted reports of violent dreams, and focused her investigation instead on questions of nutrition. But with the exception of one bracero—who was found to have been poisoned by organic phosphate—and another, who, she said, starved himself to death in order to save money, the majority of the deaths remained a mystery. And though press attention soon waned, unexplained deaths remained a feature of the bracero program until it was finally closed down at the end of 1964.[13]

Plenty of other deaths of braceros were easily explained. For example, like one of the mysterious cases Dr. West examined, braceros died of insecticide and pesticide poisoning at historically high rates. Malnutrition and (as investigations showed) even starvation was a constant feature of bracero life and of the lives of other farmworkers and their families, who also died at elevated rates from diseases linked to poor sanitation in labor camps.[14] Others died of workplace injuries in what was at the time (and which remains) one of the most dangerous professions, in which the (illegal) use of untrained braceros on dangerous farm equipment was common.[15] And hundreds of braceros (as well as other farmworkers) were killed over the course of the program while being transported to or from harvests in unsafe vehicles (including thirty-two killed and twenty-five injured in one gruesome crash between a farm labor bus and a train in Chualar near Salinas in 1963).[16]

All these deaths were not just an unfortunate side effect of the bracero program. They were integral to its working. Any number of contemporaneous investigations, and much later historical scholarship, showed that a main effect (and it is not unreasonable to surmise, a main goal) of the bracero program over the twenty-four years of its operation was to drive out relatively stable, so-called "domestic" (that is, non-bracero) workers—families, longer-term immigrants, African Americans, and so forth—and replace them with what was in essence an indentured labor force. But it was a kind of indenture that was as historically innovative as it was devastating to worker power: it relied on both the constant cultivation of a labor *oversupply* and the use of very short-term contracts, typically no more than six weeks.[17] The oversupply was accumulated in three places: in Mexican towns hosting bracero recruiting stations, where hundreds and thousands of aspirants would gather each year in hopes of getting a contract (sometimes perishing from starvation, malnutrition, and exposure as they waited); in the quite un-euphemistically named labor supply camps built explicitly to house bracero labor before and after they were deployed to specific farms; and in the other labor camps, ditch bank encampments, and skid rows into which displaced workers were pushed.[18] This labor oversupply was created by heavily recruiting workers in Mexico to come to recruiting stations in numbers far in excess of what would actually be needed. As recruiters knew well, and counted on, a good number of these workers could then cross the border illegally, adding to the labor supply on the US side. The oversupply was also created through selecting more workers than were truly required (through a highly corrupt labor shortage certification process), continually pushing domestic workers onto the road in search of any work they could get, and (through a "shape-up" recruiting process on skid rows in cities throughout the agricultural region) encouraging the congregation of large numbers of surplus workers—the reserve army of labor, as Marx put it—in specific places where they could be deployed (or not), rapidly and as needed. Often, such workers were desperate for any work they could get. They were, in many (if not all) ways, the forerunners of today's urban homeless. Together, braceros, displaced domestic workers, and the marginally employed on skid row created what the great mid-twentieth century activist lawyer and writer Cary McWilliams described as a growers' "dream of heaven."[19]

It was a dream of heaven, as labor economist Lloyd Fisher argued at the height of the program, because it created the conditions of possibility not only for cheap labor, but especially for *controlled* labor.[20] The combination of cheapness and control was made possible in many ways. Growers avoided many of the costs associated with relying on a temporary and mobile labor force by ensuring that workers were not *reproduced* (as is necessary for the reproduction of capital) but rather *replaced* and by ensuring that what reproduction costs there nonetheless were, were largely borne elsewhere (Mexico) or covertly socialized (public health nurses deployed to halt epidemics of dysentery before they spread to the general population; charities operating soup kitchens on skid row; public hospitals footing the bills for gruesome workplace injuries). Growers ensured control by seeing to it that labor was highly mobile, capable of being deployed almost instantaneously to areas of need, or by, conversely, ensuring that when labor was contracted it was basically unfree, tied to a particular contractor and unable to easily switch jobs of its own volition. And finally, growers could avail themselves of deep, if largely publicly unrecognized subsidies by ensuring that the government picked up many of the opportunity costs of such a system (border inspections of incoming braceros, much of the transportation bill, negotiating agreements and treaties with labor-supplying countries, sending dead bodies back to Mexico or burying them in paupers' graves, and so forth). But the possibility of replacement was key, and the ever-looming presence of death thus served as a vital disciplinary mechanism, especially when coupled with that other disciplinary mechanism: the constant threat of deportation, as six-week contracts were terminated without notice or simply not renewed. If the primary alternative to working under the conditions as they were evolving was dying (whether in the US or in Mexico), then one would do anything to work—put up with nearly any conditions, accept any indignity. And if one did not? It did not matter, since replacements had already been recruited and set in place. This was normal life and death, what the anthropologist and doctor Paul Farmer later insightfully called "modal suffering," part and parcel of the ordinary state of affairs—precisely the patterns through which people were *made* to die (as I put it above).[21] It is death adapting itself to "culture's preoccupations," in this case ensuring that cheap food did not come at the expense of, but positively enhanced, the galloping profits of agribusiness. However, clearly, it is not some "culture" at work but rather the very material machinations of capitalist accumulation.

In other words, the bracero program pioneered a mode of labor control and deployment—as well as a model for cheapness—that is now not just familiar but understood as a *good* in the current global, neoliberalized age. It has become the very basis on which value is produced, through which profits are generated, and by which wealth is transferred ever upward. Under neoliberal capitalism, which has come to dominate the globe since the 1970s (and really took off after the fall of socialist Eastern Europe and the Soviet Union), we are all braceros now. And by "we" I mean not only the braceros' direct descendants—like the South Asians building expat apartments and luxury hotels in Dubai and World Cup stadiums in Qatar, undocumented Central American workers trapped on mega-dairies along the US–Canada border in upstate New

York, or Peruvian miners, and farmworkers in Chile[22]—but most of the rest of us.[23]

Whether we are highly trained professionals (professors, nurses, chefs) or employed in essential work (day-laboring trash collectors, dollar-store workers, janitors), if we are lucky we are expected to survive (or not) on a succession of short-term contracts (sometimes as long as a semester, but perhaps now only lasting minutes, at least if you find your work on Task Rabbit) or on "zero hour" fast-food contracts that only rarely provide sufficient work, require one to always be on call, and all but prohibit movement to other employers.[24] If we are less lucky, we get displaced, forced to join the ever more tenuous ranks of the reserve army, perhaps eventually to join Charly Keunang and the hundreds of thousands of others on the skid rows and in the urban encampments that increasingly mark cities in the Global North.

And for the reserve army, as for an increasing number of other tranches of the working class,[25] mere survival is becoming ever more tenuous. At the height of the bracero program—when the very models of today's hegemonic labor relations were being forged—there was, at least for a significant number of people (sorted, of course, by race, gender, and nationality) a somewhat supportive welfare state to backstop social reproduction. There was also a "grand compromise" between capital and labor that ensured lifelong employment for a significant portion of the working class, a sharing of productivity gains in some industries, relatively strong unions that could curb some of capital's basest instincts, and, as uneven as this certainly was, rising standards of living for many. At the lowest ends of the working class, there was public housing, which, though never robust in the United States, was important nonetheless. The modal suffering of the braceros—from their mysterious deaths to their totally explicable ones to the everyday injuries and deprivations that defined the program—was absolutely part of this system (allowing for the production of cheap food, which helped shore up the grand compromise), but it was not yet dominant. Now it is.

Dead Surplus Labor: Or, We Are All Charly Keunang Now

The dominance of this kind of modal suffering is most clearly signaled by the ongoing assault on the social safety net. There has been no new net investment in public housing in the United States since the Carter administration, and

President Bill Clinton eliminated a long-standing requirement that any public housing unit destroyed had to be replaced, freeing local housing authorities to rip down public housing projects without having to worry about building new ones.[26] This rule change was justified as a first step in "decanting" poor people and thereby "deconcentrating" poverty, and housing authorities across the country have latched onto it and to a related program called HOPE VI to free up land for higher-income development. Between 1992—when it began as a pilot program—and 2010, HOPE VI demolished 95,200 public housing units and replaced them with 107,800 mixed-income units, of which only 56,800 were slated for low-income residents. In other words, this program alone led to a net loss of 39,400 units.[27]

Concurrent with the assault on public housing, the Clinton administration eliminated welfare "as we know it"—as an entitlement program—replacing it with a "workfare" program and stringent lifetime time limits on eligibility, work requirements, and a whole range of contradictory policies that make it exceedingly difficult, and immensely time-consuming, to comply with requirements and thus maintain eligibility for any benefits whatsoever.[28] More recently, the Council of Economic Advisors declared in 2018 that the war on poverty had been won, justifying itself both in terms of fiscal responsibility (necessary after handing yet another huge tax cut to the very wealthy) and with the argument that poor people are basically feckless. Following this declaration, the Trump administration began rolling out work requirements for food stamps, public housing eligibility, medical care, and more, as well as engaging in a concerted effort to purge people from the rolls of the disabled and force them into work.[29]

Here, the United States is merely following the United Kingdom's lead. Under the "New Labour" governments of Tony Blair and Gordon Brown, the British government "consolidated" the attack on welfare as a universal right that began under the Conservative governments of Margaret Thatcher and John Major. They transformed it into a "much broader program" of labor market coercion geared toward "steering individuals towards more active labor market participation"—in other words, to encourage a reactivation of what had been a largely latent reserve army of labor.[30] Such coercive policies were implemented in a context that can best be described as a state of (near) permanent "worklessness" for many, marked by a growing *absence* of jobs, especially ones that provide any security at all.[31] In other words, under New Labour and the subsequent Coalition and Conservative governments, labor market policy has in many ways devolved into a simple "coercion for coercion's sake"—a punitive regime of policy regulation that produced little more than misery, and, not infrequently it seems, death.[32]

And when this regime managed to achieve something else—some degree of job training, for example—then it did so at the cost of real immiseration. In Glasgow, for example, managers of a job training scheme linked to city center redevelopment argued that there will never again be jobs paying between £10 and £20 an hour, as there had been in the shipyards before deindustrialization. Therefore, their offer of jobs paying £3 to £5 an hour would *"educate"* workers in the reality of the labor market and prepare them to accept eventual work paying between £5 and £7 per hour (at a time when the national minimum wage was £4.85).[33] Rarely do such programs lead to secure, full-time employment paying a living wage. More often, they prepare workers to take whatever work they can, under whatever conditions, with any residual welfare benefits closely tied to the "willingness" to do so. Increasingly, lack of availability of work is no argument against "willingness."

And neither is disability. The Coalition and Conservative governments that followed New Labour doubled down on this consolidated and coercive regime, now under the presumed need for "austerity." Soon after coming to power in 2010, the Coalition government, citing the need for fiscal restraint (and engaging in a broad-based ideological attack on benefit claimants), changed the rules on fitness for work for those claiming disability. This required hundreds of thousands of people to submit themselves to a new "work capabilities assessment," the outcome of which would determine their eligibility for benefits. Tens of thousands of people were newly found "fit for work," frequently after a long delay (due to administrative snafus and the general incompetence of the outsourcing firm hired to conduct the capabilities assessments). When the government was forced to release data in 2015, these showed that between 2011 and 2014, an average of eighty people a month died within a month of being declared fit for work. The causes of death were surely many and not all could be linked to the decision to deny benefits, but it is perhaps telling that the British government fought long and hard to suppress these data.[34]

A LATE NEOLIBERAL HOLOCAUST

Much more certain is that since the Conservative-led Coalition government came to power, suicide rates have soared, and there is a direct link between benefit cuts and other aspects of the austerity regime and suicide. Social psychologist China Mills has studied coroner reports, suicide notes, and news accounts and finds that "the relationship between austerity and suicide is compelling." She argues that "if much of the world's population lives in conditions of chronic poverty and inequality that are killing them then there is a need to illuminate the environment from which 'welfare reform suicides' appear to represent a form of escape." Further, "Suicide is a significant social problem. Over 800,000 people commit suicide every year [globally]. Many of these are understood to be 'economic suicides' because they take place against a background of structural adjustment policies, rampant neoliberal market-led reforms and settler colonialism that serve to unsettle and dislocate the experiences of individuals within these economies."[35] Suicide is now part of the modal suffering of neoliberal austerity, in Britain and around the world.[36] The United Kingdom's Department of Works and Pensions (DWP), which handles disability benefits, seems to understand this even as it continues to deny any culpability. Between 2012 and 2017, the DWP "peer-reviewed" sixty complaints related to the denial of benefits. Forty-nine of these involved the death of a claimant, of which forty by suicide, suggesting that the DWP at least apprehended that suicide was possibly linked to the denial of benefits. Even as it admitted to undertaking these reviews, the government pushed through further cuts to benefits of disabled people deemed fit to "prepare" for work, while refusing to put into place systems to monitor the number of people who kill themselves (or otherwise die) after receiving the cut.[37]

Benefit cuts have been accomplished largely through the Coalition/Conservative government's landmark austerity-driven reform called "Universal Credit." Announced in 2010, legislated in 2012, and set to be fully operative by 2017 (though this has now been delayed until 2022), Universal Credit replaces six means-tested benefits programs (from housing subsidies to jobseekers' allowances to child tax credits) with a single, typically smaller payment (made even smaller by significant cuts to the program in 2015, which specifically reduced child support, especially to families with more than two children).[38] Among other effects, the introduction of Universal Credit has greatly increased debt loads on very poor people, as there is usually a six-week gap between the end of the old benefits and the first payment of the new. Evictions for rent arrears have increased, and with these so has homelessness.[39] By the end of 2018, one in two hundred Britons had become homeless, and tent cities had become a common sight in cities up and down the country. The aptly-named former housing secretary, James Brokenshire, denied that the government's policies could in any way be blamed, saying that "family breakdown" is at fault.[40] Food pantry patronage is likewise rapidly increasing. Finally, net incomes are dropping for the majority of benefits recipients, even as increasing numbers are being purged from the rolls.[41] The rationale for these changes is, of course, to save money (even as taxes continue to be cut for the wealthy and the government, already facing a Brexit backlash from companies and investors, does little to plug tax loopholes or stem the flow of profits and capital gains to offshore tax havens). It is also, however, to encourage people into work, even if in practice—as is becoming obvious—it actually discourages work because benefit cuts are linked to even the smallest successes on that front. In effect, this rationale seems to mostly deepen immiseration, and thus presumably pressures people to take any work at any price and under any conditions—either that, or commit suicide.

Besides direct cuts to social security benefits, the Conservative government has launched an all-out war on the institutions of social reproduction, from libraries and swimming pools, to services for the physically handicapped and developmentally disabled, to funding for schools and—resisted though it is—the National Health Service (even police department budgets have been cut!). Meanwhile, it has strongly encouraged the disposal of publicly owned land (also a policy of New Labour, though now accomplished with even greater vigor)—which is often sold at cut-rate prices to developers and other private interests[42]—while providing incentives to the growth of a predatory housing market. The result (among other things) has been a metastasization of the affordable housing crisis across the entire country.

The predatory private rental market in the UK affects the very poor (who often work contingently) and new immigrants enticed into the country by the possibilities of work (even if on the very lowest rungs of the economy), most perniciously. The vigorous recruiting of Polish, Czech, Romanian, and Roma workers has served a similar purpose to that served by the bracero program in the United States two generations earlier (as well as to the earlier recruiting of workers from the colonies to the UK), although it was never quite formalized as a guest worker program in the same way. Such a program was unnecessary, as poorer eastern European countries joined the EU and their citizens were entitled to free movement into Great Britain's farming, hospitality, janitorial, and other industries. This allowed for a much deeper casualization of work through the development of labor oversupplies, smoothing the entrance of the gig economy and its spread through ever more sectors of the economy. The EU migrants are supplemented—as braceros always were—by "illegal" workers recruited either directly by employers or by contractors, some linked to global human-trafficking gangs. This was tragically brought to light in February 2004, when twenty-three poorly trained, vastly underpaid Chinese cockle pickers, who had been smuggled into England in shipping containers, drowned in Morecambe Bay when they were overcome by a rapidly rising tide. If their deaths—which, as with those killed in the Chualar bus and train crash during the bracero program, were both extraordinary in the attention they received *and* fully integral, that is modal or normal to the working of the political economy of food—pricked at the conscience of official Britain, they did little to disrupt the system that allowed them to happen. Indeed, ten years later, according to a Durham University study, human trafficking into Britain for purposes of labor exploitation continued to grow and was set to surpass, in terms of numbers of people involved, trafficking into Britain for sexual exploitation.[43]

Both EU migrant workers and undocumented workers from elsewhere (when not fully enslaved) tend to find housing, if they find it at all, in the private rental market, itself significantly a result of the now forty-year-old attack on social welfare. An early, marquee program of the Thatcher government, the "Right to Buy" allowed tenants to buy formerly council-owned housing and was meant to unleash the freedom and entrepreneurialism that property ownership inevitably allows, at least according to its ideologues. In the UK, the Right to Buy program has certainly done the latter—unleashed entrepreneurialism—but largely *not* for its former tenants. It was not just that Right to Buy—coupled with the wholesale transfer of other council housing assets to housing associations—signaled the state's abdication of any responsibility for a right to housing, but even more that it paved the way for the opening of a private rental market that preyed particularly (though hardly exclusively) on immigrants who had little recourse to remaining stocks of social housing. An expanded landlord class quickly returned as a significant player in British cities. As when Engels wrote about the Housing Question in the 1870s, many members of this class were local petty bourgeoisie, sometimes with deep ties to the communities they worked in, but no less exploitative for that.[44]

Yet increasingly, these local players have been joined by more distanced ones: property-owning LLCs, real estate investment trusts, hedge funds, and others whose primary—indeed only—goal is to harvest rents, preferably at ever-increasing rates. Across British cities, such landlordism has had profound effects, as original Right to Buy owners have been induced to sell to these more distanced landlords (who themselves are frequently masked by layers of shell companies). The new owners then have every incentive to subdivide their properties, transforming family homes into so many bedsits with minimal facilities, which they then overcrowd. The kind of hot-bedding Engels (and so many labor historians in Britain and around the industrializing world) described as being so common during the prewelfare, liberal-capitalist era has returned with a vengeance. Such housing, deeply exploitative but also highly profitable, is not just housing of last resort, but is in many cases housing of *only* resort for new immigrants and longer-standing working-class people alike. And it does not come cheap. In the working class district of Govanhill in Glasgow, single bedsits with shared toilets were renting for £800 month in 2011, with heat and electricity not included. For many, the only option has been to share such small spaces with as many as six or seven other residents.[45]

As Universal Credit is taking hold, ratcheting down housing subsidies, demand for these bottom-rung housing options is expected to increase by a third in the next decade and double in twenty-five years.[46] The number of rough sleepers—Glasgow's Charly Keunangs—are rising concomitantly. While undoubtedly some are from Africa, like Mr. Keunang, more are Roma and other eastern European immigrants who have arrived on the promise of work and maybe a better life than was possible at home, just like the Chinese cockle pickers. And yet more are longtime Glaswegians—or residents of Cardiff, Liverpool, Nottingham, or London—finding that their new Universal Credit just does not stretch far enough to pay for housing. Like Charly Keunang, they search for somewhere to pitch a tent.[47] Like Charly Keunang and an inordinate number of his streetmates, they are dying on the streets at shocking rates.[48] And, like Charly Keunang and so many others, they are subject to an increasingly brutal regime of law and policing, making their mere survival all but impossible.[49] And yet, to the degree that the total casualization, if not elimination, of work portends a similarly grisly fate—to the degree that we are all subject to becoming mere surplus labor, more than just a reserve of labor—"they" is not the right term. "We" is more like it. We are *all* Charly Keunang now, at least potentially and assuming that, in the throes of austerity, we do not kill ourselves first.

A Late Neoliberal Holocaust: Or, We Are All Jane Doe Now

Hedge funds, private equity firms, real estate investment trusts, and other distanced investors are betting big on Glasgow bedsits for the same reason they are converting Los Angeles's Skid Row single room occupancy (SRO) hotels into fabulously expensive condos. While there is still lots of money to be made the old-fashioned way—deeply exploiting workers like the bracero farmworkers of the 1950s or the cockle pickers of the 2000s, while allowing death and replacement to substitute for sustenance and reproduction—even more can be made, it seems, from harvesting rents.[50] Rent harvesting, though, only deepens the deeply contradictory processes that are making us all braceros or—rather, *and*—Charly Keunangs.

Capitalism has a big reinvestment problem. All capital being produced—the size of the global economy doubles every thirty-five years—has to be reinvested *somewhere*, otherwise it becomes useless.[51] As industrial production matures (returns on innovation decline and/or markets become saturated), capital looks for new profitable outlets, commodifying ever-new realms of social life by, for example, turning childcare and playtime into bought-and-paid-for services, or even turning our most intimate thoughts into something bought off the shelf. But this too has its limits and contradictions, and the production–sale–return-on-investment cycle spins ever more rapidly. As a result, more new outlets for investment must be found. Hence the increased interest in the built landscape: the Glasgow bedsits and the Los Angeles SROs.

On the one hand, the invention of securities, credit default swaps, and all manner of other ingenious financial instruments has meant that land and the buildings and infrastructure on it are increasingly "treated as a pure financial asset, a form of fictitious capital" (that is, a kind of capital in which value circulates "ahead of itself" in the form of promissory notes).[52] This allows the built environment—itself a "geographically ordered, complex, composite commodity"—both to be fully financialized and to "give up" (as it were) its value nearly instantaneously, as if it were the most insubstantial commodity ever, no different from a song bought from a streaming service.[53] Yet on the other hand, the built landscape *is* different from a streamed song because it is *there*, solid and (nearly) immovable. While fictitious value can certainly be released to travel ahead of itself in the form of promissory notes and debt, the landscape is also, and importantly, a *store* of value that "turns over" (releases all its stored value) only very slowly—on a timescale of decades. This slow turnover time is important for a lot of reasons, one of which is surely that "trapping" actual value in slow-turning assets can cool the economy, serve as a break on the quickening pace of the turnover of capital as a whole, and ensures that the economy does not double in size any faster (or at least that the speedup in doubling time is moderated), which is crucial for maintaining the solvency of the global economy as a whole.[54]

This is why at moments of intense overaccumulation in the economy, investors frequently and quickly shift their capital into the so-called secondary circuit of investment in the built environment: into gentrifying skid rows, redeveloped brownfield sites, greenfield developments on the edge of town, new ports and airports, and so forth. And this is why wealthy and superwealthy capitalists have increasingly sought to park their capital in superexpensive chalets in Davos or Jackson Hole, luxury flats and townhouses in London and New York, and beach compounds the world over. The dual pressure of superwealthy capitalists looking to park their cash and organized hedge funds seeking both protection from an overheated economy and good, rapid returns is transforming cities. And it is doing so in two ways. The first is in the sort of urban restructuring—SROs into luxury hotels, right-to-buy apartments into bed-sits—described above. The second is by concomitantly *disinvesting* from—pulling capital out of—certain places (like the deindustrialized cities of the northeastern United States and northern England) perceived to be less of a safe, long-term investment.

For—and this is crucial—capital frozen in the landscape, slowly turning over, is not only something of a solution to the reinvestment problem facing capital as a whole, but constitutes a problem to it as well, since capital stored is capital at risk. First, there are the risks of overproduction (overbuilding), which mean that skyscraping luxury flats on 57th Street in New York just might not sell (at least at prices approaching $100 million, as they were a few years ago), that this or that golf course–centered gated community might stand empty, or that the new SRO conversions might find few ready buyers. Second, landscapes also become obsolete through technological or other changes (as with the tens of thousands of "ghost malls" that now mark the American landscape), are destroyed by war, natural disaster, or fire, or succumb to other forces of fashion and economy that make them, now, useless. They must be destroyed. As with austerity suicides, the killing of homeless people by the cops, and other modal, normal modes of suffering and death, the destruction of landscapes—and the values in them—is not accidental but is, in fact, integral and necessary to the working of the capitalist economy.[55]

Important in this regard is that capital is fractionalized. Those who own the circulating capital (all that fictitious capital that rules the world) are not necessarily identical to those who own the buildings—or the lives and businesses housed in them—as such. Different fractions of capital have different social and economic needs, desires, and logics. Capital that is rooted in place requires the building up, rather than the destruction, of values all around it (while footloose capital is much more sanguine about destruction). It is in the interests of some fractions of capital to ensure that the asset-stripping private equity fund does *not* land in their neighborhood, while at the same time courting inward investment of capital perceived and hoped to be relatively stable. Hence, rooted capital and its representatives in the state offer all manner of inducements to attract footloose capital, from free land to tax breaks to the provision of elaborate, state-funded infrastructure. To this fraction, mobile capital is something deeply desired and an existential threat at the same time.

What this looks like socially can be seen in any local development authority or chamber of commerce meeting, or at the mayor's office as she figures out how to attract marquee projects *and* fill the potholes and repair the aging infrastructure, or how to manage the growing numbers of homeless people who seem to be scaring the tourists, residents, and footloose capital alike away from the newly gentrified warehouse districts or just-about-to-turn skid row. For the existential threat of footloose capital is not only felt by other capitalists or by those who use (or live on) the streets, but in the tax coffers as well. As the neoliberal revolution has rolled back taxes on high-income and high-net-worth individuals, but especially on corporations,[56] localities have become ever more dependent on revenues from property and sales taxes. Both are in turn dependent on the "success" of the urban landscape, on its development and redevelopment. Property tax is particularly dependent in this way, not only because property values are relational—a function of the overall rent surface—but also and increasingly because the development tool of choice in American cities (and more and more in Britain and elsewhere) is tax-increment financing. With tax-increment financing, eventual repayment for public investment in preparatory infrastructure (and any new revenue) is derived solely from that portion of the property value that is an *increase* over values that prevailed before redevelopment, not the total value of a districts' properties. City revenues are dependent on continually increasing the value of the built environment.

Anything that threatens such increases must be confronted and neutralized. Mr. Charly Keunang, like all homeless people—like all surplus people—by his and their very presence, by his and their very desire to live, threaten such increases. So do partially employed eastern European immigrants escaping their cramped bedsits in Govanhill and hanging out on the street corners.[57] He and they have to be confronted and neutralized. And he was—as so many others just like him have been. Remember the five thousand homeless people arrested on LA's Skid Row in 2007 alone. Remember the $87 million spent on *policing* the homeless in LA in 2014. Mr. Charly Keunang was extraordinary only in that his name became somewhat well known and his killing a point of significant journalist investigation and activist organizing. Millions of others whose names we never learn die, or are made to die, or are left to die, or are killed outright, known nowhere outside of their circle of immediate family and acquaintances.

And sometimes not even known by them. Down along the California border with Mexico, out in the Imperial Valley in the small town of Holtville, a part of the town cemetery has been set aside for bodies of folks who have died trying to cross the border but who have never been identified, never returned to their families and friends, and were only ever given the name Jane Doe, John Doe, or even Baby Doe, stamped onto a small, brick-sized and brick-red headstone placed low on the brushed-clean desert floor. There are now around three hundred Jane Does, John Does, and Baby Does buried in Holtville; desperate workers who have tried to make it to—and make it in—the heartland of a neoliberal economy pioneered by the bracero program, which proved the value of hyperexploitation. Another five or six hundred small bricks mark the graves of identified border crossers, some of them perhaps the literal descendants of *braceros*, whose families were too poor to afford either the repatriation of their loved ones' bodies or anything more than a pauper's burial. Together, these gravestones are just a small bit of evidence of the late neoliberal holocaust, as are the markers, if any, memorializing the growing number of austerity suicides; a holocaust that is at once multifaceted *and* unified. They are evidence of what the geographer Ruth Wilson Gilmore has rightly identified as the *organized* abandonment of entire places and peoples that is a hallmark and a necessary component of the neoliberal global economy.[58]

These deaths are, in this respect, not so different from all the other excess deaths neoliberal capitalism produced, such as those caused by elevated rates of cirrhosis and liver cancer (up 65 percent since 2008) that have hit younger men particularly hard—or just the significantly elevated rates of mortality and morbidity linked to increased suicides, alcoholism, hypertension, and drug overdoses (increasingly called "deaths of despair" in the literature) that have continued to increase *even when the economy is no longer in crisis*.[59] These are normal, modal deaths—from Holtville to Glasgow, and in every small and large town in between and well beyond, stretching to the villages of Romania and Cameroon to the towering, not quite affordable apartment blocks of London (threatened by regeneration and fire alike), and even in Sweden, where center-left Social Democratic Party leaders of city councils now say that the presence of homeless Roma on the streets means that we are now forced to "make an exception regarding our principal stance concerning the equality of all human beings,"[60] and are thus permitted to do nothing that will allow them to live. They are modal deaths just as Charly Keunang's was, just as those bracero deaths were that Dr. Irma West was careful not to attribute to "voodoo," just as Jane Doe's was. Together, they are exactly what a late neoliberal holocaust looks like.

Endnotes

1. The best reporting on Charly "Africa" Keunang is Jeff Sharlet, "The Invisible Man: The End of a Black Life that Mattered," *GQ*, July 7, 2015, https://www.gq.com/story/skid-row-police-shooting-charly-keunang.
2. George Lipsitz, "Policing Place and Taxing Time on Skid Row," in *Policing the Planet: Why the Policing Crisis Led to Black Lives Matter*, eds. Jordan T. Camp and Christina Heatherton (London: Verso, 2016), 123–39.
3. Lipsitz, "Policing Place," 126.

4 Sharlet, "The Invisible Man."
5 Sharlet, "The Invisible Man."
6 Racism certainly shapes this pattern—is deeply integral to it—but it is not the only factor at work.
7 Per the *Oxford English Dictionary*.
8 Mike Davis, *Late Victorian Holocausts: El Niño Famines and the Making of the Third World* (New York: Verso, 2001).
9 No nationwide records of the annual number of people who die on the streets (from exposure, violent assault, lack of medical care, car accidents, etc.) are kept in the United States, but extrapolating from occasional city counts suggests it is likely in the thousands (in the UK, more than six hundred homeless people died on the streets or in shelters in 2017). Similarly, no nationwide study has yet been undertaken of the "excess deaths" that homelessness promotes, though some city-level studies exist. For example, a study in San Francisco calculated that homeless youth die at a rate more than ten times higher than youth in California as a whole. Colette L. Auerswald, Jessica S. Lin, and Andrea Parriott, "Six-Year Mortality in a Street-Recruited Cohort of Homeless Youth in San Francisco, California," *PeerJ* 4 (April 14, 2016): e1909. Other research suggests that the rate of mortality among homeless adults is three to four times that of the general population. See J. O'Connell, *Premature Mortality in a Homeless Population: A Review of the Literature* (Nashville, TN: National Health Care for the Homeless Council, 2005).
10 I am hardly alone in making the claim that we are living through a slow, diffuse, but nonetheless systemic destruction of lives. See especially Rob Nixon, *Slow Violence and the Environmentalism of the Poor* (Cambridge, MA: Harvard University Press, 2013); James Tyner, *Dead Labor: Towards a Political Economy of Premature Death* (Minneapolis: University of Minnesota Press, 2019).
11 Rachel Aviv, "The Apathetic: Why Are Refugee Children Falling Unconscious," *The New Yorker*, April 3, 2017, 72. Aviv draws especially on the work of philosopher of science Ian Hacking, "Making Up People," *London Review of Books*, August 7, 2006, 23–26.
12 Among others, see Gregg Mitman, *Breathing Space: How Allergies Shape Our Lives and Landscapes* (New Haven, CT: Yale University Press, 2007); Julie Guthman, *Weighing In: Obesity, Food Justice, and the Limits of Capitalism* (Berkeley: University of California Press, 2011); and Nancy Langston, *Toxic Bodies: Hormone Disrupters and the Legacy of DES* (New Haven, CT: Yale University Press, 2010).
13 Don Mitchell, *They Saved the Crops: Labor, Landscape, and the Struggle Over Industrial Farming in Bracero-Era California* (Athens: University of Georgia Press, 2012), 314.
14 Mitchell, *They Saved the Crops*, 142–155.
15 Mitchell, *They Saved the Crops*, 315–17; Don Mitchell, "Commentary: Dead Labor: The Geography of Workplace Violence in America and Beyond," *Environment and Planning A* 32 (2000): 761–64.
16 Ernesto Galarza, *Tragedy at Chualar: El Crucero de las Treinta y dos Cruces* (Goleta, CA: Kimberly Press, 1977); Lori A. Flores, "A Town Full of Dead Mexicans: The Salinas Valley Bracero Tragedy of 1963, the End of the Bracero Program, and the Evolution of the Chicano Movement," *The Western Historical Quarterly* 44 (2013): 124–43; and *Grounds for Dreaming: Mexican Americans, Mexican Immigrants, and the California Farmworker Movement* (New Haven, CT: Yale University Press, 2016).
17 Even mainstream economists showed no hesitation in describing bracero labor as indentured labor. See Lloyd Fisher, *The Harvest Labor Market in California* (Cambridge, MA: Harvard University Press, 1953). This form of indenture was innovative, because older forms of indenture tended to form under conditions of labor shortage and involve contracts that lasted for years.
18 Ernesto Galarza, *Farm Workers and Agri-Business in California, 1947–1960* (Notre Dame, IN: University of Notre Dame Press, 1977); *Merchants of Labor: The Mexican Bracero Story* (Santa Barbara, CA: McNally and Loftin, 1964); and *Strangers in Our Fields* (Washington, DC: United States Section, Joint United States–Mexico Trade Union Committee, 1956).

19 Quoted in Kitty Calavita, *Inside the State: The Bracero Program, Immigration, and the I.N.S.* (New York: Routledge, 1992), 21.
20 Fisher, *Harvest Labor Market*.
21 Paul Farmer, *Pathologies of Power: Health, Human Rights, and the New War on the Poor* (Berkeley: University of California Press, 2004).
22 Mike Davis, "Sand, Fear, and Money in Dubai," in *Evil Paradises: Dreamworlds of Neoliberalism*, eds. Mike Davis and Daniel B. Monk (New York: The New Press, 2007), 48–68; Kathleen Sexsmith, "Milking Networks for All They're Worth: Precarious Migrant Life and the Process of Consent on New York Diaries," in *Food Across Borders*, eds. Matt Garcia, E. Melanie Dupuis, and Don Mitchell (New Brunswick, NJ: Rutgers University Press, 2017), 201–18; Christián D. Reveco, "Chile Turns Rightward on Immigration," *Migration Information Source*, Migration Policy Institute, https://www.migrationpolicy.org/article/amid-record-numbers-arrivals-chile-turns-rightward-immigration.
23 Only 25 percent of global labor is in any sort of stable labor relationship, according to the International Labour Organization (ILO), and more than 40 percent of all American workers are now contingent (up from 17 percent in 1989). In China, less than 10 percent of internal migrant workers have contracts. Andrew Herod, *Labor* (London: Polity, 2017), 81–82.
24 Guy Standing, *The Precariat: The New Dangerous Class* (London: Bloomsbury, 2011); Tracy Vargas, "Dollar Store Economy: Reproducing Inequality within the Organization of Retail Service Work" (PhD Diss., Syracuse University, 2018); Gretchen Purser, *Labor on Demand: Dispatching the Urban Poor* (Berkeley: University of California Press, forthcoming); Herod, *Labor*.
25 A meta-analysis conducted by Columbia University's Mailman School of Public Health, surveying published research between 1980 and 2007 (that is, for the period of neoliberal entrenchment, but before the Great Recession), found that about 4.5 percent of all deaths in America could be attributed to "poverty." In 2000 alone, "approximately 245,000 deaths in the United States . . . were attributed to low levels of education, 176,000 to racial segregation, 162,000 to low social support, 133,000 to individual-level poverty, 119,000 to income inequality, and 39,000 to area-level poverty." "How Many U.S. Deaths Are Caused by Poverty, Lack of Education, and Other Social Factors?" *Press Release*, Columbia Mailman School of Public Health, July 5, 2011, https://www.mailman.columbia.edu/public-health-now/news/how-many-us-deaths-are-caused-poverty-lack-education-and-other-social-factors. See also Sandro Galea et al., "Estimated Deaths Attributable to Social Factors in the United States," *American Journal of Public Health* 101 (2011): 1456–65.
26 Jason Hackworth, *The Neoliberal City: Governance, Ideology, and Development in American Urbanism* (Ithaca, NY: Cornell University Press, 2007), 50.
27 United States Department of Housing and Urban Development, "FY2010 Budget: Road Map for Transformation," June 20, 2010, https://archives.hud.gov/budget/fy10/fy-10budget.pdf.
28 Jamie Peck, *Workfare States* (New York: Guilford, 2001). The still classic and absolutely relevant account of the dynamics of welfare expansion and recession is Francis Fox Piven and Richard Cloward, *Regulating the Poor: The Functions of Public Welfare* (New York: Pantheon, 1972).
29 Jim Tankersley and Margot Sanger-Katz, "Declaring War on Poverty 'Largely Over', White House Urges Work Requirements for Aid," *New York Times*, July 13, 2018, A14.
30 Gesa Helms and Andy Cumbers, "Regulating the New Urban Poor: Local Labor Market Control in an Old Industrial City," *Space and Polity* 10 (2006): 68.
31 Stephen Nickell, "Poverty and Worklessness in Britain," *Economic Journal* 114 (2004): 1–25, cited in Helms and Cumbers, "Regulating the New Urban Poor."
32 A 2017 study found that cuts to welfare, housing, and other benefits beginning in 2010 led to more than 45,000 excess deaths by 2014, and that the number was likely to climb to another 152,000 between 2015 and 2020—a hundred deaths a day—though to the degree the governing Conservatives "relaxed" austerity, the number could fall to 120,000.

The study was conducted before the newly introduced "Universal Credit" welfare system (discussed below) took effect, which will likely increase excess deaths. Alex Matthews-King, "Landmark Study Links Tory Austerity to 120,000 Deaths," *Independent*, November 16, 2017, https://www.independent.co.uk/news/health/tory-austerity-deaths-study-report-people-die-social-care-government-policy-a8057306.html.

33 Helms and Cumbers, "Regulating the New Urban Poor," 80, emphasis in original.
34 Patrick Butler, "Thousands Have Died after Being Found Fit for Work, DWP Figures Show," *The Guardian*, August 27, 2015, https://www.theguardian.com/society/2015/aug/27/thousands-died-after-fit-for-work-assessment-dwp-figures; Frances Ryan, "Death Has Become Part of Britain's Benefit System," *The Guardian*, August 27, 2015, https://www.theguardian.com/commentisfree/2015/aug/27/death-britains-benefits-system-fit-for-work-safety-net.
35 China Mills, "Suicides Linked to Austerity: From a Psychocentric to a Psychopolitical Autopsy," *Discover Society*, February 1, 2017, https://discoversociety.org/2017/02/01/suicides-linked-to-austerity-from-a-pychocentric-to-a-psychopolitical-autopsy/.
36 Suicide was also a not insignificant problem in the bracero program. In my research, at least, I found continual hints of it in the archival record.
37 Mills, "Suicides Linked to Austerity." John Pring, "DWP Secrecy Over Benefit-Related Suicides," *Disability News Service*, March 10, 2016, https://www.disabilitynewsservice.com/dwp-secrecy-over-benefit-related-suicides/. In the United States, suicide rates have grown 30 percent since 1999, according to the Centers for Disease Control, which also notes that rates of suicide are tightly correlated with economic downturns and yet still growing during the current "recovery," as misery has settled in in so many corners of the country. On a related note, it would not be hard to also begin talking of "austerity overdoses."
38 These cuts were very slightly rolled back the following year.
39 Patrick Butler and Matthew Holmes, "Councils Fear Surge in Evictions as Universal Credit Rollout Accelerates," *The Observer*, October 8, 2017, https://www.theguardian.com/society/2017/oct/08/councils-fear-surge-in-evictions-as-universal-credit-rollout-accelerates.
40 Patrick Butler, "One in Every 200 People in UK Are Homeless, According to Shelter," *The Guardian*, November 7, 2018, https://www.theguardian.com/society/2017/nov/08/one-in-every-200-people-in-uk-are-homeless-according-to-shelter; Alan Cowell, "U.K.'s Homeless Problem Is Growing, and Spreading, Report Finds," *New York Times*, November 22, 2018, https://www.nytimes.com/2018/11/22/world/europe/uk-homelessness.html; Robert Booth, "Rise in Homelessness Not a Result of Our Policies, Says Housing Secretary," *The Guardian*, December 18, 2018, https://www.theguardian.com/politics/2018/dec/18/rising-homelessness-is-not-due-to-tory-policies-says-james-brokenshire.
41 See "Universal Credit Cuts Hit Families with Children Hardest, Study Finds," *The Guardian*, March 1, 2017, https://www.theguardian.com/society/2017/mar/01/universal-credit-hits-families-with-children-hardest-study-finds.
42 Brett Christophers, *The New Enclosures: The Appropriation of Public Land in Neoliberal Britain* (London: Verso, 2018).
43 Andrew Glover, "Slavery 'Worse' 10 Years after Morecambe Bay Tragedy," *BBC News*, February 5, 2014, https://www.bbc.com/news/uk-england-25914594. More generally, see Parvis Mahdavi, *Gridlock: Labor, Migration, and Human Trafficking in Dubai* (Stanford, CA: Stanford University Press, 2011).
44 Frederick Engels, *The Housing Question*, ed. C.P. Dutt (Moscow: The Co-operative Publishing Society of Foreign Workers, 1935).
45 See Don Mitchell, Kafui Attoh, and Lynn Staeheli, "Policing-Centered Community Cohesion in Two British Cities," in *Policing Cities: Urban Securitization and Regulation in a 21st Century World*, eds. Randy Lippert and Kevin Walby (New York: Routledge, 2013), 58–75.

46 "Number of Homeless People in Scotland Expected to Double in Next Twenty-Five Years," *Glasgow Live*, August 10, 2017, https://glasgowlive.co.uk/news/glasgow-news/number-of-homeless-people-scotland-predicted-13456607.
47 Cowell, "U.K.'s Homeless Problem Is Growing."
48 May Bulman, "Nearly 600 Homeless People Died Last Year, Figures Show," *The Independent*, December 20, 2018, https://www.independent.co.uk/news/uk/home-news/homeless-deaths-2017-last-year-figures-streets-rough-sleeping-a8692101.html.
49 Don Mitchell, *Mean Streets: Homelessness, Public Space, and the Limits to Capital* (Athens: University of Georgia Press, 2020); FEANTSA, *Mean Streets: A Report on the Criminalization of Homelessness in Europe* (Brussels: FEANTSA, 2013).
50 Neil Smith, "New Globalism, New Urbanism: Gentrification as Global Urban Strategy," *Antipode* 34 (2002): 427–50; Don Mitchell, "From Boise to Budapest: Capital Circulation, Compound Capitalist Destruction, and the Persistence of Homelessness," in *Gentrification as Global Strategy: Neil Smith and Beyond*, eds. Abel Albet and Núria Benach (London: Routledge, 2017), 99–111; Ismael Yrigoy, "State-Led Financial Regulation and Representations of Spatial Fixity: The Example of the Spanish Real Estate Sector," *International Journal of Urban and Regional Research* 41 (2018): 594–611. More generally see Brett Christophers, Rentier Capitalism: Who Owns the Economy and Who Pays for it? (London: Verso, 2020).
51 David Harvey, *Seventeen Contradictions and the End of Capitalism* (New York: Oxford University Press, 2014).
52 David Harvey, *The Urban Experience* (Oxford: Blackwell, 1989), 97.
53 David Harvey, *The Limits to Capital* (Chicago: University of Chicago Press, 1982), 233.
54 Harvey, *Seventeen Contradictions*.
55 It is somewhat fashionable to refer to such destruction as "creative," but for those who live in landscapes being destroyed, there is little that is creative about the process. Rather, it is both cruel and banal. See Mitchell, "From Boise to Budapest," from which these paragraphs derive.
56 In the US, corporate tax revenues as a share of GDP are now at "historically low levels"; lower than at any point since the Depression. Jim Tankersley, "How the Trump Tax Cut Is Helping to Push the Federal Deficit to $1 Trillion," *New York Times*, July 25, 2018, https://www.nytimes.com/2018/07/25/business/trump-corporate-tax-cut-deficit.html.
57 Mitchell, Attoh, and Staeheli, "Policing-Centered Community Cohesion."
58 Ruth W. Gilmore, "Forgotten Places and Grassroots Planning," in *Engaging Contradictions: Theory, Politics, and Methods of Activist Scholarship*, ed. Charles R. Hale (Berkeley, CA: Global Area and International Archive, 2008), 31–61; and *Golden Gulag: Prisons, Surplus, Crisis, and Opposition in Globalizing California* (Berkeley: University of California Press, 2007). On Holtville, see Don Mitchell, "Work, Struggle, Death, and Geographies of Justice: The Transformation of Landscape in and beyond California's Imperial Valley," *Landscape Research* 32 (2007): 559–77.
59 Nicholas Balakar, "More Americans Are Dying of Cirrhosis and Liver Cancer," *New York Times*, July 18, 2018; https://www.nytimes.com/2018/07/18/health/cirrhosis-liver-cancer.html. Anne Case and Angus Deaton, "Mortality and Morbidity in the 21st Century," *Brookings Papers on Economic Activity*, Spring, 2017, 397–443, https://www.brookings.edu/bpea-articles/mortality-and-morbidity-in-the-21st-century/.
60 Quoted in Erik Hansson and Don Mitchell, "The Exceptional State of 'Roma Beggars' in Sweden," *European Journal of Homelessness* 12 (1) (2018): 15–40.

SETTLER COLONIAL URBANISM

From Waawiyaataanong to Detroit at Little Caesars Arena

Andrew Herscher

> *It is through this black hole that the West will disappear into the singularity of catastrophe, only to reemerge, on the other side . . .*
>
> —Mike Davis, "'White People Are Only a Bad Dream',"
> Dead Cities: And Other Tales, *2001*

Settler Colonial History at Little Caesars Arena

In the summer of 2017, a forty-five-block development near downtown Detroit branded "The District" opened for business. The District will comprise a vast complex of buildings rivaling the size of downtown Detroit itself; its first completed part was Little Caesars Arena, a new stadium for Detroit's professional hockey and basketball teams. The District is the largest outcome to date of the destruction of the historic Cass Corridor neighborhood and its incorporation into "Midtown," a spatial product qua urban neighborhood for the creative class professionals that the corporate interests, philanthro-capitalist foundations, and municipal officials controlling Detroit's development see as vital to the city's renewal.

Figure 1: Little Caesars Arena at The District, Detroit, 2018. Photograph by Adam Bishop.
Creative Commons license: https://commons.wikimedia.org/wiki/File:Little_Caesars_Arena_panorama.jpg

Little Caesars Arena includes the 1701 Pub, named for the year when French explorer Antoine de la Mothe Cadillac established a trading post and fort on the spot where the city of Detroit would subsequently develop. A map and plaque outside the pub describe, in word and image, how "the city of Detroit was founded in 1701 by European settlers and quickly became one of the industrial powerhouses of North America."[1] The plaque continues with a compressed history of beer brewing in Detroit:

> By the mid-1800s, small brewers started popping up to fill demand at local saloons. During prohibition, many of these brewers survived by producing non-alcoholic beer (ending immediately afterward). Local brewing returned again in the 1990s and continues to thrive—firmly establishing Detroit as a world class beer destination.

Here, narrative compression is accomplished by historical deletion—the deletion of industrialized beer brewing and its unionized labor that was vibrant in Detroit from the end of the nineteenth century until the 1960s.[2] While contemporary "local brewing" is intimately connected to urban redevelopment and its dispossession of communities of color, at the 1701 Pub local brewing is instead inserted into a mytho-history of artisanal brewing, first for mid-nineteenth century settlers and now for the early twenty-first century creative class. The omission of the intersection of beer brewing and industrial production—itself an aspect of Detroit's status as an "industrial powerhouse" referenced in the beginning of the plaque's narrative—thereby yields a depoliticized history of courageous arrivals and triumphant returns with no forced departures and no displaced exiles.

Figure 2: Map of Detroit at 1701 Pub, Little Caesars Arena, Detroit, 2017. Photograph by author.

With its name, plaque, and map, the 1701 Pub explicitly refers to the violent colonization of Indigenous space—Waawiyaataanong in the Anishinaabemowin language spoken by many of the Three Fires people who traversed, inhabited, and sustained that space. In so doing, the pub implicitly connects the dispossession of Indigenous people by European and American settlement in the eighteenth and nineteenth centuries to the dispossession of Cass Corridor's multiracial working-class communities by real estate development in the twenty-first century. From the 1960s to the 1980s, the Cass Corridor was also the "Red Ghetto," the site of the most well-known Native American community in Detroit.[3] Not only is the Cass Corridor the site of *multiple* dispossessions of marginalized people, then, but it is also the site of *repeated* dispossessions of Indigenous peoples. Therefore, at the 1701 Pub, Detroit's present is enmeshed in the city's colonial past in ways both avowed and disavowed.

In the last twenty years, the concept of "settler colonialism" has emerged as a name for a distinctive form of colonialism that develops in places where settlers permanently reside and assert sovereignty.[4] The relationship between settler colonialism and capitalist urbanism that the 1701 Pub foregrounds has been central in contemporary urban activism but has been only tentatively, if increasingly, explored in contemporary urban studies. On the one hand, prompted by the violence that occurs in the course of what is typically euphemized as "gentrification," Right-to-the-City, Indigenous, and Black liberation activists have vigorously framed contemporary urban displacement in the context of ongoing settler colonialism. For Right to the City Montreal:

> A colonial project . . . remaps itself at smaller scales in processes of gentrification of inner cities and these emerge as battlegrounds, although in more nuanced ways. We are reminded of this every time systemically disadvantaged and repressed peoples are further displaced, and their citizenships revoked, as city (re)settlers take on the self-appointed task of (re)colonizing and "taming" the "urban wilderness" of the inner-city, and its peoples.[5]

Indigenous activist Briana L. Urena-Ravelo has pointed out that "naming gentrification as the current manifestation of colonialism . . . means acknowledging that Black people experiencing gentrification have since slavery little to no say regarding where (they) went and lived."[6] And in *As Black as Resistance,* Zoé Samudzi and William Anderson write that "gentrification . . . is not a new form of colonization but rather a continuation of settler colonial dispossession in an urban setting."[7]

On the other hand, scholars in critical urban studies and critical Indigenous studies have been much more circumspect in their attempts to understand if and how settler colonial dispossession persists in contemporary urban contexts.[8] In critical urban studies, far more attention has been paid to differentiating the settler colonial city from the cities of extractive or exploitive colonialism than to analyzing the former in the context of contemporary urbanism;

in critical Indigenous studies, the dispossessions of capitalist urbanism have been foregrounded when they specifically involve Indigenous communities.[9]

I take the differentiated yet parallel engagements of activism and scholarship with settler colonialism in contemporary settings as testimony to a specifically postindustrial urban condition. While it was land that was expropriated from Indigenous peoples and labor from enslaved African peoples in the emergence and spread of settler colonialism in North America, it is now land that is expropriated from working-class and disadvantaged communities of color—sometimes also including Indigenous communities—that no longer supply reserve labor in postindustrial cities. *Replaced* rather than *exploited*, communities of color dispossessed in those cities occupy the position of Indigenous peoples in earlier stages of settler colonialism and are subject to processes that emerged and developed in those stages.[10]

The 1701 Pub in Little Caesars Arena already asserts a relationship between settler colonialism and contemporary urban redevelopment. In this essay, I take this assertion as an opening to explore the way in which Little Caesars Arena fits within Detroit's settler colonial history and, more generally, the way in which the urban history of cities in the United States can be understood as a history of land seizures, dispossessions, and displacements that repeatedly reprise US colonial settlement.[11]

Capitalism, Colonialism, and Urbanism

Emerging out of Marxist theory, critical urban studies has inherited that theory's critique of capitalism and struggled with its understanding of colonialism as a mere stage in capitalism's history. Marx understood colonialism in the frame of "primitive accumulation" ("ursprüngliche Akkumulation" in his original German)—the seizure of land, resources, and labor from spaces outside of capitalist management or control for the production of surplus value.[12] In *Capital*, he described a series of processes that accomplished these seizures in the course of colonization, including the dispossession of Indigenous people, the destruction of Indigenous forms of production and consumption, the enclosure of Indigenous commons, and the commodification of labor power:

> The discovery of gold and silver in America, the extirpation, enslavement and entombment in mines of the aboriginal population, the beginning of the conquest and looting of the East Indies, the turning

of Africa into a warren for the commercial hunting of black-skins, signaled the rosy dawn of the era of capitalist production. *These idyllic proceedings are the chief moments of primitive accumulation* ... The different moments of primitive accumulation distribute themselves now, more or less in chronological order, particularly over Spain, Portugal, Holland, France, and England. In England at the end of the 17th century, they arrive at a systematical combination, embracing the colonies, the national debt, the modern mode of taxation, and the protectionist system. These methods depend in part on brute force, e.g., the colonial system.[13]

Since the publication of *Capital* and arguably into the present, Marxist theory has been preoccupied with the registration of primitive accumulation as an ongoing or even permanent process. However, it has persistently accounted for the permanence of primitive accumulation via economic dynamics supposedly immanent to capitalism and removed from colonialism's "brute force."[14] In so doing, a central trajectory of Marxist theory has avoided analysis of the way in which colonial logics and practices of displacement, dispossession, and accumulation have come to structure those immanent dynamics.[15]

In the early twentieth century, Rosa Luxemburg's *The Accumulation of Capital* posed primitive accumulation as a structural process *within* capitalism—a form of accumulation that was actually not "primitive" at all. For Luxemburg, so-called primitive accumulation solved what she understood to be the problem of "underconsumption": a problem connected with the inability of structurally exploited workers to adequately consume the output of capitalist economies.[16] According to Luxemburg, the "capitalist desire for imperialistic expansion ... has the economic tendency ... to subjugate all the riches of the earth and all means of production to capital, to turn the laboring masses of the peoples of all zones into wage slaves."[17] The predominant methods for this subjugation, she writes, are "colonial policy, an international loan system ... and war."[18] As Hannah Arendt described Luxemburg's critique,

> Marx's "original accumulation of capital" was not, like original sin, a single event, a unique deed of expropriation by the nascent bourgeoisie, setting off a process of accumulation that would then follow "with iron necessity" its own inherent laws up to the final collapse. On the

contrary, expropriation had to be repeated time and time again to keep the system in motion.[19]

Arendt later expanded on Luxemburg's critique in her 1968 book *Imperialism*, writing that "the original sin of simple robbery, which centuries ago had made possible 'the original accumulation of capital' (Marx) and had started all further accumulation, had eventually to be repeated lest the motor of accumulation suddenly die down."[20]

More recently, scholars have accounted for the persistence of primitive accumulation in late or advanced capitalism by reference to "overaccumulation"—another problem posited as inherent to capitalism. For David Harvey, for example, the problem fundamental to capitalism is the search for opportunities for profitable investment of accumulated capital. Harvey therefore rereads the colonialism highlighted by Luxemburg and Arendt as a means to not only expand demand for consumption but also, and more importantly, to expand possibilities for profitable investment. Because this expansion must be undertaken constantly, primitive accumulation is, Harvey argues, an ongoing process:

> A general reevaluation of the continuous role and persistence of the predatory practices of "primitive" or "original" accumulation within the long historical geography of capital accumulation is, therefore, very much in order ... Since it seems peculiar to call on ongoing process "primitive" or "original" I shall, in what follows, substitute these terms by the concept of "accumulation by dispossession."[21]

Harvey describes "accumulation by dispossession" as taking place in spaces either not yet under capitalist control or separated from their owners by force: "capitalism can either make use of some pre-existing outside ... or it can actively manufacture it ... if those assets, such as empty land or new raw material sources, do not lie to hand, then capitalism must somehow produce them."[22] This difference between colonial dispossession in a "pre-existing outside" and contemporary dispossession in a manufactured outside renders the latter a kind of colonialism without colonialism: a "capture of valuable land from low-income populations that may have lived there for many years" that possesses all the salient features of colonialism-as-such.[23] This posits a conceptual distinction between a "manufactured" paracolonial outside and the "preexisting" outside of colonialism-as-such. In this way, the critical theory of capitalism registers its own inability to engage historical movements of colonial logics and practices.

Nasser Abourahme registers just these movements as he points out that "the colonial project (is) not just ... a 'constitutive outside' or subtending foil of liberal-metropolitan power, but also ... a returning political technology that eventually 'contaminates' the interior."[24] Moreover, the enmeshment of colonialism and capitalism suggested here has been foregrounded by both the colonized and those writing in solidarity with them. In *Discourse on Colonialism*, for example, Aimé Césaire defined colonization as "a form of civilization which, at a certain point in its history, finds itself obliged, for internal reasons, to extend to a world scale the competition of its antagonistic economies."[25]

Similarly, in accounting for the Indigenous experience of colonialism, critical Indigenous theory has supplemented the Marxist theory of accumulation to pose the persistence of primitive accumulation as the persistence of settler colonialism—the latter being understood as a structuring condition *of* capitalism rather than an event *within* capitalism.[26] To date, this supplementation has been most thoroughly advanced by Glen Coulthard in *Red Skins, White Masks*. For Coulthard,

> A settler-colonial relationship is one characterized by a particular form of domination; that is a relationship where power—in this case, interrelated discursive and nondiscursive facets of economic, gendered, racial, and state power—has been structured into a relatively secure or sedimented set of hierarchical social relations that continue to facilitate the dispossession of Indigenous peoples of their lands and self-determining authority.[27]

Focusing on dispossession rather than proletarianization, then, Coulthard recognizes settler colonialism to be "territorially acquisitive in perpetuity."[28] For Coulthard, this recognition keeps faith with "the subject position of the colonized vis-à-vis the effects of colonial dispossession" and opens onto critiques of the Marxist disregard of Indigenous territoriality, a recuperation of Indigenous dispossession as a way station on the historical journey to a redistributive commons, and a focus on the exploitation of people as labor power over the exploitation of land as property.[29]

Coulthard turns to an analysis of the contemporary city to register the persistence of Indigenous dispossession:

> The dispossession that originally displaced Indigenous peoples from their traditional territories either onto reserves or disproportionally into the inner cities of Canada's major urban centers is now serving to displace Indigenous populations from the urban spaces they have increasingly come to call home . . . Through gentrification, Native spaces in the city are now being treated as *urbs nullius*—urban space void of Indigenous sovereign presence.[30]

But this *urbs nullius*—a reprise of the *terra nullius* produced by the settler dispossession of Indigenous peoples—includes not only Native spaces, but also spaces inhabited by a whole range of working-class and disadvantaged communities—in particular communities of color whose labor has become dispensable in postindustrial capitalism. Thus, while Indigenous and African peoples were expropriated in fundamentally different ways in frontier and industrial settler colonialism, the position of Native and African American communities is becoming increasingly similar in postindustrial settler colonialism.[31] The Indigenous supplementation of Marxist theory, then, keeps faith not only with the Indigenous experience of settler colonization but also with contemporary urban development in situations of ongoing settler colonialism. A settler colonial framing of contemporary urbanism thereby shows that this urbanism is not simply a generic "accumulation by dispossession" but suggests that the latter might be better understood as specifically *settler accumulation*.[32]

Settler Accumulation in the Cass Corridor

The District in Detroit's Cass Corridor not only fits itself into the city's colonial history through the 1701 Pub, but also through its coming-into-being. The Cass Corridor developed along Cass Avenue in the late nineteenth century as an elite White residential neighborhood just north of downtown Detroit. As Detroit rapidly urbanized in the early twentieth century, affluent White families moved to neighborhoods further from downtown, and the presence of rooming houses, multifamily houses, and businesses increased. After the Second World War, working-class communities of color who had been dispossessed in so-called "slum clearances" often relocated to the Cass Corridor. By the 1960s, the neighborhood was one of the most racially diverse, culturally vibrant, and politically active in the city, with alternative schools, a community printing press, a food co-op, and underground galleries, theaters, and music venues. Precisely as such, however, the Cass Corridor was also a site of corporate and municipal disinvestment. Corresponding to this disinvestment, the city began to locate a number of social service providers in the area in the 1980s, including soup kitchens, homeless shelters, and mental health clinics, further driving down property values and contributing to the area's impoverishment.[33]

The Cass Corridor entered the twenty-first century as the second-poorest census tract in the city—a neighborhood at once accessible to the city's most marginalized people and communities and a site of social and economic disadvantage. Adjacent to Detroit's downtown—the first and primary site of postindustrial reinvestment in the city—the Cass Corridor was also a real estate "frontier" and, precisely as such, a site where both private and public land was targeted for "investment," which functioned as both a means and a cover term for resettlement. The largest such investment was made by a consortium of companies owned and managed by the billionaire Ilitch family, one of the major protagonists in real estate development in Detroit since the 1980s.

Investment began at the end of the 1990s and resulted not only in Little Caesars Arena and The District, but also in the dispossessions that allowed these areas to be built: while the 1701 Pub references the triumph of settler colonialism in Detroit, the real estate development that includes the pub references that colonialism's violence. Two aspects of that development in particular testify to the contemporaneity of settler colonialism in Detroit: the rendering of the enclosure of collectively held assets—including publicly owned property—as "improvements" and the rendering of resettlement as settlement.

Enclosure as Improvement

The seizure of Indigenous land in the context of settler colonialism was accomplished by, among other things, law underwritten by philosophy, most prominently John Locke's theory of property.[34] Locke's theory assigned the right of ownership to those who could use land in the most "industrious and rational" manner. This theory justified the dispossession of English rural populations through the enclosure of commons as well as the dispossession of Indigenous peoples by European settler colonists across the globe. As Allan Greer writes, Lockean "'improvement' is equally at odds with common land in England and uncleared forests in America."[35] In both European and colonial contexts, that is, Locke's references to industrious and rational land use were understood in relation to capital-based productivity—the use of land to raise crops, graze livestock, mine natural resources, and, most generally, create property—so that "productivity" was determined by the race- and class-based structures through which capital circulated.[36]

A Lockean understanding of property rights also shaped the work of the framers of the US Constitution and subsequent US laws and policies regarding the possession of property.[37] In the US, a posited "public use" justifies governmental exercise of eminent domain or transfer of publicly owned property to private owners for development. In effect, tying the right to property to the supposed capacity to use that property productively has served to legitimize land transfers for the accumulation of surplus value—framed as a public good in terms of increased property values and tax revenues—just as effectively as it served to legitimize the colonial seizure of Indigenous land in what Locke called "the inland vacant places of America."[38]

In the Cass Corridor, the Ilitch family deliberately created the contemporary version of those "vacant places"—a space of falling property values, depopulation, disinvestment, and their related consequences—by surreptitiously purchasing property and leaving it unmaintained and undeveloped.[39] This de-development strategy involved the purchase of some seventy properties for around $50 million over a fifteen-year period; purchases that were secret because of nondisclosure agreements that sellers were required to sign.[40] Withdrawing their own development plans from the Cass Corridor just as systematically as they withdrew capital, the Ilitches were then able to pose The District as an urgently needed development project that deserved public subsidy, even as it was their own disavowed de-development that exacerbated the problem this would solve: "desolate blocks (in) ...an economic dead zone."[41] As Chris Ilitch put it in an interview from 2014, after The District development had been publicly announced and approved, "It's been painful to not be able to develop some of that property because every time we made a move, the price for other property would shoot way up. But we had to wait..."⁴²

Along with paying for 58 percent of the construction of Little Caesars Arena, the public—in the guise of the Detroit City Council—subsidized the project with the largest land transfer in Detroit's posttribal treaty history: thirty-nine public properties sold for $1 to the Ilitches to assemble the parcel for The District.⁴³ Though this land transfer was questioned because it took place in the midst of the city's bankruptcy, this bankruptcy—forced by the city's Emergency Financial Manager—was also an engineered crisis that animated the enclosure of public assets; the transfer of public land to the Ilitches was just one of the city's many bankruptcy and postbankruptcy enclosures.

Detroit itself was a development made possible by the enclosure of Indigenous land by European and American settlers, legitimized by the latter with formal legal procedures. The enclosure of land that enabled The District both fits in and is naturalized by this history. In the US's "frontier" era, legal procedures were also enforced through physical violence: as Patrick Wolfe writes, "rather than something separate from or running counter to the colonial state, the murderous activities of the frontier rabble constitute its principal means of expansion."⁴⁴ This dimension of enclosure also had its contemporary counterpart in the numerous fires, whose causes were rarely ascertained, gutting buildings around the proposed Little Caesars Arena in the years that properties for it were being acquired.⁴⁵

Resettlement as Settlement

Settlements made at the origin of settler colonialism were, more precisely, resettlements: replacements of Indigenous inhabitation of land with settler inhabitation of property. As Patrick Wolfe writes, settler colonialism "strives for the dissolution of native societies" in order to "erect a new colonial society on the expropriated land base": "settler colonialism destroys to replace."⁴⁶ Wolfe describes settler replacement as not only replacing Indigenous presence, but also continually denying Indigenous absence: "The process of replacement," he writes, "maintains the refractory imprint of the native counter-claim."⁴⁷

The properties on the so-called "desolate blocks" that were seized to develop The District actually housed many of Detroit's most marginalized people and communities.⁴⁸ These properties included so-called "vacant lots," many of which were occupied by homeless people who used social services in the Cass Corridor; so-called "unoccupied buildings," many of which were squatted by dehoused people; and occupied buildings, most of which were apartment buildings rented by working-class and disadvantaged people and a large number of elderly people on pensions. The dispossession of the individuals who lived on these properties took place through eviction notices, nonrenewal of leases, and the condemning and destruction of buildings. In this way, the "desolation" of the district upon which The District arose was entirely produced.

The refractory imprint of the Cass Corridor's destroyed communities bears heavily on The District. Planned for the area around Little Caesars Arena, "The District" consists of four "neighborhoods" defined around a series of "local" sites: a park (Cass Park), two sports stadiums (Comerica Park and Ford Field), two theaters (Fox Theater and the Fillmore), and an area of "bars and restaurants."

Figure 3: Advertisement of new residential neighborhoods at The District, Detroit, 2017. Photograph by author.

The planning consultant for The District, Richard Heapes of StreetWorks, declared that "what we want is a great walkable, personable neighborhood made of as many people living their lives as possible."[49] "Great walkable personable neighborhoods" primarily occupied by working-class communities of color "living their lives" are precisely what was destroyed to make way for gentrified versions; pointing out that "people living in the district are the key to making it work," Heapes also pointed to the dispossession of the district's former residents—a dispossession that was equally key to making the project work.[50]

Gentrification, Settler Colonialism, and Decolonizing the Right to the City

The dynamics surrounding the development of Little Caesars Arena—the financial ambitions that motivated the project, the real estate transactions through which it took place, and the community displacements that it resulted in—all conform to dominant understandings of "gentrification." At the same time, these dynamics also conform to the way in which settler colonial territoriality, values, and violence have been distributed across the globe and live on in contemporary urban development. And yet, in spaces originating in settler colonialism as such, "gentrifying" property development and community displacement have specific histories in which the enclosure of Indigenous commons is continually reprised and the rematriation of Indigenous land is continually deferred.[51]

In Detroit as elsewhere, activists and communities concerned with the exploitation and dispossession that make projects like Little Caesars Arena possible have turned to the right to the city as a way to articulate demands for just and equitable urban development.[52] David Harvey, one of the leading theorists of this right, argues that "since the urban process is a major channel of surplus use, establishing democratic management over its urban development constitutes the right to the city."[53]

Harvey argues that this right needs to be claimed by "the dispossessed," but this term solicits decolonization. The right to the city is a concept drawn from the work of Henri Lefebvre in post-1968 France, where dispossession did not take place on colonized Indigenous land; in the United States, by contrast, "the commons" that the dispossessed can "reclaim" is Indigenous land expropriated by a settler colonial state.[54] *To recognize the ongoing state of settler colonialism, then, is to at once historicize and theorize dispossession*—to recognize dispossession as a practice that takes specific forms in settler colonialism even as, in the course of settler colonial history in the United States, that practice has targeted a range of marginalized and expropriated communities along with Indigenous peoples.

Writing in the *Michigan Citizen* in 1999—just as the Ilitch family was beginning to secretly de-develop the Cass Corridor—Omowale Diop Ankobia answered a letter from a reader who, quite unlike Ankobia, was "so happy that the White people are back and rebuilding the city."[55] While Marx and many of his successors left the transformation of soil into property unexamined, Ankobia wrote with awareness of the long history of this transformation in settler colonialism. In his response, then, he articulated his unease with Detroit's rebuilding and animated community resistance to it by staging it as nothing less than the contemporary form of settler colonial urbanism:

> It's about the LAND . . . If we never build nothing on it, we should not give it away. Nor should we invite enemies in to build on it. The Iroquois, Senaca, Ojibway, Mohawk, etc. did that and where are they now. We should protect it with our lives because our life as a people depends on it. That's what all the hullabaloo is about. The LAND . . . All the hullabaloo is about the LAND.[56]

Endnotes

1   On Detroit's colonization, see Tiya Miles, *The Dawn of Detroit: A Chronicle of Slavery and Freedom in the City on the Straits* (New York: New Press, 2017). The Indigenous contribution to the building of Detroit, which has around the tenth-largest Native American population among US cities, falls outside this essay's scope; on this contribution, see Edmund Jefferson Danziger, *Survival and Regeneration: Detroit's American Indian Community* (Detroit: Wayne State University Press, 1991) and Kyle T. Mays, "Indigenous Detroit: Indigeneity, Modernity, and Racial and Gender Formation in a Modern American City, 1871–2000" (PhD diss., University of Illinois at Urbana-Champaign, 2015).

2   The Altes Brewing Company operated from 1948 to 1954; the Ekhardt and Becker Brewing Company from 1881 to 1962; the Goebel Brewing Company from 1873 to 1964; the Koppitz-Melchers Brewing Company from 1891 to 1947; the National Brewing Company from 1954 to 1967; the Pfeiffer Brewing Company from 1889 to 1966; the Tivoli Brewing Company from 1898 to 1948; the Schmidt Brewing Company from 1933 to 1951; and, outlasting all the preceding, the Stroh Brewing Company remained in operation until 1989. On beer brewing in Detroit, see Peter H. Blum, *Brewed in Detroit: Breweries and Beer since 1830* (Detroit: Wayne State University Press, 1999).

3   On the Indigenous population of the Cass Corridor, see Danziger, *Survival and Regeneration,* 109; Tom Pawlick, "The Abandonment of the Indian in Detroit's Red

Ghetto," *Detroit News*, March 5, 1970, 2–4; Tom Nugent, "Leave Us Alone: Detroit's Indian Population Caught Between 2 Worlds," *Detroit Free Press*, February 20, 1972, A1, A3.

4 On settler colonialism, see Patrick Wolfe, *Settler Colonialism and the Transformation of Anthropology* (London: Cassell, 1999); Patrick Wolfe, "Settler Colonialism and the Elimination of the Native," *Journal of Genocide Research* 8, no. 4 (2006): 387–409; James Belich, *Replenishing the Earth: The Settler Revolution and the Rise of the Anglo World, 1783–1939* (New York: Oxford University Press, 2009); Lorenzo Veracini, *Settler Colonialism: A Theoretical Overview* (Hampshire, England: Palgrave Macmillan, 2010); Glen Sean Coulthard, *Red Skin, White Masks: Rejecting the Colonial Politics of Recognition* (Minneapolis: University of Minnesota Press, 2014); and Lorenzo Veracini, *The Settler Colonial Present* (Hampshire, England: Palgrave Macmillan, 2015).

5 Right to the City Montreal, "Colonizing the Inner City—Gentrification and the Geographies of Colonialism," August 15, 2012, https://righttothecitymtl.wordpress.com/2012/08/15/colonizing-the-inner-city-gentrification-and-the-geographies-of-colonialism/.

6 Briana L. Urena-Ravelo, "It's True, Gentrification Isn't the New Colonialism, It's Just the Old One," *Medium*, August 4, 2017, https://medium.com/@AfroResistencia/its-true-gentrification-isn-t-the-new-colonialism-it-s-just-the-old-one-daf7e97a86f0. See also Matt Remle, "Gentrification is NOT the New Colonialism," *Last Real Indians*, https://lastrealindians.com/gentrification-is-not-the-new-colonialism/.

7 Zoé Samudzi and William C. Anderson, *As Black as Resistance: Finding the Conditions for Liberation* (Oakland, CA: AK Press, 2018), 42.

8 This is, of course, in sharp contrast to the rich scholarly literature on the urbanism of extractive or exploitive colonialism; on this contrast, see David Hugill, "What is a Settler-Colonial City?" *Geography Compass* 11, no. 5 (2017): https://doi.org/10.1111/gec3.12315.

9 On the intersection of contemporary urbanism and settler colonialism, see Sherene Razack, "Gendered Racial Violence and Spatialized Justice: The Murder of Pamela George," in *Race, Space, and the Law: Unmapping a White Settler Society*, ed. Sherene Razack (Halifax, Canada: Between the Lines, 2002), 121–56; Nicholas Blomley, *Unsettling the City: Urban Land and the Politics of Property* (New York: Routledge, 2004); Penelope Edmonds, "Unpacking Settler Colonialism's Urban Strategies: Indigenous Peoples in Victoria, British Columbia, and the Transition to a Settler-Colonial City, *Urban History Review/Revue D'histoire Urbaine* 38, no. 2 (2010): 4–20; Coulthard, *Red Skin, White Masks*, especially 173–76; Natalie J. K. Baloy, "Spectacles and Spectres: Settler Colonial Spaces in Vancouver," *Settler Colonial Studies* 6, no. 3 (2016): 209–34; Lisa Kim Jackson, "The Complications of Colonialism for Gentrification Theory and Marxist Geography," *Journal of Law and Social Policy* 27 (2017): 43–71; and Hugill, "What is a Settler-Colonial City?"

10 On the distinction between replacement and exploitation in settler colonialism, see Wolfe, "Settler Colonialism and the Elimination of the Native."

11 In so doing, I aim to build on Rebecca Kinney's analysis of Little Caesars Arena in the context of "the White possessive"; see "'America's Great Comeback Story': The White Possessive in Detroit Tourism," *American Quarterly* 70, no. 4 (2018): 777–806. I also aim to build on the project defined by Ananya Roy as "unearthing how old mercantile and industrial histories can be traced in contemporary urban transformations, such that seemingly new and novel formations are in fact long-standing inscriptions" by advancing that project in the specific settler colonial context of the United States; see "What is Urban About Critical Urban Theory?" *Urban Geography* 37, no. 6 (2015): 814.

12 "The employment of surplus-value as capital, or its reconversion into capital, is called accumulation of capital." Karl Marx, *Capital: A Critique of Political Economy, vol. 1*, trans. Ben Fowkes (Harmondsworth, England: Penguin Books, 1976), 725.

13 Marx, *Capital*, 915–16. After the collapse of the Paris Commune in 1871, Marx began to rethink historical teleology and, correspondingly, his understanding of Indigenous societies; on this rethinking, see Kevin Anderson, *Marx at the Margins: On Nationalism, Ethnicity, and Non-Western Societies* (Chicago: University of Chicago Press, 2010).

14. As early as 1899, Kropotkin pointed to the "erroneous division" in Marx "between the primary accumulation of capital and its present day formulation." Peter Kropotkin, "The Collectivist Wages System," in *Kropotkin: 'The Conquest of Bread' and Other Writings*, ed. Marshall S. Shatz (Cambridge: Cambridge University Press, 1995), 221.
15. On this structuring, see Nikhil Pal Singh, "On Race, Violence, and So-Called Primitive Accumulation," *Social Text* 34, no. 3 (2016): 27–50; and Nasser Abourahme, "Of Monsters and Boomerangs: Colonial Returns in the Late Liberal City," *City* 22, no. 1 (2018): 106–15.
16. Rosa Luxemburg, *The Accumulation of Capital*, trans. Agnes Schwarzschild (1913; repr. New York: Monthly Press, 1964).
17. Rosa Luxemburg, "The Junius Pamphlet: The Crisis of German Social Democracy," in *Rosa Luxemburg Speaks*, ed. Mary-Alice Waters (1915; repr. New York: Pathfinder Press, 1970), 325.
18. Luxemburg, "Junius Pamphlet."
19. Hannah Arendt, "Rosa Luxemburg: 1871–1919," in *Men in Dark Times* (New York: Harcourt Brace and Company, 1983), 39.
20. Hannah Arendt, *Imperialism* (New York: Harcourt Brace Janovich, 1968), 15, 28.
21. David Harvey, "Accumulation by Dispossession," in *The New Imperialism* (Oxford: Oxford University Press, 2003), 144. Harvey offers a more expansive discussion of overaccumulation elsewhere, for example in *The Urban Experience* (Baltimore: The Johns Hopkins University Press, 1989).
22. Harvey, "Accumulation by Dispossession," 141.
23. David Harvey, "The Right to the City," *New Left Review* 53 (2008): 34; Harvey, "Accumulation by Dispossession," 137–82.
24. Abourahme, "Of Monsters and Boomerangs," 107.
25. Aimé Césaire, *Discourse on Colonialism*, trans. Joan Pinkham (1955; repr. New York: Monthly Review Press, 2000), 30.
26. In the words of Patrick Wolfe, settler colonialism is "a *structure* rather than an *event*"; Wolfe, "Settler Colonialism and the Elimination of the Native," 387.
27. Coulthard, *Red Skin, White Masks*, 6–7.
28. Coulthard, *Red Skin, White Masks*, 152.
29. Coulthard, *Red Skin, White Masks*, 10, 11.
30. Coulthard, *Red Skin, White Masks*, 175, 176.
31. On the differing racializations of Native Americans and African Americans, see Wolfe, "Settler Colonialism and the Elimination of the Native," 387–88.
32. I borrow the term "settler accumulation" from Nicholas A. Brown, though I render it in somewhat different terms; see Nicholas A. Brown, "The Logic of Settler Accumulation in a Landscape of Perpetual Vanishing," *Settler Colonial Studies* 4, no. 1 (2014): 1–26. My use of the term intersects with Ghassan Hage's "savage accumulation"; see Ghassan Hage, "État de siege: A Dying Domesticating Colonialism?" *American Ethnologist* 43, no. 1 (2016): 38–49.
33. For a (problematically affirmative) history of the Cass Corridor, see Armando Delicato and Elias Khalil, *Detroit's Cass Corridor* (Mt. Pleasant, SC: Arcadia, 2012).
34. John Locke, "On Property," in *Two Treatises of Government*, ed. Peter Laslett (1689; repr. Cambridge: Cambridge University Press, 1988), 115–25. On Locke and colonialism, see James Tully, "Rediscovering America: The *Two Treatises* and Aboriginal Rights," in *An Approach to Political Philosophy: Locke in Contexts*, ed. James Tully (Cambridge: Cambridge University Press, 1993), 137–78; Barbara Arneil, *John Locke and America: The Defence of English Colonialism* (Oxford: Oxford University Press, 1996); Duncan Ivison, "Locke, Liberalism and Empire," in *The Philosophy of John Locke: New Perspectives*, ed. Peter R. Anstey (London: Routledge, 2003), 86–105; David Armitage, "John Locke, Carolina, and the *Two Treatises of Government*," *Political Theory* 32, no. 5 (October 2004): 602–27; James Farr, "Locke, Natural Law, and New World Slavery," *Political Theory* 36, no. 4 (August 2008): 495–522; and Judith Whitehead, "John Locke, Accumulation by Dispossession, and the Governance of Colonial India," *Journal of Contemporary Asia* 42, no. 1 (2012): 1–21.

35 Allan Greer, "Commons and Enclosure in the Colonization of North America," *American Historical Review* 117, no. 2 (2012): 365–86.
36 On these structures, see Cheryl I. Harris, "Whiteness as Property," *Harvard Law Review* 106, no. 8 (June 1993): 1707–91.
37 See, for example, Harris, "Whiteness as Property," and Richard A. Epstein, *Takings: Private Property and the Power of Eminent Domain* (Cambridge, MA: Harvard University Press, 1985).
38 Locke, "On Property."
39 Tom Perkins, "How the Ilitches Used 'Dereliction by Design' to Get Their New Detroit Arena," *Detroit Metro Times*, September 12, 2017, https://www.metrotimes.com/news-hits/archives/2017/09/12/how-the-ilitches-used-dereliction-by-design-to-get-their-new-detroit-arena.
40 Louis Aguilar, "Detroit's Midtown Land Deals Spark Speculation," *Detroit News*, March 19, 2010, A1.
41 Joe Guillen and J. C. Reindl, "Council Votes Today on Arena Land Deal," *Detroit Free Press*, February 4, 2014, 1, 3.
42 Louis Aguilar, "LCA's To-Do List Gets Smaller and Smaller," *Detroit News*, September 1, 2017, https://www.detroitnews.com/story/news/local/detroit-city/2017/09/01/little-caesars-arena-todolist/105205002/.
43 In fact, to avoid paying property taxes, the Ilitches arranged for the properties to be sold to the Detroit Downtown Public Authority, from whom they have leased Little Caesars Arena for ninety-five years. The bulk of the public financial subsidy comes from tax increment financing in the Downtown Development Authority district.
44 Wolfe, "Settler Colonialism and the Elimination of the Native," 392.
45 Critmom, "Gentrification in the Cass Corridor," *Critical Moment*, June 21, 2014, https://critical-moment.org/2014/06/21/gentrification-in-the-cass-corridor/.
46 Wolfe, "Settler Colonialism and the Elimination of the Native," 388.
47 Wolfe, "Settler Colonialism and the Elimination of the Native," 389.
48 See, for example, Critmom, "Gentrification in the Cass Corridor"; Matt Helms, "What Will Happen to Cass Corridor Homeless as Arena District Moves In?" *Detroit Free Press*, August 8, 2015.
49 Bill Shea, "'Residential Everywhere': Thriving Neighbors Seen as Key to District Detroit's Sustainability," *Crain's Detroit Business*, 31, no. 47 (2015).
50 Shea, "Residential Everywhere."
51 Asher Ghertner, "Why Gentrification Theory Fails in 'Much of the World,'" *City* 19, no. 4 (2015): 552–63.
52 On the right to the city, see Peter Marcuse, "Reading the Right to the City," *City* 18, no. 1 (2014): 4–9.
53 Harvey, "Right to the City."
54 As Coulthard argues, "by ignoring or downplaying the injustice of colonial dispossession, critical theory and left political strategy . . . risks becoming complicit in the very structures and processes of domination that it ought to oppose": see *Red Skin, White Masks: Rejecting the Colonial Politics of Recognition*, 12.
55 Among the White people the reader named are Ilitch, Karmanos, Adamany, and Duggan; see Omowale Diop Ankobia, "Calling It Like It Is: What Detroit Is Giving Away," *Michigan Citizen*, December 25, 1999, A7.
56 Ankobia, "Calling It Like It Is."

STEEL BLOOM

Lineages and Landmarks of Borderland Violence

Ana Muñiz

Now.
In the Borderlands.
In 1987, Gloria Anzaldúa wrote of the US–Mexico border,
"This is my home/ this thin edge of/ barbwire."[1]
When I was young, the border in much of Arizona's Sonoran Desert was a spiked metal string limply tied between rotting wooden posts. In a few places, it still is. For the most part, however, the barriers have become increasingly formidable. Over the years, hunks of metal have been hauled in. Motion sensors have been implanted in the ground. Cholla cactuses drop fat yellow fruit under infrared, watch towers, choppers, drones, and semi-automatics.

And now, as the US government calls for proposals to build a reinforced border wall, the barrier seems set for another, more expansive iteration.[2] A home bent on exile.

As long as it has existed, the southern border has been a "1,950 mile-long open wound" hovering between brown land and blue sky.[3] Hunters walk the curve of this wound singing commands into the static of a radio. Some of them are in government-issued green polyester. Others have no badges but rather are self-appointed defenders of the frontier.[4] Perched atop off-roading vehicles, they destroy migratory trails established over centuries. Border Patrol agents lay traps for crossers by sweeping the sand with a large brush hitched to the back of a pickup truck. It is easier to see footprints that way. I imagine this is what the jaw of a whale looks like, millions of delicate bristles washing over prey.

Surrounding the brutality is a beauty of shattering clarity.

"The land stretched out under me the way a lover would."[5]

The days are warm and languid until the sun sets in an explosion, evacuating heat from the valley floor and draping the skyline in shameless tones. At dusk, the mesquite trees dissolve into one another like a single organism.

"The people live in the desert and so they move across the desert."[6]

Drawn by its beauty, some people migrate to this land through Arizona's northern border, from Iowa, Wisconsin, and Ohio. Sometimes, these immigrants buy houses on this land. Sometimes, they rip out ocotillo, aloe vera, and centuries-old creosote bushes from their front yard. Instead, a lawn is installed in the 116°F desert. Sometimes, the people from the northern border pay the people who live in the southern borderlands less than a minimum wage to tear out the ocotillo, aloe vera, and ancient creosote for them.

I used to sit in the cab of a white Chevy truck, the old ones with the gear shift on the steering wheel, and watch my father, a lover of soil, dig his hands under the root ball, trying to extract the plant intact. Border Patrol would interrupt groups of laborers at work with precise regularity, walking down the line of hunched backs to ask, "Where are you from?" The words seep into your mind like chimes from somewhere far away,

Where are you from?

It is the same question members of warring neighborhoods ask one another to tease out enemies from allies. It is the same question police officers on the streets of Los Angeles ask youth they stop for questioning.

I am from here.

In the heat of the afternoon, anyone whose response was dressed in an accent was loaded into the white-and-green van and checked for documents. A driver's license would not do. A birth certificate or green card were the only acceptable currency here.

They tried to hack the dignity out of you. They tried to get you to wield the weapon and hack it out of your own wild skin.

But some things remain "wild enough to survive."[7]

The US government would like a contractor, at a low-going rate, to construct a wall from San Diego to Brownsville. The US government issues one call for proposals to build a "Solid Concrete Wall Prototype," which, as stated, is to be constructed of concrete. They also issue a second call for an "Other Border Wall Prototype," which is to be constructed of materials other than concrete. In calling for a concrete border, a wall is defined as "a contiguous, physical wall or other similarly secure, contiguous, and impassable physical barrier" with anti-dig and anti-tunneling protection.[8]

In the second call, for a border made of anything but concrete, a wall is considered to be "an 18–30ft. tall barrier designed to prevent illegal entry and drug"[9] That is it. The definition ends with "drug" and without punctuation. It is unclear why the definition is unfinished. It is also unclear why an Other Border Wall is a drug-repelling instrument while a Solid Concrete Wall is not. The definitions are perpetually in flux, shifting, collapsible, or expandable, depending on the objective at hand. This Wall is never simply a structure, but also represents a "ritual repository"[10] for refracted fears, anxieties, and cruelties. Narratives of dominance and submission are sunken into its structure.

The US government would prefer if the contractor could perform this task independently, with "little or no Government intervention."[11] They encourage minority-owned and woman-owned businesses to apply. At some point in the application process, the contractor may be asked to describe their experience "executing high profile, high visibility and politically contentious design-build projects."[12] Ideally, this wall would incorporate portions of see-through components without compromising the wall's capacity to withstand "external attack" by "sledgehammer, car jack, pick axe, chisel, battery operated impact tools, battery operated cutting tools, propane or butane or other similar hand-held tools."[13]

But this thirty-foot high wall in the desert is not to look too conspicuous. The US government would like the contractor to aesthetically treat the US-facing side of this wall so that its appearance is pleasing and integrated into the surrounding environment. The contractor is to remember that the US government intends "environment" to be a broad term that "includes not just elements like the geography and location, but also the nature of the law enforcement mission near the border."[14] After all, Border Patrol vehicles have become as much a part of the natural environment as prickly pear cactus.

I may be getting a new home, made of concrete or a yet to be named non-concrete alternative. Maybe a wall of mud would do. While the prototypes are constructed, the National Guard is redeployed to the borderlands to reunite with the web of local, county, state, federal, and military agencies tasked with standing guard.[15] As the soldiers ride into the beautiful south, I realize that some longer process in me has been ultimately rendered,

This is my home
This obscene expanse of steel
Blooming in the desert sun

Much has been made of The Wall. It has made its presence acutely known in my own life. It does material damage to the people trying to cross it, to the land, and to the animals that rely on it. Nonetheless, its immediate physicality is not its only, or perhaps even principal, imposition. Rather, The Wall is significant because of the diffusion of its function, and its violence—both sensual and symbolic—throughout myriad institutions.

Racial subjugation takes various forms historically, including the explicit brutality of racialized state violence perpetrated and enabled by law enforcement and other government officials, at times, in concert with white supremacist vigilantes.[16] Additionally, less spectacular formations of "state organized race crime"[17] perpetuate subjugation, such as the "slow violence"[18] of cumulative disadvantage, the "plunder" of property,[19] and normalization of "legal violence," wherein members of marginalized groups are routinely denied legal protections.[20]

What follows are three interwoven vignettes; nonfiction stories from three different points in time, moving closer to the present but remaining enmeshed in familiar dynamics of border violence—a multifaceted violence, expressed physically and institutionally, in which components are mutually constituted across time and space.[21] One of these stories focuses on a 1976 case in which three ranchers were accused of torturing three border crossers. The second examines the aftermath of a 1977 police murder of a young Chicano in Tucson, Arizona. The third vignette takes place inside a Los Angeles courtroom in 2016, where a deportation decision hinges on a gang allegation by local police. As the stories travel temporally, they also take us over the geographic space of a common migration circuit, across the southern border, north through Arizona, and then to Los Angeles. Finally, we are returned to the borderlands, to consider the latest iterations of racial control and violence.

1976.
1.5 Miles North of the Border.
Six Men.

Late summer is the height of monsoon season in Southern Arizona. Temperatures regularly break 110°F through the early afternoon until black and purple storm clouds roll in heavy with rain. The smell comes first, then the wind and thunder, and finally, the downpour.

On the morning of August 18, 1976, Manuel Garcia Loya, Eleazar Ruelas Zavala, and Bernabe Herrera Mata approached the international boundary separating Agua Prieta, Sonora, Mexico, from Douglas, Arizona, United States, as the heat ascended.[22] The land hinted at the post-monsoon wildflower bloom. They crossed into the US through some desert scrub and agave next to a copper smelter. The trio's destination was a farm in Elfrida where the men hoped to work, located a little over 25 miles north of Douglas up US Route 191.[23] After crossing, the three men stopped at a reservoir to refill their water jugs.[24] The sun pushed higher into the sky, a pure yellow orb.

On the horizon, another yellow object, a pickup truck, began to materialize through waves of dust. Manuel, Eleazar, and Bernabe assumed it was a Border Patrol truck. On its arrival, a boot emerged from the open door, then the arm, shoulder, and mustachioed face of an Anglo[25] man. Next, his right leg appeared and finally, his right hand, holding a pistol. Manuel, Eleazar, and Bernabe were all in their twenties. This Anglo man, Tom Hanigan, looked to be about their age, maybe a bit younger.[26]

According to Manuel, Eleazar, and Bernabe, Tom addressed them in Spanish, using a derogatory term for people who cross from Mexico into Texas by wading through the Rio Bravo.[27] The Rio Bravo, however, was far from Arizona, having made a hard turn away from the border in New Mexico to run north toward the Rocky Mountains.

"You all come here to rob," Tom allegedly muttered as he instructed them to get into the camper of his truck.[28] Tom drove the men a few minutes away to a ranch house and ordered them out of the truck to sit near a porch. Another truck pulled up, out of which a man in his sixties wearing business attire emerged, shotgun in hand.²⁹

A third truck pulling a camper arrived. Tom's brother Pat, older by a few years and taller by a few inches, hopped out of the driver's side. Pat reportedly pulled a handgun from the waist of his jeans and swung the barrel at Manuel, "I know you. You stole three rifles and a pistol from me."³⁰

Over Manuel's insistence that this accusation was untrue, the elder George Hanigan, having changed into a plaid work shirt and jeans, and his two sons, Pat and Tom, ordered the three Mexican men into the yellow truck.³¹

When they were pulled from the vehicle back into the sunshine, Manuel, Eleazar, and Bernabe recognized the arroyo as being near the spot where they had stopped for water a short time ago. They reported that the three Anglo men allegedly gathered each of the three Mexican men's limbs into a point behind their backs, binding each set of hands and feet together in the way a rancher would tie cattle.³² With a hunting knife, the Hanigans stripped the clothing from the Mexican men's bodies and the hair from their scalps.³³ As Bernabe's pants were torn, a single dollar flickered to the ground. The Anglo men discovered $30 in Manuel's pants and another $7 in one of his socks. Pat gathered the money and shoved it in into his own pocket.³⁴

The Hanigans reportedly spent the next several hours conjuring well-worn white supremacist traditions. They threatened castration by running a knife around the testicles of the Mexican men. The soles of Eleazar's feet were branded using a metal rod that had been heated in a fire built from felled mesquite branches.³⁵ Of course, there was attempted lynching.³⁶ Ultimately, the Mexican men reported that their nooses were slashed so that the Hanigans could hunt moving targets: "Let's see how good you are at running."³⁷

Bernabe received 47 birdshot pellets to the back. Manuel was hit with 125. Eleazar tripped while sprinting south through the desert, pellets barely missing the top of his newly sheared hair.³⁸

1977.
59 Miles North of the Border.
Joe.

So many things in Tucson seem to have two names—restaurants, plants, people. Like the place that serves greasy spoon breakfasts in the morning as "Franks" and in the afternoons switches their sign to "Francisco's" for Mexican dinners. I recall my confusion when I first heard someone refer to a *javelina* as a *peccary* and call a *creosote* bush *chaparral*. There are also two Tucsons, and not only in the metaphorical sense. South Tucson is its own official city, a jurisdiction of approximately one square mile, separate from the City of Tucson, into which Mexican immigrants and their descendants have been historically segregated.[39]

My father remembers growing up in South Tucson with a friend who everyone called Joe, even though his given name was Jose. Jose, or Joe, always seemed to be laughing. The rigid vigilance that people often develop to survive rough neighborhoods somehow missed him. He played in a band and studied art at the community college.[40] Joe's blood was Opata, through his mother's line, from the indigenous people of Northern Sonora. Joe's mother, Lupe, grew up riding horses in Southern Arizona in the 1930s. His father, Joe Sr., worked in the mines around Tucson.[41]

Shortly before Independence Day in 1977, when they were both twenty-four years old, Joe and my father went to a Jack-in-the-Box off of Interstate 10 in South Tucson. A fight broke out, and police arrived to conduct arrests, despite those involved in the altercation having already left the scene.[42] The officers' turn to persuasion by billy club only triggered more resistance from the youth, an escalating pattern that reached its climax in an officer sending a distress call to dispatch. Over forty police officers from four jurisdictions responded.[43] A South Tucson Police Department (STPD) helicopter swerved into the hot summer sky as police dogs jumped out of black-and-white Crown Victoria sedans.

Officer Ford from the Department of Public Safety was on traffic control duty. He waved a couple of kids in a 1954 Chevy pickup truck onto 6th Avenue, a main thoroughfare in South Tucson.[44] The kid driving the truck, Joe, and his passenger, Mario, were traveling south, in the direction of the Veteran's Administration Hospital, where Joe would later bleed out.[45]

Officer Christopher Dean had been on the job with STPD for two months, having recently been fired from the Pima County Sherriff's Department for allegedly beating a man in a cemetery during a narcotics investigation.[46] Holding a young Chicano man by the arm on his way to a police van, Dean stepped in front of Joe's truck. According to multiple witnesses, the truck stopped, idled momentarily, and then passed by Dean.[47]

Officer Dean said that the Mexican kid twice tried to run him over in his '54 Chevy. So he took those numbers and reversed them, added a dot up front, and assuming a kneeling position, fired off rounds from his department-issued .45. A handful of bullets went into the back of the truck. One breached the metal of the cab at a full gallop, went through the seat, went through Joe's skin, went through the muscles of his lower back, and settled into his spine.[48] The truck and its occupants rolled two more blocks down South 6th Avenue before colliding with a curb.[49] Officer Dean got into his partner's patrol car, and they drove to the South Tucson Police Station to fill out their incident reports together.[50]

The cabs in those old Chevys had one long seat made of blue or brown leather. Chicano guys used to upholster them with seat covers that scratched the back of your thighs, woven with harsh rope in Southwest designs of recurring stripes, zigzags, and diamonds. Under Joe's cab seat, a homicide investigator scraped together a few marijuana seeds that did not have Joe's blood on them and started to use terms like "intoxication" and "justifiable homicide."[51]

1977.
7.5 Miles North of the Border.
Six Men Become Five.

The patriarch George Hanigan was dead.
Though all three Hanigans pleaded "not guilty" to the torture of Manuel Garcia Loya, Eleazar Ruelas Zavala, and Bernabe Herrera Mata in January 1977, by the start of the three-week trial on September 20, 1977, George had been felled by a heart attack.[52] Only the Hanigan sons, Tom and Pat, would be judged in Bisbee, Arizona, by a Cochise County Grand Jury on eleven felony counts each, including kidnapping, assault with a deadly weapon, armed robbery, and conspiracy.[53] The defense argued that the torture accusations were an attempt by the three Mexican men to appropriate, through legal channels, the money that they originally intended to steal from the Hanigan property, pointing to a pending civil lawsuit in which Manuel, Eleazar, and Bernabe sought $1.2 million each in punitive damages.[54]

For months, Douglas newspapers had run long-form investigative pieces on burglaries in the area, relaying Border Patrol suspicions that every "illegal alien" was a latent burglar. One local journalist calculated the net cost of Douglas area burglaries in 1975 at $135,000.[55]

At some point during the first week of October, the presiding judge in the case received a note from the jury, which inquired as to whether the felony "assault with a deadly weapon" charges could be reduced to simple assault charges. The judge denied the jury's request. On October 7, 1977, the jury returned the verdict of "not guilty" on all charges.[56]

The US Department of Justice (DoJ) announced that they would not pursue charges under the Civil Rights Act because the citizenship status of Manuel, Eleazar, and Bernabe put them outside of federal jurisdiction.[57] DoJ representatives stated that federal civil rights prosecution would require either that the victim(s) of violence have legal status or that the perpetrator of violence be a law enforcement official. Thus, it was not legally possible for noncitizens on US soil to have their civil rights violated as a result of private citizen vigilante violence, an example of the way in which American law constructs migrants as punishable subjects while simultaneously pushing them outside the law.[58]

1978–79.
61–62 Miles North of the Border.
Joe and the Officer.

Officer Dean stated that he shot at the truck in self-defense. Joe ran him over once, and then backed up his truck to try to run him over again, so Dean shot at the tires. He was not sure how the shots swerved so far upward, but he was sure that he did not intend to kill anyone.[59] And anyway, Officer Dean reasoned, he had shot to stop a fleeing felon.[60]

At the time, homicide by a police officer was considered legally justifiable in the case of one of the following parameters: "(a) In overcoming actual resistance to the execution of some legal process, or in the discharge of any other legal duty. (b) In retaking felons who have been rescued or who have escaped. (c) In arresting persons charged with felony who are fleeing from justice or resisting arrest."[61] Officer Dean's claim that his actions were consistent with these criteria prompted some confusion among the eight-person all-white jury.[62] Joe did not have a felony on his record. He had not been fleeing from prison.

The felony, Officer Dean clarified, was the attempt to run him over.[63] Thus, during the seconds it took to pass by Officer Dean on South 6th Avenue, Joe had become a felon, a fleeing felon, and a justifiably dead felon. The law works quickly under the right circumstances.

A fellow officer backed up Dean's account, but most of the other witnesses were baffled as to why he had fired his weapon. Although Officer Dean claimed to be run over by Joe's truck, he sustained no injuries. One witness, an Arizona State Corrections Officer, characterized Officer Dean's shot as "well aimed" and accomplished with his "arm held horizontal" to Joe's back.[64] Witnesses claimed that only after the fatal shot did Dean lower his arm to aim at the tires of Joe's truck.

On January 23, 1978, the jury acquitted Officer Dean of involuntary manslaughter charges.[65]

During the last week of June 1979, Joe's family hosted their forty-second weekly vigil outside of the Federal Building in downtown Tucson.[66] The purpose of the vigil had been to pressure the DoJ to prosecute Officer Dean under federal civil rights statutes after the Arizona state trial ended in acquittal. The Assistant Attorney General for the Civil Rights Division wrote that the DoJ was unlikely to file federal charges: "As I know you are aware, criminal civil rights prosecutions are generally difficult cases because of the government's burden of proof beyond a reasonable doubt and because of the necessity of proving, under current federal law, that the defendant specifically intended to violate the victim's federal civil rights."[67]

The threshold of willful intent has long provided a steep barrier to successful antidiscrimination litigation and allowed the US criminal justice system to function according to a "penology of racial innocence."[68] As antidiscrimination law has developed to require proof of specific individual intent, coded manifestations of racism have simultaneously made intent progressively more difficult to prove.[69] Thus, racialized punishment wears a façade of neutrality as people of color are expelled to the fringes of legal protection while they are disproportionately subjected to legal retribution.

Nonetheless, as June transformed into July and outrage over Joe's case spread across the nation, the DoJ announced that it would reverse its position and convene a grand jury to investigate whether civil rights charges applied. As a result of mass mobilizations following several murders by police in the

Southwest,[70] the DoJ decided that it was open to pursuing a "dual prosecution" strategy, in which federal charges could be brought against police officers for civil rights violations independent of the state's decision to prosecute.[71] Joe's family announced that they would move the weekly vigil to the front yard of the family home in South Tucson.

1980.
Less than 1 Mile North of the Border.
Five Men.

Enlightened Nationals United for Freedom, or E.N.U.F.!, could be reached through the US mail at Box HH in Douglas, Arizona. Hanigan supporters had organized the group to protest the legal action taken by the government against the three ranchers.[72]

They wanted nothing of the talk of dual prosecution and distinct jurisdictions. The district attorney, the United States attorney, the federal investigator—they were all the government. Individuals appeared in specific roles and then were promoted, transferred, or retired, and a new face took the place of the old one. Ranchers knew the things that did not change; the constancy of the land, the grazing patterns of the cattle, and the feel of a horse directed with a squeeze of the knees.

Those who formed E.N.U.F.! believed the land to be their birthright, one that was being pilfered from all sides. They grieved the "torturous" conditions endured by the Hanigans as they awaited trial back at the ranch house, "The Hanigans will never be able to recover from the mental torture they have had to endure over the past four years, nor would any citizen under the circumstances. It is time that WE, the silent majority, stand up for our rights while we have some left."[73]

That George Hanigan was a central figure in the Cochise County Republican Party and enmeshed in the local structure of governance to such an extent that the judge in the first Hanigan trial, a close friend of George's, was forced to recuse himself, did not upset this anti-government ideology.[74] Helming the structure of governance while advocating vigilantism amounted to a closed system of logic almost elegant in its elasticity and elusiveness.

Although they previously claimed that the federal government had no jurisdiction to investigate private citizens for violence against noncitizens, eventually the DoJ responded to public pressure and convened a grand jury to investigate the Hanigan torture case. It may have been the first time the federal government investigated American citizens for violation of a noncitizen's civil rights.[75]

Federal prosecutors, however, eschewed any charges relating to violations under the Civil Rights Act. They also chose not to prosecute the Hanigans for violating prohibitions against "Concealing" and "Transporting Undocumented Aliens," essentially smuggling charges, or unlawfully assuming the authority of immigration agents, which constituted a violation of statutes prohibiting the "Private Enforcement of Immigration Laws."[76] Instead, the remaining two Hanigans were charged in US District Court with violating the Hobbs Act, an interstate commerce statute most commonly used to target white-collar and organized crime.[77]

Prosecutors argued that, first, the Hanigans had interfered with interstate commerce, by preventing the three Mexican men from traveling to the peanut farm in Elfrida where they would have participated in the labor market. Second, the $38 that the Hanigans reportedly confiscated during the torture would have entered interstate commerce had it stayed on the bodies of Manuel, Eleazar, and Bernabe.[78] Perhaps seeking charges under statutes pertaining to the disruption of interstate commerce was the most effective prosecutorial strategy at the time. Nonetheless, the approach obscures both the brutality and the racialized aspect of the torture and, instead, subsumes racialized violence under economic imperatives.

The evidence against Pat and Tom was heard by two separate, all-white juries. On the witness stand, Pat's ex-wife straightened her blue-and-white polka dot dress as she described how the Hanigan brothers occasionally grabbed their shotguns to hunt for immigrants crossing the border.[79] The jury tried to discern the degree to which $38 impaired the national economy.

1980.
59 Miles North of the Border.
Joe.

The narrow concrete walkway led to a small A-line porch. A couple of men in casual button-downs and jeans lingered under the awning, loosely crossing their hands at the waist. The rest sat on metal lawn chairs, looking across the walkway at the white-robed holy man on the other side. As he did every Thursday evening, the priest cupped his hands next to an altar constructed atop a table smothered in white lace, candles, flowers, a rendering of La Virgin de Guadalupe, and a photograph of Joe. In the front yard of their South Tucson home, the Sinohui family vigil pressed into its 108th week.[80]

The US Department of Justice had agreed to investigate whether to bring charges against Officer Dean under federal civil rights legislation. But the Sinohuis' expressed suspicion regarding the rigor with which the DoJ would pursue a subsequent indictment and conviction. Daniel Haro, a graduate of the Antioch School of Law who helped draft several bases for the prosecution of the Hanigans that federal prosecutors ultimately ignored, characterized the response of the DoJ to both the Hanigan prosecution and Joe's case as follows:

> First they do nothing. Then we form a committee, meet with them and they tell us they are also concerned. Later we meet again to convince them they must investigate. They agree, but the investigation drags on and on. We meet again to complain, but they explain they are working full speed, but that the case is difficult. Finally they decide to take no action. They time their announcement for a day when they have some positive civil rights news to announce so they can stick the bad news at the bottom of the good story.[81]

Putting flesh on the scaffolding is a different animal. In the case of the murder of Joe Sinohui by Officer Christopher Dean, US attorneys presented partial evidence, which did not include the transcripts of key witness statements. The jury then went on a fifteen-month break from the case. On their return, they received a four-hour summary of the evidence previously presented.[82]

Jack Greenberg, director of the NAACP Legal Defense and Education Fund, wrote, "we are disturbed by the delay and lack of aggressiveness that appears to have characterized the Justice Department's investigation into the Sinohui killing."[83]

Regarding the missing transcripts of witness testimony that contradicted Officer Dean's account of the killing, a collection of civil rights leaders lamented, "If a simple request for a transcript could only be accomplished as quickly as the taking of an Hispanic's life, there would have been no delay."[84]

In the intervening months, as the result of a favorable ruling in a civil wrongful death case, the Sinohuis had received $150,000 in compensation against Dean and the City of South Tucson and an additional $50,000 against Dean for unjustifiable homicide. In order to pay the damages, Dean sold his house. Some Tucsonans mumbled disapproval that the government and some Mexicans could so easily take away a man's home.[85]

On October 17, 1980, the DoJ announced that the grand jury had not found sufficient cause to indict Officer Dean for the murder of Joe Sinohui.[86]

1981.
124 Miles North of the Border.
Five Men.

On February 23, 1981, the juries in the Hanigan cases returned unanimous verdicts from Phoenix, Arizona, where the trial had been moved. The distance from the border was supposed to deflate the case's tense racial overtones.

The first jury found Tom Hanigan not guilty.

The second jury found Pat Hanigan guilty as charged, for which he was sentenced to three years' prison time.[87]

1981.
59 Miles North of the Border.
Joe.

The new year signaled the expiration of the grand jury term to investigate Officer Dean for the murder of Joe Sinohui in South Tucson, and, for the time being, the closing of Joe's case.[88]

2016.
537 Miles North of the Border.[89]
A Woman and an Officer.

When entering a place like this,

"You put your heart in your back pocket."[90]

The early-morning dew stuck to the outdoor benches is the only thing that reminds me that downtown Los Angeles is not completely exempt from the laws of nature. Inside the federal courthouse, the lobby has a refined austerity about it, with marble columns and a security apparatus to rival an international airport, all presided over by the portraits of the sitting United States president and vice president. The courtrooms themselves, however, look more like conference rooms than trial venues. The floor is carpeted. The administrative staff always seem cold, adjusting long shapeless cardigans in muted tones. Each surface has Xerox boxes full of paper, enough paper to suffocate the city.[91]

It is into a room like this that the voice of a young Los Angeles Police Department (LAPD) patrol officer arrives over the telephone to testify in the bond hearing of a Mexican woman, who at the time of her arrest resided in Los Angeles City.[92] The immigration judge will summon her image from a detention center via a videoconferencing screen. Both of them—the police officer and the woman—have been brought here by a joint operation conducted in the early months of 2016 between the LAPD and US Immigration and Customs Enforcement (ICE). The purported purpose of the operation was to search a residence where a robbery occurred.[93]

Already, there is a sleight of hand here; something obvious that is difficult to see. The LAPD has celebrated itself as an immigrant-friendly department.[94] The Los Angeles Mayor's Office of Immigrant Affairs vigorously defends the LAPD as the model sanctuary city policing agency. The LAPD describes their joint operations with ICE as targeting transnational criminal violations, including human trafficking, drug operations, and gangs, and *not* as conducted for the purposes of immigration enforcement. However, white supremacist narratives—including those that pervade law enforcement agencies—and the securitization-era frameworks that define immigration enforcement as a dire national security issue, conflate drug trafficking, transnational gang activity, and terroristic threats with nonwhite immigrants such that targeting one seamlessly justifies targeting the other.[95]

Always remember,

"*The soldiers wear guns,* not *in their back pockets.*"[96]

On February 24, 2016, LAPD officers entered a residence and arrested everyone inside, including the woman at hand.[97] She was taken to LAPD's Rampart station, questioned, and not charged with any crime.[98] The LAPD then transferred her to ICE custody, describing her as a gang affiliate.[99]

The young LAPD officer with the round face and buzz cut has been called to bear witness, to tell the immigration judge that the woman lives in a gang area. He has seen her talking to people who he thinks are gang members.

No, he had not met her before the day he arrested her, but he thinks he once, years ago, saw her use a sweatshirt to pick up something from the ground, probably drugs or a gun. He conjectures that her tattoos might be gang related.[100]

The criteria by which law enforcement determines gang membership are frequently based on subjective, loosely defined guidelines that are informed by racial stereotypes and fail to meet basic evidentiary standards.[101] Gang labeling practices are particularly prone to overreach in the immigration enforcement system, where procedural protections—including compulsory legal representation and rights of prior discovery to prepare for allegations—are dramatically cabined or absent.[102] Thus, in immigration proceedings in which hearsay is permitted, immigration authorities can successfully label an immigrant as gang affiliated based on little to no evidence.

Consequently, the statements by the police officer shift the burden to the woman on the screen. She needs to produce proof of what she is *not*. She needs to figure out how to prove that she is not a gang member at this moment, without an attorney, through a Spanish interpreter, struggling to master the procedural regularities of the court.

She says that her tattoos consist of her children's and grandchildren's names and an LA Dodgers logo. The ink does not endorse any gang. She is admonished for making this statement. She is supposed to only question the officer, not argue with him. She is supposed to undermine his logic using the interrogation tactics of an attorney.

But she is not an attorney. The presiding judge sets her bond at $60,000, based on concerns about her continued presence in a gang area.[103] Largely based on the officer's statements, she becomes a deportation priority. His words bring her very close to the border.

"*Do not forget for a minute that the soldiers wear guns.*"[104]

Now.
Location Indeterminate.

The US government would like a contractor, at a low-going rate, to construct a wall that starts at the base of the earth and runs an infinite distance into the sky. Do not let your imagination limit you. This wall can go in every direction, beyond what the eye can see. This wall should consist solely of invisible components, without compromising its capacity to withstand external attack.

A border can be many things. A border can be a monstrous home. It can be a foreign invader that disrupts the desert ecosystem. It is a probing scalpel that cuts through the Tohono O'odham nation. It is a method of deciding who gets to live and who does not.

A border wall can be steel, concrete, or, as is increasingly the case, digital. Whether or not a steel barrier blooms among borderland cactus may ultimately prove to be less relevant to immigration enforcement than the construction of digital infrastructure to classify and surveil migrants. Information technology is as much a part of the border environment as prickly pear cactus. Law enforcement agencies have an insatiable need for information; they want more and more.[105]

"Desire is a machine"[106]

And so, the government is now seeking a contractor to conduct continuous monitoring of hundreds of thousands of immigrants: their name(s); aliases; dates of birth; phone numbers; addresses; nationality; citizenship; driver's license information; Alien Registration Numbers; Social Security Numbers; Vehicle Registration Information; Individual Taxpayer Identification Numbers; passport numbers; travel and visa information; employment records; educational history; immigration history; criminal records; gang allegations; height; weight; eye color; hair color; scars, marks, and tattoos; health data; housing information; utility subscriptions; marriage history; bond information; case management information; information on relatives, associates, and spouses; wire transfer data; social media activity; credit history; insurance claims; property information; payday loan information; fingerprints; DNA; and photographs.[107]

This is the border in its evolving form—as a series of roaming elastic spheres that attach to targeted people, simultaneously bulging with digital information and collapsing down into a tiny package, a digital "data double,"[108] that can be moved across jurisdictions and nation-states. This border is mobile, omnipotent, ever-present, diffuse; not a singular site but instead encountered at various points, carried in the body.[109] It is inhaling and pulsing and growing.

I am getting a new home, made of code.

Now.
Back in the Borderlands.

If you walk along the Yuma line, or the one that splits Nogales, Arizona, and Nogales, Mexico;

If you walk the space between San Diego and Tijuana or Douglas and Agua Prieta;

If you ride into Columbus from Palomas, or into Palomas from Columbus;

If you drive near El Paso and Juarez; Brownsville and Matamoros;

"Capitals like cactus beneath the sky.
Cactus like green suns, radiating pointed
rays and steeped in poison."[110]

Stop the car, the tires screeching to a stop in a sharp violin note cutting upward, and on both sides of the international boundary you will see prehistoric reefs of flesh and thorns.

"It is noontime. The sun is at its zenith. Let time stand still."[111]

Only along a limited ribbon of Southern Arizona and Northern Sonora grows the most iconic of these creatures—the saguaro, those desert lighthouses with ivory flowers that bloom in the dark. Even in death are they beautiful, stripped down to ribs like clusters of golden towers.

Yes, you will see green cacti. You will see people whose green uniforms say, "Border Patrol." You will even see them crossing into the First Nations. Their guns say, ".40." Since the Hanigan and Sinohui cases, the numbers have changed. So has the skin color of some of the agents. The systemic brutality has not.[112] The color of the skin under the uniform is largely irrelevant, as are the intentions. Well-intentioned or malicious, the pictures on the altar at the vigil are the same.

"The river of blood rises, breaks through the surface, and courses boldly
through the desert."[113]

As power sings a sermon of Law and Order, I watch Arizona bleed out into the rest of the nation, knowing that the dash across the border, if one makes it past the tear gas and line walkers, is only the start. The borderlands bubble up away from the border, in systems of policing, prosecution, and punishment that act as filtering systems for people who were not skimmed out at the physical nation-state barrier. Police who empty their weapons into backs will likely not answer for their destruction but instead, "will receive pensions."[114] One court system, and then another, will dismiss charges against purveyors of white supremacist violence. A woman will be expected to contest a flimsy allegation by engaging in an adjudicative process without the preparation of legal training. Civilian vigilantes will take the function of filtering upon themselves. Social control is ultimately backed by the threat of violence, and made stronger when deployed from multiple locations.

The border moves inward. I fear it will accelerate in this motion until there is oblivion.

Acknowledgments

The author would like to thank brilliant writers Adam Vine, Josh Green, Aisha Alfa, Eric Thomas, and Luis Fernandez for their feedback and encouragement.

Endnotes

1. Gloria Anzaldúa, *Borderlands/La Frontera: The New Mestiza* (San Francisco: Aunt Lute Books, 1987), 3.
2. Exec. Order No. 13767, 3 C.F.R. 8793 (2017).
3. Anzaldúa, *Borderlands/La Frontera*, 2.
4. Justin Akers Chacón and Mike Davis, *No One Is Illegal: Fighting Racism and State Violence on the U.S.-Mexico Border* (Chicago: Haymarket Books, 2006), 249.
5. Barbara Kingsolver, *Animal Dreams* (New York: HarperCollins Publishers, 1990), 321.
6. Charles Bowden, *Desierto: Memories of the Future* (New York: W.W. Norton and Company, 1991), 190.
7. Rick Bass, *The Ninemile Wolves* (New York: Mariner Books, 1992), 24.
8. Exec. Order No. 13767, 3 C.F.R. 8793 (2017).
9. United States Customs and Border Protection, *Other Border Wall*, 8.
10. Elana Zilberg, "Gangster in Guerilla Face: A Transnational Mirror of Production between the USA and El Salvador," *Anthropological Theory* 7 (2007): 49.
11. United States Customs and Border Protection, *Solid Concrete Border Wall*, 55.
12. United States Customs and Border Protection. *Other Border Wall*, 39.
13. United States Customs and Border Protection. *Solid Concrete Border Wall*, 4.
14. United States Customs and Border Protection. *Solid Concrete Border Wall*, 54.
15. Pres. Memorandum, *Securing the Southern Border of the United States* (April 4, 2018), https://www.whitehouse.gov/presidential-actions/presidential-memorandum-secretary-defense-attorney-general-secretary-homeland-security/.
16. Geoff Ward, "The Slow Violence of State Organized Race Crime," *Theoretical Criminology* 19 (2015): 299–314; Joy James, *Resisting State Violence: Radicalism, Gender, and Race in US Culture* (Minneapolis: University of Minnesota Press, 1996); Brent M. Campney, "'The Most Turbulent and Most Traumatic Years in Recent Mexican American History': Police Violence and the Civil Rights Struggle in 1970s Texas," *Southwestern Historical Quarterly* 122 (2018): 32-57.
17. Ward, "Slow Violence," 300.
18. Ward, "Slow Violence," 300.
19. Ta-Nehisi Coates, "When Plunder Becomes a System of Governance," *Atlantic*, October 25, 2013, https://www.theatlantic.com/international/archive/2013/10/when-plunder-becomes-a-system-of-governance/280885/.
20. Cecilia Menjívar and Leisy J. Abrego, "Legal Violence: Immigration Law and the Lives of Central American Immigrants," *American Journal of Sociology* 117 (2012): 1385.
21. Menjívar and Abrego, "Legal Violence," 1385.

22 United States v. Patrick W. Hanigan, 681 F.2d 1127 (9th Cir. 1982).
23 Christine Marin, "They Sought Work and Found Hell: The Hanigan Case of Arizona," *Perspectives in Mexican American Studies* 6 (1997): 101.
24 Toni Breiter, "They Sought Work and Found Terror," *Agenda, A Journal of Hispanic Issues* 8 (1978): 23.
25 Throughout this essay, I use the terminology consistent with the era being described.
26 Breiter, "They Sought Work," 23.
27 Marin, "They Sought Work," 102.
28 Breiter, "They Sought Work," 22.
29 Tom Miller, *On the Border: Portraits of America's Southwestern Frontier* (Tucson: University of Arizona Press, 1981), 144.
30 Breiter, "They Sought Work," 23.
31 Miller, *On the Border*, 145.
32 Breiter, "They Sought Work," 23.
33 Katherine Benton-Cohen and Geraldo Cadava, "Back to the Border: A Historical Comparison of U.S. Border Politics," *Immigration Policy Center*, 2010, 15. https://www.americanimmigrationcouncil.org/sites/default/files/research/Back_to_the_Border_090210.pdf.
34 Marin, "They Sought Work," 104; Miller, *On the Border*, 147.
35 Benton-Cohen and Cadava, "Back to the Border," 15; Marin, "They Sought Work," 104 – 195.
36 Campney, "Most Turbulent and Most Traumatic Years," 43.
37 Marin, "They Sought Work," 105.
38 Varn, Gene, "Prosecution Ends Case against Hanigans after 16 Days, 35 Witnesses," *Arizona Republic*, July 19, 1980, B1.
39 City of South Tucson, https://www.southtucsonaz.gov/
40 Edward Bassett, "Slain Man's Family to Challenge Police Story on Shooting," *Tucson Citizen*, July 4, 1977, 1A.
41 Carmen Duarte, "Social Justice Advocate Guadalupe Sinohui, Known for Acts of Kindness, Dies," *Arizona Daily Star*, July 4, 2017, https://tucson.com/news/local/social-justice-advocate-guadalupe-sinohui-known-for-acts-of-kindness/article_9ad82573-38cb-5fb2-a436-a86938d05ad5.html.
42 In addition to archival materials, this section is based on an oral history with my father. In the tradition of Hazel V. Carby, I use family narratives to unsettle archives by contrasting subaltern narratives with official accounts. See Hazel V. Carby, *Imperial Intimacies: A Tale of Two Islands* (New York: Verso, 2019), 2.
43 Tom Miller, "Pistol Justice: White Cops and Chicano Corpses," *The Nation*, November 4, 1978, 471.
44 *In Re the Matter of the Killing of: Jose Sinohui, Jr., Request for New Grand Jury Submitted to Honorable Charles B. Renfrew Deputy Attorney General, U.S. Department of Justice*, 1980. Herman Baca Papers, MSS 0649. Special Collections & Archives, UC San Diego, 10.
45 Bassett, "Slain Man's Family," 1A.
46 *Brutality by Law Enforcement Agencies: Case Summaries, Part II*, n.d. Herman Baca Papers, MSS 0649. Special Collections & Archives, UC San Diego, 11; Bassett, "Slain Man's Family," 1A; National Minority Advisory Council on Criminal Justice, *The Inequality of Justice*, 1981, 96, https://files.eric.ed.gov/fulltext/ED218384.pdf.
47 Brian D. Behnken, "The Next Struggle," in *Civil Rights and Beyond: African American and Latino/a Activism in the Twentieth-Century United States*, ed. Brian D Behnken (Athens: University of Georgia Press, 2016), 204.
48 Behnken, "The Next Struggle," 204; *In Re the Matter of the Killing of*, 1.
49 Bassett, "Slain Man's Family," 1A.
50 *In Re the Matter of the Killing of*, 4.
51 *In Re the Matter of the Killing of*, 12.
52 Benton-Cohen and Cadava, "Back to the Border," 15.
53 Miller, *On the Border*, 155.

54 Breiter, "They Sought Work," 26.
55 Breiter, "They Sought Work," 25.
56 Miller, *On the Border*, 164.
57 *Coalition Leaders Give Views on Hanigan Trial*, n.d. Herman Baca Papers, MSS 0649. Special Collections & Archives, UC San Diego.
58 Menjívar and Abrego, "Legal Violence," 1385; Charles R. Babcock, "Arizona Ranchers Indicted," *Washington Post*, October 17, 1979. https://www.washingtonpost.com/archive/politics/1979/10/17/2-arizona-ranchers-indicted/0ea8ce2d-16e0-4daf-aa48-f6bae28eaf2f/.
59 Behnken, "The Next Struggle," 204.
60 *In Re the Matter of the Killing of*, 6-7.
61 *In Re the Matter of the Killing of*, "Exhibit 'A.'"
62 *In Re the Matter of the Killing of*, 1.
63 *In Re the Matter of the Killing of*, 7.
64 *In Re the Matter of the Killing of*, 7–8.
65 *In Re the Matter of the Killing of*, 1; *Coalition*, n.p.
66 *Coalition*, n.p.
67 *Letter by Drew S. Days, III, Assistant Attorney General, Civil Rights Division*, 1978. Herman Baca Papers, MSS 0649. Special Collections & Archives, UC San Diego.
68 Naomi Murakawa, and Katherine Beckett, K., "The Penology of Racial Innocence: The Erasure of Racism in the Study and Practice of Punishment," *Law & Society Review* 44 (2010): 695.
69 Murakawa and Beckett, "Penology of Racial Innocence," 700–701.
70 Campney, "Most Turbulent and Most Traumatic Years," 48; *Brutality by Law Enforcement Agencies: Case Summaries*, n.d. Herman Baca Papers, MSS 0649. Special Collections & Archives, UC San Diego.
71 Juan Vasquez, "Killings of Chicanos by Police Protested," *The New York Times*, October 12, 1977, 17; Tom Miller, "Pistol Justice: White Cops and Chicano Corpses," *The Nation*, November 4, 1978, 471.
72 *Enlightened Nationals United For Freedom E. N. U. F.!*, n.d. Herman Baca Papers, MSS 0649, Special Collections & Archives, UC San Diego.
73 *Enlightened Nationals United For Freedom*.
74 Marin, "They Sought Work," 101, 107.
75 Roger Langley, "Arizonan Fans Flames of 'Hanigan Case,'" *The Arizona Republic*, October 2, 1979, A7.
76 *Bases for Prosecution in Hanigan Case*, n.d. Herman Baca Papers, MSS 0649. Special Collections & Archives, UC San Diego.
77 United States v. Patrick W. Hanigan, 681 F.2d 1127 (9th Cir. 1982).
78 Varn, "Prosecution Ends Case," B1.
79 Louis Sahagun, "Patrick Hanigan's Ex-Wife Tells of Threats," *Tucson Citizen*, n.d. Herman Baca Papers, MSS 0649. Special Collections & Archives, UC San Diego.
80 *Prayers Seek Action in Tucson Slaying*, 1980. Herman Baca Papers, MSS 0649. Special Collections & Archives, UC San Diego.
81 Roger Langley, *Hispanic Beat*, 1980. Herman Baca Papers, MSS 0649. Special Collections & Archives, UC San Diego, 1.
82 *Letter from Civil Rights Organizations to Honorable Charles B. Renfrew*, November 7, 1980.
83 Jack Greenberg, *Investigation into the Shooting Death of Jose Sinohui, Jr.*, October 31, 1980. Herman Baca Papers. MSS 0649. Special Collections & Archives, UC San Diego.
84 *Letter from Civil Rights Organizations*.
85 *In Re the Matter of the Killing of*, 3.
86 *In Re the Matter of the Killing of*, 3; Langley, *Hispanic Beat*, 2.
87 Benton-Cohen and Cadava, "Back to the Border," 16; United States v. Patrick W. Hanigan, 681 F.2d 1127 (9th Cir. 1982).
88 Langley, *Hispanic Beat*, 2.

89 Distance measured from the Agua Prieta/Douglas crossing.
90 Cherríe Moraga, *Loving in the War Years* (Boston: South End Press, 2000), 60.
91 In addition to archival material, this section is based on data collected through observation of the case at hand, interviews with attorneys involved in the case, and interviews with nineteen legal advocates who practice in the Southern California region at the intersections of criminal, juvenile, and immigrant defense work, specifically with clients accused of gang membership or affiliation. Interviews were conducted between August 2016 and May 2018.
92 *Office for Civil Rights and Civil Liberties, U.S. Department of Homeland Security, Complaint Concerning ICE Arrest and Intended Deportation of L.A. Resident Xochitl Hernandez*, October 18, 2016. National Day Laborer Organizing Network, 3, https://ndlon.org/abuela-xochitl-files-civil-rights-complaint-against-lapd-and-department-of-homeland-security/; Hernandez v. Sessions, No. 16-2323 (2d Cir. 2018), 12.
93 *Internal Affairs Group, Los Angeles Police Department, Complaint Regarding Civil and Human Rights Violations in the Case of Xochitl Hernandez*, October 18, 2016. National Day Laborer Organizing Network, 2, https://ndlon.org/abuela-xochitl-files-civil-rights-complaint-against-lapd-and-department-of-homeland-security/
94 Robert M. Arcos, "We're Here to Protect and Serve Immigrants, Not Help ICE Deport Them," *Zócalo Public Square*, August 8, 2017, https://www.zocalopublicsquare.org/2017/08/08/protect-serve-immigrants-not-help-ice-deport/ideas/nexus/ ; Los Angeles Police Department. *The Los Angeles Police Department and Federal Immigration Enforcement: Frequently Asked Questions, Version 2.0*, 2018, http://assets.lapdonline.org/assets/pdf/immigrationfaq.pdfhttp://assets.lapdonline.org/assets/pdf/immigrationfaq.pdf.
95 Jennifer M. Chacón, "Unsecured Borders: Immigration Restrictions, Crime Control and National Security," *Connecticut Law Review* 39 (2007): 1831; Robert Pallitto and Josiah M. Heyman, "Theorizing Cross-Border Mobility: Surveillance, Security and Identity," *Surveillance & Society* 5 (2008): 317.
96 Moraga, *Loving in the War Years*, 60.
97 David Noriega, "The LAPD Says It Won't Work with Feds on Deportations, But It Already Does," *Buzzfeed News*, December 8, 2016, https://www.buzzfeednews.com/article/davidnoriega/the-lapd-says-it-wont-work-with-feds-on-deportations-but-it.
98 *Internal Affairs Group*, 1.
99 *Internal Affairs Group*, 3.
100 *Office for Civil Rights and Civil Liberties*, 3, 6.
101 Mike Davis, *City of Quartz: Excavating the Future in Los Angeles* (New York: Verso, 2006), 284; Jennifer M. Chacón, "Whose Community Shield? Examining the Removal of the 'Criminal Street Gang Member'," *University of Chicago Legal Forum* 2007 (2007): 337.
102 Jordan B. Woods, "Systemic Racial Bias and RICO's Application to Criminal Street and Prison Gangs," *Michigan Journal of Race & Law* 17 (2012): 349; Chacón, "Whose Community," 340.
103 Hernandez v. Sessions, 12; *Internal Affairs Group*, 4.
104 Moraga, *Loving in the War Years*, 60.
105 Christian Parenti, *The Soft Cage: Surveillance in America from Slavery to the War on Terror* (New York: Basic Books, 2003), 178.
106 Gilles Deleuze and Félix Guattari, *Anti-Oedipus: Capitalism and Schizophrenia* (Minneapolis: University of Minnesota Press, 2000), 26.
107 United States Department of Homeland Security. *EID*, 7-9, 21; United States Department of Homeland Security, *ENFORCE*, 23276; United States Immigration and Customs Enforcement, *Targeting*, 1. For a more extensive discussion of information collection see Ana Muñiz, "Secondary Ensnarement: Surveillance Systems in the Service of Punitive Immigration Enforcement," *Punishment & Society* (forthcoming).
108 Kevin D. Haggerty and Ricard V. Ericson, "The Surveillant Assemblage," *British Journal of Sociology* 51 (2000): 606.

109 Irus Braverman, "Civilized Borders: A Study of Israel's New Crossing Administration," *Antipode* 43 (2010): 265; David Lyon, "The Border Is Everywhere: ID Cards, Surveillance, and the Other," in *Global Surveillance and Policing: Borders, Security, and Identity*, eds. Elia Zureik and Mark B. Salter (Portland, OR: Willan Publishing, 2005), 66; Louise Amoore, "Biometric Borders: Governing Mobilities in the War on Terror, *Political Geography* 25 (2006): 338; Katja F. Aas, "Analysing a World in Motion: Global Flows Meet 'Criminology of the Other'," *Theoretical Criminology* 11 (2007): 296. For more on digital technology and border formation, see Ana Muñiz, "Bordering Circuitry: Cross Jurisdictional Immigration Surveillance," *UCLA Law Review* (forthcoming).
110 Jean Genet, *Our Lady of the Flowers* (New York: Grove Press, 1963), 141.
111 Bernard E. Harcourt, *Language of the Gun: Youth, Crime, and Public Policy* (Chicago: University of Chicago Press, 2006), xiii.
112 Irene Vega, "Empathy, Morality, and Criminality: The Legitimation Narratives of U.S. Border Patrol Agents," *Journal of Ethnic and Migration Studies* 44 (2016): 2547.
113 Charles Bowden, *Blues for Cannibals* (New York: North Point Press, 2002), 277.
114 Ta-Nehisi Coates, *Between the World and Me* (New York: Spiegel & Grau, 2015), 9.

WHERE DID THE FUTURE GO?

Notes on the Fantasies and Strategies of the Hyper-Right from the United States to Brazil

Bruno Carvalho

> To catastrophe, searching
> For survival, we are born.
> —Murilo Mendes,
> "The Ruins at Selinunte" (1949–50)[1]

During the Second World War, Stefan Zweig famously hailed Brazil as the "land of the future."[2] As the country's promises failed to materialize, this became a running joke: "Brazil is the country of the future, and always will be." It might be easy to dismiss Zweig's paean as naïve if we forget the conflicts that engulfed much of the Global North. The Jewish-born writer moved to Brazil after escaping the rise of Nazi fascism in Europe. He thought that the tropical society could provide a model for "peaceful coexistence on earth, in spite of all the different races, classes, colors, religions and convictions."[3] We might think of the history of modernity as a series of competing visions over what the future ought to be like. Excavating the futures past of urban modernity in Brazil yields rich visions of alternative civilizational models: in Lina Bo Bardi's public architecture, in the eruptions and organization of carnival, in the poetry and music of the Doces Bárbaros (*Sweet Barbarians*) . . . At various moments, the dynamism and utopian potentials of Brazilian popular culture worked to destabilize structures of inequality, broadening and opening up horizons of possibility. A succession of events leading to the government of Jair Bolsonaro left us with the question of where those futures might have gone.

Brazil may not be "the land of the future," but its land contains a key to planetary futures. The actions of Bolsonaro and allies to encourage deforestation and further unleash extractivist pressures produce catastrophe for life in Amazonian ecosystems—and beyond. Intensifying the destruction of wetlands and rain forests will likely disrupt climate patterns in Southeast Brazil, for example—there is evidence connecting the expansion of the soybean frontier to drought in the São Paulo metropolitan region. Although many of Brazil's more widely circulating images pertain to natural landscapes, it is one of the world's most urbanized countries. And Brazil's cities provide increasingly fertile ground for dystopian, apocalyptic imaginaries—including exterminationist, murderous practices enacted by military police and other armed groups. Even so, for someone coming from a Latin American tradition—where pro-city biases have historically been the norm—Mike Davis's indictments of urban America can be unsettling: another US intellectual against the city. My own tendency has been to approach cities as sites of violence, segregation, and environmental degradation, but also of creative possibilities, communities, and vitality. I for one still believe in the role of street corner sociabilities against the encroaching logics of turbo-capitalist productivity. But street corners can only do so much against prevailing tides.

In *Evil Paradises* (2007), Daniel Bertrand Monk and Mike Davis asked, "Toward what kind of future are we being led by savage, fanatical capitalism?"—a question they reframe as: "What do contemporary 'dreamworlds' of consumption, property, and power tell us about the fate of human solidarity?"[4] The eventful years following these questions provide a host of gloomy answers. The consolidation of global patterns of consumption, property, and power—along with the explosion of new forms of social media—suggests that the task of understanding local realities needs to be increasingly connective. It appears that the "dreamworlds" of globalization have forged urban political subjects more synchronically and perhaps less diachronically comparable—in several ways more like their contemporaries across the planet than their immediate predecessors. Bolsonaro has been compared to Orbán, Duterte, Trump, and others. To be sure, for every similarity there are many differences. But it seems to me that to make sense of Brazil's political landscapes, it pays to look at connections and correspondences, and in particular to turn to the United States.

Despite very different institutional contexts for right-wing cultures in Brazil and the US, some general points of contact emerge from shared Atlantic histories: the whitewashing of violent settler colonialism, denial of the legacies of slavery, the pursuit of car-centric and segregated built environments, grievances against the expansion of rights, and the instrumentalization of neo-pentecostalism for electoral purposes. We should speculate, nonetheless, about how the historical roots and political continuities that help to explain the rise of figures like Trump and Bolsonaro can also hinder our understanding of the extent and depth of contemporary transformations. The urban forms and spatial logics of the globalized world, saturated with cheapened telecommunications technologies, gated communities, widespread segregation, and miserably long commutes (especially for the poor) all lend themselves to social lives and encounters with difference mediated by screens—and help to create conditions for the hyper-right. Hyper-right stands for intensity and extremism as much as for the digital, interlinked, "hyperreality" of its basic patterns of operation, by no means exclusive to the partisan right, and with analogues in urban development and design: when it is the image or the representation that triggers and drives socioeconomic forces, desires, and political processes, rather than the material or empirical realities to which the image supposedly refers.[5]

It appears that certain right-wing fantasies and strategies that reshaped postwar US politics and found fertile ground online have been remaking Brazilian politics—and that more and more, these vast Americas convert from privileged spaces for future-production into places onto which we project dystopias. It is always too early to tell what will happen, but we should be ready for the unimaginable. Mike Davis's work has been criticized for hyperbole. He prepares us for the world ahead.

"It's Not Your Fault"

In 2018, Brazilian voters caused the latest electoral shock, but Jair Messias Bolsonaro was certainly not an unknown quantity. In 1998, Chilean general

Augusto Pinochet was arrested in London. He was accused of, among other crimes, the torture and murder of political opponents. Bolsonaro, a second-term congressman at the time, did not seem to believe in the innocence of the former dictator. In fact, he stated that "Pinochet should have killed more people."[6] Since then, evidence of the atrocities committed under Pinochet's rule has only mounted. Even so, in 2015 Bolsonaro still maintained that "Pinochet did what had to be done."[7] These assertions neatly fit with others made by Bolsonaro: "During the [Brazilian military] dictatorship, they should've killed about thirty thousand corrupt people, starting with President Fernando Henrique [Cardoso]" (on corruption under Pinochet's regime, no comment).[8] "The dictatorship's mistake was to torture without killing" (the dictatorship both tortured and killed). As for himself: "I'm an army captain, my mission is to kill"[9] (that is not what the Constitution says).

In a democracy, a proponent of mass murder should not be a part of serious discussions about the direction of the country. A week before the elections, speaking via cell phone to rallying supporters while his image was being projected on screens, Bolsonaro reinforced his fascistic bona fides: "They will lose ... and the cleansing now will be much broader. Either they go away or they go to prison. These red outcasts will be banished from our fatherland."[10] With former president Lula of the Workers' Party (PT) in jail, on October 28, 2018, a plurality of the Brazilian electorate voted for Bolsonaro. Throughout the year, he proved to be the only political figure able to galvanize a considerable cross-section of the country. While Brazilian society has authoritarian leanings and was undergoing intense political polarization, I doubt that all that many people wanted to see political opponents exterminated or banished. As much as a death cult and self-destructive drive animate some Bolsonaro enthusiasts, I am inclined to believe that relatively few would welcome the torture of pregnant women, which happened under Latin American dictatorships like Pinochet's. So, how do we make sense of the massive support for Bolsonaro among people who see themselves as civilized, Christian bearers of moral values?

There are a number of plausible interpretations. There is certainly no lack of historical precedents: the protagonists or passive witnesses of the greatest horrors of humanity usually believed themselves to be decent, honorable people. I would like to develop a less obvious hypothesis. In an essay published in Brazil's *piauí* magazine, João Moreira Salles analyzes the phrase "Não fui eu" (it wasn't me), which has been spray-painted, enigmatically, across Rio de Janeiro. At one point, he quotes anthropologist Luiz Eduardo Soares, who observes how in Brazilian political culture, people often place the blame on the third person plural: "they don't even care," "they are ruining the country,"[11] etc. Some of the power and draw of *bolsonarismo* (or Bolsonarism) lies in this fantasy.

Bolsonaro's campaign slogan could well have been "It's not your fault." As if to say, "If *they* weren't ruining everything, this country would be great." This line of thinking allows voters to feel brave and worthy, even as they skirt responsibility. In a complicated, confusing world, Bolsonaro and other emerging far-right figures beckon to a fantasy of justice and heroism. Rejecting institutional politics becomes a sign of purity. Like Trumpism, Bolsonarism offers the expiation of guilt and the transfer of responsibility, feats worthy of a *mito* (myth, or legend), as his supporters call him. We cannot underestimate the appeal and destructive potential of this phenomenon—or its ability to transfer from one figure to another. Despite the many differences, there were strikingly comparable dynamics behind the candidacies of Trump and Bolsonaro.

In March 2018, I arrived in Rio, my hometown, a day after the assassination of city councilor Marielle Franco and her driver Anderson Gomes. I met with some of her friends and colleagues. The prevailing feeling was that whoever stood up to police corruption and Rio's militias (paramilitary groups), like Marielle did, might be next. Later that week, during a lunch with a different group, someone casually asked: "Did you know that Marielle was married to Marcinho VP?" (Marielle, an openly gay woman, was never married to convicted drug trafficker Marcinho VP.) When I tried to understand where this rumor originated, I discovered that in the social circles of the person who had passed it on, the political discussion was completely monopolized by Bolsonaro supporters. People who could not have cared less about electoral politics fifteen years ago were now passionately defending his candidacy on Facebook and in WhatsApp groups. Like many others, I had been watching this phenomenon from a distance. Many specialists dismissed his chances. There seemed to be whiffs of Trumpism. I decided to systematically read

Bolsonaro supporters' posts, to engage them in conversation, and to listen to what they had to say.

In conversations on the left, the so-called Bolsominions, Bolsodummies, Bolsonazis, and so on were overwhelmingly associated with the candidate's misogyny, racism, and homophobia. But it quickly became clear that for many of his followers, these issues seemed virtually irrelevant. What Bolsonaro's black-and-white views offered was clarity. To some, you can be attracted to what Bolsonaro had to offer without buying the whole package. If the problem with Brazil is criminals and corruption, then you have to elect someone honest like him and wipe out the bad guys. If you disagree, then you are defending the crooks. His campaign took advantage of distortions created by the spotlight on corruption in Brazil. According to an Instituto Ipsos poll conducted during the elections, for example, 75 percent of Brazilians attributed deficits in the social security system to corruption and embezzlement, ignoring structural issues, including a very regressive tax system.[12] Bolsonarism, averse to complexity and reflection, offered voters the comfort of unshakable certainties and the conviction that responsibility always lies elsewhere. The country is in crisis? "It's not your fault." A steady diet of fake news, antileftist memes, and pro-Bolsonaro clichés gets in the way of a grounded view of material problems, but can be good for self-esteem.

How Con Men Obfuscate

We must try to understand why people who do not desire mass murder might support someone who thinks Pinochet should have killed more. Let us be generous, insofar as possible: when Bolsonaro hails Pinochet, he is, in the eyes of many of his supporters, not advocating for the latter's crimes. We can assume that many Brazilians are unaware of the extent of the atrocities committed by the Chilean dictator, or even by Brazil's own military dictatorship (1964–85). My impression, however, was that initially, most of Bolsonaro's followers sought to relativize and downplay his most extremist positions. If you cannot make out the "real meaning" behind what the "myth" says, you are accused of being too sensitive, humorless—a snowflake. The downplaying, however, is nearly always selective, disproportionate, and self-congratulatory. So Bolsonaro praises criminal dictatorships. For the casual Bolsonarist, his statements should not be taken literally. For those who are more dedicated to the cause, the problem lies with those who do not understand that threats from the left (or "red outcasts") justify any and all measures.

This procedure repeats ad nauseam. A comment in poor taste offends and dehumanizes minorities? The fault lies with those who did not get the joke, or cannot take it. By this logic, criticism of Bolsonaro becomes an assault on the right to crack a joke. And who, after all, dislikes jokes? Those who belong to marginalized groups or who defend human rights (a common target) have to be able to take jabs on the chin and laugh it off. But when the target is Bolsonaro, though, suddenly it stops being funny. In a radio interview, presidential candidate Marina Silva was asked to compare politicians to animals, and said that Bolsonaro would be a hyena. In a video response, he cried out: "If I'd called Marina Silva a hyena... the whole world would come crashing down on me."[13] Playing the victim is a frequent move in this playbook. "As far as I can see, no legislator takes as much of a beating as me,"[14] he says. "They show me elbowing someone, but when I get tackled from behind nobody shows that."[15] The implication: they just play the victim card; we are the true victims.

In the United States, this tactic has been used to great effect by the right wing for some time. Historically, as we know, the state privileged white groups over minorities. With the advances of the civil rights movement, as the government rolled back racist legislation and embraced full citizenship for African Americans, it increasingly became painted as the villain. (The echoes in an emergent anti-government libertarianism or "classical" liberalism of convenience in Brazil are obvious.) Savvy segregationists saw that an open campaign against civil rights was no longer the best strategy, as we learn in works like Kevin Kruse's *White Flight*.[16] Instead of saying that black people should not be allowed to buy the house next door or enter universities, segregationists found a positive framing, supposedly focused on individual freedom: what right does the government have to force me to live with people I do not want to be around? In this way, the oppressors position themselves as the victims.

Since the 1960s, the war on drugs and mass incarceration have targeted African Americans in practice, but not necessarily in their rhetoric. The Republican Party, in particular, gradually perfected dog-whistle politics: by insisting on punitive measures and hardline approaches to law and order, candidates signaled to segregationists whose side they were on. Statements, however, had to be sufficiently veiled in order to make them acceptable for those uncomfortable with open racism.

Trump saw that dog whistling would no longer do the trick for certain dissatisfied groups, especially white men who feel that they are losing status. He smashed through the discretion and "civility." During the campaign, Trump's bigoted comments received broad coverage in the press and sparked indignation in liberal and leftist circles. At the rallies, however, flattering and self-aggrandizing laudatory comments about his base were probably more frequent than prejudiced remarks. Some Trump followers heard the praise louder than the hate. Critics recoiled at the racism, misogyny, and xenophobia in his speeches. But many of his voters heard an appealing message: "Do you feel like you're falling behind? It's the Mexicans' fault. Your son didn't get into their dream school? Blame affirmative action. Not your fault." For some, the media's constant coverage of Trump's "controversial" statements was a form of persecution that they took personally. For those who think that accusations of racism are worse than actual racism, the media's coverage seemed unfair, and defending Trump became a way of preserving self-regard.

Bolsonarism sets up a similar trap. Like Trumpism, it feeds off confrontations with the press and an obsession with political correctness. "Controversial" comments generate widespread coverage, leading to accusations of media bias, which in turn reinforce the impression that Bolsonaro is being persecuted. "They play the victim, and we get persecuted." And if our hero bothers people so much, it is because he is not like other professional politicians. The thinking goes: "All politicians talk the same way, except mine. He's authentic, he doesn't beat around the bush, he calls it like it is." In Brazil, this strategy helped to make up for the fact that Bolsonaro and his three sons earn a living off politics. Unlike Trump, after all, he was a career politician. In theory, he should have had a harder time selling himself as an outsider.

Political correctness is an integral element in the construction of this image. On the one hand, Bolsonaro relied on the backlash against the "PC patrol." On the other, his campaign benefited from politically correct coverage. Legacy media's need to appear neutral, leading it to prefer restrained language, helps to mask extremism. Since journalists have to avoid the impression of bias, they opt for the politically correct "controversial," which benefits Bolsonaro and those like him. A sober but factual description, after all, makes anyone sound as if they are persecutorial. Extremist candidates have found an effective strategy: to act so out of the mainstream that it becomes difficult to describe their record to casual observers without coming across as tendentious or unfair. In order to avoid confrontation or the appearance of partiality, academics and journalists often rely on euphemisms. We might speak of "populism" when a behavior directly caters to elite desires, or would be better characterized as theocratic, sectarian, or exterminationist. Adjectives such as "controversial" and even "conservative," in turn, can give the impression that murderous positions are serious, bold, even courageous.

Of course, actual controversies should be marked by disputes, a grasp of baseline facts, and recognition of the opposing stance. Defending heliocentrism in the seventeenth century, for example, was controversial. Unlike Galileo, Bolsonaro-like figures do not tend to regard empirical evidence. It would be more accurate to describe them as demagogues. But then we fall into the trap of confirming the narrative of persecution. And for the commercial press, what to do when a demonstrable con man has considerable buy-in among high-income groups? Editorial lines are of course not immune to the pressure of advertisers or consumers—media groups would rather avoid challenging or insulting viewers and sponsors. Hence the preference for covering the inoffensive (sports, weather) and events void of moral complexity (the do-gooder or serial killer striking again).

Con men explore these cracks—in obfuscation, "strong" or "controversial" leaders appear to stand apart from "the system," while unpopular policies and powerful economic interests stay above the fray. Capitalists can be savages and fanatics, but their "dreamscapes" can also seem magical. In magical capitalism, anyone can become a deserving one-percenter through hard work and the fairy dust of meritocracy. That these fantasies strain credulity is part of the point: once the leap of faith is taken, it is hard to turn back. It is easier to find a scapegoat or internalize a flattering story line than to face hurtful truths. The pretense that anyone could become the boss stimulates entrepreneurial subjectivities. The fact of wage labor as a means to stuff someone else's pockets makes for a tough pitch: class consciousness can be humiliating.

How the Hyper-Right Wins

We cannot yet fully grasp the extent of the ongoing epistemological revolution. It is definitely not being televised. Democratic systems are made of conflicts and have always been susceptible to rumors and fake news, but digital social networks introduced unpredictable dynamics. Online logics seem to lead some people that previously ignored politics to feel compelled to pick a side. At the same time, we are still learning about how much ground traditional media and party machines have lost to social media in electoral races. The fact that Trump was so over-the-top and had highly unfavorable ratings made many specialists downplay his chances. The same happened in Brazil. In scenarios of generalized disillusionment and low participation, a low ceiling seems to matter less than an energized base. A number of established politicians, including several from the PT, declared that they preferred Bolsonaro as an opponent in a second round, which in Brazil takes place if no candidate gets 50 percent of the valid votes during a first round. We know who Hillary Clinton preferred to run against in 2016. Seasoned professionals did not take the hyper-right seriously enough.

When Trump and Bolsonaro faced candidates identified with partisan politics, the antiestablishment pitch worked. In his 1928 autobiography, Mussolini wrote that fascism should always "assume the characteristics of being anti-party."[17] In a time of disillusionment with institutional politics, the ability to play politics while pretending to reject it is a considerable advantage. Of course, reliance on clichés and stock phrases is a tactic that precedes the world of memes. Hannah Arendt wrote that clichés serve to "protect us from reality," seeing them as a key part of the working of totalitarian regimes. The novelty now is that digital tools can supplant more one-dimensional or expensive forms of propaganda (pamphlets, TV ads, rallies, etc.). Although Bolsonaro, unlike Trump, did not have a major party behind him, *bolsonarismo* was tailor-made to triumph online.

Many of us underestimated the extent to which Trump and Bolsonaro would manage to position themselves as agents of change while also representing entrenched forces within traditional political systems. Bolsonaro counted on the active or tacit support of significant segments of the military, media, finance, industry, agribusiness, congress, and evangelical churches. In São Paulo's main newspaper, Patricia Campos Mello exposed a multimillion-dollar

WHERE DID THE FUTURE GO?

illegal scheme in which business owners appear to have bankrolled a massive fake-news campaign against Bolsonaro's opponents via WhatsApp.[18] Early evidence indicated well-organized efforts, with particular fantasies tailored to specific audiences. WhatsApp is perhaps even more of a gated community than other social media platforms: only members of a group can add others and share and view content. Yet people might be part of a host of groups: family, work, childhood friends, school parents, and so on. It has become a nearly ubiquitous communication tool in Brazil; a space of personal networks through which *bolsonarismo* formed a social movement. Pro-Bolsonaro and antiestablishment mass media content—disseminated at an unprecedented scale, frequently through WhatsApp channels—helped generate hyperrealities that effectively appealed to feelings, superseding the evidentiary or verifiable. These recall Baudrillard's famous idea of a simulacrum as a copy without an original, which itself becomes a form of truth, or hyperreality. In the realities of the hyper-right, which included many former Lula voters, PT candidate Fernando Haddad promoted incest and pedophilia, and his party had a plan for the state to take ownership of children and decide their gender. Or the press was paid 600 million dollars to take down Bolsonaro, and the voting machines were rigged by Venezuela.

Like others in the hyper-right, the Trump and Bolsonaro campaigns mastered new media's potential to project different images depending on the circumstances and desires of particular constituencies: as pro-market or protectionist, as far-right agitators or conservatives, as champions of eliminationist punitiveness or anticorruption crusading, homophobia or family values. Bigoted one day, posing with a minority the next. After the election, Bolsonaro affirmed his respect for the Constitution on national television. Online, for his followers, he attacked the press, quoted the Bible, and encouraged students to film teachers in the classroom to keep them in line. This is a sophisticated, multipronged, cross-platform strategy. The connecting thread is an absolutely cynical instrumentalization of evidentiary bases and a disdain for the pursuit of ascertainable truths.

Hyper-right movements use legitimate disillusionment with the "system" to discredit investigative journalism and dismiss critical analyses as fake, partial, bought. The hyper-right new media keep legacy media under the whip with constant threats and accusations of "bias." Brazil's *Record* TV, part of a media conglomerate owned by the founder and leader of the diabolically wealthy neo-pentecostal Universal Church of the Kingdom of God, now vies for the chance of becoming the Fox News of the tropics. Likewise, several public figures seemed afraid to criticize Bolsonaro during the elections. Many established politicians sided with him to ride the waves of discontentment and anti-PT sentiment or to avert a deluge of online attacks. Those complicit in the demonization of the left, or those who tolerated Bolsonaro because they saw his candidacy as the lesser evil, helped hatch the serpent's egg. A chorus of voices from across the ideological spectrum did rise to the occasion and sounded the alarm. Yet even among them there was little reflection on the nature and extent of Bolsonaro's appeal.

Like Trumpism, Bolsonarism adopts a series of procedures that the right often attributes to the left, not always wrongly: acritical relativization, self-victimization, the PC ploy, and the primacy of individual, subjective perspectives. The inviolable right to one's own opinion is a way out for those who want to deny facts, do not know what they are talking about, or have a fanatic attachment to simplistic solutions. So your argument collapses when confronted with evidence? Blame people for not respecting different opinions. Eliane Brum speaks of "self-truths":[19] the overestimation of personal, self-proclaimed truths. Indeed, since winning the election and as a way of skirting the factual, Bolsonaro and members of his team have aggressively stated that, unlike others, "they speak the truth." Some Bolsonarists also frame identity-related agendas as assaults on individual achievement. So you are a minority and you worked hard and overcame challenges? In that case, they say *it was all you*. Forget the collective, ignore history, *speak your truth*. To some extent, the hyper-right is capable of absorbing and neutralizing identitarian, positionality-based discourse. The candidate compares descendants of maroon communities to lazy livestock? Counterattack with the personal: a photo-op with a black supporter "proves" that he cannot be racist.

The hyper-right is less vulnerable when we take on opinions or personal stances than when we question policies and the consequences of specific actions. But the imperative of clicks leaves little space for that. On September 6, 2018, in an intrusion of the real into hyperreality, a deranged man with a messianic complex who claimed to follow orders from God stabbed Bolsonaro. This set off a conspiratorial frenzy: some claimed the assassination attempt was forged by right-wingers, many others that the would-be killer was part of a leftist plot. It also activated an even more intense version of the Christian redemption template: persecution legitimizes the savior. The PT had been counting on that strategy for Lula, but being the victim of a murder attempt trumps imprisonment. Once Bolsonaro recovered, after being hospitalized for weeks, his health and physical integrity became the ideal shields to avoid scrutiny. Coverage privileged the personal. Bolsonaro refused to take part in debates or to detail proposals, and only engaged with friendly outlets. This provided cover for much of the news media to return to its preferred "neutral" position—if Bolsonaro is an extremist, he was also the target of extremism: *both sides do it.*

False equivalences, whether on the right or on the left, help weaken democracy. Polarization, however, is not necessarily symmetrical. In our economic order, marked by shifts from unionized industrial societies to winners-take-all global finance, the right acquired a substantial financial advantage and a disproportionate influence in shaping policy. This is not clear to the casual observer. In Brazil, soccer has become a well-worn source of metaphors for political polarization. But in sports—unlike in congress or the judicial system—the rules are clear and generally recognized; there are common denominators, and some consensus can be found about concrete facts. Sports coverage relies less on newscasts' "he said, she said" mode. Even the most die-hard fan cannot deny a stellar performance by the opposing team's player, or the scoreboard at the end of the game. The combination of political illiteracy and an unflinching conviction of the moral superiority of one side over the other has no parallel in sports. For all the bad blood in Brazilian soccer, we accept that our adversary is legitimate and has the right to play. In politics, where the stakes are higher, the consequences spill over the bounds of the game. And there are never just two sides.

In order to justify defending the unjustifiable, the representation of "the other side" has to become increasingly grotesque and unreal, until opponents become disqualified, unworthy, expendable. In a confrontation with Maria do Rosário, a congresswoman and former Minister of Human Rights, Bolsonaro stated that he would not rape her because she did not deserve it. When people object that no one ever deserves to be raped, there are three basic responses available to his supporters: they claim it is her fault, since she pushed his buttons, deflect by saying it was just a joke, or point fingers to the left of their hyperreal imaginaries, which promotes pedophiles and incest.

The far right does not have a monopoly on some of these procedures, of course. The PT, for example, waged a wildly dishonest, Karl Rove–style campaign against Marina Silva, Lula's former Minister of the Environment, during the 2014 presidential elections. She was presumed to be a stronger second-round contender than Aécio Neves, a center-right candidate who discredited the results, after he lost to the incumbent Dilma Rousseff, of the PT. But this was all before the explosion of WhatsApp and the rise of the hyper-right. In this new-media cyberwarfare, unlike in sports, winning can be a matter of perspective. Part of the point is to operate in the realm of the unverifiable. It takes less energy to attack by making lies go viral than it does to refute attacks. That helps to explain the hyper-right's particular fondness for unfounded accusations of pedophilia. There is no winning strategy for the accused.

On the more mundane turf of building coalitions in Brazil's fragmented multiparty system, during the PT's time in the presidency (2002–16), its governments often opted to team up with the corruption-fueled "center" and right-wingers rather than with the non-PT left or the liberal center-right. Once corruption investigations got closer to some very powerful people, committed above all to the ideology of money-making, former allies sought to sabotage the PT so they could "contain the bleeding," as one notoriously unsavory senator put it in recorded private conversations. Legacy media reported on PT involvement in corruption schemes with gusto. Brazilians, particularly those from the middle and upper classes, took to the streets in protest, often donning the jersey of the national soccer team, itself run by a notoriously corrupt federation. A broad coalition pushed for the impeachment of Dilma Rousseff. It included her vice president and the center-right PSDB (both mired in corruption scandals) as well as financiers, industrialists, and evangelical groups. In 2018, ultracorrupt politicians ran on fighting against the PT's corruption. Many of them predictably supported the nominally anticorruption Bolsonaro. It is hard to blame much of the public for not keeping up with such convoluted plotlines. While print media uncovered leads and evidence of corruption schemes involving Bolsonaro and his circle, Brazil's main media group, *Rede Globo*—responsible for the most-watched newscast in the country—largely looked the other way.

WHERE DID THE FUTURE GO?

In the hyper-right fantasies, those fighting on behalf of orchestrated disinformation campaigns often see themselves as insurgents against fake news. From where they stand, the digital sphere *feels* democratic. It allows them to rebel against changing norms as well as evidence-based political debates that they might have felt excluded from because they did not *know* enough. Elsewhere they might just feel like a cog in the machine, frustrated by futures that never came, overwhelmed by information. The hyper-right empowers people to offend and self-affirm, to seek revenge and find communities, to speak their truths and fight the system.

Unsurprisingly, *bolsonarismo* constantly taps into discomfort with gender fluidity. Perhaps the most recurrent trope of Bolsonaro's campaign was the idea that only he and his allies could save Brazilian children from a PT-backed governmental "gay kit" to be distributed in schools—this was tame in comparison to other made-up claims, like news of baby bottles shaped like penises. Reproduced without regard for referents, these bottles and kits only exist in hyperreality. But they shaped the electorate. According to polls, over 80 percent of Bolsonaro voters believed in the "gay kit." Opposing it allowed people to fashion themselves as bastions of moral superiority, against deviants. On one level this remains a facade, an assertion of personal truths to ward off the gender revolutions happening all over. It is easier to reject the *gay kit* than to confront repressed desires or an LGBT+ person in the family or neighborhood. The "anything goes" attitude behind the diffusion of hyper-right content in a way reacts to the perception that now "anything goes" in gender relations. It operates as a feat of dissimulation. We might channel Perry Anderson: the hyper-right adopts *methods* of postmodernism to create defenses against *experiences* of postmodernity.

As postmodern, post-truth, self-truth methods erode pillars of civic life, Republics of the Real collapse into Republics of Spam, YouTubers, WhatsApp groups, Electoral Infomercials. The hyperreal of course does not operate in a world detached from material conditions—we know that the hyper-right brings disaster to the most vulnerable. In Brazil, Bolsonaro fared best among those self-identifying as white and male, with a higher income and formal education. He still appealed to a substantial part of the working class, and not just evangelicals. What Achille Mbembe identifies as lumpenradicalism overlaps with the hyper-right: the taking of a "culture of brutality" and a "desire to subjugate" public spaces through "the use of verbal violences typical of far-right movements, the colonization of internet forums, and . . . the intimidation of opponents and critics through the absence of limits in language and behavior."[20] He adds that these movements are marked by a belief that "winners are always right" and by "exacerbated hypermasculinity."[21] Mbembe's characterizations of African contexts are at home in Trump's United States and Bolsonaro's Brazil.

It's the Racism, Stupid

We should not imagine that the activities of online trolls or bots was enough to propel Trump or Bolsonaro into office. In the United States, Trump relies on widespread ignorance about the government's role in the formation of a postwar white middle class, favored by investments that largely excluded minorities. As we know, at the same time, the nation publicly celebrates the advances of civil rights. This combination creates the impression, among groups of whites who feel stuck, that the government and the media are more interested in helping minorities and immigrants. Aided by trolls and bots, Trump masterfully tapped into a deep-seated resentment of diversity and globalization, transforming it into a positive identity: "I'm white and I'm proud."

In the United States, though many areas remain ultrasegregated, the sites (and sights) of economic prosperity have gained in demographic diversity. In Brazil, racial and xenophobic cleavages have not been exploited in electoral politics to the same extent as in the United States and Europe, and for obvious reasons: Brazil has a comparatively smaller immigrant population and more people identify as black or brown than as white. And yet, the spaces where the rich live remain almost exclusively white. Race-based revanchism or race-inflected backlash politics constitute a key element of right-wing movements across the world, and Brazil is not an exception.

There are some on the left who argue that the hatred for Lula and his PT does not stem from missteps while in government (2002–16), but rather from the threat that certain social advances during that period represented to the upper classes, such as increased socioeconomic mobility and expanded access to higher education. There has been plenty of talk about the "new middle class," but how to take the measure of the middle and upper-middle classes that remained stagnant, declined, or simply believe they deserve

WHERE DID THE FUTURE GO?

better? Bolsonarism is, in part, a reaction of those who feel that they have lost guarantees and status in recent years; and, like Trumpism, it promises to convert rancor and resentment into pride and affirmation. The boom years produced refrains like: "too many poor people are taking planes," or "who can afford a maid these days?" Many who felt life getting harder could find solace in Bolsonarism: it is not your fault.

Some in the left, however, often caricature and overestimate the relevance of "the resentful white middle class." It is, after all, a relatively small portion of the Brazilian electorate. If we attach too much importance to it, we run the risk of overlooking how Bolsonaro appeals to a variety of voting groups, including the working-class "new middle class," affected by unemployment and a stagnant economy. More significantly, the sense of insecurity produced by rising crime rates, shared by almost everyone, became a driving force behind Bolsonaro's rise. There is no cognitive dissonance or right-wing fantasy in the general diagnostic: the impact of urban violence is real. The fantasies, in this case, lie in the solutions peddled by Bolsonaro. But what alternatives are championed by the left, the center, or the nonfascistic right? In this context, Bolsonaro was the only candidate who gave the impression of truly caring about impunity, widespread corruption, and violence.

In an interview with Rio newspaper *O Globo* before the elections, he said: "We've got to let everyone have guns, just like in the United States. I'd let truck drivers and vigilantes have guns, for example. It's like the Wild West out here, but only one side is allowed to shoot."[22] This is not controversy; it is bluster. Of course he distorts facts when he says that everyone in the United States can have guns and that "only one side is allowed to shoot" in Brazil. The less detail, the better. We know that the Brazilian police shoot often, and that they are one of the most lethal security forces in the world. Likewise, we know that drug traffickers' weapons do not fall out of the sky, and that the drug trade, paramilitary groups, and corruption (including in the police and the military) are interconnected problems. We know that the experiences of other countries suggest that the decriminalization of drugs produces better results than a build-up of arms and violent conflict. These are complex, challenging discussions. To some, Bolsonaro's simplistic, steadfast approach is comforting. To them, others are ideological, while they have common sense.

BETWEEN CATASTROPHE AND REVOLUTION

In practice, Bolsonaro's vision for public safety doubles down on failed approaches and ultimately offers more of the same: endless war (the arms and prison industries rejoice). To suggest that more gun ownership will solve the problems of public security is little more than exploiting others' despair. For Bolsonaro's supporters, he is a messiah (his middle name is Messias, after all) who promises salvation without sacrifice. This does not seem like a bad deal, but to buy it you have to find it normal for the police and the military to enter favela neighborhoods and kill with impunity, leaving mostly black and poor victims. These deaths, which include police officers, many of them also black and poor, are collateral damage in a supposedly just and necessary war. For them, military intervention and sacrifice; for us, law and order.

Brazil's version of the dog whistle is less about affirming white pride, but Bolsonarism also rests on a hierarchy where the lives of the black, the poor, and favela residents matter less, when they are not seen as expendable. In a event hosted by financial firm BTG Pactual (sometimes regarded as the "Goldman of the Tropics"), Bolsonaro reportedly received applause for the following proposal: helicopters would shower Rocinha (a densely populated favela) with pamphlets warning that criminals would have six hours to turn themselves in. Once time was up, the police would open fire on the favela. Many of those who applaud such a proposal would say that they are not racist and would be offended if someone accused them of being so. So our country has not overcome the legacies of slavery. So our society is wildly unequal, inequality has a racial dimension, the police arrest and kill black and poor people at a disproportionate rate. Bolsonarism consoles you: it's not your fault.

The analytical category of redundant racism might be useful here: in a society where racial inequality is structural, racism is redundant. In other words, if we woke up tomorrow in a country with no racists, we would still be living in a racist country. A regressive tax system, for example, helps perpetuate racial inequalities by taking more from wage earners and less from the intergenerational wealth of the ultrarich. To paraphrase Angela Davis: in contexts where racism is institutional, there is no such thing as not being racist. Either you are anti-racist and fighting actively to reduce racial inequalities within institutions, or you are racist. This demands that we take collective responsibility for inequalities that stem from contexts that precede us. It is not an easy task.

When the Hyper-Right and the Real Collide

When Bolsonaro defends the idea of gun-wielding vigilantes, some hapless supporters imagine Chuck Norris types saving the day. That must be an insult to upstanding police officers and members of the military who believe that Brazil should remain a democratic, law-abiding society. To think that there are not enough shots fired in Brazil is to show great contempt for those whose lives are most affected by armed conflict, including the police and military members on the front lines of public safety. In the abovementioned interview with *O Globo*, Bolsonaro says that Marielle Franco's murder "doesn't mean anything for democracy," and that "it's just another death in Rio de Janeiro." "We have to wait for the results of the investigation," he concludes.[23] When Santiago Andrade, a videographer, was struck by a flare and killed during protests in Rio in February 2014, Bolsonaro had not shown the same restraint, accusing the leftist Socialism and Liberty Party (PSOL) of being behind his death. This goes way beyond having a double standard; it is a form of absolutist relativism used to justify violence from the "good" side and any conclusion that damns the "other" side. Someone fired shots at the pro-Lula protesters camped outside the prison where he was held? They were asking for it.

The comment about Marielle may seem inconsequential for those who have seen homicides become a routine in Rio de Janeiro. In some sense, it is just another death. But for democracy, it means a lot: the assassination of an elected city councilor. A young, courageous, black woman. Who killed Marielle? Who wanted her dead? A lot of evidence leads to Bolsonaro's allies, and to his family. They have been working hard to stonewall investigations. In Bolsonaro's comments about Marielle's case, the dog whistle is active. The message is heard by those who are on the side of the murderers, but not by those who would be turned off by it. The cynical or the naïve may deny it, but no corrupt police officer, paramilitary group member, aspiring vigilante, or hitman would doubt for a moment what side Bolsonaro is on. He whistles; the hyenas laugh.

Marielle was a member of a socialist party, but she also represented qualities that many on the right claim to prize. She fought against adversity and seized her few opportunities. She helped renew politics in a society prone to electing members of political dynasties. Marielle represented a threat to the same old Brazilian politics and was the opposite of the career politicians of the Bolsonaro clan. In her master's thesis, she shows the importance of recognizing differences but does not reduce life to a clash between two sides: "The drug trade is cruel, violent, and ravages communities, but the State can't compete with it by fighting to see who can exert the most violence," she wrote.[24] "There can be no hierarchy for pain, no room to believe that it is only felt by the mothers of young victims from the favelas. This militarized, warlike State is also responsible for the pain haunting the families of the sixteen police officers who have been killed since the start of the UPP [Pacifying Police Unit] program."[25] She defended her thesis in 2014.

Marielle names the police officers who died in the line of duty, something that memes criticizing her for "defending criminals" rarely do. She does not call for more government but for a better government. Marielle had much of the courage that *bolsonarismo* projects onto idols with feet of clay. She met challenges head-on. Her campaign slogan, "I am because we are," is the antithesis of "it wasn't me" or "it's not your fault." Instead of advancing a withdrawn individualism, Marielle inserts herself into the collective. She recognizes the limits of any single person and the potentials of drawing strength from being within a community.

Bolsonaro, like Trump, is more of a symptom than a cause. Both, however, already had an important impact, distorting the political spectrum by legitimating extremist positions and pushing the center to the right. In an article in the *Folha de S. Paulo*, Antonia Pellegrino and Manoela Miklos—basing themselves on a study from social scientist Esther Solano—conclude that Bolsonarism is not a passing phenomenon. It would be all too easy to delegitimize the opinions of his followers and claim the higher ground, but, Miklos and Pellegrino insist, it would not do us much good. They argue that despite increasing aggression against feminism, feminists should seek dialogue.[26] It is always easier to divide the world into two sides: good (us) versus bad (them). Facing the full complexity of our problems and recognizing that there are no magical solutions is much more difficult. Obviously, this also applies to the tempting comfort of anti-Bolsonarism (or anti-Trumpism). We all have our share of responsibility. After all, the inability of the left and of institutional politics as a whole to present viable visions for the future is part of what fuels Bolsonarism and its variants.

WHERE DID THE FUTURE GO?

The Future is Already a Thing of the Past

As we know, Bolsonarism and Trumpism are not isolated phenomena. Since 2009, Slovakian artist Tomáš Rafa has been documenting street protests, mostly in central Europe. Using direct cinema methods, he records the activities of neo-fascist, homophobic, and xenophobic groups as well as those supporting refugees and minorities like the Roma, who are often targets of far-right organizations. The project is called "New Nationalisms," and some of Rafa's work is available on his website.[27] These "new nationalists" often resort to the age-old tack of evoking an illusory past. Slovakian nationalists seek legitimation in fascist collaborator Jozef Tiso, celebrating him as a benign founding father who fought against globalizing forces in the name of his people. This nostalgia is not so distant from that of conservatives in the United States who protest the removal of monuments to defenders of slavery on the grounds that they are part of a cultural heritage. In Brazil, this illusory past surfaces when some claim that there was no corruption under the military dictatorship.

Struggles over historical memory are nothing new, but regressive imaginaries that idealize the past seem to be expanding in the public sphere. The internet provides fodder for any fantasy-fueled opinion about Nazism, slavery, or Pinochet, undermining responsible debate and pulverizing historical knowledge. At the same time, our contemporary impasses pose obstacles to progressive visions and reflections about the future and about what can be done to overcome the past. The ecological crisis and increasing labor precariousness are upon us. One of the most beautiful slogans of the protests of June 2013 in Brazil, "tomorrow will be greater," seems to have fizzled out. From a catastrophist point of view, it is as if the dire future, not the past, is already a given—seemingly inalterable, fixed, irrevocable.

The absence of political platforms, projects, or alternative visions sweeping and seductive enough to broaden the horizons of possibility only strengthens the appeal of Bolsonarism and the "new nationalisms" of the far right. If all seems lost, it may be encouraging to recall our terrible track record when it comes to predictions. Who foresaw the advances of the LGBT+ movements over the past few decades, for example? On the other hand, the campaign slogan of Brazil's clown-turned-politician Tiririca—"It can't get any worse than this"—is never true. Things can always get worse, and what *bolsonarismo* unleashed represents an incalculable threat.

BETWEEN CATASTROPHE AND REVOLUTION

Trotsky wrote in 1930: "If the Communist Party is the party of revolutionary hope, then fascism, as a mass movement, is the party of counter-revolutionary despair."[28] Bolsonarism may be the movement of counterrevolutionary hope, or revolutionary despair. It represents those who yearn for the return of the dictatorship's "law and order" or who just want to watch everything go up in flames. Fears of extermination policies may seem far-fetched, but are these not already being carried out in the name of a war on drugs that is doomed to failure? In *The Origins of Totalitarianism*, Hannah Arendt writes: "What runs counter to common sense is not the nihilistic principle that 'everything is permitted' ... What common sense and 'normal people' refuse to believe is that everything is possible."[29]

Bolsonarism, like Trumpism, is for those who cannot face the music and prefer to offload their responsibility. We must have the courage to face it patiently and compassionately, but firmly. Those who allow themselves to be seduced or acquiesce may be tomorrow's perpetrators, or tomorrow's victims.

Now What? The Politics of Streets and Screens

It might be tempting to think that in Brazil, we have witnessed something along the lines of the Reagan alliance in the US, bringing together anti-working-class policies and the moral issues dear to evangelicals. That would be optimistic. Bolsonaro borrows directly from Trump's playbook. He seeks to govern via hyperreality: the Amazon is not really burning, and if it is, NGOs and indigenous people did it to make the government look bad. The truth arrives on WhatsApp. Meanwhile, dissenting media outlets and businesses are threatened through more old-fashioned means. A number of critics of the government have received "warnings" that their family members would be murdered if they did not relent.

Differences between Brazil and the US should also assert themselves, though we cannot predict how. Brazil does not have the geopolitical standing to get away with bravado. Nor does it have the same tradition as the US of racialized partisan behavior. How do Bolsonaro supporters react to a lack of improvement in public safety? To a pandemic? Brazil has a political culture of taking to the streets—and of harsh police suppression of left-leaning manifestations—as well as weaker institutions.

WHERE DID THE FUTURE GO?

So far, capitalism has not provided all that much resistance to neo-fascist developments. What sorts of recriminations and scapegoating do we get in a scenario of ecological catastrophe or a major economic downturn? How far do draconian measures go with GDP growth and an ever greater concentration of wealth? *Late Victorian Holocausts*[30] is, among many other things, full of lessons about how unaccountability might be a condition for capitalist expansion.

If contemporary political subjects have become more synchronically than diachronically comparable, this of course corresponds to transformations in our built environments. Political fantasies and strategies seem to be more comparable across the globe, not unlike how our cities themselves have become increasingly similar. The urban spaces and spatial logics of São Paulo might be more like those of suburban Lagos or Singapore than like those of São Paulo a century ago. In a world of social lives increasingly mediated by screens, we should ask whether digital platforms like Facebook and WhatsApp do not supersede just "old" media—newspapers, radio, TV. Rather, they also supersede more familiar forms of urban social experience: the bus stop, the public square, and so on. What happens when screens displace streets as the primary interface for social encounters?

Days before the first round of the Brazilian elections, hundreds of thousands, perhaps millions of people took to the streets as part of protests led by women under the hashtag #*EleNão* (Not Him). Feedback loops between screens and streets occurred—anti-Bolsonaro manifestations, organized through digital tools. Almost immediately, WhatsApp groups became flooded with memes claiming that the protests were not actually taking place, that birds-eye images of crowds circulating in social media and on television screens were in fact from carnival. It is easy to imagine that these hyperreal factoids thrive better among those living in the sorts of cities that we have been building for some time in modern Brazil—cities of enclaves, segregated and car-centric; of superhighways rather than streets. The hyper-right hacked the information superhighway. But street corners remain among the cornerstones of freedom. It is unclear whether the memes purporting to debunk #EleNão managed to persuade significant numbers of Bolsonaro supporters, but on screens and streets alike, it became clear that the movement reignited a sense of solidarity and possibility—festive, and with a purpose. People return to the streets, always again, searching for life amid catastrophe. If and when massive protests against this and comparable regimes arise, they will likely not only face the wrath of the hyper-right, but also batons, bullets, bombs.

Endnotes

1 In *Contemplação de Ouro Preto (1949–1950)*, published in 1954, quoted from a translation by Luciana Stegagno Picchio.
2 Stefan Zweig's book with that same title, published in German as *Brasilien: Ein Land der Zukunft* (Stockholm: Bermann-Fischer, 1941), was later translated to several languages.
3 Stefan Zweig, *Brazil, Land of the Future* (New York: Viking, 1943), 1.
4 Mike Davis and Daniel Bertrand Monk, *Evil Paradises: Dreamworlds of Neoliberalism* (New York: New Press, 2007), 1.
5 This can be associated with what has been called postmodernity, with Guy Debord's "the society of the spectacle," or with what others deem late capitalism. It should resonate with Mike Davis's own work in *City of Quartz* and *Ecology of Fear*, for example, including the notion of "counterfeit urbanity." Here I will try to articulate later stages and variations in familiar phenomena. The use of "hyperreal" draws on Baudrillard's notion of "the generation by models of a real without origin or reality" (*Simulacra and Simulation*, Ann Arbor: University of Michigan Press, 1994), 1.
6 My translation. In *Revista Veja*. Veja Essa. Edição 1575, (December 2, 1998): 39 [2]. Much of the reflection on the emergence of Bolsonaro was published in a Brazilian magazine during the election ("Não foi você: uma interpretação do bolsonarismo," *revista piauí*, Ed. 142, July, 2018). Flora Thomson-DeVeaux translated that essay, which I have substantially revised and rewritten here. I am also thankful to Etyelle Pinheiro de Araújo for her help finding the original sources for citations.
7 My translation. In T1, "Pinochet fez o que tinha que ser feito', dispara Jair Bolsonaro," YouTube video, 6:42, March 2, 2015, https://www.youtube.com/watch?v=REoW-ZWQEU-o.
8 My translation. In Thais Gianni, "Jair Bolsonaro defendendo guerra civil, fim do voto e fechamento de congresso [COMPLETO]," YouTube Video, 35:38, April 10, 2016, https://www.youtube.com/watch?v=qIDyw9QKIvw. The PSDB of former president Fernando Henrique Cardoso, which made it to the second round in every election won by the PT, underperformed dramatically. The PT and Bolsonaro's previously insignificant party elected most members to congress, though each with only about 10 percent of the total.
9 My translation. In Poder, "Bolsonaro diz que, no Exército, sua 'especialidade é matar'," *Folha de S. Paulo*, June 30, 2016, https://www1.folha.uol.com.br/poder/2017/06/1897435-minha-especialidade-e-matar-diz-jair-bolsonaro.shtml.
10 My translation. In Eduardo Bolsonaro, "Jair Bolsonaro por telefone para a av. Paulista em 21/OUT/2018," YouTube Video, 7:53, "Eduardo Bolsonaro", October 21, 2018, https://www.youtube.com/watch?v=KznEhYR9NeA.
11 My translation. In João Moreira Sales, "Anotações sobre uma pichação: Inocência, culpa e responsabilidade nas ruas do Rio de Janeiro," *Piauí*, 139 edition, April, 2018, https://piaui.folha.uol.com.br/materia/anotacoes-sobre-uma-pichacao/.
12 "Pulso Brasil", FENAPREV, Ed 157, April 2018, http://midias.cnseg.org.br/data/files/EB/71/46/1E/3FF746100A1DC546F98AA8A8/Apresentacao_Ipsos_Press_Kit.pdf.
13 My translation. In Bolsonaro TV, "MARINA SILVA CHAMA BOLSONARO DE HYENA," YouTube Video, 1:08, April 24, 2018 https://www.youtube.com/watch?v=hxh5G1niYRM.
14 Bolsonaro TV, "MARINA SILVA."
15 My translation. In Carlos Bolsonaro, "BOLSONARO NA REDETV (2015): SEMPRE ESCLARECEDOR," YouTube Video, 40:12, March 02, 2015 https://www.youtube.com/watch?v=1BIJyvlTbUM
16 Kevin M. Kruse, *White Flight: Atlanta and the Making of Modern Conservatism* (Princeton, NJ: Princeton University Press, 2005).

17 Benito Mussolini, *My Autobiography* (Mineola, NY: Dover, 2006), 53.
18 Patricia Campos Mello, "Empresários bancam campanha contra o PT pelo WhatsApp," *Folha de S. Paulo*, October 18, 2018, https://www1.folha.uol.com.br/poder/2018/10/empresarios-bancam-campanha-contra-o-pt-pelo-whatsapp.shtml.
19 Eliane Brum, "Bolsonaro e a autoverdade - Como a valorização do ato de dizer, mais do que o conteúdo do que se diz, vai impactar a eleição no Brasil," *El País*, July16, 2018, https://brasil.elpais.com/brasil/2018/07/16/politica/1531751001_113905.html
20 My translation. In Achille Mbembe, "O lumpenradicalismo e outras doenças da tirania," *Flanagens* (blog), December 31, 2017, https://flanagens.blogspot.com/2017/12/o-lumpenradicalismo-e-outras-doencas-da.html.
21 Mbembe, "O lumpenradicalismo."
22 My translation. In *O Globo*, "Saiba quais são as propostas de Bolsonaro e Haddad para Segurança Pública", October 10, 2018, https://oglobo.globo.com/brasil/saiba-quais-sao-as-propostas-de-bolsonaro-haddad-para-seguranca-publica-23145171
23 My translation. In *O Globo* "Caso Marielle: presidenciáveis comentam morte de vereadora", April 23, 2018, https://oglobo.globo.com/brasil/caso-marielle-presidenciaveis-comentam-morte-de-vereadora-22619562
24 My translation. Marielle Franco, "UPP – A redução da favela a três letras: uma análise da política de segurança pública do Estado do Rio de Janeiro"(Master's thesis, Universidade Federal Fluminense, 2014), 98, https://app.uff.br/riuff/bitstream/1/2166/1/Marielle%20Franco.pdf.
25 Franco, "UPP," 99.
26 Antonia Pellegrino and Manoela Miklos, "E agora, Maria? Como o feminismo deve reagir diante da simpatia por um candidato misógino?" *Folha de S. Paulo*, April 30, 2018, https://www1.folha.uol.com.br/colunas/antonia-pellegrino-e-manoela-miklos/2018/04/e-agora-maria.shtml.
27 Tomáš Rafa's work is available on: http://your-art.sk/.
28 Leon Trotsky, "The Turn in the Communist International and the German Situation, 1930," in *Fascism: What It Is and How to Fight It*, ed. George Lavan Weissman (Pioneer Publishers 1969), 26.
29 Hannah Arendt, *The Origins of Totalitarianism* (London: George Allen and Unwin, 1958), 568.
30 Mike Davis, *Late Victorian Holocausts: El Niño Famines and the Making of the Third World* (London: Verso, 2001).

ERUPTIONS OF RAGE

Mustafa Dikeç

> *None of this was doing anybody any good.*
> *It would have been better to have left the plate glass*
> *as it had been and the goods lying in stores.*
>
> *It would have been better, but it would also have been*
> *intolerable, for Harlem had needed something to smash.*
>
> —*James Baldwin,* Notes of a Native Son

Urban uprisings of late have exposed the fractures and inequalities in the cities of the so-called developed world. These fractures and inequalities are not the products of paltry efforts or lack of resolve on the part of those whose urban lives are marked by hardship and suffering but of ongoing histories of colonialism and uneven urbanization. Such uprisings, then, are not signs of individual pathologies but of interlinked histories of rage, class, and "race," as Mike Davis once put it, referring to the 1992 Los Angeles uprising. From Paris to Baltimore and London to Ferguson, such histories are exposed in and through uprisings. These are not necessarily revolutionary moments, but they are political ones in their exposure of ongoing histories of violence and oppression.

Seen this way, urban uprisings are not signs of wanton criminality but of rage that has built up over the years. It is the eruption of this rage and the exposure of its sources that gives a political aspect to such uprisings. Informed by urban uprisings in the liberal democracies of the West in the past decade or so, I would like to present four arguments in this chapter.[1]

First, urban uprisings are not just looting and burning; they connect and speak to broader dynamics including injuries of the past, difficulties of the present, and anxieties about the future. They are marked by violence, but they are also responses to different forms of violence such as discrimination, police brutality, structural unemployment, stigmatization, and other forms of inequality. To put this another way, they are episodic incidents of violence against structural violence.

This leads to a second argument: there are structural reasons, not individual pathologies, behind urban uprisings; reasons that have to do with the routine workings of our cities. This implies that the episodic violence of urban uprisings can be put in perspective rather than dismissed as criminal or pathological once we get a sense of other forms of violence that build resentment and lead to these eruptions of rage. Rather than demonizing and brutalizing participants in urban uprisings, it is important, it seems to me, to try to understand what enrages and leads them to such destructive rage, risking their lives and freedom.

The third argument follows from this observation about the structural reasons behind urban uprisings and emphasizes its temporal dimension. As Omi and Winant put it, following the 1992 Los Angeles uprisings, even though the spark is usually a single incident, "rage is not born in a moment."[2] These uprisings are outcomes of deep-rooted grievances, of long histories of exclusion of and violence perpetrated against particular populations. Los Angeles was no exception, as *City of Quartz* had already demonstrated a couple of years before rage finally erupted. Or—to take a more recent example—following the August 2016 uprising in Sherman Park, Milwaukee, after the police shot an African American man to death, community resident Sharlen Moore had this to say: "This isn't just, 'Oh, my gosh, all of a sudden this happened.' It's a series of things that has happened over a period of time. And right now you shake a soda bottle and you open the top and it explodes, and this is what it is." Milwaukee is one of the most segregated cities in the United States, with some of the highest incarceration and unemployment rates for African American men in the country.[3] Urban uprisings, then, are not reactions to isolated incidents but to injustices that have become routine and normalized. The rage that erupts in these incidents is not a reaction to isolated cases of bad practice; it is rage against sustained oppression and has many sources.

My final argument is about the political significance of urban uprisings. Even when there are no explicit demands or immediate political programs, urban uprisings are political in that they expose patterns and dynamics of exclusion and oppression that have become routinized. As eruptions of accumulated grievances, they are like "a revealing flash of lightning," as Alain Locke described the 1935 Harlem riot: not only disrupting but also exposing routinized injustices. As Don Mitchell puts it, they "arise out of the very social and physical structure of the city, and when they do, they suddenly illuminate it," bringing to light "the structure and exercise of power" in cities.[4] The occurrence of burning and looting, unfortunate as it is, does not render urban uprisings less or not political at all. As an indignation about unequal treatment of groups and other forms of injustice, these revolts are calls for justice and equality, even when these are not always expressed explicitly. This signals a politics of rage that is bent on survival, not destruction; guided by cognitive states, not impulses; affirming equality, not inferiority.

This political aspect of urban uprisings, it seems to me, gets overshadowed by the occurrence of looting and burning. Urban uprisings, however, do not start as gratuitous burning and looting. They are triggered by a specific, usually tragic incident that symbolizes the sufferings and hardship of oppressed populations. The triggering incidents are not one-off occurrences, as I have noted above, but part of systematic injustices. In other words, the incident that triggers an uprising is neither rare nor unprecedented, but is one that perhaps has gone awry and finally "overflowed the unimaginably bitter cup," as James Baldwin put it in 1966.[5] Such an incident occurred in August 2014 in Ferguson. Rage erupted, revealing years of unsavory law enforcement practices designed to generate revenue for the city by preying on African Americans, at once exploiting and criminalizing them.

"Race," Class, and...

The triggering incident for the Ferguson uprising was police violence: on August 9, 2014, white police officer Darren Wilson repeatedly shot an unarmed African American teenager, Michael Brown, and killed him. His dead body was left on the street for several hours. The uprising began the following day and continued for about two weeks, with peaceful protests as well as burning, looting, and clashes with the police. The uprising was repressed by police officers equipped with military-grade weapons, with the National Guard referring to the protestors as "enemy forces" and the city declaring a state of emergency—an extreme measure that was also taken in April 2015 during the Baltimore uprising, in August 2016 in Milwaukee, and a month later in Charlotte.[6] Ferguson experienced another week of unrest in November 2014 after a grand jury decided not to indict Wilson, and smaller-scale protests took place on the anniversary of Brown's killing.

Ferguson is an inner suburb of St. Louis, Missouri. A "sundown town" until the mid-1960s—which meant that African Americans could not enter the city after dark—Ferguson is now a majority African American city, although this is not reflected in the city's administration and police force. From 1990 to 2010, the city's African American population increased from 25 to 67 percent, while the white population decreased from 74 to 29 percent. During the 2000s, St. Louis and its suburbs were hit by a process that affected almost every major US metropolitan area: the suburbanization of poverty. This process was partially caused by the dismantling of public housing projects and the shift to the voucher system, which tended to concentrate poverty in certain areas, such as the one where Michael Brown lived and was killed.[7] Coupled with a trend of inner-city revival and gentrification, this shift pushed the inner-city poor out toward the suburbs. Ferguson's poor population doubled from 2000 to 2012. One in four Ferguson residents lived below the poverty line in 2012.

A higher number of poor residents meant less revenue for the City of Ferguson, but the latter had a "business model" that helped generate revenue. This model was based on the joint operation of Ferguson's police department and its municipal court, and involved targeting African Americans for revenue generation through fines and court fees. Police officers wrote up to eight, and in one instance fourteen, citations during a single encounter, and the police department used the number of citations as a sign of productivity in its officer evaluations and promotions. This, then, was not a matter of bad apples; it was a deliberate and systematic exploitation of African Americans through the coordinated efforts of the police department and the municipal court, urged by city management, as the Department of Justice (DoJ) investigation following the uprising revealed.[8] In March 2000, for example, the city's finance director contacted the police chief to express his concern about the expected sales tax shortfall and to ask him to offset this through fines. "Unless ticket writing ramps up significantly before the end of the year," he wrote, "it will be hard to significantly raise collections next year." In the year leading up to the uprisings, in March 2013, the finance director wrote the following to the City Manager: "Court fees are anticipated to rise about 7.5%. I did ask the [police] Chief if he thought the PD [police department] could deliver 10% increase. He indicated they could try."

Municipal fines and fees are the second-largest source of income for the City of Ferguson after sales tax. In the five years leading up to the 2014 uprising, the share of fines and fees in Ferguson's municipal revenue went up from 8 to over 13 percent. Between 2010 and 2014, about 90,000 citations and summonses were issued for Ferguson municipal code violations—22,500 citations and summonses a year in a city with a population of 21,000 and with a municipal court judge working for a grand total of twelve hours per month. In the year before the uprising, the court generated more than $2.5 million through municipal fines and fees.[9] The DoJ investigation found that this upsurge was not due to a rise in serious crime (serious crimes such as assault, stealing, and driving while intoxicated have remained constant or declined in Ferguson over the last ten years) but to the concerted efforts of city management, the police department, and the municipal court to generate revenue for the city. As the DoJ report put it: "Ferguson's law enforcement practices are shaped by the City's focus on revenue rather than by public safety needs." This focus led to unconstitutional policing and dubious practices at the municipal court, both of which reflected and exacerbated racial stereotypes and discrimination.

Ferguson police disproportionately targeted African Americans: 85 percent of vehicle stops and practically all pedestrian stops involved African Americans. African Americans also accounted for 90 percent of citations, 93 percent of arrests, 92 percent of cases with arrest warrants, about 90 percent of cases of use of force, and all police dog bites. Data also show that certain municipal charges applied almost exclusively to African Americans. The five most common charges brought against them were also the ones that gave the widest discretion to police officers: Manner of Walking in Roadway, Failure to Comply, Resisting Arrest, Peace Disturbance, and Failure to Obey. Between

2011 and 2013, African Americans accounted for 95 percent of Manner of Walking in Roadway charges, and 94 percent of Failure to Comply charges.

"Partly as a consequence of City and FPD [Ferguson Police Department] priorities," the DoJ report put it, "many officers appear to see some residents, especially those who live in Ferguson's predominantly African American neighborhoods, less as constituents to be protected than as potential offenders and sources of revenue." Michael Brown lived and was stopped and killed in such a neighborhood, probably in another attempt by a Ferguson police officer to generate revenue for the city. The killing of Brown was the triggering incident, but the 2014 Ferguson uprising was not a reaction to an isolated incident; it was a response to years of institutionalized racism, oppression, and exploitation.

African Americans are not a racialized minority in Ferguson, but they are not represented in the police department and city government. Baltimore, which erupted a year after Ferguson, is a different story. Unlike in Ferguson, African Americans hold prominent positions in the police department and city government. Baltimore's population is 63 percent African American. The mayor is African American, her police chief is African American, the majority of the city council, including its president, is African American, the top prosecutor is African American, and practically half the police force is African American too.

Rage erupted in Baltimore in April 2015 after Freddie Gray's funeral, a twenty-five-year old African American man who was arrested for no apparent reason and put in a police van in Sandtown, one of the most deprived—and stigmatized—neighborhoods in the already quite deprived, 96 percent African American West Baltimore area. When Gray came out of the police van, he was no longer conscious. He died in hospital a week later. The six officers involved in his arrest, three of them African American, were indicted on charges including second-degree murder but were not convicted in the end.[10]

As the Ferguson example suggests, urban uprisings are not triggered by some isolated police action but by police practices that have become routine. Baltimore in 2015 was similar. The police action that cost Gray his life was part of an established pattern of police brutality. An investigation by the *Baltimore Sun* revealed that between 2011 and 2014, the City had to pay about $6 million in settlements to more than one hundred victims of police violence, most often African Americans, including a twenty-six-year old pregnant woman and an eighty-seven-year old grandmother. Injuries inflicted by police officers ranged from broken bones to organ failure and led to death in some cases. Serious injuries during police van rides were not unprecedented either. Baltimore police had an established practice of going for a "rough ride"—driving to harm handcuffed but unbuckled detainees in the back of the police van—which had already left several people paralyzed by fracturing their necks.[11]

In Baltimore, aggressive policing of poor and stigmatized neighborhoods sowed the seeds of rage. The city's previous mayor, Martin O'Malley, targeted such areas with a zero-tolerance policy. This policy got so out of control that in a single year, the Baltimore police arrested practically one in six people in the city: in 2005, more than 100,000 arrests were made in a city of about 640,000, of which about one-fourth led to no charges. This policy of mass arrest was challenged with a lawsuit filed in 2006, and Baltimore agreed to pay a $870,000 settlement.[12]

This policy had lasting effects on the poor and African American population of the city. Arrest records make it very difficult to get a job or to qualify for housing. Moreover, this mass arrest policy turned residents of areas like Sandtown into criminal suspects in the eyes of the police, who—just like in Ferguson—were under pressure to perform. Even the police officers who arrested Freddie Gray could not provide an account suggesting that he was involved in any wrongdoing. Heavy-handed policing of such areas aggravated material difficulties and created more resentment among residents.

The Baltimore uprising suggests that class plays an important role as well. The context for the uprisings in both Ferguson and Baltimore was prepared by inequalities, poverty, and aggressive and discriminatory policing. These were the results of policy choices that hit racially stigmatized groups hardest, rather than outcomes of inevitable trends, cultural peculiarities, or individual pathologies. Let us now look at the French example, which shows the role that colonial legacies play in addition to class and racialization.

. . . the Colonial Present

The 2005 uprising in the *banlieues* of France was unprecedented in its magnitude and geographical extent. It lasted for three weeks, touching about three hundred communes. The state response to it—declaration of a state of emergency—was unprecedented as well. That the state of emergency was based on a 1955 law dating from the Algerian War, and that it was invoked only twice before in France's former colonies but never on mainland France, exposed the colonial nature of the French state's treatment of working class *banlieues*—social housing estates in the peripheral areas of cities.

Although the term *banlieue* is commonly used to refer to a certain form of housing (social housing estates) associated with certain kinds of populations (immigrants and nonwhite French), this is not empirically accurate. Originally an administrative term, *banlieue* designates a geographical area, not specific forms of housing or certain groups of the population. The peripheral status of the *banlieues* suggests an image of exclusion, but the term is not necessarily negative and not all *banlieues* are poor. Yet the dominant and stereotypical image of *banlieues* is one of social housing estates in the peripheral areas of cities—"badlands" that do not quite fit in the French Republic. This image is fed by France's colonial past as well as by the dystopian images of American ghettos, which is why the main groups associated with this badlands image are Arabs and black people, even when they are born and raised in France. The fear of the formation of ethnic communities and ghettos—incompatible with France's self-image as a "one and indivisible" Republic—makes the poorer and more ethnically diverse *banlieues* objects of much policy and debate, even though ethnic concentration is stronger among white than among nonwhite French. It is, however, the latter's concentration that seems to pose a problem.

The colonial imaginary is still dominant in France. Hence the title of this section, "colonial present," to emphasize how the colonial imaginary persists and is played out in French *banlieues*.[13] Through its policies and discourses, "the State perpetuates, indeed reproduces, forms of colonial domination" in the French *banlieues*.[14] One example of this imaginary is the use of military language such as "reconquest," which is a term recurrently used in connection with *banlieues* and more recently in urban redevelopment projects aimed at the demolition of social housing estates.[15] Policies and discourses that frame *banlieues* as the "badlands of the Republic" that are incompatible with its values exacerbate the already entrenched prejudices.[16] The persistence of this strong colonial legacy in France is divisive; the projected image of the Republic as "one and indivisible" only adds insult to injury. The French children of immigrants from the former French colonies are still seen as immigrants and foreigners, and they are treated like that socially, economically, and politically. Turks suffer the same fate.[17] This is the beast confronting children like Zyed, Bouna, and Muhittin—and their children as well.

Zyed Benna (seventeen years old, family from Tunisia), Bouna Traoré (fifteen years old, family from Mauritania), and Muhittin Altun (seventeen years old, Kurdish family from Turkey) were three teenagers who were electrocuted in an electricity substation in Clichy-sous-Bois, a *banlieue* to the northeast of Paris, while trying to escape identity checks by the police—a form of daily harassment not uncommon for youth of working-class *banlieues*, especially if they have darker skin. The police who were chasing them saw the three entering the electricity substation to hide, but rather than warning them or calling someone to cut off the electricity, they blocked the exit. The teenagers were electrocuted shortly after. Muhittin, the only survivor, managed to get out and reach his neighborhood despite his burns, and the firefighters were finally called—by the youth, not by the police. This was the triggering incident for the uprising, and the initial official statements portraying the three teenagers as thieves only fueled the anger. A silent march was organized a couple of days later, and the situation seemed to get calmer. A day after the march, however, a police tear-gas grenade exploded in the local mosque. This was the turning point that rekindled the fire in Clichy and turned the local uprising into a national one.

There is a disturbing, if unsurprising coincidence here. As two official studies found, the descendants of immigrants from North and sub-Saharan Africa—like Zyed and Bouna—and from Turkey, like Muhittin, are economically the most vulnerable in French society, although they are born and raised in France. Even when factors such as educational level, social status of parents, and place of residence are controlled for, these studies showed that they still have higher risk of unemployment compared to white French or the children of European immigrants, simply because of who they are (something Muhittin would probably not be able to escape in Turkey either, because he is Kurdish).[18] In other words, Zyed, Bouna, and Muhittin had origins that made them more likely to live in a poor *banlieue*, face hardship at school, end up unemployed or underemployed, and suffer discrimination—including in relations with the police, as the tragic incident exposed. This was the insight into structural inequalities in France that were once again exposed by an eruption of rage. This rage, however, was not a reaction to a single incident. As Mechmache put it, although the death of the teenagers was a trigger, the source of the uprising was the accumulation of years of injustice perpetrated through state policies, policing practices, and inflammatory language used by state officials.[19] This feeling of injustice was only exacerbated by the illusions of the French republican model—with its alleged commitment to equality—and the French state's failure, or unwillingness, to come to terms with its colonial past and present.

From Pathology to Politics

The rage that erupts in urban uprisings builds up from systematic exclusion and oppression, which go beyond police violence and expand to all areas of urban life, including housing, employment, social encounters, and political worth—none of which suggest a causal relationship between uprisings and the pathological disposition of those who participate in such insurrections. Yet, references to "scum," "criminals," "feral youth," "people with a twisted moral code," and "marauders and marginals" were repeatedly made by politicians in power during the uprisings in France, the United States, and the United Kingdom. This pathological interpretation of urban uprisings rests on nineteenth-century social theories concerned with the alleged emotional volatility and irrationality of the crowd, which was seen as a threat to the ideal of the modern, rational individual—a view that has a long lineage in Western philosophy, dating all the way back to Plato, which is marked by an unease about emotions.[20] Historical research into riots showed that this pathological interpretation is empirically inaccurate.[21] My brief survey above suggests that such pathological name-calling is still not empirically warranted. Urban uprisings are destructive outbursts of rage produced by—and intended to halt—violence inflicted on excluded urban citizens, whose actions are "not bent upon destruction, but upon survival," to borrow from Audre Lorde.[22]

This suggests a politics of rage—a politics, in other words, of the emotions of the excluded, as I use the term here—that does not equate emotions with irrationality. What, then, defines rage as a political emotion rather than a pathological reaction?

My understanding of the politics of rage is premised on three general arguments on the nature of emotions.[23] First, the supposed emotion/reason and emotion/rationality dichotomies do not hold, because reason is not some pure power that is untainted by emotions and guides us to rational decisions. Second, emotions are not just individual eccentricities, because they are deeply embedded in specific social and cultural practices. They are, in other words, shaped in and by particular cultural and social contexts. Finally, emotions are, in turn, part of how we perceive and interpret these contexts. As Nussbaum put it, "[e]motions are not irrational pushes and pulls, they are ways of viewing the world. They reside in the core of one's being, the part of it with which one makes sense of the world."[24] Individuals whose urban lives are marked by recurrent and unaddressed humiliation (for example, perpetrated by police officers, as in the incidents explored in this chapter) will likely develop a hostile perception of the outside world, channeling their rage, when it erupts, in particular ways.

Emotions, therefore, are political if "politics is about forms of perceiving the world and modes of relating to it," as I have argued elsewhere.[25] There is, however, more to suggest that we should be thinking about emotions politically rather than pathologically. If, for example, I am angry, my anger is directed at an object; I am angry at or about someone or something (say, a person or a "system" that has wronged me). This object-directedness—or "aboutness"[26]—is a sign of intentionality in so far as it implies a power to discern what has wronged me (a sign of cognition, not impulse) and is a sign of a capacity to make judgments (about what is bad, wrong, unjust, unfair, etc.). Emotions also require certain beliefs for them to exist—for example, beliefs in equality, justice, and freedom from oppression are bound up with the kind of rage explored in this chapter.[27] Indeed, expressing anger can be an act of affirming equality when it allows the dominated or subordinate groups to establish themselves as moral and political agents by showing their capacity to make judgments about wrongs.[28] Emotions, therefore, are not irrational or uncontrollable impulses, because they involve cognition, rest on beliefs, and evidence judgment. The fact that such judgments about wrongs have had to be expressed in rage through revolt is a sign of failure—not of the moral disposition of the individuals involved but of our democracies, which have neglected to address recurrent wrongs and attend to the resentment they produce and reproduce.

This theoretical rectification goes beyond an academic endeavor; the pathological approach has political perils as well. It encourages a limited, punitive response to urban uprisings. As long as urban uprisings remain confined to a pathological framework, they will be addressed by state violence. These outbursts of rage, however, are related to the structures and dynamics of society and to how people see their place and future in it. When they feel excluded and are reminded of their exclusion every day in their urban lives, the recent incidents suggest that what we get is a profound sense of disenfranchisement and resentment. This will reach a point where they engage in acts that indicate they have little or no stake in their community. Rather than insisting on individual pathologies of participants, it would be more politically progressive to look at the sources of their resentment.[29]

Police violence, we have seen, is a major source of resentment and a frequent trigger for rage to erupt. It would be a mistake, however, to let police violence detract from other sources of exclusion and resentment, including the historical and structural sources of urban rage. Government policies, private developers, urban renewal programs, and real estate firms all play their role in the formation of areas of concentrated poverty, which then become targets for aggressive and discriminatory policing. "This is not a rogue officer problem," as Charles M. Blow put it; "this is a rogue society problem."[30] It is, therefore, futile to search for a single reason behind urban uprisings. As Mike Davis put it, following the 1992 Los Angeles uprising:

> You can't reduce the events to a single essence—one major characteristic or identity. L.A. was a hybrid social revolt with three major dimensions. It was a revolutionary democratic protest characteristic of African-American history when demands for equal rights have been thwarted by the major institutions. It was also a major postmodern bread riot—an uprising of not just poor people but particularly of those strata of poor in southern California who've been most savagely affected by the recession. Thirdly, it was an interethnic conflict—particularly the systematic destroying and uprooting of Korean stores in the Black community. So it was all of those things at once and issues of rage, class, and race cannot be separated out.[31]

Urban uprisings, once again, are not signs of individual flaws or cultural traits of certain groups behaving irrationally, but manifestations of grievances that expose forms of exclusion and the violence suffered. Thus, they are political events. Continuing to brutalize, kill, or lock people up when they revolt is the pathological response. The political one would be to listen to their voices as equal, legitimate, political ones, even if—or perhaps especially if—they elude the norms and spaces of established institutions of mainstream politics.

Endnotes

1. This chapter draws from my *Urban Rage: The Revolt of the Excluded* (New Haven, CT: Yale University Press, 2017). I am grateful to Daniel Bertrand Monk and Michael Sorkin for inviting me to this collection and for helping me develop the idea of a politics of rage.
2. Michael Omi and Howard Winant, "The Los Angeles 'Race Riot' and Contemporary U.S. Politics," in *Reading Rodney King/Reading Urban Uprising*, ed. Robert Gooding-Williams (New York: Routledge, 1993), 109.
3. John Eligon, "Milwaukee's Unrest Was No Shock to Some Residents," *International New York Times*, August 16, 2016, 5.
4. Alain Locke, *The Works of Alain Locke*, ed. Charles Molesworth (Oxford: Oxford University Press, 2012), 307; Don Mitchell, "Introduction: The Lightning Flash of Revolt," in *Revolting New York: How 400 Years of Riot, Rebellion, Uprising, and Revolution Shaped a City*, eds. Neil Smith and Don Mitchell (Athens: University of Georgia Press, 2018), 1. I owe the Locke description to this chapter.
5. James Baldwin, "A Report from Occupied Territory," *The Nation*, July 11, 1966, https://www.thenation.com/article/report-occupied-territory/.
6. Joanna Walters, "Troops Referred to Ferguson Protestors as 'Enemy Forces,' Emails Show," *The Guardian*, April 17, 2015, https://www.theguardian.com/us-news/2015/apr/17/missouri-national-guard-ferguson-protesters-email.
7. Elizabeth Kneebone, "Ferguson, Mo. Emblematic of Growing Suburban Poverty," Brookings Institute blog, August 15, 2014, http://www.brookings.edu/blogs/the-avenue/posts/2014/08/15-ferguson-suburban-poverty.
8. Unless stated otherwise, this section is based on this report: Department of Justice, *Investigation of the Ferguson Police Department*, United States Department of Justice, Civil Rights Division, March 4, 2015, https://www.justice.gov/sites/default/files/opa/press-releases/attachments/2015/03/04/ferguson_police_department_report.pdf.
9. City of Ferguson, Missouri, *Comprehensive Annual Financial Report for the Year Ended June 30, 2014*, http://www.fergusoncity.com/DocumentCenter/View/1752/2014-COFM-CAFR?bidId=.
10. The prosecutors failed to obtain a conviction after four trials, and the remaining charges were eventually dropped. See Baynard Woods, "Freddie Gray Death: Remaining Charges Dropped against Police Officers," *Guardian*, July 27, 2016, https://www.theguardian.com/us-news/2016/jul/27/freddie-gray-police-officers-charges-dropped.
11. Mark Puente, "Undue Force", *The Baltimore Sun*, September 28, 2014, https://data.baltimoresun.com/news/police-settlements/; Doug Donovan and Mark Puente, "Freddie Gray Not the First to Come Out of Baltimore Police Van with Serious Injuries," *The Baltimore Sun*, April 23, 2015, https://www.baltimoresun.com/maryland/baltimore-city/bs-md-gray-rough-rides-20150423-story.html.
12. Paul Schwartzman and John Wagner, "As Baltimore Mayor, Critics Say, O'Malley's Police Tactics Sowed Distrust," *Washington Post*, April 25, 2015, https://www.washingtonpost.com/local/dc-politics/as-mayor-of-baltimore-omalleys-policing-strategy-sowed-mistrust/2015/04/25/af81178a-ea9d-11e4-9767-6276fc9b0ada_story.html; Catherine Rentz, "Arrests for Minor Crimes Spur Resentment in Some Baltimore Neighborhoods," *The Baltimore Sun*, August 23, 2015, https://www.baltimoresun.com/news/investigations/bs-md-ci-minor-arrests-20150823-story.html.
13. Derek Gregory, *The Colonial Present: Afghanistan, Palestine, Iraq* (London: Blackwell, 2004). This is also the interpretation of some of the activists in the *banlieues*.

14 Saïd Bouamama, *Les classes et quartiers populaires: Paupérisation, ethnicisation et discrimination* (Paris: Editions du Cygne, 2009); Sadri Khiari, *Pour une politique de la racaille: Immigré-e-s, indigènes et jeunes de banlieues* (Paris: Textuel, 2006); Pierre Tévanian, *Le ministère de la peur* (Paris: L'esprit frappeur, 2003). The quote is from Mogniss H. Abdallah, *Rengainez, on arrive!* (Paris: Libertalia, 2012), 15.
15 Stefan Kipfer, "Neocolonial Urbanism? La Rénovation Urbaine in Paris," *Antipode* 48, no. 3 (2016): 603–25.
16 Mustafa Dikeç, *Badlands of the Republic: Space, Politics and Urban Policy* (London: Blackwell, 2007).
17 Saïd Bouamama, "Transmettre l'histoire de nos luttes" (interview), *Mouvements* 83 (2015): 154–65; Saïd Bouamama, "L'expérience politique des Noirs et des Arabes en France: Mutations, invariances et recurrences," in *Race Rebelle: Luttes des quartiers populaires des années 1980 à nos jours*, eds. Rafik Chekkat and Emmanuel D. Hoch (Paris: Editions Syllepse, 2011), 29–45.
18 Pierre-Yves Cusset et al., "Jeunes issus de l'immigration: Quels obstacles à leur insertion économique?" Note d'analyse, France Stratégie, March 2015, https://www.strategie.gouv.fr/sites/strategie.gouv.fr/files/atoms/files/na26_27022015_bat12_0.pdf; INSEE, *Données sociales. La société française* (Paris: INSEE, 2006). France Stratégie is an economic research and strategy unit that reports to the Prime minister. INSEE is the national statistics bureau.
19 Mohamed Mechmache, "Les révoltes de 2005, une prise de conscience politique," *Mouvements* 83 (2015): 17–21.
20 Eric Van Rythoven, "Fear in the Crowd or Fear of the Crowd? The Dystopian Politics of Fear in International Relations," *Critical Studies on Security* 6, no. 1 (2018): 33–49; Elizabeth V. Spelman, "Anger and Insubordination," in *Women, Knowledge, and Reality: Explorations in Feminist Philosophy*, eds. Ann Garry and Marilyn Pearsall (New York: Routledge, 1992), 263–73.
21 George Rudé, *The Crowd in History: A Study of Popular Disturbances in France and England, 1730–1848* (1964; repr., London: Serif, 2005).
22 Audre Lorde, "The Uses of Anger," *Women's Studies Quarterly* 25, no. 1/2 (1997 [1981]): 278–85.
23 Emma Hutchison, *Affective Communities in World Politics: Collective Emotions After Trauma* (Cambridge: Cambridge University Press, 2016).
24 Martha C. Nussbaum, "Emotions and Women's Capabilities," in *Women, Culture, and Development: A Study of Human Capabilities*, eds. Martha C. Nussbaum and Jonathan Glover (Oxford: Clarendon, 1995), 375.
25 Mustafa Dikeç, *Space, Politics and Aesthetics* (Edinburgh: Edinburgh University Press, 2015), 1.
26 Spelman, "Anger and Insubordination," 265.
27 Which are clearly different from the beliefs that constitute the rage that mobilizes nationalist, supremacist, and fascist movements.
28 As Spelman puts it, "the systematic denial of anger can be seen as a mechanism of subordination, and the existence and expression of anger as an act of insubordination." Spelman, "Anger and Insubordination," 270.
29 As Linklater put it: "A central issue at present is how far liberal 'civilized' societies react to 'illiberal anger' by representing it as evidence of a gulf between self-restrained, 'modern' subjects and impulsive, 'pre-modern' peoples who can only be restrained by force, against recognizing its close connection with justice for the groups involved." Andrew Linklater, "Anger and World Politics: How Collective Emotions Shift over Time," *International Theory* 6, no. 3 (2014): 577.
30 Charles M. Blow, "America's Problem with Policing," *International New York Times*, September 27, 2016, 7.
31 Mike Davis, "Uprising and Repression in L.A.," in *Reading Rodney King/Reading Urban Uprising*, ed. Robert Gooding-Williams (New York: Routledge, 1993), 142–43.

A THEORY OF THE MIDDLE EAST

Oil for Insecurity, Permanent War, and the Political Economy of Late Imperial America

Jacob Mundy

As the second decade of the new millennium drew to a close, the American foreign policy establishment increasingly questioned whether the Donald J. Trump administration was as committed to maintaining Washington's historical involvement in the Middle East as his predecessors were.[1] On the one hand, the Trump administration not only abandoned a 2015 nuclear disarmament agreement with Iran and reimposed sanctions on Tehran, but it also reinforced US relations with Iran's main regional opponents—Saudi Arabia and Israel—notably by inking a nearly half-trillion dollar arms deal with Riyadh and by recognizing Jerusalem as Israel's capital during its first year in power. Trump even continued to voice strong support for the regime in Saudi Arabia after it was revealed that Crown Prince Mohammad bin Salman had ordered the torture, execution, and dismemberment of Jamal Khashoggi, a Saudi journalist and *Washington Post* columnist, in the Kingdom's Istanbul consulate in early October 2018. In a candid admission, Trump asserted that the United States was unable to criticize, let alone sanction, Saudi Arabia because American jobs in the US arms industry were on the line. Yet even with the global outrage generated by Khashoggi's murder, Congress proved unwilling to stop US military support to Saudi Arabia. Support consisted notably of material and logistical backing for the ongoing Saudi intervention in the civil war in Yemen, which had become the world's largest humanitarian crisis according to the United Nations.

In late 2018, on the other hand, Trump announced his intent to withdraw US troops from Syria and Afghanistan, an act that triggered a nearly unprecedented event in US history: the immediate resignation of the secretary of defense in protest. An even earlier indication of the Trump administration's ambivalence toward historical US involvement in the Middle East was its refusal to consider the ongoing conflict in Libya a foreign policy priority. There was a bit of irony in Trump's disinterest in the Libyan civil war. For six years, reactionary political forces in the United States—those that would eventually back Trump during his run for president—had become obsessed with the Obama administration's handling of the postrevolutionary situation in Libya, above all the administration's response to the 2012 attacks on US diplomatic and intelligence facilities in Benghazi. But as this chapter will later demonstrate, the increasingly reactionary character of the last fifty years of American electoral politics can be explained by the growing entanglement of the late American empire's political economy in the Middle East since the 1970s.

This increasing entanglement tends to be explained in two prevailing ways. For some, there is a tragic theory of American involvement in the region. At the center of this theory lies a series of unfortunate yet necessary alliances with countries like Libya (until 1969), Saudi Arabia and its satellites in the Gulf, Iran (until 1979), and Iraq (at various times). As the story goes, these relations were forged during the early Cold War so as to advance Washington's strategic and economic interests in the emerging conflict with the Soviet Union. The ostensible premise of these otherwise unsavory relationships was an "oil for security" deal, one in which the United States would help protect certain regimes from domestic and foreign threats irrespective of their commitment to basic human rights. In exchange, these regimes would guarantee the free flow of oil, particularly to aid in the reconstruction of Western Europe and—after its own domestic production began to decline in the 1970s—the United States. Some of these alliances were further entrenched through arms sales, as US protection began shift to more indirect forms of promoting oil for security in the wake of Vietnam and the so-called Arab oil embargoes of 1973. The necessity of security versus the luxury of democracy thus also explains why the United States has heavily invested in authoritarianism in the Middle East. Occasional direct interventions, such as the first and second Gulf Wars, were nonetheless necessary measures to address challenges to these arrangements. These challenges, whether they come from other governments in the region or nonstate actors, are often described as *blowback*: the unintended and problematic consequences of otherwise well-intentioned policies aimed at promoting political stability and energy security. Hence the tragedy.[2]

More cynical interpretations of the entwined fates of the late American empire and the Middle East often posit a different mechanism at the heart of these relationships: growing geopolitical concerns about an impending decline in worldwide oil production. What animates these oil-for-security arrangements, therefore, is not just a mutually beneficial pact between democracies in the North Atlantic and authoritarians in the Middle East. They are in fact driven by increasingly desperate attempts to find and control dwindling petroleum-based sources of energy so as to sustain three things: one, the hyperconsumptive lifestyles of North Atlantic societies that no mainstream politician is willing to challenge; two, the global systems of production and exploitation that feed those lifestyles; and, three, American military supremacy as the foundation of the first two. As with the tragic accounts, these cynical ones tend to paint endogenous challenges to these relationships, from the Iranian Revolution to the Islamic State, as monsters of our own making. If the rallying cry of tragedians is *energy independence*, then the mantra of the cynics is *no blood for oil*.[3]

Though these two accounts have much in common, both fail to account for the broader patterns of repeated US efforts to reconstitute American hegemony in and through the Middle East since the 1970s. For starters, there is no historical or contemporary documentary evidence of any explicit US oil-for-security deals in the Middle East or North Africa, as political historian and US-Saudi relations expert Robert Vitalis has recently argued.[4] It should also be noted that the United States has done as much, if not more, to protect those states in the region with marginal or nonexistent domestic oil production, particularly when measured in terms of military, security, and development aid (i.e., Pakistan, Turkey, Israel, Egypt, and Morocco). Since 2001, the United States has spent more on statebuilding in Afghanistan than on the entire Marshall Plan for European reconstruction after the Second World War.[5]

In as far as any tacit oil-for-security logic might exist on either a country-by-country or a regionwide basis, this logic also has to contend with the fact that these implicit provisions have generally been a disastrous arrangement for all those involved. Two-thirds of all international wars that have emerged since 1970 have occurred either in the Middle East or in regions directly adjacent to it. Seven of the ten occupational wars recorded between 1970 and 2010 were all in the Middle East as well. Of all the low- and high-intensity internal conflicts to emerge since the end of Second World War, those in the Middle East experienced a rate of internationalization that was 10 percent higher than the worldwide average. Of the five countries that have experienced the most fatalities in armed conflict since the end of the Cold War, three are in the Middle East. Since 2012, the Middle East (excluding the states of North Africa) has accounted for more fatalities in warfare than all other regions combined. Of all the interstate conflicts since the Vietnam War, the Iran-Iraq war still easily ranks as the most destructive in terms of combatant fatalities.[6] Meanwhile, the 2003 Anglo-American occupation of Iraq was such a disaster for regional security that even the US Army War College, in its recently published official two-volume history of that war, concluded that the only country to have gained any benefit was Iran.

Just as it is difficult to interpret US actions in the Middle East as driven by a desire for security at the level of either particular states or the region as a whole, it is similarly difficult to understand American policy as driven by impending oil scarcity. From the late nineteenth century to the present, the defining characteristic of the political economy of oil has been its overabundance. In a capitalist energy system, this means finding ways of calibrating oil extraction, refinement, circulation, and distribution in such a way as to realize profits. The early decades of the oil industry are thus replete with domestic monopolies, interfirm cartels, exclusive intraimperial markets, and the use of state power to open new global frontiers of extraction and, more importantly, keep others closed. As historian Timothy Mitchell has argued, any account of the modern Middle East and its vexed relationship with North Atlantic capitalism has to take these things into account.[7] More recent oil price "shocks" in the late 1970s and during the lead-up to the 2007–08 financial collapse were easily "corrected" by new geographies and technologies of extraction. As will be argued below, periods of apparent *overabundance*—1986–2000 and 2014–present—have been just as important to the history of the Middle East since 1970 as the more famous periods of apparent scarcity and peak oil hysteria in the later 1970s and the years leading up to the 2011 Arab Spring.

Another problem with oil-for-security theories is the unclear relationship between the security and oil. The United States was more directly involved in providing security for oil-producing regimes in Libya, Saudi Arabia, and Iran well before domestic US oil production peaked in the late 1970s.[8] Almost twenty more years would pass before the United States reached the point of true foreign oil dependency in the mid-1990s. There are also important cases where oil lagged behind security. The American airbase in Tripoli, one of the largest outside of mainland United States, was established at the end of the Second World War, well over a decade before Libya became a major oil exporter. Moreover, Libyan oil production matched that of Saudi Arabia in the late 1960s; yet the Nixon State Department did not initially interpret the 1969 military coup in Libya as a catastrophe for the United States. This should be surprising for oil-for-security theorists, given Libya's geostrategically advantageous location facing Europe on the Mediterranean side of a then blockaded Suez Canal.[9] Last, Saudi Arabia's unique status as the world's leading "swing producer" of oil (i.e., the only country with abundant high-quality conventional reserves and low domestic demand) only became a reality in the 1970s, which raises questions as to what conditions made this possible and for what reasons.[10]

Finally, it should be noted that the Chinese economy, especially in the last two decades, has neither required ad hoc oil-for-security deals nor direct military intervention in the Middle East to fend off challenges to its energy supply. Today, China not only boasts the world's largest economy, along with increasingly consumptive middle and upper classes, but also the world's largest fleet of motor vehicles and almost as many personal cars as the United States. While it could be argued that the Chinese economy has matured under the same global security umbrella provided by US oil-for-security deals since the 1970s, it is revealing that China—unlike America's NATO allies under Obama and Trump—has never been berated by Washington for such massive free riding.[11]

More importantly, Chinese state power has been able to secure a globe-spanning petroleum energy system that has supported levels of social change that are unprecedented in the history of the modern world. All of this has been accomplished without direct or threatened interventions in the Middle East in the name of oil for security. This, in turn, raises important questions about the different political economies of hegemony that underwrite the declining American empire and the now apparent Chinese one. While the unique political economy driving Chinese ascendancy has become a growing preoccupation of leading critics of US imperialism—from historian Alfred McCoy[12] to geographer David Harvey[13]—most analyses of the terminal crisis in the American empire and its decisive relationship with the Middle East have so far failed to develop a viable interpretive framework, as the paragraphs above suggest.

In order to address these explanatory deficits, this chapter revisits Mike Davis's 1984 article "The Political Economy of Late Imperial America."[14] Therein Davis mainly documented the domestic side of the Reagan administration's solution to the multidimensional crises of American hegemony in the 1970s. Nonetheless, the framework of analysis Davis used to understand how American hegemony was internally reconstituted in the late Cold War is just as useful when it comes to decoding its rearticulation globally. As Davis argues,

> Conventional definitions of American post-war "hegemony" have focused on the sheer preponderance of economic and military power concerted through an atomic-military monopoly, monetary sovereignty, overseas investment, and historic differentials of productivity and mass consumption. . . . In truth, a simple "balance of power" approach frustratingly yields more dilemmas of this type than it provides clear-cut answers. A better methodology, in my opinion, is to define "hegemony" not as a single, all-embracing power relation—radiating through various instances—but as a dynamic system which *unifies accumulation, legitimation and repression* on a world scale. In this sense, American hegemony is a historically specific form of adequation between the capitalist state system and the world economy.[15]

This chapter therefore proposes to account for the reconstitution of American hegemony in the 1970s through an analysis of the mechanisms by which crises of accumulation, repression, and legitimation found partial resolution in the Middle East.

The central crisis of accumulation examined here was the need for the North Atlantic world's petroleum-based energy systems to find new ways of functioning according to capitalist principles. This crisis followed the imposition of new profit-sharing agreements by the producer states, notably in the Middle East, in the late 1960s and early 1970s. In the aftermath of Vietnam, a crisis of international repression occurred and with it the need to find new ways of engineering control across the Middle East through indirect means of suppressing opposition at national, subnational, and transnational scales. The solution to both of these crises was found in a new system of *oil for insecurity* premised on *permanent war* in the region. Building on racial prejudice, this nonsystem of repression and accumulation initially succeeded in legitimating itself by pretending not to exist or by presenting its effects as the primary reason for its necessity. While legitimating these arrangements proved increasingly difficult—as contradictions in the system gathered strength in the 1980s and 1990s—the events of September 11, 2001, successfully validated a renewed emphasis on sustained and direct US military intervention under the Bush-Cheney reunification of accumulation (oil for insecurity), repression (permanent war), and legitimation (counterterrorism). Though the Bush-Cheney restoration of American hegemony proved to be the most successful alignment of these forces since the crises of the 1970s, the contradictions it produced and exacerbated have rendered any further reunification of accumulation, repression, and legitimation impossible. Rather than confront the realities and legacies of these arrangements, the American polity has grown increasingly insular in the face of a reactionary politics born of oil for insecurity's diminishing returns.

Accumulation: Oil for Insecurity

The accumulatory crisis of the 1970s with respect to oil in the Middle East emerged around the same time as two related crises, those of stagflation and the US gold standard, posed serious threats to the vitality of North Atlantic capitalism as a whole.[16] The North Atlantic world's petroleum-based capitalist energy systems began to face significant resistance in the postcolonial world, as producer states started demanding a greater share of profits from the international oil companies in the 1940s and 1950s. These demands were soon joined by additional ones for more direct involvement in the processes of locating, extracting, moving, refining, and exporting oil and financing oil production, which would necessitate the development of native technological, scientific, and managerial expertise. The founding of the Organization of the Petroleum Exporting Countries (OPEC) in 1960, largely as a countercartel to the historical collusion of the dominant European and American oil companies, also posed a significant challenge to the ability of North Atlantic states and their petroleum industries to control the conditions under which profits could be realized. Industry efforts to isolate or punish threats of nationalization in the Middle East (e.g., in Iran in 1953) were no longer effective by the 1970s for three main reasons: intergovernmental solidarity among the oil producers across the Middle East, the weaker bargaining position of the smaller independent oil companies, and the increasing number of successful precedents of oil "nationalization" in Latin America. A case in point was Libya in the early 1970s. Emboldened by Algeria's successful bid in 1971 to secure majority ownership of its French-held operations, Libyan threats of nationalization were resisted by the major international oil companies but accommodated by smaller independent ones, whose loss of investment in Libya would have been catastrophic. But once the new normal of national ownership or preeminence had been established, the major companies were forced to play along or get out. That said, these new profit-sharing burdens for US oil companies operating abroad were largely subsidized by taxpayers at home, through framing these new agreements as taxes paid to a foreign government.[17] This, coupled with other industry-specific tax breaks and subsidies—today totaling nearly $1 trillion annually for companies based in the European Union and United States—has helped maintain the profitability of the industry.

Though it was clear that European and North American governments were willing to engage in substantial financial intervention to prop up their private oil industries, the question of profitability was as much relative as it was absolute. As economists Jonathan Nitzan and Shimshon Bichler have consistently demonstrated, in a series of studies spanning nearly three decades, the ability of the major international oil companies to achieve differentially higher rates of profit than other dominant sectors—the index by which vitality is measured and rewarded under capitalism—has been dependent on there being wars and other threats to the security of oil extraction and exportation in the Middle East.[18] What became apparent in the wake of the 1967 and, more importantly, the aftermath of the 1973 Arab-Israeli wars was the ability of regional insecurity to sustain a dramatic increase in oil prices. This effectively restored the comparative levels of profitability that major North Atlantic oil firms had enjoyed in prior decades; the years before Middle Eastern states had leveraged significant concessions. Periods when there appeared to be significant threats to major oil production centers in the Middle East (1973-76, 1979-84, 1990-91, 2001-12) were periods when the profits of the major international oil companies outpaced other sectors within North Atlantic capitalism. In other words, the solution to the crisis of accumulation within the capitalist energy system was permanent war in the Middle East. An added benefit of this system, as Nitzan and Bichler's work shows, is that it generated massive amounts of petrodollars that could be used to finance private military sales to the regimes in the Middle East, whether by arms manufacturers in the Eastern Bloc or the North Atlantic. Oil for insecurity thus solved two accumulatory crises: one in the oil industry and another in the arms industry. More on this latter point will be said in the next section.

These new mechanisms of profitability initially succeeded in addressing the accumulatory crisis in the North Atlantic world's petroleum-based energy systems from the mid-1970s onward. In important ways, however, it was a pyrrhic victory of sorts. As one could imagine, numerous destabilizing contradictions were produced by these efforts to relocate oil pricing in a new market, whose most successful condition of relative profitability became permanent war in the Middle East. A leading contradiction produced by these efforts to induce unnatural scarcity was oil for insecurity's unexpected capacity to produce debilitating surpluses. Since the emergence of the oil-for-insecurity regime in the 1970s, two extended periods of apparent scarcity and higher prices were met with two extended periods of the opposite. The first such cycle occurred between 1970 and 2000. Permanent war in the Middle East successfully increased oil prices in the 1970s, but it also incentivized the significant expansion in traditional areas of production (Saudi Arabia's annual exports had more than doubled by the end of the decade). Higher prices also helped develop new geographies and technologies of extraction. Such innovations and incentives made production in difficult yet strategically advantageous locations possible (e.g., Alaska, the North Sea, and Siberia).[19] For the Soviet Union, unprecedented levels of oil production and extravagant arms sales also became an important financial lifeline, just as Reagan and Thatcher began to reintensify the Cold War. Globally expanded production then led to an extended period of oversupply and price declines, gradually from 1980 onward and then dramatically in 1986. Despite a brief panic over Iraq's invasion of Kuwait in 1990 and the 1991 Gulf War, fourteen years would pass before prices would begin to climb back up.

The second cycle was effectively launched by the events of September 11, 2001, and was reinforced by the Anglo-American invasion of Iraq less than two years later. The first decade of the global war on terror became a period of unparalleled relative profitability in the international oil sector, surpassing the rates achieved in the late 1970s. But as in the previous cycle, oil for insecurity became a victim of its own success. It first of all saw post-Soviet Russia, then stabilized under the growing power of Vladimir Putin's regime, rejoin the ranks of the world's top producers. Rising prices also incentivized a technological renaissance in unconventional oil and gas extraction, techniques popularly known as "fracking" (hydraulic fracturing). This led to an unexpected resurgence of production across the contiguous United States. By the end of 2018, these technologies had allowed the United States not only to resume its position as the world's leading oil producer (a position it last held in 1973), but also to boast of billions of barrels of now viable reserves. These technologies had also contributed to a new period of overabundance that began to undermine oil prices. Though the entire Middle East was seemingly engulfed in a new round of conflicts following the revolutions and counter-revolutions of 2011 and 2012, the international oil companies saw their differential profits enter a period of unprecedented decline in 2013, a downturn that even newly internationalized civil wars in Syria, Iraq, Libya, and Yemen were unable to correct.[20] We will return later to this disarticulation of repression and accumulation—keys to understanding the crisis of US hegemony that begot Trump—by way of conclusion.

Repression: Permanent War

The crisis of international repression afflicting American hegemony in the early 1970s was the prospect of a new geopolitical reality in which the United States could no longer use direct military intervention to counter resistance in the postcolonial world. This was also a crisis of accumulation, because it was a threat to powerful defense industries. Rearming Europe and fighting Communism in East Asia had helped stabilize the capitalist weapons manufacturers after their massive expansion during the Second World War. But with the collapse of the European empires and the specter of a post-Vietnam drawdown of US forces, arms manufacturers and their government sponsors needed ways to justify and, more importantly, finance the sale of weapons—publicly, privately, or both—in new markets. Thus, the solution to the crisis of accumulation—permanent war in the Middle East— also became the solution to the crisis of repression.

The prospect of outsourcing repression to reliable client states, all in the name of a Kissingerian balance-of-power approach to the Middle East,[21] was vital to the creation of a viable international market in weapons systems. Flush with petrodollars, the Middle East was the most obvious frontier for a new age of privatized arms sales. The allure and profitability of weapons would be all the more enhanced if there were actual conflicts and insecurities to motivate the acquisition of some of the North Atlantic world's most expensive weapons systems. Needless to say, Soviet arms manufacturers were drawn to the new Middle East market as well. Thus, during the 1970s and 1980s leading arms manufacturers, like the international oil industry, also became dependent on permanent war in the Middle East in order to sustain their dominant position within North Atlantic capitalism.[22] Militarizing the region would thus solve, temporarily at least, the accumulatory crisis facing defense industries in the North Atlantic world. At the same time, it would address the crisis of repression afflicting US hegemony in two ways. Beyond the military empowerment of regional clients, oil for insecurity created a regionwide system of instability that would impede coordinated action against North Atlantic interests by both enemies and allies in the Middle East.[23] The imperative to fashion such a system was all the more apparent after the 1973 oil "embargoes."[24]

Skyrocketing oil prices in the 1970s helped finance the rapid and intensive militarization of the Middle East, a transformation without parallel in the postcolonial world. At the start of the 1970s, East Asia and Europe unsurprisingly accounted for nearly two-thirds of all arms imports worldwide; less than one-fifth went to the Middle East. By the early 1980s, the Middle East accounted for over 40 percent of all the world's arms imports. This was in a context where military sales worldwide had grown from $300 billion in 1972 to roughly $820 billion ten years later, in unadjusted dollars. Whereas the governments of the Middle East collectively spent $1.26 billion on arms in 1963, a decade later their expenditures were already over $10 billion (again, in unadjusted dollars). This reflected an annual growth rate of 14.7 percent, far ahead of East Asia (7.5 percent), South Asia (2.9 percent), all of Africa (6.5 percent), and Latin America (3.9 percent). From 1972 to 1982, this growth rate slowed to 11.5 percent, with Latin America (13.9 percent) and all of Africa (8.9 percent) witnessing marked increases in the context of the widening Cold War. In 2017 dollars, Middle East arms imports went from below $7.5 billion in 1971 to over $18 billion in 1975, and then to over $30 billion in 1977.[25]

By the end of the 1970s, almost all countries in the world whose military expenditures registered as 10 percent or more of their GDP were in the Middle East: both Yemeni states, Egypt, Jordan, Oman, Syria, Qatar, Israel, and Saudi Arabia. In North Africa, even the resource-poor agricultural state of Morocco was spending somewhere between 5 and 10 percent of its GDP on arms, largely as a result of its US-backed occupation of Western Sahara. Oil-rich Algeria and Libya were spending between 2 and 5 percent, the latter increasingly being drawn into its own quagmire in French-backed Chad. Unsurprisingly, the ten countries with the highest ratio of military expenditures to central government expenditures in 1982 were all in the Middle East. In the years that followed, most governments in the region continued to outpace all other "middle-income" countries in terms of military spending and arms imports, from low population oil exporters to those with high populations and limited natural resources. These spending trends have been dominated, especially since 2001, by Saudi Arabia, Israel, Turkey, the United Arab Emirates, and Iran. While some of these states saw acute bursts of exorbitant military outlays during times of war, others used military spending to prop up elaborate internal security forces. Meanwhile, foreign military sales and financing to the region, led by the North Atlantic powers and Russia since the 1970s, has never abated and outpaces all other regions combined. Funds that could have otherwise gone to education, health, and civil infrastructure were massively diverted to defense, which served to reinforce the authoritarian tendencies and capacities of regimes dominated by the bureaucratic logic and institutional structures of their disproportionately large security sectors.[26]

The rapid and intensive militarization of the Middle East contributed to the insecurity that came to define the region in the 1970s. This system of insecurity translated into a system of indirect control—the temporary solution to the post-Vietnam crisis of repression—through several mechanisms, notably the initiation, exacerbation, and prolongation of conflicts in the region. Though the end of the Cold War created new opportunities for the direct use of force by the United States, the primary infrastructure of the system continued to be the maintaining of regional tensions and the prevention of peace.

First of all, militarization helped sustain and exacerbate preexisting tensions. This was not just the case for "core" Middle East conflicts in the Levant (Arab-Israeli, Israeli-Palestinian, Lebanon), Mesopotamia (Iran-Iraq war, Kurdish rebels), and the Gulf (various wars in Yemen, the Saudi-Iranian "cold war" from 1979 onward). Instead, an arc of interconnected conflicts came together, stretching from the western edge of the Sahara to the western Himalayas. Though these conflicts could be neatly overlaid onto the Cold War map of the region, it would be misleading to think of them as simply proxy wars driven by geopolitics. This constellation of insecurity was also made possible by the fact that the Soviet Union was just as willing to cash in on the oil boom by selling weapons to the region. Indeed, Libya was the worldwide leading arms importer in the final year of the 1970s, with a bill of $2.1 billion in military goods (or about $7 billion in 2017 dollars), ahead of both Iraq and Syria. The vast majority of these Libyan purchases were from Soviet manufacturers.

In cases where warring countries lacked oil wealth (e.g., Morocco, Israel, Egypt, Turkey, and Pakistan), other means of supporting their militarization were found. Ingeniously, hypermilitarization was often rationalized in terms of the very insecurity that arms sales and military financing were ostensibly meant to address. And apart from the important cases of Egypt, Iraq, and Iran, the patterning of the region in the 1970s into permanent antagonists of North Atlantic interests (Algeria, Libya, Sudan, and Syria) and durable Western allies (Morocco, Tunisia, Israel, Lebanon, Saudi Arabia, Turkey, and Pakistan) has remained more or less unchanged since the fall of the Berlin Wall, when enemy states simply became pariahs or rogue states. The same could be said of Yemen and Afghanistan, which have continuously functioned as important sacrifice zones in the ongoing reproduction of insecurity across the region. It is equally telling that the upheavals of 2011 have only served to reinforce this geography of insecurity. While Tunisia's largely symbolic transition was supported by its Franco-American patrons, aggressive anti-revolutionary action by Morocco in Western Sahara and Saudi Arabia in Bahrain barely registered any significant international opposition. Meanwhile, Egypt soon saw the popular restoration of its military regime, while highly destructive civil conflicts in Syria, Libya, and Yemen were aggravated by multilateral outside involvement.

This system of indirect repression has also been maintained by preventing the peaceful resolution of conflicts whenever possible. Exacerbating wars and preventing peace, often two sides of the same coin, are important elements in the oil-for-insecurity system. The most conspicuous cases where US involvement has seemed to be driven by logics of exacerbation, prolongation, or malign neglect are Afghanistan since 1979, the Iran-Iraq war (1980–88), and Israel's occupation of Palestinian and Syrian territories since 1967.[27] Equally prominent examples are Washington's uninterrupted devotion to Saudi Arabia, the various ways in which US administrations sought to solve the Iraq problem from 1990 onward, and America's prolonged confrontation with postrevolutionary Iran. Less well-known cases of conflict exacerbation and prolongation, though equally illustrative, are the Moroccan occupation of Western Sahara since 1975, Libya's war in Chad in the 1980s, the civil conflict in 1990s Algeria, and Turkey's repression of the Kurds. Interestingly, the greatest progress toward peace in both Palestine and Western Sahara occurred in the 1990s, a period that also saw an overall decline in the relative profits of the international oil sector during the Clinton administration. In the face of this crisis of peace in the 1990s, the Bush-Cheney White House, in the name of supporting Israel's and Morocco's wars on terrorism, quickly reversed all the painstaking progress that had been made under the Oslo process in Palestine and the UN effort to organize a referendum on independence in Western Sahara. Where peace was allowed to happen, notably in South Sudan and Libya in 2005, the logic of oil and arms sales was as patently obvious.[28]

Legitimation: Terrorism

Oil for insecurity represented an effort on the part of the United States to restore its status as the world's hegemonic power in the 1970s. Solutions to related crises of accumulation, repression, and legitimation afflicting the American empire would be found in the Middle East, a region that happened to contain significant quantities of high-quality petroleum that could be easily obtained through conventional means of extraction. As described above, solutions to the crises of accumulation within the North Atlantic world's capitalist energy and defense industries were both found in this region through the mechanism of permanent war. In this way, the Middle East also provided an example par excellence of indirect suppression of opposition to US imperialism, which became the solution—albeit temporary—to the post-Vietnam crisis of repression. By promoting war and militarization across the Middle East, and thereby reinforcing authoritarianism when not directly investing in it, American hegemony was partially reconstituted on the basis of outsourced coercion in the context of regionwide destabilization. The greatest domestic challenge to this reconstitution of American hegemony in and through the Middle East has been at the level of legitimation. An effective solution to the problem of legitimation was provided by the events of September 11, 2001, an event that paved the way for a return to direct forms of repression, and which in turn addressed growing weaknesses in the oil-for-insecurity regime that had accumulated in the 1980s and 1990s.

Domestic legitimacy has indeed been the weakest link in this system, especially during its initial years of formation in the late 1970s. As a system constructed in reaction to an excess of direct intervention in Southeast Asia, assembling and exercising US hegemony in the Middle East through indirect repression was often met with tenuous, ambivalent, and contingent legitimations. Yet for the most part, oil for insecurity was justified by its disavowal. In the shadow of Vietnam, American efforts to reconstitute US hegemony in and through the Middle East were never understood, and even less presented, as such. The Middle East policies of the United States, from the Suez crisis to the rise of the Islamic State, have been overwhelmingly framed as being driven by the allegedly innate nature of the region's persistent insecurity, above all by those who devised these insecuritizing policies in the first place. In this way, oil for insecurity drew on latent Orientalism in Western political and intellectual life as much as on the immediacy of the oil "embargoes" of the 1970s, the visceral drama of Palestinian militancy on the international stage, successive American hostage crises, the emergence of "political Islam," and the growing US identification with Israel. Nevertheless, indirect involvement in conflicts in the Middle East in the 1970s and 1980s never elicited broad public support in the United States, nor were there intensive efforts to cultivate it. Touting clandestine US support for the insurgents fighting the Soviet Union in Afghanistan was more of an exception than the rule. The Reagan administration's double-dealing in the Iran-Iraq war, so as to illegally finance secret proxy wars in Central America, was viewed as so egregiously cynical by the US public that it threatened to bring down the entire administration in its final years. In the 1990s, the Clinton administration was often accused of using airstrikes in Iraq, Afghanistan, and Sudan (if not Serbia as well) to distract the US public from its various scandals.

Where American lives were threatened, direct intervention was highly circumscribed (e.g., Iran in 1980 and Libya in 1986), apart from the ill-fated peacekeeping mission in Lebanon. And while threats to the world's energy security might have legitimated offshore naval action in the Strait of Hormuz in the late 1980s, the push for war against Iraq had to be hastily reframed in late 1990 as a humanitarian intervention to protect Kuwait in the face of wavering US public support. While this meant redescribing a former Cold War ally—Saddam Hussein—as a new Hitler, this humanitarian framing elicited more US public support for war against Iraq than initial claims of energy security. But there were also political limits to this humanitarian framing, especially when the lifeless bodies of US soldiers dominated twenty-four-hour news cycles (e.g., Beirut in 1983 and Mogadishu in 1993). It should also be recalled that the impending Anglo-American invasion of Iraq in 2003 triggered the single largest coordinated day of protest in the history of the world, notably in London and cities across the United States. Yet it is equally important to underscore the fact that widespread popular opposition to the Iraq war, from March 2003 onward, stopped well short of taking any practical steps to domestically sabotage the war effort, a fact which we will return to shortly.

In the now five-decades-long history of the oil-for-insecurity regime, it has become clear that the Bush-Cheney administration achieved unparalleled success in their unification of repression, accumulation, and legitimation. This is evidenced in the dramatic expansion of the national security state in the North Atlantic world, the sprawling global war on terror, the robust health of the international oil industry between 2001 and 2009 (which saw US exports increase tenfold), and the growing insecurity across the Middle East throughout the first decade of the new millennium.

This reassertion of US hegemony from 2001 onward is likewise indicative of the extent to which terrorism—or, to be more precise, counterterrorism—offered a powerful form of legitimation that prior administrations were unable to access or effectively wield. Terrorism as an often contradictory framework for understanding particular forms of armed resistance by particular kinds of actors, and so responding to those things in particular ways, gained prominence in the 1970s as a new field of security practice and expertise.[29] That said, academic and political interest in the burgeoning field of terrorism studies and counterterrorism practices declined significantly in the early 1990s, as much of this interest was actually driven by the extent to which the concept of terrorism could be instrumentalized in the fight against the Soviet Union by linking Moscow to various opposition movements and pariah states in the Middle East.[30] Though the botched demolition of the World Trade Center in 1993, massacres in Algeria, suicide bombings in Israel, vague threats issued from caves in Afghanistan, and the rubble of US embassies in East Africa did little to reinvigorate America's commitment to oil-for insecurity in the Middle East in the 1990s, these events did important work in terms of creating an interpretive framework constructed around terrorism as a form of implacable violent resistance practiced mainly, if not exclusively, by Muslims. Thus, the events of 9/11 not only worked to resuscitate interest in the concept of terrorism—and dramatically so—by rendering it as an existential threat to North Atlantic polities, but these events also generated new understandings of the past thirty years that seemed to suggest that the North Atlantic world had always been at war with *terrorism* in one way or another.

The Bush-Cheney unification of legitimation, repression, and accumulation—one that allowed for a spatially and temporally limitless presidential mandate to confront terrorism—thus succeeded in making sustained direct military intervention a possibility again. In so doing, this reunification not only addressed the 1990s crisis of peace facing arms manufacturers after the

Cold War but also the crisis of profitability that had antagonized oil companies and producer states from the late 1980s through most of the 1990s. What the Bush-Cheney reunification addressed was the fact that the oil-for-insecurity system established in the 1970s had become a victim of its own success. While oil for insecurity had temporarily helped solve several aspects of the crisis of US hegemony by the late 1970s, it had also failed to anticipate the contradictions it would create. On the one hand, oil for insecurity's emphasis on indirect control through permanent destabilization had produced oppositional forces in the 1980s and 1990s (e.g., Al-Qaeda) that warranted a return to direct forms of repression in Afghanistan in 2001 and Iraq in 2003.

On the other hand, international oil companies and producer states struggled throughout the 1980s and 1990s to address the excess quantities of oil that had been produced following the stunning rise in oil prices in the 1970s. The new international political economy of oil of the 1970s had precipitated a significant geographical and infrastructural expansion of production that produced an overabundance of oil, which had to be managed throughout the 1990s. Even with important oil-producing regimes under sanctions (Iran, Iraq, and Libya) and with other states in the region facing either widespread civil conflict or terrorist provocations (Algeria, Egypt, Turkey, Afghanistan), oil prices remained relatively depressed throughout the 1990s. Prior to the outbreak of the second Palestinian intifada in 2000 and the events of September 11, 2001, the international oil companies had largely failed to outperform their peers within the dominant sectors of North Atlantic capitalism. The only year during which the international oil companies had registered relatively higher rates of profit of a significant magnitude had been 1991, as a result of direct US intervention in the Gulf.[31]

At the same time, the end of the Cold War raised the prospect of declining fortunes in the armament industries once more. Having militarily blundered in Somalia and Bosnia, the Clinton administration opted to use economic coercion as much as possible and airstrikes when convenient. The Democratic Party's embrace of neoliberal economics and its abandonment of labor coincided with a closer alignment to sectors within North Atlantic capitalism that had prospered since the end of the Cold War. These were in fact manufacturing and service industries whose political economy of accumulation was antagonistic to the kinds of widespread global conflict that underwrote arms and

A THEORY OF THE MIDDLE EAST

oil.[32] Unsurprisingly, those sectors seeking the opposite—a return to the market conditions that had underwritten the golden years of oil for insecurity in the late 1970s and early 1980s—found common cause in the neoconservative movement and willing political engineers in the Bush-Cheney administration. The attacks of September 11, 2001, organized by marginal political forces that had nonetheless helped articulate the original oil-for-insecurity regime of the late 1970s and early 1980s, provided the ever-elusive element of explicit legitimation for permanent war and never-ending intervention.

That said, the apparent acquiescence of the American polity to permanent war and intervention in the Middle East has as much to do with counterterrorism as a legitimating framework as with the instruments of political and economic control that emerged in the 1970s and 1980s to disable the possibility of mass domestic opposition in the United States. In this way, it is perhaps a question of whether Americans are unwilling or, more importantly, effectively unable to oppose US interventions in the Middle East. The emergence and implementation of these instruments of political and economic control in the 1970s and 1980s are masterfully accounted for by Davis throughout *Prisoners of the American Dream*. His account goes a long way toward helping us understand the difference between the last great rupture in the US polity—that of the late 1960s and 1970s, where imperial intervention in Vietnam played a significant role in the organization of dissent—and the current rupture in the US polity since 2008, where permanent war in the Middle East has become increasingly incidental to dissent across the political spectrum. That is to say, the difference between the American polity in 1970 and forty years later is the fact that oppositional movements have been largely de-skilled and become antipolitical in the interim.

The de-skilling of opposition in the United States owes much to the ways in which the US military solved the crisis of international repression in the 1970s. While the effects of the neoliberal resolution of the "labor problem" have been well understood in terms of its broader impact on the possibility of organizing lower- and middle-class resistance in the United States, another factor is the end of military conscription. Apart from a small corps of professional activists, most US citizens lack any basic training in strategy and tactics that they would have otherwise received as members of a labor union or as members of the US armed forces. Other outcomes of the "all-volunteer" army have been well documented, such as the effective "poverty-draft" tactics of the US military in impoverished rural or deindustrializing white and migrant communities as well as the loosening of political constraints on the executive use of force absent congressional approval. But what is worth highlighting is the generalized *de-skilling* of opposition in the United States that comes with neither being raised in a militant working-class household nor having any personal experience in organizing and conducting an effective fight—simulated or actual, violent or not.

This unlearning of strategic skills has been reinforced by a growing aversion to questions of power among grassroots social movements in general. At one level, there is perhaps no better illustration of this antipolitical tendency than the intellectual and social—and increasingly governmental—insistence on nonviolent forms of protest as the only legitimate means of resistance that "global civil society" should tolerate. Ironically, at the heart of "nonviolence" is an absurd amount of epistemic violence: almost the entire history of anticolonial resistance and labor struggle has been simply recoded in apolitical terms as either successful or unsuccessful episodes of a reified category of conflict called nonviolence, wherein the politics of the conflict is inconsequential to the tactics in use.[33] As anarchist theorists have noted in response, the widespread insistence on nonviolence in American social movements of the last fifty years—as an understandable reaction to the kinds of means-ends justifications that have motivated domestic terror campaigns—has nonetheless led to an antipolitics of protest, where the means have become the ends.[34]

The antipolitics of contemporary opposition to the American empire, to the extent that it exists, reflects the profound depths of acquiescence that the neoliberal project has secured in relation to both determining the conditions of resistance as well as constraining the horizon of the ideologically possible. There was perhaps no better illustration of the absurdity of this antipolitics of opposition to war, as political anthropologist Mahmood Mamdani noted, than the campaign to "Save Darfur," a movement that had formed in response to an intensifying conflict in western Sudan between the government and pro-independence rebels. By the middle of the first decade of the 2000s, the Save Darfur campaign had arguably become the largest globally oriented social movement on university and college campuses in the United States. The movement's objective was to pressure Western governments, especially the

United States, to intervene and stop the armed conflict, by force if necessary. Leading human rights organizations and intergovernmental agencies deemed the Darfur conflict the most important humanitarian crisis in the world, and Secretary of State Colin Powell went as far as to call it a "genocide" in 2004. Thus, one of the most visible antiwar social movements in the United States was, at the height of the Anglo-American war in Iraq in 2005–06, effectively appealing for US intervention in another Arab country at a time when the Bush-Cheney administration was becoming engulfed in the most destructive and expensive military blunder since Vietnam.[35] Under Anglo-American occupation, thousands of Iraqi civilians were slaughtered by the rampant bombing campaign of a rogue Al-Qaeda branch, massacred by Sunni insurgents, or tortured by the thousands at the hands of US-trained death squads run by the Shia-dominated Interior Ministry. In the middle of all of this were the flailing counterinsurgency efforts of US and British soldiers, their associated intelligence forces, other Iraqi and Kurdish allies, and countless mercenary firms. Basic notions of democratic responsibility suggest that the Iraq war should have been a far greater concern to the US public than the Darfur conflict, and yet mass domestic opposition—the kind capable of physically sabotaging the Iraq war effort—collapsed as soon as President George W. Bush opted to simply ignore the millions of people who marched on February 15, 2003. For the most part, opposition to the Iraq war was channeled through the Democratic Party, which put forward presidential candidates in 2004 and 2008 who promised to manage the global war on terror—the new oil-for-insecurity regime—in a way that would be less disruptive to social order at home and global order abroad. On both accounts, Obama failed.

Conclusion: Obama, Trump, and the New Disunity

The success achieved by the Bush-Cheney administration in their effort to restore American hegemony through a reunification of accumulation (oil and arms), repression (direct intervention), and legitimation (counterterrorism) proved to be as unsustainable as the previous iteration, as new contradictions emerged and old ones were exacerbated. Most important was the wave of mass popular opposition to the oil-for-insecurity regime's dependence on reliable dictators, which coalesced in late 2010 across the Arab world after years of diffuse protest.[36] The second most important contradiction produced by the Bush-Cheney reunification was a technological revolution in the unconventional extraction of oil that had come about as a result of increasing oil prices in the 2000s. These contradictions, however, would most visibly manifest themselves during the Obama administration, whose (non)response to them reflected a continued misunderstanding of their origins and consequences for US hegemony. The Obama administration simultaneously pursued renewed oil production at home, a new foreign policy ostensibly refocused on East Asia, and an approach to permanent war in the Middle East based on a return to indirect forms of outsourced control, lower levels of intervention, and selective peacemaking. It thereby inadvertently aggravated the new crisis of American hegemony as accumulation, repression, and legitimation increasingly lost their synchronicity.

While the Obama administration had come to power in 2008 by rejecting the use of large-scale expeditionary force as a means to manage the war on terror, the president's commitment to permanent war in the Middle East was such that, by the time his successor took office, the region boasted three of the five deadliest armed conflicts since the end of the Cold War. By 2017, the Syrian civil war had become the most lethal episode of mass organized violence since the 1994 massacres in Rwanda, followed closely by Afghanistan (third), Iraq (fifth), and even Sudan (seven). Indeed, the year 2012 marked the first time since 1989 that the percentage of armed-conflict fatalities in the Middle East not only outranked all other world regions but also all other world regions combined.[37] Peace processes in Palestine and Western Sahara continued to be viewed as hopeless endeavors, held hostage by implacable forces emerging entirely from within the region. The Syrian, Libyan, and Yemeni civil wars were largely sustained through lower-level forms of intervention, while the occupation of Afghanistan was mostly escalated. Special Forces operations swelled to include regular operations in 150 countries,[38] while vastly expanded drone wars over Afghanistan, Pakistan, Yemen, Libya, and Somalia saw thousands of strikes whose targeting procedures often amounted to little more than behavioral profiling from ten thousand feet up.

At the same time, domestic opposition to US involvement in the Middle East largely collapsed. Throughout this period, none of the major American social movements to emerge during the Great Recession—the Tea Party, Occupy Wall Street, Black Lives Matter, or Me Too—centered the American empire in their critique of contemporary US politics or the economy.[39] What had largely barred Hillary Clinton from becoming the Democratic candidate for president in 2008—her vigorous support for the 2003 invasion of Iraq— no longer seemed to matter by 2016. In acquiescing to permanent war in the Middle East, the Obama administration and the American polity also acquiesced to new regimes of intensive domestic electronic surveillance,[40] along with the dramatic expansion of a national security state that no longer abided by longstanding distinctions between its domestic and foreign functions. Any ostensible limits imposed on the war on terror by the 2001 congressional authorization to use military force were casually flaunted, as in NATO's war in Libya in 2011 or in the ongoing support for the Saudi war in Yemen that started in 2015. Meanwhile, Pentagon budgets—so purposefully Byzantine that even the world's largest private accounting firms have been unable to audit them[41]—regularly increased beyond the US military's capacity to absorb them. By 2018, the total cost of occupying Afghanistan since 2001—the longest war in the history of the American republic—surpassed the price tag of the Marshall Plan when adjusted for inflation.[42]

The 2011 Arab uprisings presented the American empire with a moment to rethink the traditional relationships that had underwritten its power since the 1970s. However, the prevailing response of the Obama administration—continuing to pursue permanent war in the Middle East, albeit without deploying large-scale expeditionary force beyond the Afghan theater—was more consistent with the powerful historical momentum that oil for insecurity had obtained. This momentum helped the Egyptian national security state return to full power by 2013 and, to a lesser extent, Tunisia. Civil wars in Libya and Syria were prolonged through multilateral interventions from regional and extraregional powers, notably competing powers in the Gulf, Turkey, and Russia. This was a clear indication that Obama's efforts to outsource control had become an invitation for other states to pursue their own kind of hegemonic or counterhegemonic initiatives in the Middle East.

The one instance where the Obama administration seemed intent on de-escalation was Iran. Here, it is also interesting to note the most prevalent criticisms leveled at the Obama administration from the US foreign policy establishment and the punditariat: one, the White House's putative reluctance to intervene—or intervene more substantially—in Syria; two, its efforts to begin a process of normalizing relations with Iran by addressing the nuclear question first. Despite having shown a sincere and sustained commitment to permanent war in the Middle East, the Obama administration's attempt to create a more hybrid regime of oil for insecurity through direct and indirect intervention failed to maintain the extraordinary rates of relative profits that the international oil companies had enjoyed since 2001. Starting in 2013, the North Atlantic world's petroleum-based energy industries began to face a period of unprecedented decline in their relative rates of profit. Obama's legacy in the Middle East was thus a paradox: the region was more embroiled in conflicts than ever before, yet—from the perspective of major energy companies—the prices and profitability of oil began to respond in disastrously negative ways.

As mentioned above, this was due in large part to the so-called fracking revolution in the United States. Increasing prices throughout the first decade of the new millennium not only funded investment in new geographies and geologies of production; they also incentivized the development and deployment of technologies that allowed a diverse and uncoordinated array of oil companies to revisit old zones of extraction.[43] But, as in the mid-1980s, these new forms and zones of production quickly overshot apparent demand. The real price of oil, which finally surpassed its 1980 peak in 2008 and then again in 2011, collapsed in the face of new production in the United States in 2014, taking a substantial portion of the new fracking production down with it. But as prices slowly recovered in the years that followed, so too did production in the United States, which tended to offset any cuts that occurred deliberately—within OPEC—or accidentally, because of civil conflict (e.g., Libya, Nigeria, and Venezuela). With aggregate global demand in doubt—given the oncoming threat of entire energy systems abandoning carbon-based fuels at the municipal, provincial, or national level—both the oil companies and the producer states entered a new and uncertain reality, where proven mechanisms of profitability no longer seemed to work.

Compounding this crisis of accumulation were two independent but related crises of legitimation. At the international level, there was a crisis of self-confidence in the American empire; at the level of polities across the North Atlantic world, there were increasingly fierce struggles over economic policy and national identity. With respect to the latter crisis, it was interesting that struggles only seemed to be spreading and intensifying as the 2007–08 financial collapse receded into the background, as North Atlantic capitalism ostensibly entered a recovery.[44] That these economic and identitarian struggles were so rhetorically ferocious yet so inconclusive in their political outcomes was indicative of the extent to which the reordering of social relations in the North Atlantic world since the 1970s—largely through economic discipline and internecine cultural warfare—had largely succeeded in achieving one of the original objectives of the neoliberal movement, which was to limit the horizon of the political.[45] Disabling the ideational and material conditions under which *any* mass-based opposition could emerge as a viable threat to the neoliberal order, whether in the form of mercantilist ethnonationalism or socialist multiculturalism, had rendered neo-fascistic movements in the North Atlantic world more of a farce than a tragedy. But this also meant that neoliberalism had just as much rendered the possibility of more humane and democratic alternatives equally incapable of imagining and building durable hegemonic political coalitions based on solidarity across lines of class, race, and sexuality.

As noted above, the crisis of self-confidence in the American empire often found voice in criticisms of the Obama administration's putative unwillingness to use direct military intervention and to maintain longstanding antagonisms in the Middle East. Though there was ample evidence of Obama's willingness to use lower levels of direct intervention and to empower semireliable proxies across the region, other indicators—the nuclear agreement with Iran or looking for "the future of politics"[46] in Asia—suggested efforts to find new ways of unifying accumulation, repression, and legitimation that did not necessitate prolonged and intensive military interventions in the Middle East. As the Obama administration contended with the contradictions of oil for insecurity's most successful decade (2001–11), the incentives it had created angered elements in the US foreign policy establishment. The latter lamented the White House's refusal to find new ways of restoring the Bush-Cheney reunification, albeit in a far more challenging context of accumulation, repression, and legitimation. It was a context where US oil production had overtaken imports, where the Middle East had experienced an intensification of conflicts for over a decade (joined by Nigeria and Venezuela), and where increasingly volatile and insular polities in the North Atlantic world no longer viewed counterterrorism as a reason for launching large-scale military deployment in the Middle East (e.g., in Syria, Iran, or both).

To what extent an alternative to the Bush-Cheney unification seemed possible for the Obama White House—given the new realities of domestic oil production, the emergent potentialities of the Arab Spring, or the American polity's acquiescence to the new transnational US security state—are all moot points by now. In the end, it was the Obama administration's inability to comprehend the fracking revolution, the Arab revolutions, and the Islamic State revolution as contradictions produced by the oil-for-insecurity system. This is exactly why oil for insecurity defined Obama's foreign policy legacy, despite his efforts to do otherwise.

Interestingly, it could be argued that Donald J. Trump was the only leading candidate in the 2016 presidential elections to espouse positions that seemed to call into question the necessity of the post-9/11 American empire in the Middle East. This was a conservative position normally relegated to marginalized voices on the libertarian right. By comparison, the foreign policy positions of Bernie Sanders—the leading candidate of the progressive and socialist left—were largely indistinguishable from his opponent's, Hillary Clinton, Obama's former secretary of state and a supporter of the 2003 invasion of Iraq. In important ways, Trump's resonance with *just enough* of the electorate owed much to the fact that he was willing to define himself in opposition to the Bush-Cheney and Obama administrations, particularly in reference to their efforts to reconstitute American hegemony vis-à-vis the Middle East. This, of course, is not to say that Trump, in his efforts to make America great again, intends or is willing to forge a new unification of autarkic accumulation, isolationist repression, and racial legitimation with or without the Middle East at its center.

All of this is to say that the reactionary character of late American politics has been conspicuously animated by the Middle East since the original articulation of the oil-for-insecurity regime in the 1970s: Nixon-Ford and the oil embargos; Carter and the Iran hostage crisis; Reagan-Bush and Iran-Contra; Clinton's retreat from oil for insecurity; Bush-Cheney and Iraq; Obama and the Islamic State.[47] If Trump and his administration are so ideologically derivative as to seem inchoate, if not vacuous, this should be understood as an effect of having emerged from a long line of reactionary begettings dating back to the Nixon-Ford administration's early elaborations of the oil-for-insecurity regime. This, however, is not to say that what Trump represents is a politics so inbred as to be unviable. There are always profound dangers in the potential collapse of imperial systems. As already fractured North Atlantic polities cleave under the weight of neoliberal capitalism's contradictions, it is a question of whether reactionary minoritarian movements will even seek to create a new unification of accumulation and repression. In many ways, it seems as if these movements are seeking to influence politics through an approach that is more like the antithesis of Davis's theorization of hegemony. Here we need only cite the referendum on Brexit and Trump's election in 2016 as evidence of a new and possibly antihegemonic mode of power rising in the North Atlantic world.

Endnotes

1. It will become obvious that this chapter uses a rather expansive understanding of the Middle East as incorporating not only the commonly accepted areas of the Levant, Egypt, Mesopotamia, Arabia, and Persia, but also the entirety of Northern Africa (Mauritania to Egypt, Sudan to Morocco), as well as Anatolia, Afghanistan, and Pakistan. It also mentions such peripheral zones as the Sahara-Sahel, the Horn of Africa, and the Central Asian Republics. A forthcoming companion paper in the journal *Civil Wars* explains the rationale for this approach. On the relationship between the growth of US power and Middle East studies after the Second World War, see Osamah F. Khalil, *America's Dream Palace: Middle East Expertise and the Rise of the National Security State* (Cambridge, MA: Harvard University Press, 2016). For the ambivalent relationship between Middle East studies and Maghrib (North Africa) studies, see Robert P. Parks, "American Research Centers in North Africa and Sahara-Sahel Studies," paper presented at the conference West Africa and the Maghreb: Reassessing Intellectual Connections in the 21st Century, Harvard Divinity School, September 13–15, 2018.
2. See, e.g., David S. Painter, *Oil and American Century: The Political Economy of the U.S. Foreign Oil Policy* (Baltimore: Johns Hopkins University Press, 1986); Rachel Bronson, *Thicker Than Oil: America's Uneasy Partnership with Saudi Arabia* (New York: Oxford University Press, 2006); John Duffield, *Over a Barrel: The Costs of U.S. Foreign Oil Dependence* (Stanford, CA: Stanford Law and Politics, 2007); Steven A. Yetiv, *The Petroleum Triangle: Oil, Globalization, and Terror* (Ithaca, NY: Cornell University Press, 2011); Charles L. Glaser and Rosemary Ann Kelanic, *Crude Calculus: Reexamining the Oil Security Logic of America's Military Presence in the Persian Gulf* (Washington, DC: Georgetown University Press, 2016). Citations courtesy of Jeff Colgan.
3. See Michael Klare, *Blood and Oil: The Dangers and Consequences of America's Growing Dependency on Imported Petroleum* (New York: Metropolitan Books, 2004); Chalmers Johnson, *Blowback: The Costs and Consequences of American Empire* (New York: Holt, 2004); David Harvey, *The New Imperialism* (New York: Oxford University Press, 2005); Andrew Bacevich, *America's War for the Greater Middle East: A Military History* (New York: Random House, 2016). For a more nuanced analysis of the relationship between US political economy, foreign policy, and national identity vis-à-vis overconsumptive lifestyles, see David Campbell, "The Biopolitics of Security: Oil, Empire, and the Sports Utility Vehicle," *American Quarterly* 57, no. 3 (2005): 943–72.

4   Robert Vitalis, "Oilcraft," paper delivered at the 2017 Political Economy Summer Institute, George Mason University, June 11, 2017.
5   SIGAR, "Quarterly Report to the United States Congress (July)" (Arlington, VA.: SIGAR Special Inspector General for Afghanistan Reconstruction, 2014).
6   See Meredith R. Sarkees and Frank Wayman, *Resort to War: 1816–2007* (Washington, DC: CQ Press, 2010); Therése Pettersson, and Kristine Eck, "Organized Violence, 1989–2017," *Journal of Peace Research* 55, no. 4 (2018): 535–47.
7   Timothy Mitchell, *Carbon Democracy: Political Power in the Age of Oil* (New York: Verso, 2011).
8   On Saudi Arabia, see Robert Vitalis, *America's Kingdom: Mythmaking on the Saudi Oil Frontier* (Stanford, CA: Stanford University Press, 2007); on Iran, see Roham Alvandi, *Nixon, Kissinger, and the Shah: The United States and Iran in the Cold War* (New York: Oxford University Press, 2014); on Libya, see Geoff L. Simons, *Libya and the West: From Independence to Lockerbie* (London: I. B. Tauris, 2003).
9   See "Memorandum from Harold Saunders of the National Security Council Staff to the Special Assistant to the President's Assistant for National Security Affairs (Lake) for the President's Assistant for National Security Affairs (Kissinger), Washington, September 2, 1969," National Archives, Nixon Presidential Materials, NSC Files, Box 1239, Saunders Files, Libya, 1969; "Memorandum From the Assistant Secretary of State for African Affairs (Newsom) to the Acting Secretary of State (Richardson), Washington, September 4, 1969," National Archives, RG 59, Central Files 1967–69, POL 23-9 Libya. Secret. Sent for action. Drafted by Robert Allen Jr. (AF/N). Cited in Jacob Mundy, "A Useful Enemy? Libya, the United States, and the Making of Insecurity," *The Prize? Energy, Security, and Expertise*, paper presented at the Society of Historians of American Foreign Relations Annual Meeting, Washington, DC, June 22, 2017.
10 Timothy Mitchell, "McJihad: Islam in the U.S. Global Order," *Social Text* 20, no. 4 (2002): 6.
11 One needs to only skim the 2018 National Defense Strategy of the United States to see why China, which is accused of seeking "Indo-Pacific regional hegemony in the near-term and displacement of the United States to achieve global preeminence in the future," will not be asked by the Trump administration to share more of the global energy security burden. See United States Department of Defense, "Summary of the 2018 National Defense Strategy of the United States of America: Sharpening the American Military's Strategic Edge" (Washington, DC: United States Department of Defense, 2018). Compared to the final *Quadrennial Defense Review* of the Obama administration from 2014, the increased hostility toward China in Trump's "Security Strategy" only reinforces this point. As much as the Trump administration complained about European free riders (such that it appears Trump has contemplated leaving NATO on a number of occasions, while Germany and France have had to revive the old idea of an EU army in response), the unthinkability of a Sino-American alliance for oil and security reveals the extent to which this is as much a question of political economy as military strategy.
12 Alfred McCoy, "2030: The End of U.S. Empire," *Alternative Radio*, October 25, 2017, https://www.alternativeradio.org/collections/spk_alfred-mccoy/products/mcca007.
13 For example, see Harvey's commentary included in Utsa Patnaik and Prabhat Patnaik, *A Theory of Imperialism* (New York: Columbia University Press, 2016).
14 Mike Davis, "The Political Economy of Late-Imperial America," *New Left Review* 143 (1984): 6–38. It was later republished in Mike Davis, *Prisoners of the American Dream: Politics and Economy in the History of the US Working Class* (1986; repr., New York: Verso, 1999). Davis's most recent treatment of the American polity, particularly the resubordination of the working class, suggests that most of his analysis from the mid-1980s holds true today: Mike Davis, *Old Gods, New Enigmas* (New York: Verso, 2017).
15 Davis, "Political Economy of Late-Imperial America," 6–7, emphasis added.
16 See Giovanni Arrighi, *The Long Twentieth Century: Money, Power, and the Origins of Our Times* (New York: Verso, 2010), 309–55.
17 For background, see Francisco Parra, *Oil Politics: A Modern History of Petroleum* (London: I. B. Tauris, 2004), 17–21.

18 See Shimshon Bichler and Jonathan Nitzan, "Still About Oil," *Real-World Economics Review* 70 (2015): 49–79; Jonathan Nitzan and Shimshon Bichler, *The Global Political Economy of Israel: From War Profits to Peace Dividends* (New York: Pluto Press, 2002), Chapter 5.
19 Mitchell, *Carbon Democracy*, 170–72.
20 For a recent update of their findings, see Shimshon Bichler and Jonathan Nitzan, "Arms and Oil in the Middle East: A Biography of Research," *Rethinking Marxism* 30, no. 3 (2018): 418–40. Bichler and Nitzan fail to consider the extent to which the fracking revolution in the United States of the last decade, discussed later in this chapter, explains the collapse of their otherwise consistently accurate model.
21 See Salim Yaqub, *Imperfect Strangers: Americans, Arabs, and U.S.–Middle East Relations in the 1970s* (Ithaca, NY: Cornell University Press, 2016).
22 See Nitzan and Bichler, *Global Political Economy of Israel*, 208–16.
23 Ian Lustick examines specific cases—Egypt and Iraq—where Western policies were specifically calibrated to prevent the emergence of a regional hegemon. Ian S Lustick, "The Absence of Middle Eastern Great Powers: Political Backwardness in Historical Perspective," *International Organization* 51, no. 4 (1997): 653–83.
24 On the myths of the 1973 oil "embargos," see Mitchell, *Carbon Democracy*, 173–77, 184–85.
25 Statistics in this paragraph are drawn from the regular reports of the US Arms Control and Disarmament Agency published in 1975, 1982, and 1984. See also Salim Yaqub, *Containing Arab Nationalism: The Eisenhower Doctrine and the Middle East* (Chapel Hill: University of North Carolina Press, 2004).
26 Statistics in this paragraph are drawn from the regular reports of the US Arms Control and Disarmament Agency published in 1982 and 1984, as well as from Melani Cammett et al., *A Political Economy of the Middle East* (Boulder, CO: Westview Press, 2015), 357–66.
27 Mitchell, *Carbon Democracy*, 215–20.
28 While Libya's "nuclear disarmament" was framed as a vindication of a more aggressive US policy of preemptive military action against rogue states, the push for South Sudanese independence, facilitated by a Khartoum unnerved by the invasions of Afghanistan and Iraq, was just as much a gift to the evangelical Christian base of Bush-Cheney. On the latter point, see Rebecca Hamilton, "The Wonks Who Sold Washington on South Sudan," *Reuters*, July 11, 2012, https://www.reuters.com/article/us-south-sudan-midwives/special-report-the-wonks-who-sold-washington-on-south-sudan-idUS-BRE86A0GC20120711.
29 This correlation—the emergence of "terrorism" with oil for insecurity—is no mere coincidence, though there is not enough space here to unpack it.
30 See Lisa Stampnitzky, *Disciplining Terror: How Experts Invented "Terrorism"* (New York: Cambridge University Press, 2013). For a general background, see Joseba Zulaika and William Douglass, *Terror and Taboo: The Follies, Fables, and Faces of Terrorism* (New York: Routledge, 1996).
31 Bichler and Nitzan, "Arms and Oil in the Middle East," Figure 1.
32 Nitzan and Bichler, *Global Political Economy of Israel*, 271–72.
33 As a leading example, see Erica Chenoweth and Maria J. Stephan, *Why Civil Resistance Works* (New York: Columbia University Press, 2011). This antipolitical reinterpretation of social movements mirrors the similarly antipolitical reinterpretation of nearly all forms of armed resistance by nonstate actors as terrorism, such that a desperate tactic has effectively become an entire ontology of organized violence on par with international, civil, and imperial wars.
34 Ward Churchill and Michael Ryan, *Pacifism as Pathology: Reflections on the Role of Armed Struggle in North America*, 3rd ed. (Oakland, CA: PM Press, 2017).
35 Mahmood Mamdani, "The Politics of Naming: Genocide, War, Insurgency," *London Review of Books* 29, no. 5 (2007): 5–8.
36 On the groundwork that paved the way for the Arab Spring, see Joel Beinin, *Workers and Thieves: Labor Movements and Popular Uprisings in Tunisia and Egypt* (Stanford, CA: Stanford University Press, 2015).

37 Marie Allansson, Erik Melander, and Lotta Themnér, "Organized Violence, 1989–2016," *Journal of Peace Research* 54, no. 4 (2017): 574–87; Pettersson and Eck, "Organized Violence, 1989–2017."
38 Nick Turse, "The Golden Age of Black Ops," *Tom Dispatch*, January 20, 2015, http://www.tomdispatch.com/post/175945/tomgram%3A_nick_turse,_a_shadow_war_in_150_countries/
39 These movements' insularity stands in particularly sharp contrast to the internationalism of ten years prior, the "anti-globalization" movements and the antiwar movements.
40 Elizabeth Stoycheff, "Under Surveillance: Examining Facebook's Spiral of Silence Effects in the Wake of NSA Internet Monitoring," *Journalism & Mass Communication Quarterly* 93, no. 2 (2016): 296–311.
41 Dave Lindorff, "The Pentagon's Massive Accounting Fraud Exposed," *The Nation*, November 27, 2018, https://www.thenation.com/article/pentagon-audit-budget-fraud/
42 J. J. Messner, ed. *2018 Fragile States Index* (Washington, DC: The Fund for Peace, 2018).
43 For an optimistic take on these trends, see Meghan L. O'Sullivan, *Windfall: How the New Energy Abundance Upends Global Politics and Strengthens America's Power* (New York: Simon and Schuster, 2017).
44 Adam Tooze, *Crashed: How a Decade of Financial Crises Changed the World* (New York: Viking, 2018).
45 As historian Quinn Slobodian has recently argued, the original objective of the neoliberal intellectual movement was to reorganize sovereignty and production in such a way as to inhibit political power from subordinating capitalism to any totalitarian project. Despite whatever contradictions exist between its vision of an optimal political economy of social reproduction and the realities of North Atlantic capitalism's evolution after the 1970s, the neoliberal movement nonetheless succeeded in disabling to a large extent the ability, if not the willingness, of industrial democratic societies to engage in mass collective opposition. See Quinn Slobodian, *Globalists: The End of Empire and the Birth of Neoliberalism* (Cambridge, MA: Harvard University Press, 2018).
46 Hillary Clinton, "America's Pacific Century," *Foreign Policy*, October 11, 2011, https://foreignpolicy.com/2011/10/11/americas-pacific-century/.
47 Beyond the Islamic State, Obama deemed the international failure to secure Libya's transition after the 2011 revolution—what had become a "shit show," in his words—as the greatest mistake of his administration. It is also worth noting that the September 11, 2012, attack on US diplomatic and intelligence facilities in Benghazi, Libya, became a cause célèbre of American conservatives and a linchpin in their strategy to delegitimize the 2016 presidential campaign of Hillary Clinton, a campaign premised on her foreign policy credentials and thus her ability to safely manage the American empire after Obama. This campaign to preemptively delegitimize Clinton not only included eight different investigations by the US Congress, but also a $50 million Hollywood production dramatizing those events in Libya, which was released in early 2016.

MAXIMALIST ELITES AND THE ECOLOGICAL BURDEN OF SOUTHERN HISTORY

Christian Parenti

> *New England, the West, and other regions are occasionally permitted to speak for the nation. But the South is thought to be hedged about with peculiarities that set it apart as unique.*
>
> —C. Vann Woodward

> *Anything south of the Canadian border is "The South."*
>
> —Malcolm X

> *All progress in capitalist agriculture is a progress in the art, not only of robbing the worker, but of robbing the soil; all progress in increasing the fertility of the soil for a given time is progress towards ruining the more long-lasting sources of that fertility . . . undermining the original sources of all wealth—the soil and the worker.*
>
> —Karl Marx

It is an old, even out-of-date question, but it never seems to go away: why is the US South different? In literature and popular culture, the American South is the cradle of racism and a peculiarly violent, hedonistic, but also religiously devout culture. Beneath the lush and genteel surface lurks something sinister. The Southern Gothic captures this sensibility: the quest for control always fails; humiliation, heartbreak, illness, insanity, and defeat always win out over illusions of propriety, heroism, and progress. Like the placid muddy water of its swamps and rivers, the region has an aura of sensuality but also of gloom and danger.

Traditional explanations tended to ascribe the South's difference to its climate. Thomas Jefferson called Southerners: "aristocratical, pompous, clannish, indolent, hospitable . . . fiery, voluptuary . . . unsteady, jealous for their own liberties, but trampling on those of others, generous, candid, without attachment or pretensions to any religion but that of the heart." In matters of business he found Southerners "careless of their interests" and "thoughtless in their expences." He ascribed these traits "to that warmth of their climate which unnerves and unmans both body and mind."[1]

By contrast, Jefferson saw Northerners as "cool, sober, laborious, independent, jealous of their own liberties, and just to those of others, interested, chicaning, superstitious and hypocritical in their religion." To Jefferson's mind, these characteristics grew "weaker and weaker by gradation from North to South and South to North, insomuch that an observing traveller, without the aid of the quadrant may always know his latitude by the character of the people among whom he finds himself."[2]

With the benefit of hindsight, we can see that the South is different from the North, not because of anything innate in its people or deterministic about its climate, but rather because of the extremely unequal and exploitative class relations that helped produce, and were reproduced by, Southern patterns of economic evolution; patterns that are best described with the rather out-of-fashion idea of *underdevelopment*—as in, "having a relatively low economic level of industrial production and standard of living."[3] These conditions are not an original state or a local failing but rather the consequence of historical capitalism, or what Andre Gunder Frank called "the development of underdevelopment."[4] The "indispensable component of modern underdevelopment," explained Walter Rodney, "is that it expresses a particular relationship of *exploitation*."[5]

MAXIMALIST ELITES AND THE ECOLOGICAL BURDEN

While it is correct to foreground human agency in the economic story of the South, the role of nonhuman nature—the Southern environment—is also important. Yet, even as environmental history has blossomed in the study of other regions, the environmental history of the US South remains stunted. This is due, in part, to the progressive rejection of older traditions in Southern historiography that used environmental determinism to justify racist conclusions.[6]

Below, I attempt to read back into Southern history the dialectical relationships between class formation, class struggle, and environmental causality. Central in all this will be the role of the South's uniquely maximalist ruling class.

Tell about the South...

Even today, the South shows fading signs of underdevelopment.[7] The US Census defines four major regions: Northeast, Midwest, South, and West. Of these, the South has the lowest median household income; it also has "the largest share of counties with high income inequality." The South remains the region with the lowest median wages;[8] has "maintained the highest rates of poverty over the past 40 years," and has "the largest share of Americans living in poverty of all regions." Food insecurity is highest in the South. It has the highest adult and infant mortality rates and the greatest prevalence of illnesses like cardiovascular disease, obesity, and HIV/AIDS. Southerners suffer higher occurrences of occupational fatalities, and the South has many of the highest rates of incarceration.[9]

Despite its history of widespread economic hardship, the South also produced an extremely rich and politically powerful ruling class. During the eighteenth and nineteenth centuries, economic inequality was greatest in the South. And while most of the region's population, both Black and white, was grindingly poor, the region's economic elite was not only wealthier than the common folk of their region but also tended to be wealthier than the elites of other regions.[10] This ultrarich Southern ruling class always placed domineering control over labor above all else, even development itself. From the birth of the Republic onward, the Southern ruling class has punched above its weight in national politics and often did so on the basis of maximalist demands and threats.

BETWEEN CATASTROPHE AND REVOLUTION

Even at the Constitutional Convention, they threatened secession. As John Rutledge of South Carolina put it, while demanding defense of the slave trade: "Religion & humanity had nothing to do with this question - Interest alone is the governing principle with Nations - The true question at present is whether the Southn. [sic] States shall or shall not be parties to the Union. If the Northern States consult their interests they will not oppose the increase of Slaves which will increase the commodities of which they will become the carriers."[11] In 1818, North Carolina's Nathaniel Macon crystallized the logic of elite Southern antidevelopmentalism in one line: "If Congress can make canals, they can with more propriety emancipate."[12]

From the defense of states' rights, to nullification, to secession, to sabotaging the New Deal, to the aggressive antiunion politics of today, Southern elites have maintained a zero-tolerance-style hostility towards anything threatening their economic prerogatives, particularly their domination of the local workforce.[13] This elite Southern extremism is an important element in the New Right. As Mike Davis illustrated in *Prisoners of the American Dream*, the New Right emerged from a specific geography: the Sun Belt encompassing the Old South and the West; a geography that is very much a partial heir to elements of a Southern worldview and political economy.[14]

In this regard, and others, the story of the South takes on national and even international relevance. Du Bois saw this when he warned, "As the South goes, so goes the nation." He was not referring merely to the "solid South" of electoral politics.[15] He was referring to the whole ensemble of violent white supremacy, brutal class struggle, and the unaccountable, violent, corrupt nature of state power that has always been central to the political economy of the South. Du Bois worried that the entire nation would be dragged down to the degraded political-economic condition of the South, where labor has few rights and the environment is wantonly despoiled.

C. Vann Woodward gave us another reason to understand Southern history. For Woodward, "the irony of Southern history" was the political wisdom the region's story could provide to the nation as a whole. "For the inescapable facts of history were," wrote Woodward,

> that the South had repeatedly met with frustration and failure. It had learned what it was to be faced with economic, social, and political problems that refused to yield to all the ingenuity, patience,

and intelligence that a people could bring to bear upon them. It had learned to accommodate itself to conditions that it swore it would never accept, and it had learned the taste left in the mouth by the swallowing of one's own words. It had learned to live for long decades in quite un-American poverty, and it had learned the equally un-American lesson of submission. For the South had undergone an experience that it could share with no other part of America—though it is shared by nearly all the peoples of Europe and Asia—the experience of military defeat, occupation, and reconstruction.[16]

One might add that this fate was, very much, brought upon the region by its maximalist elites.

Writing during the height of the Cold War, as American imperialism was becoming ever more violent and globally obvious, Woodward's implicit point was that the South had a potential lesson about humility and limits that it needed to learn and teach imperial America. Alas, the lesson went unlearned. Yet, in the age of climate change, so-called "forever wars," and soaring economic inequality, the Southern message about limits, realism, and the dangers of elite extremism is more necessary than ever.

Slavery, Development, and the Southern Environment

Since the early nineteenth century, a large and politically diverse literature has argued that the South's relative underdevelopment is bound up with, and has been largely caused by, slavery. How exactly slavery did this is still debated. An old line of argument blamed environmental causes for all Southern ills. Yet, in current Southern economic history, the role of the environment is not much explored.[17]

The reason for this evasion is simple: both the history and historiography of the South have seen much pseudoscientific racism that was justified with spurious, environmentally reductionist arguments. The planters' old assertion that Africans were fundamentally different from Europeans and were "naturally" suited to fieldwork in hot weather found a more sophisticated, though still racist, reiteration in the first generation of professional Southern historians.[18] The Dunning School, famously racist, paid little attention to the environment, but one of Dunning's star students—the doyen of modern academic Southern history, U. B. Phillips—did bring environmental questions into play. In fact, Phillips blamed the entire course of Southern development on the hot weather. His 1929 book *Life and Labor in the Old South* opens: "Let us begin with the weather, for that has been the chief agency in making the South distinctive. It fosters the cultivation of the staple crops, which promoted the plantation system, which brought importation of Negroes, which not only gave rise to chattel slavery but created a lasting race problem."[19] Phillips notoriously and incorrectly defended slavery as a benevolent, not very profitable institution dedicated to the betterment of the enslaved. "The one was master," explained Phillips in a description of plantation life, "the many were slaves ... the one was teacher, the many were pupils."[20]

This close association of environmental determinism and racism among the Southern historians of the Phillips era left many later historians squeamish about discussing the environmental aspects of Southern history.[21] C. Vann Woodward entirely dismissed the environment: "The same old blinding tropical sun that readily explained a peculiar pattern of imperialist institutions in the nineteenth century shines upon a quite different pattern of institutions in the twentieth century. So it is in the South, where new and radically different institutions, architecture, crops, and styles of living flourish in the same old climate, environed by the same old geography."[22]

Most recent economic history of the South, despite having many points of disagreement, tends to concur that a central element in the South's slower and less equitable economic development has been its lower population density. So why has the South, historically speaking, been sparsely populated?

The South did not start out economically underdeveloped. As Gavin Wright points out, "in 1790, the two [regional] economies were nearly equal in population, area, and levels of wealth. Broadly speaking, they shared a similar cultural and legal heritage. So the economic competition boiled down to the essential difference between them."[23] That difference was the dominance of slavery in the South.

Regional economic divergence—or what Wright calls the sectional cold war, depending how it is measured—really began in the 1820s and 1830s, as northeastern industrialization launched into takeoff and the Northern population grew thanks to waves of European immigration. So the two questions are: what drove capitalist industrialization in the North, and what blocked it in the South?

MAXIMALIST ELITES AND THE ECOLOGICAL BURDEN

In *Slavery and Freedom,* James Oakes summarized how slavery underdeveloped the South as follows: "Slavery hindered technological innovation even where its profitability depended on the latest techniques for processing and transportation. It slowed the growth of cities and industry, hampered the growth of a consumer market, reduced the flow of savings, and promoted soil exhaustion and demographic instability by dampening interest in long-term improvements on the land."[24] Note that land use is key. We will return to that in a moment.

As for the growth of the North, Charles Post's *The American Road to Capitalism* offers a comprehensive review of the literature and a very sound explanation of the transition. For Post, the roots of the North's takeoff lie in the economic effects of the Revolutionary War, which "subordinated northern family-farming to 'market-coercionization' forcing rural household-producers to specialise output, innovate technically, and accumulate land and tools."[25] Gordon S. Wood, though having a politics very different from Post, has also noted that the war drove an expansion of market relations: "The inexhaustible needs of three armies—the British and French as well as the American—for everything from blankets and wagons to meat and rum brought into being hosts of new manufacturing and entrepreneurial interests and made market farmers out of husbandmen who before had scarcely ever traded out of their neighborhoods."[26] The war and the interventionist state policies it forced into being, brought together new producers and consumers, created new connections between previously isolated regions, and thus vastly stimulated "inland trade," while also laying the legal and physical foundations for what would later be recognized as the market revolution.[27] The fighting in the South happened later and was more irregular, or guerilla, in style, than in the North. It thus did not have the same effect of pushing household production toward petty commodity production. As Post put it: "In the North, agrarian petty-commodity production provided a growing home-market for industrial capital. In the South, the dominance of plantation-slavery blocked the deepening of the social division of labour and industrial development."[28]

The war alone did not trigger marketization. The new nation's functional system of taxation and financing also helped drive the process by driving up land values. Not until Northern land became fully commodified, which happened between 1790 and 1820, were Northern farmers fully subordinated to the competitive logic of the market and compelled to produce *for sale* rather than producing *for subsistence* with the occasional sale of surplus. This shift, in turn, drove them to specialize, innovate, invest, and generally intensify their production of value.

Again Post explains it well: "federal land-policies radically altered the relationship of rural households to landholding, making the appropriation, maintenance and expansion of land dependent upon successful commodity-production.... The federal government set minimum-prices and acreage to be purchased, but put no restrictions on the maximum size of purchase, allowing the operation of 'market-mechanisms' to set the maximum-price obtained at public auction."[29] And, importantly, the first great chunk of federal lands doled out was in the Old Northwest, and the federal law governing its disposal prohibited slavery.[30]

Patterns of Settlement

What was the political ecology of Southern land use patterns? From early on, the Southern disposal of public lands tended to be so laissez-faire, so open to elite abuse, as to be chaotic. Every colony had its own unique land disposal system; "no two were exactly alike." However, "two systems of disposal represented the extremes of the colonial experience—the New England and the southern."[31] These produced distinct social orders. As Paul W. Gates put it: "Each Colony had its own system of granting land, under which officers and men enlisted for colonial wars received bounty land." But "in the southern Colonies speculators and planters acquired large grants by bringing in laborers under the headright system."[32] This system granted fifty acres per person to whomever paid the passage of a new settler.

The New England system, on the other hand, typically involved the settlement of whole townships, generally six square miles each, occupied by pre-arranged groups of families under the leadership of a Congregational minister. Individual subplots were generally left to the town government to parcel out.[33] This approach produced a landscape of dense towns and small farms; an economy in which agriculture, simple commodity production, and trade were somewhat balanced. (Lest that sound too tidy and egalitarian, keep in mind that early New England was class-stratified, slave-owning, religiously intolerant, and committed to the violent extirpation of Native Americans.)

MAXIMALIST ELITES AND THE ECOLOGICAL BURDEN

New England farms tended to combine food crops and livestock production in patterns that, until the market revolution—or communications revolution—of the early nineteenth century, were relatively sustainable.[34] Although the problem of soil exhaustion appeared as early as the 1630s, so too did adaptations.[35] As H. Bruce Franklin details in *The Most Important Fish in the Sea*, soil husbandry using "immense shoals" of menhaden as fertilizer started not much later.[36]

In the South—Virginia and below—the land disposal systems were less rational and less equal and led to a more acute soil crisis. "Land was taken up by the use of warrants. These could be located on any unappropriated land. But the surveyors, especially the deputies, were poorly trained, and the records were carelessly kept, so that the location of several thousand acres with irregular sides was often made on some former location."[37] As a result, settlement patterns were individualistic and haphazard. Much of this was due to the aristocratic intentions, if not origins, of Virginia's early leading men. The Virginia Company sought to establish a New World version of England's hierarchal social order. An early study of the national land system found that instead of "small tracks of a few hundred acres at most, the southern planter insisted on holdings well into the thousands. This caused the dispersion of population."[38]

While few actual gentry settled in Virginia, highly profitable tobacco cultivation helped launch a new elite with Old World pretensions. The environmentally destructive qualities of tobacco monocropping also shaped settlement patterns and class structure. "Tobacco strips more than ten times the nitrogen and more than thirty times the phosphorus from the soil than do typical food crops," the geologist David Montgomery explains. In colonial Virginia, after "five years of tobacco cultivation the ground was too depleted in nutrients to grow much of anything. With plenty of fresh land to the west, tobacco farmers just kept on clearing new fields. Stripped bare of vegetation, what soil remained on the abandoned fields washed into gullies during intense summer rains. Virginia became a factory for turning topsoil into tobacco."[39]

This factory, as John Majewski's *Modernizing a Slave Economy* has shown, used "shifting cultivation"—in which farmers "burned forest growth to quickly release nutrients into the soil. After five or six years, when the nutrients had been exhausted, the old field was abandoned until it was cleared again in twenty years."⁴⁰ This burning practice and the large lots it required stemmed from several factors: the self-consciously aristocratic vision of the Virginia Company, the soil-wrecking qualities of tobacco, and, as Majewski has shown, the prevalence of the highly acidic, low-nutrient, Ultisol soils in the US South.⁴¹

The inherent weakness of the soil meant that investment in manure, marl, and fences would ultimately return less income than would the same expenditure on the less acidic, more nutrient-rich Alfisol soils that predominate north of the Mason-Dixon Line. The importance and scope of Majewski's argument seems to invite a reductionist misreading. But Majewski is not rehashing the old Phillips sequence that ran from climate to white supremacy. Rather, he is exposing a layer of environmental agency within Southern history that constrained and channeled human agency. In other words, the South's conspicuously bifurcated class and caste structure did not result from the environment. But neither did they develop in isolation from it. Rather, they were dialectically shaped by the environment and in turn helped shape it. Central to the metabolism of this Southern political ecology was a regional ruling class bred to the "habit of command." In a dangerously utopian fashion, these elite Southern maximalists maintained a zero-tolerance stance toward any infringement on their prerogatives, be those labor laws, progressive taxes, or environmental regulation.

In his classic *Soil Exhaustion as a Factor in the Agricultural History of Virginia and Maryland, 1606–1860,* Avery Craven explained the socioeconomic dynamics of Southern "soil mining" as follows: "Seeming abundance of raw materials encourages waste; the lack of capital forbids the economies of production, and the heavier burden of carriage and marketing fall upon the producer," all of which encourage maximum exploitation of the resource. "Furthermore, the abundance of land, combined with a scarcity of capital and labor—a condition which characterizes all frontiers—throws the burden of intensified production upon the soil as the cheapest factor. Only the most fertile soils will be used and only those methods employed which give greatest immediate returns regardless of future consequences."⁴² One planter described his methods as "skinning the lands."⁴³

As Craven put it, "The destruction of a little land amid such an abundance, was a matter of small consequence compared to the rapidity with which wealth and luxury were replacing privation and simplicity. . . . and the splendid life that was rising in the river valleys bore convincing testimony to the fact." The planter William Fitzhugh estimated that his Virginian investments in indentured servants, slaves, and land returned profits three times greater than could have been made by similar efforts in England.[44] Craven found that "prices were so high that in the early days a man's labor in tobacco production yielded him six times as large a return as might be secured from any other crop."[45] These amazing profits joined similar ones from other Southern commodity frontiers: sugar, rice, indigo, cotton, cattle, timber, turpentine, phosphate, coal, oil, and eventually strip malls and subdivisions. Each of these extractive and ecologically plundering booms produced a particular layer of the regional ruling class; an elite constellation that—through the political ecology of slavery and export-oriented staple monocropping—developed a uniquely aggressive and apocalyptic worldview and mode of combat.

The Permanent Frontier

Driven forward by tobacco's combination of quick wealth and soil exhaustion, Southern planters appropriated land in a remarkably chaotic fashion. State governments would issue warrants—government-sanctioned licenses to take possession of a designated amount of terrain—but in no specified pattern. The warrant owner was free to survey and claim the best lands possible and exclude others. Thus, "owners were careful in arranging their surveys to eliminate gullies, swamps, and other undesirable land, preferring level, well-drained land close to streams. The result was that boundaries commonly took fantastic shapes, although the regulations attempted to require that they be in rectangular form." The Southern speculator's habit of excluding less valuable terrain was known as "stringing," and, if executed well, "could be made to include much more than the acreage granted."[46] To make matters worse, many Southern systems lacked "proper surveys and recording."[47]

The practice of "stringing" led to the related problem of overlapping land claims, known as "shingling."[48] The haphazard Southern land disposal systems, allowing "location of warrants in any manner the owner wished, so long as he was not trespassing on Indian land or on the property of other grantees," resulted in layer upon layer of conflicting ownership claims, sometimes three to five deep.

One result of this was a proliferation of lawsuits. As Gates put it: "Such a haphazard system, which permitted individuals to run their boundaries as they saw fit so long as they did not encroach on others' possessions, and which rarely left permanent land markers, was bound to cause numerous conflicts over boundaries and overlapping claims. The courts of Virginia and Kentucky were to be cluttered with cases arising from the lack of a system of prior rectangular survey."[49]

These legal problems further undermined settlement and the development of markets. Abraham Lincoln's father, Thomas, left Kentucky for Indiana in part because of three lawsuits, the last of which stemmed from the chaotic land disposal system and the power of speculating absentee landlords.[50] This pattern of settlement was the result of undemocratic political processes and short-term economic thinking driven by superprofits and the rapid soil exhaustion of tobacco monocropping, and it ultimately became a serious impediment to economic development.

Writing about Virginia and North Carolina, Gates notes that "Neither state had developed a well-maintained land office where titles and vacant lands could be investigated and neither had any adequate local title registration system. When residents of the western portions of these states were trying to frame constitutions and to obtain admission to the Union, it was impossible to determine what amount of land was still owned by Virginia or North Carolina."[51] In Tennessee, where numerous North Carolina speculators and squatters had dispossessed Native American groups and willy-nilly claimed what would soon become federal lands, many titles remained in legal limbo until as late as 1841.[52]

The relative chaos of the Southern land disposal systems favored powerful speculators, who had the means to manipulate slow and costly legal cases. Along with racial slavery, Southern land disposal patterns created a more unequal society than that of New England. As the process of state lands cessions gathered momentum, most Southern states scrambled to give away as much land as possible before transferring the remains.

As Wilma Dunaway explains in *The First American Frontier: Transition to Capitalism in Southern Appalachia, 1700–1860*: "By 1800, absentee landholders owned three-quarters of the total acreage reported in county tax lists ... In Virginia and [what is now] West Virginia, little acreage was left for residence.

MAXIMALIST ELITES AND THE ECOLOGICAL BURDEN

After 1790, distant speculators gobbled up more than 90 percent of the land when the Virginia Assembly began to sell its frontier areas at very cheap prices." In Kentucky, absentee landlords would own more than 56 percent of the land; in the Appalachian counties of Virginia, 89 percent; and in what is now West Virginia, 93 percent.[53]

Even originally egalitarian North Carolina was eventually captured by speculators.[54] In 1783, as North Carolina was negotiating its cession of western backlands, the state government "threw open its own western sector and the lands of Tennessee for purchase at very cheap prices. Shortly, land jobbers began a speculative rampage that resulted in the disposal of 4,000,000 acres within seven months. In Tennessee, absentee merchant-investors, land companies, and distant planters amassed nearly seven-tenths of the Appalachian lands."[55]

As the lower South cotton frontier opened, a similar pattern emerged there. In *Development Arrested*, Clyde Woods put it this way: "An ideal plantation [in Mississippi] in the 1850s consisted of sixteen hundred acres, costing $90 per acre, with 135 Black workers producing one to two bales an acre. High levels of capitalization and indebtedness meant that only the wealthiest, often absentee, planters in the South or North could meet such requirements."[56]

Speculators and absentee landlords impeded development by keeping land prices too high for homesteaders and by the investment-retarding transaction cost they introduced with their "shingled" claims, leading to endless lawsuits. In those areas where geographical absentee speculators controlled the most land, population growth was slow and thus, so too, was economic activity and development.[57]

We must also consider the South's so-called open-range laws. These allowed cattle and swine to wander and forage where they saw fit. A reaction to low population density, open-range laws also perpetuated low population densities. The open range was the product of several interacting environmental and social factors. These were the region's week acidic soils; the massive economic rewards that came from the soil-stripping monocropping of staples; and the resulting shifting cultivation. Another environmental factor that perpetuated the open range was the prevalence of hot weather diseases, like the cattle tick fever that assaulted Southern livestock.[58] Thus, for a long time, crops had to be fenced in while animals wandered. As Abraham Hill

Gibson put it: "Virginia's colonists found it more time- and cost-effective to let their domestic animals fend for themselves in the woods. This was the origin of the southern range, an institution that eventually spread throughout the Southeast and which lasted another 250 years."[59]

The open range was both a product and cause of the South's relative underdevelopment. Most modernizing Southern agronomists opposed open-range laws because "improved" or more intensive agriculture required the collection and rational use of manure and the more controlled care for and breeding of animals. They also lamented that the open-range laws allowed poorer herders to benefit at the expense of wealthier landowners. The open range and low state taxes were concessions to the poorer yeomanry's struggle for subsistence and self-sufficiency.[60] As such, they helped buy political stability but also thwarted specialization, retarded a deeper division of labor, and discouraged investment in technology.

Given the many factors that led to a thinly dispersed population, it did not make sense for Southern farmers to "waste precious time, labor, and materials building fences to enclose domestic livestock," so "colonists allowed the animals to roam the Virginia landscape as they pleased."[61] In response to a claim that a horse was trespassing on unfenced land, one Southern magistrate said: "Such law as this would require a revolution in our people's habits of thought and action. . . . Our whole people . . . would be converted into a set of trespassers."[62] In fact, the open range was only fully extinguished in the 1970s. Tennessee changed its range laws in 1947, Alabama in 1951, Georgia in 1955, Missouri in 1969, and Mississippi in 1978.[63]

Plantation Self-Sufficiency

The many forces that led to low population density in the South—weak soils, shifting cultivation, highly profitable but soil-depleting staple monocrops, and land-hoarding elites—undermined the development of urbanization, transportation infrastructure, and internal markets. Another component of this dynamic was the plantation's relative self-sufficiency and the region's general self-sufficiency. In language of development economics, this self-sufficiency undermined the development of so-called backward production linkages. These are linkages connecting the agricultural point of production, the farm, to parts of the nonfarm sector that supply agricultural inputs like fertilizer,

MAXIMALIST ELITES AND THE ECOLOGICAL BURDEN

tools, seed, fuel, business services, etc. Forward production linkages refer to farm output that is used by the nonfarm sector as input: the cotton that fed the cotton mills and cotton-carrying shipping.[64]

In the North, the agricultural revolution that Post shows was central to industrialization involved the marketization not only of forward linkages but crucially of backward linkages as well. Put in Marxist terms: in the plantation South, the realm of "unpaid reproductive work" was larger than in the North. The market revolution in the North involved what Marx called "real subsumption," whereas in the South, due to plantation self-sufficiency, subsumption of reproductive labor was merely formal. That is, it was linked as an input (the production of labor power) to production for the market but was not itself governed by the logic in workings of the market.

As markets increasingly mediated the reproduction of Northern farms, the same process occurred in the South, but far more slowly. Plantation self-sufficiency meant there was no pressure to innovate, specialize, and invest in the realm of reproduction. And crucially, there was no value (exchange value) being produced to capture and reinvest. While just as much use value was being produced in the reproductive work of plantations, this happened beyond the revolutionizing dynamic of the law of value. In the North, expanded reproduction—that is to say, further accumulation of capital—became more intensive, while in the South it had to be extensive, with more land and more slaves producing more of the key staples for export.[65]

This blockage was linked to the property rights in slaves. Slaves not only produced value but were also valuable property and thus, unlike other forms of labor, could not be shed during slumps. Southern slave owners had higher fixed costs in the form of enslaved people, and so when slaves were not producing products for sale they were put to work reproducing themselves and the other means of production and subsistence. With a thinly spread population that tended to consume only the necessities and produced much of that for itself, industry and commerce remained sluggish. This, in turn, negatively impacted development of infrastructure. How would canals and railroads be paid for with few customers and a limited tax base?

This settlement pattern also created a political geography—county government was more important than town or city government. And it created a regional ruling class that was dominated not by industrialists and merchants but by landlords. After the Civil War, as Southern capitalists came to outweigh actual planters in the elite, the elite mentality and style of rule remained that of landlordism.

The Elite Southern Mind

In 1929, journalist W. J. Cash published an essay that twelve years later would become a book, *The Mind of the South*. Delivered in the style of a hot, late-night, boozy regaling, the book is lauded as a study of regional character, but it is actually something far more unusual: a ruthless class analysis of Southern political culture.[66] Cash gave constant and explicit attention to class struggle, elite hegemony, and the decisive role of white supremacy in the continual reproduction of Southern political economy. In this regard, Cash very much followed Du Bois's *Black Reconstruction*, although he did not cite the book.[67]

The Southern environment was an important recurring character in *The Mind of the South*; it was, for Cash, a deep yet indirect cause of the region's many social ills. "Leisure conspired with the languorous climate to the spinning of dreams," wrote Cash. "Unpleasant realities were singularly rare, and those which existed, as, for example, slavery, lent themselves to pleasant glorification. Thus fact gave way to amiable fiction."[68]

Southern elites were, in the eyes of Cash, parvenus conditioned by the violence and quick fortunes of the frontier.[69] "The ruling class as a body and in its primary aspect," wrote Cash, "was merely a close clique of property."[70] Almost as compensation for their lonely, hardscrabble surroundings, this frontier nouveau riche fetishized aristocracy; theirs was an imitation of the Virginian imitation of the British gentry. Add to this mix a form of slavery that allowed the *total domination* of one human by another—a condition that can elicit depravity and sadism from even normal, well-adjusted people—and a particular political culture comes into focus.

"Nowhere else in America," wrote Cash, "would class awareness in a certain very narrow sense figure so largely in the private thinking of the master group. And not only in the private thinking of the master group, for that matter. Everybody in the South was aware of, and habitually thought and spoke in terms of, a division of society into Big Men and Little Men, with strict reference to property, power, and the claim to gentility."[71]

Cash saw the DNA of Southern politics as the double helix of prepolitical class consciousness on the one hand, and a hyperindividualistic obsession with honor, status, and autonomy on the other. All of this was, for him, "rooted in the soil" or born of the South's political ecology. For example: "The plantation tended to find its center in itself: to be an independent social unit, a self-contained and largely self-sufficient little world of its own.... [O]nce the forest was cut and the stumps grubbed up, once the seeds were in a few times and the harvest home a few times, once he had a Negro or two actually at work—once the plantation was properly carved out and on its way, then the world might go hang.... [F]reed from any particular dependence on his neighbors, the planter, as he got his hand in at mastering the slave, would wax continually in lordly self-certainty."[72]

This planter mindset and the Big Men/Little Men sensitivity to rank extended all the way down the social structure—at least as fragments, distortions, and reactions—to poor whites and the enslaved. The "[f]armers and the crackers were in their own way self-sufficient too—as fiercely careful of their prerogatives of ownership, as jealous of their sway over their puny domains, as the grandest lord. No man felt or acknowledged any primary dependence on his fellows, save perhaps in the matter of human sympathy and entertainment."[73]

As always, violence was a hallmark. The fight to expropriate Native Americans dragged on for decades. Slavery was maintained by the steady use of the whip and by the slave patrol system, in which all white men had to participate as a form of corvée labor.[74] Dueling was common among elite men, while eye gouging and bareknuckle fistfights were common among the poor. Decades before the Civil War, there was a robust Southern lynching culture—"frontier justice"—that had white commoners as its primary victims.[75] Among other things, this culture of rank, honor, autonomy, and violence meant that politics and class struggle were conducted with the gloves very much off.

Class Struggle in the New South

With the end of Reconstruction, the regional ruling class revived and reconstituted itself. Even as new capitalists like R. J. Reynolds and J. B. Duke emerged from the yeoman class and other capitalists arrived from outside the region, the fantasy of the cavalier persisted. For both Black and white Southerners, the Civil War experience of military service—with its hierarchy, discipline, and constant violence—reinforced the habitual ordering of Southern society into Big Men and Little Men.

Among Black Southerners, the war and military service intensified and legitimized a very Southern ideal of violently defended honor and autonomy. As the late Clyde Woods showed, the Blues captured this sensibility when it emerged from the social rubble of the postwar South.[76] By the end of the war, the Union Army was about 20 percent African American, and in military service African Americans—like white Americans—experienced a reanimation of tropes that made up the planter's cosmology of honor, rank, autonomy, and property. Emancipation also rearticulated and re-energized these old Southern themes. But with the *de jure* hierarchy of slavery gone, Southern racism was, in Cash's view, renovated and relaunched by a wave of elite-led terror. (Decades after Cash, C. Vann Woodward would tell a similar story in *The Strange Career of Jim Crow*.)[77] In Cash's history, Southern elites did not merely ride the bloodlusting cracker mass, but stoked and guided it; all the while using the spectacle of mounting terror to discipline and divide both the Black and white elements of the working class. Sentimentality, nostalgia, rape-fixated negrophobia, resentment of the Yankee overlords (a largely mythical stand-in for local capitalists); all of this was ginned up to maintain the class hierarchy. Those who were "more set in the custom of command" led the process.[78]

The economy, however, was in ruins. While the war liberated almost four million people from slavery[79] and drove a massive process of economic growth and modernization in the North, the conflict was utterly catastrophic for the Southern economy. Eric Foner offered the tally in his classic *Reconstruction: America's Unfinished Revolution, 1863–1877*. "Thirty-seven thousand blacks," wrote Foner, "the great majority from the South, perished in the Union Army, as did tens of thousands more in contraband camps, on Confederate Army labor gangs, and in disease-ridden urban shantytowns. Nearly 260,000 men died for the Confederacy—over one fifth of the South's adult white male population.... Mississippi expended 20 percent of its revenue in 1865 on artificial limbs for Confederate veterans."[80]

With defeat, vast fortunes in the form of Confederate bonds and currency became worthless. Wealthy planters, banks, railroads, colleges, churches, and local and state governments were wiped out. Agriculture suffered too: "Between 1860 and 1870, while farm output expanded in the rest of the nation, the South experienced precipitous declines in the value of farm land and the amount of acreage under cultivation. The number of horses fell by 29 percent, swine by 35 percent, and farm values by half.... For the South as a whole, the real value of all property, even discounting that represented by slaves, stood 30 percent lower than its prewar figure."[81]

Economic revival meant a return to cotton and tobacco, but now with the addition of expensive modern fertilizer. Farmers thus needed credit, but the war had destroyed Southern banking. As Ransom and Sutch explained, and the History of Capitalism literature has elaborated, the antebellum Southern banking system was not "backward." The South had some very large banks of its own, and several of the largest European banks had operations in the South. The antebellum South also had some complex credit and insurance schemes built on the collateral of enslaved people.[82] But after the war, all that was wiped out.

Merchants stepped into the void of the collapsed Southern credit system using the crop-lien system and other forms of sharecropping, in which farmers borrowed directly from merchants and landowners. As cotton output soared, prices dropped. Both Black and white tenant farmers and independent sharecroppers sank further into destitution.[83]

"The business system prevailing with such hurtful and dangerous tendencies in the Southern States," wrote Charles H. Otken in 1894, "is enslaving the people, and, by its insidious operations, concentrating productive wealth in the hands of the few. It reduces a large body of people to a state of beggary, fosters a discontented spirit, checks consumption, produces recklessness on the part of the consumer, places a discount on honesty, and converts commerce into a vast pawning shop where farmers pledge their lands for hominy and bacon upon ruinous terms in harmony with the pawning system."[84] All of this put extreme stress on the land, accelerating erosion and depleting the soil. The soil crisis, in turn, drove up input costs, which led to further consolidation of land holdings.

The other path to economic recovery was industrialization. But here too, the region faced an uphill struggle. In "the record crop year of 1860," writes James C. Cobb, "the South contributed less than 7 percent of the value of the nation's manufactured cotton goods."[85] The total manufacturing output of all Southern states in that same year "was less than that of either Pennsylvania, Massachusetts, or New York."[86]

Labor-intensive, extractive, and processing operations defined the South's early steps into industrialization. By the late nineteenth century, textile, tobacco, lumber, and other industries began to grow. In a pattern "typical of an underdeveloped economy . . . cheap labor and abundant raw materials" led the way, with processing and transport clustering near the resources.[87] Cotton processing developed in the Piedmont above the croplands; Georgia had fifty-three cotton mills by 1890. Petroleum and sulfur refining arose in Texas and Louisiana. Appalachia produced the coal. The pine barrens stretching across the lower South produced turpentine and about one-third of the nation's raw timber by 1900. Fertilizer production arose in South Carolina not far from major phosphate deposits. The Red Mountain Formation, a long ridge of rust-colored rock faces holding seams of red hematite iron ore, were mined by the Sloss Mines; this drew in railroads and leased convict labor, all of which launched Birmingham and its iron industry in Alabama.[88] Each of these commodity chains produced more sudden new fortunes. Capital that was reinvested in local credit networks further proletarianized both white and Black commoners.

With industrialization came robust, usually violent, but too often hopelessly futile working-class resistance. In this struggle, Cash saw something noble yet absurd, something particularly Southern. His original 1929 article "Mind of the South"—referring to white Southerners—resorted to appallingly orientalist language:

> Another excellent reason, then, for the failure of Southern strikes is the impossibility of holding in organization the individualized yokel mind. The peon, to be sure, will join the union, but that is only because he is a romantic loon. He will join anything, be it a passing circus, a lynching-bee, or the Church of Latter Day Saints. He will even join the Bolsheviks (as at Gastonia, where the strikers were organized by the National Textile Workers' Union), though he is congenitally incapable of comprehending the basic notion of communism. The labor-organizers, with their sniffling pictures of his dismal estate, furnish him with a Cause for which he can strut and pose and, generally, be a magnificent

galoot. And the prospect of striking invokes visions of Hell popping, the militia, parades, fist-fights and boozy harangues—just such a Roman holiday as he dotes on. By all means, he'll join the union![89]

"How this characteristic reacts with industrialism is strikingly shown by the case of the cotton-mill strikes in the Carolinas," wrote Cash in 1929. "Of the dozen-odd strikes which flared up a few months ago, not one now remains. All failed."[90]

While violence had occurred at many of these strikes, Cash saw the Southern political imagination as the real key:

> The native baron simply closes his mill and sits back to wait for nature to take its course. He understands, that is, that the strikes may be trusted to go to pieces in the mind of the striker himself. That mind is, in every essential respect, merely the ancient mind of the South. It is distinctly of the soil. . . . There again, it strikes back to the Old South, to the soil. The South is the historic champion of States' Rights. It holds Locke's 'indefeasibility of private rights' as axiomatic. Its economic philosophy is that of Adam Smith, recognizing no limitations on the pursuit of self-interest by the individual, and counting unbridled private enterprise as not only the natural order but also the source of all public good. *Laissez-faire* is its watchword.[91]

Class Power as Southern Gothic

This planter mindset, this ideology born of a specific political ecology of slavery and export staples, took form as policy when Southern elites "set in the custom of command" inhabited political office. Recall Rutledge's threats at the Convention and Macon's willingness to forgo federally funded canals for fear of loosening master-class control of the workforce. From the Constitution's three-fifths clause onward, Southern elites enjoyed disproportionate amounts of power in the national government. Through its disenfranchisement of African Americans—by way of the Constitution's three-fifths clause, then by the poll tax and Klan terror—the Southern political class fought less competitive elections than most other American politicians. This translated into greater political longevity for elected politicians, which meant seniority within the committee structures of the US House and Senate, and seniority allowed Southerners to control committees and appointments. The great muckraker Stetson Kennedy summarized the process: "there had been no truly free elections in the South for generations, thanks to such institutionalized frauds as the poll tax and white primary, which kept masses of people—white and black—from voting. Thus the small manipulated electorate was able to send back, term after term, the same old racist, feudalist, reactionary demagogues to House and Senate, where, by virtue of seniority, they controlled key committees and literally 'ruled the roost.'"[92]

The capitalist elites of the New South used this power to direct their zero-tolerance-style hostility toward any form of progress that might empower labor and raise wages. Open commitment to being a low-wage region was the norm. During the New Deal, this meant that elite Southern extremism blocked and modified laws that threatened the role of the South as the land of poor and politically weak workers. Most infamously, Southern Dixiecrats helped exclude farmworkers and domestic labor from coverage under the Fair Labor Standards Act. As the political scientist Marian D. Irish correctly noted, Roosevelt had both "his staunchest supporters and his strongest opponents within the ranks of his own party south of the Mason-Dixon line."[93]

Southern political elites, displaying the worldview of landlordism even when they were industrialists, went as far as blocking publicly supported industrial development efforts for fear of empowering the working class. Thus, in Georgia, Governor Eugene Talmadge "vetoed an appropriation bill passed by the state legislature to match funds donated by the chemical foundation to build a promising experimental pulp mill that could create jobs and a lucrative pulp and paper industry in the state."[94]

In New Deal Georgia, wealthy landowners passed state laws making it illegal for cities and towns to offer "subsidies to attract outside business." So complete was their commitment to dominating labor that, like Macon before them, they would oppose capitalist developmentalism for fear of rising wages! Business groups, particularly the Southern States Industrial Council, fought the New Deal on all fronts, even opposing the Tennessee Valley Authority, "which offered cheap electricity to consumers and possibly an incentive to industry looking for plant locations in the region." Reactionary elites committed to maintaining the low wages of the South "included not just planters but lumber and sawmill operators, textile mill owners, and other employers."[95]

MAXIMALIST ELITES AND THE ECOLOGICAL BURDEN

With the New Deal completed, the Southern elite pushback focused on "right to work" legislation that allowed workers to receive union benefits without joining or paying union dues. The first states to pass such laws were Arkansas and Florida in 1944. In both campaigns, the "right to work" champions such as the business-supported Christian American Association stoked racist fears. Texas followed a year later, and eleven more states passed similar legislation before Section 14(b) of the 1947 Taft-Hartley Act legally sanctioned a state's right to undermine organized labor in this fashion.[96]

Today, the Southern elites' zero-tolerance, maximalist quest to dominate labor is alive and well. As then Governor Nikki Haley put in 2014: "We discourage any companies that have unions from wanting to come to South Carolina because we don't want to taint the water."[97] Even when employers do not at first oppose unionization, as was the case with Volkswagen, the Southern political class has led the charge against worker organizing. During the 2014 unionization drive at Volkswagen's plant in Chattanooga—"the only VW factory worldwide to have no formal mechanism for representing workers' interests"—Tennessee governor Bill Haslam intervened uninvited. He offered Volkswagen $300 million in state subsidies if the company would expand production in Tennessee, but made the subsidies "subject to works council discussions . . . being concluded to the satisfaction of the State of Tennessee." Meaning: the money was available only if the unionization effort was defeated. Bob Corker, the US senator from Tennessee, also got involved and falsely claimed on the eve of the union vote that Volkswagen managers had told him they would allocate more work to Chattanooga "only if workers rejected a union."[98]

The missing piece of the liberal Southern Gothic is the region's vicious and fantasy-prone ruling class. Many writers have noted how a Southern "sense of place" is conditioned by the apocalyptic worldview of Southern religion. The dominant strains of Southern Protestant fundamentalism have a social critique (this world is corrupt and evil, stalked by Satanic forces), but the religious solution is the apocalypse, the rapture, the end of this world. Based on this sensibility, literary scholar Anthony Dyer Hoefer has suggested that "the South, in its most frequent manifestations, is brought to life out of the fear of its own inevitable disappearance."[99] Southern political ecology—the socioeconomic system's interaction with the environment, the low population density, the harsh labor regimes, and the continual exhaustion of resources on one commodity frontier after another—helped produce a violently intolerant elite jealous of its prerogatives. As a vanguard element of the New Right, the Southern political class has been instrumental in pushing this not-so-peculiar class agenda onto more and more of the nation as a whole.

The postbellum reunion of the Southern elite's apocalyptic ruthlessness with the instrumental rationality of their Yankee brothers—the shippers, financiers, and industrialists—translated into a globalizing logic of domination, disregard for long-term outcomes; and, in the age of neoliberal hegemony, a campaign of enforced underdevelopment of economies of the Global South. This is America, at home and abroad. Thus, to some extent, we all belong to the South.

Endnotes

1 "From Thomas Jefferson to Chastellux, with Enclosure, 2 September 1785," *Founders Online,* National Archives, http://founders.archives.gov/documents/Jefferson/01-08-02-0362. [Original source: *The Papers of Thomas Jefferson, vol. 8, 25 February–31 October 1785,* ed. Julian P. Boyd. Princeton, NJ: Princeton University Press, 1953, 467–70.] Having been in France for already a year, perhaps Jefferson was homesick and thus prone to nostalgic self-Orientalizing—something Southerners are known to do. It is tempting to assert that Jefferson's depiction of Southerners referred only to white Southerners, but that is not at all clear. While clearly a racist, the patriarch of Monticello lived much of his life as the head of an isolated African American community, cohabitating with an African American woman who gave birth to Jefferson's children, some of whom passed as white and some of whom lived as black. For an intimate and complicated portrait of Jefferson's relationship to race, see the fantastic Annette Gordon-Reed, *The Hemingses of Monticello: An American Family* (New York: W. W. Norton & Company, 2009).
2 "From Thomas Jefferson to Chastellux." Jefferson presented his collection of regional traits in a vertically arranged comparative list. I have adjusted the format for readability.
3 *Webster's Dictionary*, online.
4 Andre Gunder Frank, *The Development of Underdevelopment* (New York: Monthly Review Press, 1966).
5 Walter Rodney, *How Europe Underdeveloped Africa* (New York: Verso, 2018), 16.
6 Christopher Morris, "A More Southern Environmental History," *The Journal of Southern History* 75, no. 3 (August 2009): 582.
7 See "Percentage of People in Poverty by State Using 2- and 3-Year Averages: 2013–2014 and 2015–2016." For a clearer display of states ranked by poverty rate, see "Interrelationships of 3-Year Average State Poverty Rates: 2014–2016." Both can be found at https://www.census.gov/library/publications/2017/demo/p60-259.html.
8 See *Governing* magazine's ranking of states by wages as calculated by the Bureau of Labor Statistics. Of the seventeen states with the lowest wages, fourteen are Southern and the other three are Western. Only Virginia has median wages above the national average and that is thanks in large part to Northern Virginia's wealthy suburbs, which are part of the high-wage Washington DC Metro area. "Median Wages by State," *Governing*, May 2016, http://www.governing.com/gov-data/wage-average-median-pay-data-for-states.html.
9 Regina S. Baker, "Poverty and Place in the Context of the American South" (PhD diss., Duke University, 2015), 1–3. The South, as defined by the US Census, is made up of the states of the old Confederacy, plus Delaware, Maryland, West Virginia, Kentucky, Missouri, and Oklahoma, which, during the Civil War, was one territory.

MAXIMALIST ELITES AND THE ECOLOGICAL BURDEN

10 For details on regional comparisons, see David H. Fisher, *Albion's Seed: For British Folkways in America* (New York: Oxford University Press, 1989), 374.
11 *James Madison—His Notes on the Constitutional Debates of 1787, vol. 2 of 2* (Create Space Independent Publishing Platform, 2014), 232.
12 Quoted in Daniel Walker Howe, *What Hath God Wrought: The Transformation of America, 1815–1848* (New York: Oxford University Press, 2009), 221.
13 Macon to Bartlett Yancey, April 15, 1818, Battle, "Letters of Nathaniel Macon," II, 47. See Noble E. Cunningham, Jr., "Nathaniel Macon and the Southern Protest against National Consolidation," *The North Carolina Historical Review* 32, no. 3 (July, 1955): 376–84. On Southern inequality, see Rudolf Heberle, "The Changing Social Stratification of the South," *Social Forces* 38, no. 1 (Oct., 1959): 42–50.
14 Mike Davis, *Prisoners of the American Dream: Politics and Economy in the History of the U.S. Working Class* (London: Verso, 1986). Mike Davis has not written much, or really anything at all, about the US South, yet most of his writing is infused with something Southern in both subject matter and form, that is to say, sinister, apocalyptic, yet also luscious. Davis's natal terrain, Southern California, is profoundly influenced by the South and, as part of the Sun Belt, remains very much bound up with Southern patterns of development and politics. Starting in the 1890s, cotton cultivation was extended to California's Central Valley by old Southern families like the Boswells. Then, the Depression and Dust Bowl pushed hundreds of thousands of Southern Oakies to California. Immediately afterward, industrial mobilization for the Second World War recruited hundreds of thousands of African Americans, mostly from Louisiana and East Texas, to work in the factories, mills, and shipyards of Democracy's Arsenal.
15 Angie Maxwell makes this point in her excellent introduction to: Angie Maxwell and Todd Shields, *The Ongoing Burden of Southern History: Politics and Identity in the Twenty-First-Century South* (Baton Rouge: Louisiana State University Press, 2012), xii.
16 C. Vann Woodward, *The Burden of Southern History* (Baton Rouge: Louisiana State University Press, 1993), 190.
17 The first to make this point was Otis L. Graham, "Again the Backward Region? Environmental History in and of the American South," *Southern Cultures* 6, no. 2 (Summer 2000): 50–72; a decade later, Christopher Morris followed up on these points and found the field still underdeveloped. "If there is an emerging environmental history of the South, it is not yet integrated into the general field of Southern history. And Southern history is not yet integrated into U.S. environmental history." See Morris, "A More Southern Environmental History," 582.
18 For the classic Southern construction of race, see Thomas Jefferson, *Notes on the State of Virginia, 1853* (Richmond, VA: J. W. Randolph, 1853), 150. Fredrick L. Olmsted wrote the following: "And as to the more common and popular opinion, that the necessary labour of cotton tillage is too severe for white men in the cotton-growing climate, I repeat that I do not find the slightest weight of fact to sustain it. The necessary labour and causes of fatigue and vital exhaustion attending any part, or all, of the process of cotton culture does not compare with that of our July harvesting; it is not greater than attends the cultivation of Indian corn in the usual New England method." See Fredrick L. Olmsted, *Journeys and Explorations in the Cotton Kingdom: A Traveler's Observations on Cotton and Slavery in the American Slave States. Based Upon Three Former Volumes of Journeys and Investigations by the same author* (London: Sampson Low, Son & Co., 1862), 265.
19 U. B. Phillips, *Life and Labor in the Old South* (Boston: Little Brown and Company, 1929), 3.
20 U. B. Phillips, *American Negro Slavery: A Survey of the Supply, Employment and Control of Negro Labor as Determined by the Plantation Regime* (New York: D. Appleton and Company, 1929), 309.
21 See, for instance, Raymond Arsenault, "The End of the Long Hot Summer: The Air Conditioner and Southern Culture," *The Journal of Southern History* 50, no. 4 (1984): 597–628; Morris, "A More Southern Environmental History," 581; Graham, "Again the Backward Region?"

22 Woodward, *Burden of Southern History*, xii–xiii.
23 Gavin Wright, *Slavery and American Economic Development* (Baton Rouge: Louisiana State University Press, 2013), 49. More specifically, Wright reports: "At the time of the Revolution, total and per capita wealth levels of the slave colonies were far greater than those of their protofree counterparts" (17). "If we exclude the value of human property—slaves—the two regions, prior to the Revolution, had similar measures of economic development... Measured by nonhuman wealth per capita (real estate, livestock, and equipment and inventories of producers' and consumers' goods), the two regions were within 5 percent of each other: 38.4 pounds sterling for the North versus 36.4 pounds sterling in the South" (57). Russell Menard put it this way: "In 1775, there was no 'South' with a single, integrated economy, a unifying culture, or a cohesive ruling class with a shared vision of the future. We are best served by recognizing diversity from the start and rejecting the notion of a 'South' in favor of a concept of 'Souths,' four proximate but separate regions with distinctive characteristics: the tobacco colonies around Chesapeake Bay; the rice and indigo districts of the Carolina-Georgia lowcountry; an area of mixed farming or "common husbandry" in the backcountry and around the periphery of the plantation districts; and a frontier zone dominated by cross-cultural trade. However, if the South was not yet a region, the factors that would give it greater unity and define its character during the early nineteenth century were firmly in place: an expansive plantation agriculture, African slavery, and an emerging planter class with a sense of purpose." Russell Menard, "economic and social development of the south," in Stanley L. Engerman, Robert E. Gallman (Ed.s), The Cambridge Economic History of the United States, Volume 1, (Cambridge, UK: Cambridge University Press, 1996), 249–297: 249.
24 James Oakes, *Slavery and Freedom: An Interpretation of the Old South* (New York: Alfred A Knopf, 1990), 37.
25 Charles Post, *The American Road to Capitalism: Studies in Class-Structure, Economic Development and Political Conflict, 1620–1877* (New York: Haymarket Books, 2012), 3.
26 Gordon S. Wood, *The Radicalism of the American Revolution* (New York: Knopf Doubleday, 2011), 248.
27 W. W. Rostow, "The Stages of Economic Growth," *The Economic History Review* 12, no. 1 (1959): 1–16; also see Lawrence A. Peskin. *Manufacturing Revolution: The Intellectual Origins of Early American Industry* (Baltimore: The Johns Hopkins University Press, Baltimore, 2003).
28 Charles Post, *The American Road to Capitalism: Studies in Class-Structure, Economic Development and Political Conflict, 1620–1877* (New York: Haymarket Books, 2012), 3.
29 Post, *American Road to Capitalism*, 83.
30 David B. Davis, "The Significance of Excluding Slavery from the Old Northwest in 1787," *Indiana Magazine of History* 84, no. 1 (March 1988): 75–89.
31 Payson J. Treat, "Land System Under the Confederation," in *The Public Lands: Studies in The History of the Public Domain*, ed. Vernon Carstensen (Madison: University of Wisconsin Press: 1962), 9.
32 Paul Gates, *History of Public Land Law Development* (Washington, DC: US Government Printing Office, 1968), 1.
33 As late as the 1830s and 1840s, "New Englanders tended to emigrate to Illinois and Michigan in groups, after careful planning and under the leadership of a Congregational minister." See Gates, *History of Public Land Law Development*, 69.
34 Brian Donahue, *The Great Meadow: Farmers and the Land in Colonial Concord* (New Haven, CT: Yale University Press, 2004); Brian Donahue, "Environmental Stewardship and Decline in Old New England," *Journal of the Early Republic* 24, no. 2 (2004): 234–41; John L. Larson and Michael A. Morrison, *Whither the Early Republic A Forum on the Future of the Field* (Philadelphia: University of Pennsylvania Press, 2012); Richard W. Judd, "The Ecologies of Frontier Farming," in *Second Nature: An Environmental History of New England* (Amherst: University of Massachusetts Press, 2014), 69–94.
35 William Cronnon, *Changes in the Land: Indians, Colonists, and the Ecology of New England* (New York: Hill & Wang, 1983), 150–51.

36 H. Bruce Franklin, *The Most Important Fish in the Sea: Menhaden and America* (Island Press: Washington, 2008), 52.
37 Payson J. Treat, "Origin of the National Land System Under the Confederation," in *Annual Report of the American Historical Association, Volume 1* (Washington, DC: Government Printing Office, 1906), 235–36.
38 Treat, "Origin of the National Land System."
39 David R. Montgomery, *Dirt: The Erosion of Civilizations* (Berkeley: University of California Press, 2007), 119. Walter Johnson, *River of Dark Dreams: Slavery and Empire in the Cotton Kingdom* (Cambridge, MA: Harvard University Press, 2013), 180–85. Also see Johnson for a good discussion of soil exhaustion, manuring, and what planters knew about both. Robin Blackburn, disagreeing with Karl Marx and David Montgomery, takes issue with any significant environmental causality to Southern expansion. He asserts that "the planters could have made better use of fertilizers as they did in Cuba." Some of them— like Jefferson and Washington—did, while others remained genuinely ignorant of how to do so. The breakthrough in soil chemistry did not happen until the mid-nineteenth century. See Robin Blackburn, *An Unfinished Revolution: Karl Marx and Abraham Lincoln* (New York: Verso, 2011), 10. Surprisingly, Baptist does not mention soil depletion in the Chesapeake as a push factor, which—along with the pull factor of new land and a cotton boom in the old South West—drove the internal slave trade. See Edward Baptist, *The Half Has Never Been Told: Slavery and the Making of American Capitalism* (New York: Basic Books, 2014).
40 John Majewski, *Modernizing a Slave Economy: the Economic Vision of the Confederate Nation* (Chapel Hill: University of North Carolina Press, 2009), 16–17.
41 Majewski, *Modernizing a Slave Economy*.
42 Avery O. Craven, *Soil Exhaustion as a Factor in the Agricultural History of Virginia and Maryland, 1606–1860* (1925; repr., Columbia, SC: University of South Carolina Press, 2006), 20–21.
43 Craven, *Soil Exhaustion*, 39.
44 Craven, *Soil Exhaustion*, 38–39.
45 Craven, *Soil Exhaustion*, 30. The full paragraph is: "Tobacco alone seems capable of lifting the colonists quickly from the severe conditions of frontier life into the comforts of former days. The European demand for this plant was rapidly increasing and the Spanish supply was far from keeping pace with the growing demand. Prices were so high that in the early days a man's labor in tobacco production yielded him six times as large return as might be secured from any other crop."
46 Gates, *History of Public Land Law Development*, 42.
47 Treat, "Land System Under the Confederation," 9.
48 Gates, *History of Public Land Law Development*, 42, 53.
49 Gates, *History of Public Land Law Development*, 57.
50 I thank Jim Oakes for bringing this fact to my attention. In his own short campaign autobiography of 1860 (it is actually presented in the third person as a biography), Abraham Lincoln describes trouble regarding land title as part of what drove his father from Kentucky. "At this time his father resided on Knob Creek," reads the text. "From this place he removed to what is now Spencer County, Indiana, in the autumn of 1816, Abraham then being in his eighth year. This removal was partly on account of slavery, but chiefly on account of the difficulty in land titles in Kentucky. He settled in an unbroken forest, and the clearing away of surplus wood was the great task ahead." Abraham Lincoln Online.org, http://www.abrahamlincolnonline.org/lincoln/speeches/autobiog.htm. Interestingly, the plaintiffs trying to eject Thomas Lincoln were Yankees. The "suit for ejectment" against Lincoln "shows that the Knob Creek farm was part of a tract of ten thousand acres surveyed in 1784, and patented in 1786 by Thomas Middleton, father of the Hannah Rhoades who was one of the parties to the suit. She lived in Philadelphia, as did Abraham Sheridan, Inn Keeper, another plaintiff." See William E. Barton, *The Paternity of Abraham Lincoln; Was He the Son of Thomas Lincoln? An Essay on the Chastity of Nancy Hanks* (New York: George H. Doran Company, 1920), 262–63.

51 Gates, *History of Public Land Law Development*, 53. The destructive individualism and short-term thinking of Southern elites is one of the defining features of that region's identity and culture. It played out as an almost suicidal propensity towards dueling, a poorly thought-out war of secession, and a Confederate government so disorganized and committed to states' rights that even procuring slave labor to build defenses was often difficult because planters resisted. Meanwhile, Confederate generals on numerous occasions stole arms shipments meant for their comrades elsewhere. When Union forces invaded the Mississippi Valley, the Confederate government ordered planters to destroy their cotton. Many refused to comply, however, preferring to smuggle cotton to the Yankees. Among these renegades was Jefferson Davis's own brother, who was caught hoarding two hundred bales in a swamp. See Bruce Levine, *The Fall of the House of Dixie: The Civil War and the Social Revolution That Transformed the South* (New York: Random House, 2013), 80.
52 Gates, *History of Public Land Law Development*, 54.
53 Wilma A. Dunaway, *The First American Frontier: Transition to Capitalism in Southern Appalachia, 1700–1860* (Chapel Hill: University of North Caroline Press, 1996), 56, Table 3.1, 57.
54 The first successful European colony there had been the democratic and autonomous settlements on the navigationally inhospitable Albemarle Sound. Established slowly over the second half of the seventeenth century by Quakers and a steady trickle of renegade runaway servants and slaves from despotic Virginia, these communities even maintained friendly relations with the Iroquoian language-speaking Tuscarora. The autonomy and democracy of Albemarle was largely ended in the early eighteenth century by the arrival of a Royal Governor and was finally exterminated in the Tuscarora War of 1712. For more on this, see Noeleen McIlvenna, *A Very Mutinous People: The Struggle for North Carolina, 1660–1713* (Chapel Hill: University of North Carolina Press, 2009). On the war, see David La Vere, *The Tuscarora War: Indians, Settlers, and the Fight for the Carolina Colonies* (Chapel Hill: University of North Carolina Press, 2013).
55 Dunaway, *First American Frontier*, 57.
56 Clyde Woods, *Development Arrested: The Blues Plantation Power in the Mississippi Delta* (1998; repr., New York: Verso, 2017), 47.
57 Dunaway, *First American Frontier*, 66. Mainstream economics recognizes the retarding effects of land speculation; see, for example, Fred E. Foldvary "Market-Hampering Land Speculation: Fiscal and Monetary Origins and Remedies," *American Journal Of Economics & Sociology* 57, no. 4 (1998): 615–37.
58 Majewski, *Modernizing a Slave Economy*, 36, 165.
59 Abraham H. Gibson, "Born To Be Feral: An Evolutionary History of Domestic Animals in the American South" (PhD diss., Florida State University, 2013), 75.
60 Post, *American Road to Capitalism*, 147–48.
61 Gibson, "Born To Be Feral," 114.
62 J. Crawford King, "The Closing of the Southern Range: An Exploratory Study," *Journal of Southern History* 48, no. 1 (February 1982): 54.
63 King, "Closing of the Southern Range," 54.
64 Carville Earle, "Why Tobacco Stunted the Growth of Towns and Wheat Built Them into Small Cities: Urbanization South of the Mason Dixon Line, 1650–1790," in *Geographical Inquiry and American Historical Problems* (Stanford, CA: Stanford University Press, 1992), 88–152.
65 James Oakes, *Slavery and Freedom: An Interpretation of the Old South* (New York: Alfred A Knopf, 1990).
66 On the discomfort with Cash's assault on the Southern elite, see for example Louis D. Rubin ,"W.J. Cash After Fifty Years," *Virginia Quarterly Review*, Spring 1991, https://www.vqronline.org/essay/wj-cash-after-fifty-years; C. Vann Woodward, "W.J. Cash Reconsidered," *New York Review of Books*, December 4, 1969, https://www.nybooks.com/articles/1969/12/04/wj-cash-reconsidered/.

67 Cash only mentions Du Bois once, and then only on page 315, but it is hard to imagine that Cash had not at least familiarized himself with the arguments in *Black Reconstruction*. W. E. B. Du Bois, *Black Reconstruction in America, 1860–1880* (1935; repr., New York: Free Press, 1998).
68 W.J. Cash, "The Mind of the South," *American Mercury* 18, no. 70 (October 1929): 185.
69 Years later, Allan Kulikoff's *Tobacco and Slaves* confirmed with deep archival documentation what Cash had merely asserted. "Though many Gentleman emigrated with the first settlers, some died in the Indian attack of 1622, and others left when they discover the difficulties of carving plantations out of forests. Since other English gentleman refused to migrate to either colony, hierarchal leadership was missing. Furthermore, planters lived scattered along the banks of rivers and streams rather than in villages where the few remaining gentleman could police their behavior. Ordinary small planters, who owned a freehold of several hundred acres and perhaps an indentured servant, filled the vacuum left by the gentlemen and came to dominate the region's population and politics." Allan Kulikoff, *Tobacco and Slaves: Development of Southern Cultures in the Chesapeake, 1680–1800* (Chapel Hill: University of North Carolina Press, 1986), 31.
70 W. J. Cash, *The Mind of the South* (1941; repr., New York: Random Books, 1991), 21.
71 Cash, *Mind of the South*, 34–35. Cash was prone to a uniquely Southern style of self-Orientalizing. "It is not without a certain aptness, then, that the Southerner's chosen drink is called moonshine. Everywhere he turns away from reality to a gaudy world of his own making.... In his own eyes, he is eternally a noble and heroic fellow. He has always displayed a passion for going to war. He pants after Causes and ravening monsters.... The lyncher, in his own sight, is ... magnificently hurling down the glove on behalf of embattled Chastity." Rather than merely condemning racist terror—an all-important but not very difficult task—Cash sought to explain racism as useful for class rule. (Modern anti-racist academics would find his argument crassly instrumentalist and perhaps even too forgiving of the rank-and-file poor whites.) In his telling, Southern Racism was, after Reconstruction, renovated and relaunched by a wave of elite-led terror articulating a newly refined, more virulent form of White supremacy. It was the same story C. Vann Woodward would later tell in *The Strange Career of Jim Crow*—the New South's epidemic of White supremacist terror and the development of *de jure* segregation that rode with it were not the result of folk mores but were rather a strategy of elite class rule.
72 Cash, *Mind of the South*, 32–33.
73 Cash, *Mind of the South*, 33. For a detailed view on this question, see Stephanie McCurry, *Masters of Small Worlds: Yeoman Households, Gender Relations, and the Political Culture of the Antebellum South Carolina Low Country* (New York: Oxford University Press, 1995).
74 Sally E. Haden, *Slave Patrols: Law and Violence in Virginia and the Carolinas* (Cambridge, MA: Harvard University Press, 2003).
75 Cash, *Mind of the South*, 43.
76 Woods, *Development Arrested*.
77 C. Vann Woodward, *The Strange Career of Jim Crow*, 3d rev. ed. (New York: Oxford University Press, 1974).
78 Cash, *Mind of the South*, 111. The postwar reign of terror was not, of course, pulled from thin air. As Cash notes, the rural South of the up-country yeoman farmers had been a "world of ineffective social control, [where] the tradition of vigilante action, which normally lives and dies with the frontier, not only survived but grew so steadily that already long before the Civil War and long before hatred for the black man had begun to play any direct part in the pattern (of more than three hundred persons said to have been hanged or burned by mobs between 1840 and 1860, less than ten per cent were Negroes) the South had become peculiarly the home of lynching."
79 The 1860 census listed the total population at 31,183,582. Of that, 3,950,528, or 13 percent of Americans, were enslaved. These people were owned by a different 8 percent of the population, or 393,975 individuals.
80 Eric Foner, *Reconstruction: America's Unfinished Revolution, 1863–1877* (1988; repr. New York: Harper Perennial, 2014), 125.

81 Foner, *Reconstruction*, 125.
82 Roger L. Ransom and Richard Sutch, "Debt Peonage in the Cotton South After the Civil War," *The Journal of Economic History* 32, no. 3 (September 1972): 641–69. Also see many of the essays in Sven Beckert and Seth Rockman, eds., *Slavery's Capitalism: A New History of American Economic Development* (Philadelphia: University of Pennsylvania Press, 2016), particularly Bonnie Martin, "Neighbor-to-Neighbor Capitalism: Local Credit Networks and the Mortgaging of Slaves," (107–21); Joshua Rothman, "The Contours of Cotton Capitalism: Speculation, Slavery, and Economic Panic in Mississippi, 1832–1841" (122–45); and Kathy Boodry, "August Belmont and the World the Slaves Made," (163–78).
83 Carolyn Merchant offers this clear summary of the various forms of this indebted farming: "Sharecropping was a loose term for several farming methods. In sharecropping, someone else, such as the planter or absentee landlord, owned the land. Often the owner also supplied the tools, seed, farming equipment, mules, and even the food, in exchange for a percentage of the crop. In tenant farming, which was related to sharecropping, the tenant owned some of the equipment—for example, the mules and the tools—and rented the land in exchange for a portion of the crop. Tenant farming was a step up from pure sharecropping, in the sense that the tenant owned some equipment and tools and could take his capital with him. A third method was the crop lien system, in which the farmer owned the land but borrowed the seed, fertilizers, and perhaps the equipment. In each case, about a third or a quarter of the crop went back to the merchant or land-owner who also appropriated clients' assets for failure to repay loans." Carolyn Merchant, *The Columbia Guide to American Environmental History* (New York: Columbia University Press, 2002), 54.
84 Charles H. Otken, *The Ills of the South; or, Related Causes Hostile to the General Prosperity of the Southern People* (New York: G. P. Putnam's sons, 1894), 28.
85 James C. Cobb, *Industrialization and Southern Society, 1877–1984* (Lexington: University Press of Kentucky, 1987), 6.
86 Cobb, *Industrialization and Southern Society*, 7.
87 Cobb, *Industrialization and Southern Society*, 17.
88 Douglas A. Blackmon, *Slavery by Another Name: The Re-Enslavement of Black Americans from the Civil War to World War II* (2008; repr., New York: Anchor, 2009).
89 Cash, "Mind of the South," 188.
90 Cash, "Mind of the South," 187.
91 Cash, "Mind of the South," 187.
92 Stetson Kennedy, *Southern Exposure* (New York: Double Day, 1946), viii.
93 Quoted in Roger Biles, *The South and the New Deal* (Lexington: University Press of Kentucky, 1994), 125.
94 Ken Fones-Wolf and Elizabeth A. Fones-Wolf, *Struggle for the Soul of the Postwar South: White Evangelical Protestants and Operation Dixie* (Champaign: University of Illinois Press, 2015), 17.
95 V.O. Key, quoted in Fones-Wolf and Fones-Wolf, *Struggle for the Soul of the Postwar South*, 17–18.
96 Chris Kromm, "The Racist Roots of 'Right to Work' Laws," *Facing South*, December 13, 2012, https://www.facingsouth.org/2012/12/the-racist-roots-of-right-to-work-laws; David Jacob and Marc Dixon, "The Politics of Labor-Management Relations: Detecting the Conditions that Affect Changes in Right-to-Work Laws," *Social Problems* 53, no. 1 (February 2006): 118–37.
97 Quoted in Rudolph Bell, "South Carolina: Union Jobs Aren't Welcome Here," *USA Today*, February 20, 2014, https://eu.usatoday.com/story/money/cars/2014/02/20/no-south-carolina-union-jobs/5642031/.
98 Phil Williams, "Haslam Offers No Apologies for $300M Volkswagen Offer," *News Channel 5 Network*, April 1, 2014, last updated September 16, 2015, https://www.newschannel5.com/news/newschannel-5-investigates/tennessees-secret-deals/haslam-offers-no-apologies-for-300m-volkswagen-offer; Steve Cavendish, "Haslam on $300M VW Deal:

'We Had an Interest in the Outcome of That Vote,'" *Nashville Scene,* April 2, 2014, https://www.nashvillescene.com/news/article/13053294/haslam-on-300m-vw-deal-we-had-an-interest-in-the-outcome-of-that-vote; Robert Wright "Works Councils at VW 'Key' for Further US Work," *The Financial Times,* February 19, 2014, https://www.ft.com/con-tent/8a5ceed0-99a3-11e3-b3a2-00144feab7de.

99   Anthony D. Hoefer, *Apocalypse South: Judgment, Cataclysm, and Resistance in the Regional Imaginary* (Columbus: Ohio State University Press, 2012), 101.

AVIATION, HIJACKINGS, AND THE ECLIPSE OF THE "AMERICAN CENTURY" IN THE MIDDLE EAST

Waleed Hazbun

"Lower Manhattan was soon a furnace of crimson flames, from which there was no escape."[1] So begins the fiery preface of *Dead Cities*, the first post-9/11 collection of essays by Mike Davis. In this chilling scene from H.G. Wells's 1908 novel, *The War in the Air*, the imperial German fleet of zeppelins bombs New York City in a surprise attack. Further down the page, we read the novel's observation that "For many generations New York had taken no heed of war, save as a thing that happened far away, that affected prices and supplied the newspapers with exciting headlines and pictures."[2] Davis goes on to trace how the American response to the 9/11 attacks "has been societal exorcism in reverse" as fear unleashed a massive, costly drive to "secure" the homeland, with efforts ranging from the "terror-proofing" of downtown public spaces to Islamophobic hate crimes of assault.[3] These fears were not contained within America's increasingly hardened borders. In the run-up to the 2003 US invasion of Iraq, Michael Ignatieff wrote: "Terror has collapsed distance, and with this collapse has come a sharpened American focus on the necessity of bringing order to the frontier zones."[4] Americans in New York, Washington, DC, and elsewhere not only "took heed" of wars in the Middle East but came to view "ungoverned spaces" abroad as threats to the homeland. They feared that nonstate terrorist groups like al-Qaeda could use territories where central state authority was limited as sanctuaries to organize attacks against Americans at home and abroad. As the US launched wars in Afghanistan and Iraq as well as counterterrorism operations across the globe, the territorial extent of American fears about external threats became boundless. The *9/11 Commission Report* notes that "9/11 has taught us that terrorism against American interests 'over there' should be regarded just as we regard terrorism against America 'over here.' In this sense the American homeland is the planet."[5]

Fear, Davis argues, drove post-9/11 security politics at home and abroad. To explain how, he suggests: "The most interesting answer, at least in the Marxist tradition, comes from Ernst Bloch."[6] In his 1929 essay "The Anxiety of the Engineer," Bloch suggests that in precapitalist or "Southern" cities (such as Naples), people did not delude themselves into thinking they could have total command over nature. Rather, Davis explains, in such societies "anxiety does not infuse daily life," as they embrace "imperfect and carnivalesque improvisation that yields to the fluxes of the dynamic Mediterranean environment."[7] In contrast, Bloch suggests that in the culture and politics of Northern industrialized societies, "The city of ever-increasing artificiality" detached from nature is "so complex and so vulnerable that it is increasingly threatened by accidents."[8] Thus, Davis concludes, "the deepest structure of urban fear is not Wells's war in the air, but 'detachment and distance from the natural landscape'" and the inability to accommodate its undirected patterns and improvisations.[9]

As Mike Davis has shown in greatest detail concerning the city of Los Angeles, anxiety and fear generate a vicious circle in which urban planners, middle class communities, and corporate interests seek constant control over processes that operate in complex environments. As a result, events outside their control generate anxiety and motivate extraordinary, but self-defeating, efforts to reengineer systems in the quest for total command over nature, society, and capital. Scaling up this argument, Davis offers an answer as to why the 9/11 attacks unleashed a "global war on terror" seeking to bring order to America's planetary homeland and in the process made "[i]mperialism ... politically correct again."[10] As Davis puts it, "The globalization of fear thus becomes a self-fulfilling prophecy ... Terror has become the steroid of Empire."[11]

Such a process is not unique to post-9/11 America. Across his many studies, Davis explores its workings in the history of global imperialism and contemporary capitalist dynamics, always aware of the resistances it engenders.

AVIATION, HIJACKINGS, AND THE ECLIPSE

Inspired by *Buda's Wagon: A Brief History of the Car Bomb*, this essay offers a brief investigation into the global politics of airplane hijackings in the 1970s and 1980s within the context of the US-backed global expansion of postwar civilian aviation. This era, which I will argue marks the rise of "terrorism" as a strategic threat in American geopolitical thinking, represents a critical phase in America's engagement in the world that also exposed anxieties about the limits of America's seemingly hegemonic global power. In *Buda's Wagon*, Davis argues that the car bomb can be understood as "a semi-strategic weapon that under certain circumstances was comparative to airpower in its ability to knock out critical urban nodes and headquarters as well as terrorize populations of entire cities."[12]

Transposing his argument from urban spaces to the global post-1945 infrastructure of civilian air travel, I view the global politics of "aeromobility" through the lens of Bloch's "The Anxiety of the Engineer." Aeromobility refers to "the dominance of flying as the normal international mode of travelling."[13] Middle East historian Yoav Di-Capua notes, "More than the train, the car and the telephone, the airplane represented a superior mastery of how nature works. No other machine drew so impressively on [modern science] in order to defy the forces of nature and subdue them to the human will."[14] And in 1942, writing in the midst of the Second World War, Alexander De Seversky's *Victory Through Air Power* popularized the notion of the geopolitical primacy of air power and the strategic importance of "control of the skies."[15]

American wartime industrial and technological capacity, combined with endeavors to establish numerous landing fields abroad, set the stage for US postwar efforts to develop civil aviation and extend American aeromobility to cover the globe. This aeromobility enabled a network of international diplomacy, commerce, migration, and tourism and was essential to the growth of American global power. It was through aviation that the United States both visualized and realized its global interests and role during what Henry Luce would term "The American Century." In the 1950s and 1960s, US airlines—backed by government assistance—built a complex system of nodes and flows that extended across the Middle East. In the midst of Middle East regional turmoil and the rise of nationalist political movements seeking decolonization and territorial sovereignty, American private firms with government support helped establish Beirut as a critical regional hub for global aviation and for US multinational firms and intelligence networks, which also served growing US interests in the oil-rich Persian Gulf states.

While 9/11 led to a major disruption of US airspace and travel flows, the fragility of the US-centered global infrastructure of air travel was not first encountered on 9/11. In the early 1970s, the adoption of hijacking as a tactic by militant Palestinian and other self-described "revolutionaries" transformed the act of illegally diverting an aircraft into a new category of violent threat: international terrorism. Because of aeromobility's centrality to American global power, disruptions to any flights and threats to any American traveler abroad were viewed as challenges to the entire system of global aeromobility. As a result, US government efforts shifted from seeking to expand aeromobility as a distributed network to securing the spaces of its flows under American control.[16]

This securitization of air travel only increased American fears of vulnerability and led to an increasingly militarized effort to police global airspaces and travel flows far beyond its borders. As Luce had noted in 1941, in words that would be echoed by the *9/11 Commission Report*, "America is responsible, to herself as well as to history, for the world-environment in which she lives."[17] In this chapter, I suggest that the rise of airplane hijackings in the 1970s, followed by a series of more violent terrorist attacks against airplanes and air travelers in the 1980s, contributed to a late Cold War anxiety about the limits of American global power. It also heightened the fear of threats to the US's "vital interests" that the expansion of new forms of political violence—Middle East terrorism—posed. Echoing Bloch, I suggest that the global aviation system the US helped build in the early postwar era became "so complex and so vulnerable that it is increasingly threatened by accidents" and that fears of this vulnerability generated anxieties that drove increasing US efforts to project military power into the Middle East. Thus, a few acts of political violence in the early 1970s helped set in motion the dynamics at work in America's militarized response to 9/11.

America's "Empire of the Air"

Wells's *The War in the Air* foreshadowed that global politics in the twentieth century would be defined by air power and aeromobility. The transformative power of global aviation was not only experienced in its military forms. As

AVIATION, HIJACKINGS, AND THE ECLIPSE

Jenifer Van Vleck shows, the expansion of civil aviation played a central role in the development of American global power and in the way Americans visualize their global role.[18] Publisher Henry Luce helped popularize this vision in his highly influential essay "The American Century," originally published in the February 7, 1941, issue of *Life*.[19] The essay defines a grand responsibility for the US. Luce projects the US "to become the most powerful and vital nation in the world" and offers a vision of the world united under the umbrella of US hegemony.[20] He celebrates the ability of the US to go anywhere in the world with its ships and airplanes and argues that the country must serve as the guarantor of global mobility. In his view, this is needed to sustain open, free economies and political systems.

The aerial optic enabled a geopolitical imaginary that could envision the globe as one space; but throughout this space, the US was uniquely positioned to serve as a global hegemon, protecting the system against hostile challenges. As Van Vleck explains, air travel provided the material infrastructure and ideological vision to sustain a nonterritorial empire, or America's "Empire of the Air."[21] Across global space, American airlines and government policies worked together to define a global order based on global trade and communications without requiring the direct control of overseas territories.

In the early post-1945 era, international travel and tourism were at the leading edge of US-led efforts to establish and expand a liberal economic order. Efforts to reduce travel barriers and establish tourism networks—including airline routes, international hotels, and (eventually) other elements of tourist industries—in Europe and across the Middle East were critical to efforts to incorporate these regions into this US-centered order.

Aviation and air travel held the potential to radically transform the global political economy. Americans could embrace these changes with the confidence that American technology, private firms, and regulatory regimes would dominate the rising global networks of mobility and commerce. Van Vleck notes that for Henry Luce's wife, Congresswoman Clare Boothe Luce, "the aerial gaze served to demarcate hierarchical distinctions between the United States and its dependencies."[22] In 1955, geopolitical strategist Robert Strausz-Hupé wrote: "The impact of aviation upon the entire economic, social, and political structure of civilization has shattered traditional concepts of space and time."[23] He suggested that global air travel "conveys to man a sense of the interdependence of people and the arbitrariness of political boundaries" but also noted that US airlines accounted for about two-thirds of all airline revenues. Global aviation would be a system that the US could use to dominate rivals (including its European allies) and extend its influence across the developing world while defining a new basis for a US-centered global order. "In the long run," Strausz-Hupé writes, "the most significant contribution of aviation to world commerce will be the opening up of hitherto inaccessible regions to continuous expansion of trade as regards to both markets and resources."[24]

The Middle East as the "Aerial Crossroad of the World"

For both American strategists and US airlines in the post–1945 era, the Middle East was a critical region to dominate from the air. American officials viewed the Middle East as a region of "strategic importance" due to the region's oil resources, US needs for military base rights, and its "strategic location . . . in terms of world shipping and air transport routes."[25] US airlines, more practically, needed to cross the Middle East to connect their European routes to Asia while avoiding Soviet-controlled Eastern European airspace. During the interwar era, American and European airlines had developed international routes serving their existing overseas territories and economic interests. While American airlines connected the US to Latin America, British-owned Imperial Airways dominated traffic across the Middle East, having built a vital air route to India. During the Second World War, however, the US military helped transform the aviation landscape of the region by supporting airport development across North Africa and the Middle East.[26] In 1945, aviation news magazine *Flight* reported that "[i]nterest in the establishment of air routes that eventually will circle the world centres on the Middle East region, which has been called that aerial crossroad of the world."[27] American airlines expected heavy tourist traffic from the US to "historic and cultural centres of the Middle East" and envisioned replacing British dominance in the region with their own.[28]

In 1940, Imperial Airways was merged with British Airways Ltd., which operated flights to continental Europe, to form BOAC (the British Overseas Airways Corporation). The British state-owned airline maintained a strong position in the Middle East into the 1950s. BOAC owned a majority share in and ran several of the smaller airlines in territories that had been or remained under British control, such as Gulf Aviation (based in Bahrain), Aden Airways, Kuwait Airways, and Arab Airways (based in Jerusalem).[29] The British saw the maintenance of commercial air service as critical to their postwar military and economic goals.

Seeking to maintain their imperial privileges and fearful of US dominance, the British challenged American efforts to liberalize international commercial aviation.[30] At the International Civil Aviation Conference in Chicago in 1944, the US proposed an "open skies" regime that would grant all carriers unhindered access to the airspace and airports of member states. As Jeffrey Engel observes: "Though American policymakers were zealous believers in the power of open skies to promote peaceful international relations, they also believed that those policies would ultimately lead to American dominance."[31] After Britain successfully opposed the open skies scheme, the US negotiated bilateral agreements for each state in which US air carriers sought to operate. Meanwhile, Britain worked to block early US efforts in the Middle East, reportedly telling American officials that they "[did] not want American airlines to operate in the Middle East."[32]

American officials, however, viewed the expansion of American aviation across the Middle East and support for regional airlines as vital for securing US military and intelligence advantages. American officials also considered aviation a useful tool for fostering a pro-American orientation on the part of regional governments at a time of rising Arab nationalism. They thus promoted an "aggressive policy" to advance US regional goals through aviation.[33] The US quickly came to challenge British dominance; not through seeking ownership or management of regional airlines but through bilateral agreements to give US flag carriers aviation rights and through encouraging US airlines to offer technical assistance to local airlines.

As Nathan Citino notes, Arab elites considered the development of aviation and aeromobility critical for their nations to become active agents in the process.[34] At the same time, Americans, in both government and the private sector, depicted efforts to incorporate the Middle East into America's "Empire of the Air" as driven by US strategic interests. US airlines and the United Nations program of technical aviation assistance, which was run though the International Civil Aviation Organization (ICAO), helped build the needed local aviation infrastructure. In 1954, the US sent a team of aviation experts to foster commercial airline development in the region. The chairman of Trans World Airlines (TWA) called the assistance program a "master stroke of geopolitics" but also "a step toward encouraging economic self-sufficiency."[35] Economist Hans Heymann Jr. of the RAND Corporation reported that in practice, however, US civil aeronautics aid policy "has been more toward enhancing the aviation contribution of the less developed countries to the international air links than it has toward aiming aviation at their own domestic development."[36] Heymann explains that "in order to make the long-haul international air routes profitable for U.S. carriers local airlines had to be created to feed 'fill-up traffic' into the intermediate stops en route."[37]

In the regional competition for control over Middle East aviation, BOAC was in a strong position in the late 1940s, while TWA seemed to be the leading US challenger, having secured aviation rights to Cairo, the regional transportation hub throughout the war and "the largest and most important base for TWA on its route from New York to the Far East" at the time.[38] TWA also established and ran the Saudi national airline, while its long-haul flights benefited from a stopover airfield in Dhahran built by the US army. TWA also had a contract to maintain the aircraft of Iranian Airways, in which it owned a 10 percent stake.[39]

In the 1950s, regional geopolitics shifted the aviation landscape in the Middle East. The region's key geopolitical players—Egypt, Syria, and Iraq—were led by "revolutionary" Arab Nationalist leaders, with state-owned airlines that maintained close ties to the military. For Egyptian president Gamal Abdel Nasser, the development of civil aviation was critical to national modernization plans, but these efforts were challenged by ongoing geopolitical changes. Egypt's Misrair was the oldest regional airline. With an order for British aircraft in 1954, Nasser worked to expand the fleet of the Egyptian flag carrier and run flights to London. However, following the US's refusal to support World Bank funding for the Aswan hydroelectrical dam project, Nasser nationalized the British- and French-owned Suez Canal in 1956. As a result, the British, French, and Israelis invaded Egypt and sought to topple its regime. Egypt soon shifted to purchasing American aircraft during a brief era of US–Egyptian accommodation. By the early 1960s, however, these efforts were constrained by foreign exchange shortages, management difficulties when Egypt, Syria, and Iraq sought to merge their national airlines, and the shift to socialist economic policies and closer ties to the Soviet Union.[40]

Beirut's Role in America's Global Aviation Network

As Nasser's Egypt rose to play a central role in regional geopolitics, the center of regional aviation shifted from Cairo to Beirut. Beirut's connections to air travel networks helped define its unique position in the region as a commercial, cosmopolitan hub. The city's aviation potential was defined by its location along the route from Europe to what would become the oil-rich Gulf states and to Asia.[41] Its value grew in the 1950s and 1960s as Beirut emerged as a leading center for urban culture, business, and entertainment. It was also a gateway to Lebanon as a tourist destination. Beirut's rise as an aviation hub was moreover a product of Lebanese government policies that encouraged aviation and facilitated private-sector development. American multinational firms began to establish regional Middle East headquarters in Beirut, which often served their growing interests in the oil-rich Gulf states. Meanwhile, the US's regional strategy came to focus on securing a regional hub for its network of political, economic, and intelligence ties.[42] Beirut's strategic value to the US was highlighted when the latter agreed to deploy Marines to help reestablish stability in Lebanon in 1958.[43]

The rise of Beirut as a regional travel hub would not have been possible without the success of the Beirut-based Lebanese air carrier, Middle East Airlines (MEA). MEA often relied on ties to European and American firms and governments, but it was never a creature of them or beholden to them like many other regional airlines. At different times, MEA had ties to British, American, and French entities. The firm was privately run, usually with some share of foreign ownership. But these ownership shares often translated into access to modern equipment, training, and close ties to global aviation and marketing networks.

MEA was founded in 1945 and used British planes and an agreement with BOAC, from which it initially gained staff and training. MEA management, however, wanted to expand its fleet with larger aircraft. BOAC opposed this plan. In 1949, MEA ended the contract and acquired American aircraft with the help of Pan American Airlines (Pan Am) in exchange for a 36 percent ownership stake.[44] The new aircraft and Pan Am–supplied pilots allowed MEA to expand its route network. Up to this point, air "traffic rights between the USA and most of North Africa and the Middle East" were dominated by Pan Am's rival TWA, which flew through Cairo.[45] But "by connecting its [global] network to that of MEA in Beirut, Pan Am regained access to these markets and broke TWA's monopoly in the region."[46] Pan Am vastly expanded its traffic through the rising regional travel hub of Beirut. The rapid development of airplane technology and demand for Middle East travel allowed for longer and more frequent flights. By 1950, Pan Am ran a weekly Stratocruiser service from New York to Beirut with only one stopover, in London.[47] By 1955, lower transportation costs and more frequent scheduled flights had made visiting the Middle East "Easy and Cheap."[48]

Pan Am's relationship with MEA was not without conflict. Najib Alamuddin, MEA's general manager at the time, reports that Pan Am's influence on MEA was much greater than warranted by its 36 percent of shares.[49] MEA's district sale managers in Beirut, Cairo, and Saudi Arabia were all Americans seconded from Pan Am. Although they were MEA employees in theory, "they rarely followed MEA instructions or sale policies where these were not approved by Pan-Am."[50] When a dispute between the head of the regional Pan Am office and MEA developed, Pan Am president Juan Trippe was called in to arbitrate. While Trippe decided to support MEA's position, Alamuddin narrates that MEA's chairman soon lost favor, as he failed to promptly comply with Trippe's request to contact Iran's Prime Minister Mohammad Mosaddegh to assist in a new oil deal.[51] Pan Am regional managers became frustrated in dealing with MEA and concerned about the profitability of the relationship. BOAC eventually took over Pan Am's shares. Pan Am's interests in Beirut persisted, as the regional aviation hub of Beirut continued to serve as Pan Am's major stopover point, where Pan Am's subsidiary InterContinental Hotels built its first overseas property outside of Latin America.

In the mid-1960s, new air fares further lowered the cost for Americans visiting the Middle East and marked the appearance of the "jet set" in the region.[52] At the time, the world was "experiencing a tourism boom, with America in the leading position in total number of tourists and dollars spent."[53] Many American officials continued to feel that "[t]ourism may play the key role in the future in providing underdeveloped nations with a much needed new source of foreign exchange required for economic development programs."[54] Van Vleck observes that "[b]etween 1958 and 1968, the jet age seemed to indicate the triumphant ascendance of the 'American Century'," in which fast jet travel "instantiated the visions of commercial empire builders such as Trippe and his friend Henry Luce—visions of a world with no distant places, in which U.S. power and influence could expand infinitely."[55]

Hijacking's Challenge to America's "Empire of the Air"

The 1967 Arab–Israeli war would temporarily disrupt American travel flows to the Middle East. More critically, however, global American travel was hit by the 1968 dollar crisis, when excessive US spending and imports led US president Lyndon Johnson to call on Americans to defer leisure travel abroad for two years. US airlines, however, were not interested in reducing the volume of US travel abroad. They had support from other travel boosters and commercial interests.[56] Meanwhile, many conservative critics refused to accept the president's scaling back of American consumerism and continued to associate "unfettered tourism with the Cold War crusade."[57] In the late 1960s and early 1970s, American bankers, industrialists, and politicians struggled with the question scholars of international political economy framed as the crisis of American hegemony. Before the mechanisms to sustain a neoliberal order were in place, the rise of airplane hijackings violently challenged American understandings about the existing order and the fate of the "American Century."

The act of unlawfully diverting an airplane was initially not viewed as a major threat to national security or air travel. Into the 1960s, Americans might have used terms such as "escapees" to refer to hijackers, as many of the most well-known cases ("Freedom Flights") involved persons who were attempting to escape communist regimes and seek asylum in the US or other Western states.[58] With the unanticipated rise of hijackings *to* Cuba following the 1959 revolution, the US government began considering antihijacking measures. Still, many policymakers remained concerned with making exceptions for those with political causes that helped reinforce the US's Cold War claims about promoting freedom of movement. At the same time, US airlines sought to avoid policies that might hamper the rapid expansion of air travel or suggest to passengers that flying was not safe. When first proposed, the airlines rejected security measures such as the screening of passengers and carry-on bags, as "the industry was convinced that enduring periodic skyjackings to Cuba was financially preferable to implementing invasive security at all American airports."[59]

The airlines were forced to change their attitude in the 1970s, as the tactics of hijackers and the way their actions were understood shifted, giving rise to the notion of "modern, international terrorism."[60] Hijacking as a political tactic was most extensively developed by followers of the Popular Front for the Liberation of Palestine (PFLP), a radical leftist element of the Palestinian national movement. While seeking to bring global attention to the Palestinian cause, the PFLP used hijackings as a means to challenge American global power abroad, exploiting a critical phase in the transformation of the American role in an increasingly interconnected and diverse global economy. The late 1960s and early 1970s were defined by the end of the Bretton Woods financial system, the rising power of European and Asian economies, and the war in Vietnam, calling the continued role of the US as a global hegemon into question. At the same time, US–Israeli ties—especially America's strong backing of Israel during the 1967 war—made the US a target for a new wave of revolutionary movements in the Middle East.

The PFLP's first hijacking was of an Israeli El Al flight from Rome to Tel Aviv in July 1968. Ordering the plane to Algiers, the hijackers held the Israeli passengers hostage and eventually won release of over a dozen Palestinians held by Israel. The PFLP would justify such actions against El Al flights by considering them military targets. This was based on the cooperation between the airline and the Israeli military,[61] which had devastated the Arab forces in the 1967 war with its overwhelming air power. The PFLP's actions were a variation of insurgent tactics (or labor disruption) such as targeting transportation and supply lines. Ali Mazuri referred to the rise of hijackings as "guerrilla warfare transferred from the forests to the skies" that could generate "an atmosphere of general insecurity."[62] Beyond the notion of these hijackings as a form of revolutionary violence, the PFLP militants would also articulate what might be called a counternarrative of aeromobility through their actions, words, and images. Not only did the Palestinian people lack a sovereign state with a national airport and flag carrier, but much of their displaced population resided in refugee camps and carried travel documents that afforded limited mobility across borders. As Davis comments about car bombs, hijackings could "terrorize populations" but also functioned as "a semi-strategic weapon" that attempts the "enfranchisement of marginal actors."[63] While their actions would contribute to broader awareness of the Palestinian struggle, by "targeting global networks of transportation"[64] they also had wider, systemic impacts, exposing American anxieties about the limits of their global aeromobility.

In 1969, a group of PFLP hijackers—including the now well-known Leila Khaled—sought to attack "imperialist America" for its support of Israel. They took over TWA Flight 840 from Rome to Athens and diverted it to Damascus. Before landing, Khaled asked the pilot to fly toward Lydda (Lod) so she could see Palestine and her hometown of Haifa for the first time since her family was expelled in 1948.[65] Flying over Israel, Khaled communicated directly with Israeli air traffic controllers and apparently took joy in forcing them to address her not as TWA 840 but as "Flight PFLP Free Arab Palestine."[66] Upon landing in Damascus, the Syrian authorities placed the hijackers under house arrest while they exchanged the Israeli hostages for Syrians held by Israel.[67]

On September 6, 1970, the PFLP—operating under the direction of Wadie Haddad—launched its most ambitious operation: a single-day, multiple-plane hijacking. A TWA flight departing Frankfurt and a Swissair flight departing Zurich, both bound for New York, were diverted to Dawson Field, an unused, former British military airfield outside of Amman, Jordan. The hijackers renamed it "Revolution Airport."[68] Meanwhile, a Pan Am 747 departing from Amsterdam also heading to New York was hijacked and first taken to Beirut for refueling. The hijackers then had the plane land in Cairo because they were unsure if the "Revolution Airport" runway was long enough to accommodate the jumbo jet. There, it was evacuated and then blown up. The two captured planes in the Jordanian desert were joined days later by a BOAC flight that was hijacked after departing from Bahrain for Beirut. For each flight, the PFLP prepared mock airline tickets, suggesting an imaginary revolutionary aeromobility. For Khaled's additional effort to hijack an El Al flight—which was foiled, resulting in her capture—the hijackers imagined a PFLP airline with the slogan "all over the world" and printed tickets that read "VALID ON PFLP AIRLINES ONLY," with a destination called "Revolution."[69] In Amman, the hijackers evacuated the passengers, about a hundred of whom were US citizens, and held them as hostages to negotiate the release of Palestinian prisoners (including Khaled) held in the UK, Switzerland, and Israel.[70]

On September 12, the evacuated planes were dynamited in front of the international media. The images of the aircraft being blown up on the Jordanian desert tarmac were circulated globally and became iconic representations of the era. They did not simply depict events in Jordan or events related to the Arab–Israeli conflict. "The shock" of these images was "felt throughout the world," David Pascoe suggests, because "the fires started here on this remote airfield were sufficiently magical to draw seemingly random acts of violence into the realm of international relations, and even war."[71]

Citino suggests that the hijackings "embodied a reimagined concept of revolutionary change as decentralized and resulting from autonomous personal and group actions."[72] While the Palestinian national struggle was largely defined as a territorial one, the hijackings articulated a counternarrative of aeromobility that sought to challenge US influence abroad and its non-territorial "Empire of the Air" that sustained its global position. President Richard Nixon would later comment that the hijackings "brought the world to an awareness of the fragility of the network of international air traffic."[73]

It is not clear, however, whether the global network of international air traffic was really that "fragile" and functionally disrupted as a global system or rather, whether the American encounter with hijackings highlighted the limits of American control over the system of international civil aviation—at a time when US airlines and US government support for them were weakening due to geopolitical change and financial crises in the US airline sector. The rejection of the American free market "open skies" regime in 1944 led to a system of civil aviation that gave all states, including developing countries, "easy access to civil aviation."[74] As a result, most countries had launched their own airlines, which by the 1970s were able to control a major share of their national market.[75] After having dominated global aviation in the 1950s, the US flag carriers' share of total international aviation measured in passenger kilometers dropped from almost 30 percent in 1963 to under 18 percent by 1980.[76] By the mid-1970s, the network of civil aviation was far more resilient than America's "Empire of the Air." American airlines were losing money on long-haul flights and would soon be turning to oil-rich states such as Iran for financial support.[77]

Meanwhile, the growing number of airlines across the Global South that operated under difficult, war-time conditions offered a different perspective on the question of fragility. In the Middle East, many regional airlines suffered far more hijackings and disruptions than American airlines.[78] Consider the experience of Lebanon's MEA. In December 1968, for example, Israeli forces responded to the attack by Palestinian militants on an Israeli El Al plane at Athens airport by sending commandos on a night raid to blow up Lebanese aircraft overnighting at Beirut airport. This attack destroyed over half of MEA's fleet. The next morning, however, the airport reopened. By combining multiple destinations on a single flight, MEA was able to serve all its planned destinations for that day.[79] While the Israeli actions were widely condemned, MEA benefited from an insurance claim and expanded its operations until the beginning of the civil war in Lebanon, in 1975, which made operating out of Beirut difficult. MEA continued to fly when it could, but suffered from the closure of Beirut airport for long stretches during the civil war and following the Israeli invasion of Lebanon in 1982. MEA pilots learned to fly in and out of war zones and cope with Lebanon's collapsed infrastructure.[80] Airline staff and other MEA employees had to cross checkpoints and avoid street battles and kidnapping attempts to get to work.[81] In line with Bloch's understanding of precapitalist Mediterranean cities, MEA aviators, managers, and engineers did not delude themselves into thinking they could have total command over the environment in which they operated.

The Challenge of an Antihijacking Regime

In 1947, TWA could run full-page advertisements that depicted a globe without national borders but with lines circumnavigating the sphere representing TWA's air travel routes, with the slogan "Where the World Is One."[82] By the 1970s, global travel sustained a complex, multinational network and Pan Am could no longer function as the so-called "chosen instrument" of the US government.[83] Both TWA and Pan Am suffered from the 1973 oil price spike (erroneously blamed on what many refer to as the "Arab oil embargo") and economic recession, just as Boeing was delivering its iconic 747 jumbo jet. This left Pan Am and TWA with a costly oversupply of airline capacity. By the late 1970s, the US began the deregulation of the airline industry, a step in the shift toward a neoliberal economic order. The end of price and route regulation would introduce fierce competition and market volatility. In the process, the self-asserted exceptionalism of the "American Century" was exposed to the limits of the US's capacity to serve as a guarantor of global mobility. The US could no longer unilaterally set the terms of global aeromobility in the Middle East or elsewhere. These limits surfaced most starkly with the air travel system's vulnerability to disruption and the challenges the US faced in trying to implement a global antihijacking regime.

The September 1970 hijackings provoked the US and other governments to develop air security measures that converted air spaces into policed security zones, with searches of passengers and armed air marshals on planes. Pan Am's initial reaction was to resist US government calls to boycott nations that were deemed to harbor hijackers. Pan Am president Najeeb Halaby said: "We are obliged by law to serve Beirut and Damascus as well as other cities around the world" and suggested that the problem of hijacking had to be solved by the world's governments.[84] At a Senate hearing on "Skyjacking" in October 1970, a representative of the American Society of Travel Agents argued that the costs of any new security measures should not be borne by the travel industry and—after invoking the use of US naval vessels to protect sea lanes—made a forceful argument that "American citizens have a right to look to their Government for safety and protection ... [so] that they can continue to enjoy their inherent right to travel freely among nations of the world."[85]

However, the policing of global travel networks now required the agreement and cooperation of all states. In the early 1970s, the US sought to promote a global antihijacking regime, but its approach assumed that other states would embrace the American understanding of "international terrorism" and view it as a threat to global order and "the delicately interwoven network of modern transportation and communications facilities on which every single country is dependent."[86] Many UN member states viewed the US's efforts as centered on Israeli concerns. They insisted that any resolution affirm the legitimacy of national liberation struggles and recognize the political contexts that gave rise to political violence and terrorism. With the 1971 Montreal Convention, the ICAO agreed to criminalize hijackings and the violent destruction of aircraft, but the US found such multilateral efforts of limited use because they lacked enforcement mechanisms and because many states refused to imprison or extradite hijackers. In 1973, the ICAO would even condemn Israel for air piracy over Lebanon. Israeli intelligence had suspected that the PFLP's leader was on board an MEA commercial airliner, operating an Iraqi Airways flight from Beirut to Baghdad, and forced the plane to land in Israel.[87]

The Israelis, who frequently suffered as the target of hijackings and other forms of political violence and terrorism (such as the attacks at the 1972 Munich Olympics), continued their unilateral approach. In 1976, Wadie Haddad's breakaway faction hijacked an Air France flight from Tel Aviv and held Israeli passengers hostage at Entebbe airport in Uganda. An Israeli raid killed the hijackers while freeing Israeli citizens and was celebrated as a great success in Israel and the US. Occurring in the wake of the US failure in and retreat from the Vietnam conflict, American policymakers and a rising set of so-called "terrorism experts" invoked the Israeli raid to reject calls for rule-based multilateral strategies that required compromise and to make the case for the unilateral use of military force and other coercive means.[88] After a spike in 1977, hijackings represented the increasingly prevalent notion of "international terrorism" as a threat to American travelers and US interests. The US began to develop a new approach that pressured states to adopt American aviation security policy and practices, which included maintaining a list of states supporting international terrorism and imposing sanctions on them. A cosponsor of the proposed 1978 Act to Combat International Terrorism noted: "In the final analysis, no modern nation can exist without international air traffic. Once you invoke such sanctions against a country . . . they will find themselves strangled, for air traffic is necessary and essential to their survival as a viable country."[89]

Late Cold War Travel Anxieties and the Eclipse of the American Century

While the US would actively sanction states it believed supported terrorism and pressure other states to enact aviation security policies, it developed an increasingly militarized approach to counterterrorism in the 1980s. In the process, the country made the final step in a shift where it went from deploying its geopolitical dominance to promote civilian aeromobility to an interventionist global security posture that often hindered international travel networks and tourist flows. This shift, however, was often justified as a response to threats against American travelers and aircraft abroad. In suggesting a connection between travel insecurities and the US projection of military power in the Middle East, I build on Melani McAlister's argument that "the discourse of terrorist threat in the 1980s focused on ... those highly visible and dramatic actions, such as hijackings and bombings, that came to dominate news coverage in the United States."[90] McAlister shows how such media events, and in particular the 1979–81 Iran hostage crisis, "worked to construct the United States as a nation of innocents, a family under siege by outside threats and in need of a militarized rescue."[91] The threats against American travelers and aircraft in the 1980s built on early 1970s hijacking experiences and exploited the continuing American notion of a "right to travel," established and popularized during the early post-1945 era of American aviation dominance.

In the mid-1980s, a series of violent attacks targeting American and other travelers, aircraft, and travel offices in Europe as well as the Middle East occurred in the wake of the traumatic Iran hostage crisis.[92] Together, they generated a powerful, late Cold War anxiety about American travel abroad. One of the most dramatic attacks was the June 1985 hijacking of TWA Flight 847 from Athens. The plane landed in Beirut—against the will of Lebanese air traffic control—where a pro-Iranian militia held the plane and passengers hostage, killing one American in the process. Their demands included the release of hundreds of captives held by Israel and the withdrawal of Israeli forces occupying southern Lebanon.[93] Following the massive car bombs deployed by pro-Iranian forces in Lebanon, which destroyed the US embassy and US Marines barracks in Beirut in 1984, American influence and leverage in Lebanon had declined.[94] At an Aviation Subcommittee hearing, conducted while thirty-eight American passengers were being held in Beirut, US Senator Frank Lautenberg declared:

> Recent events have cast doubt about whether Americans or other passengers can travel safely on international flights ... these tragedies ... have inspired possible fears that air travel just is not safe anymore ... American freedom includes the right to travel free from fear, free from threat of hijacking or bombing. If any Americans are threatened by terrorism, all Americans are at risk.[95]

In 1985, the year of the TWA 847 hijacking, twenty-eight million Americans traveled abroad, but the next year, nearly two million Americans changed their foreign travel plans as a result of the previous year's events.[96] Chris Ryan notes, "Europe, which hitherto had seemed a safe destination to US holidaymakers, began to be perceived as a dangerous location."[97] Shortly after the release of the TWA 847 hostages, secured with the assistance of Syria and its allies in Lebanon, President Ronald Reagan characterized the hijacking and other attacks as "acts of war" against the US and announced that Beirut airport—"through which have passed 15 percent of the world's hijackings since 1970"—should be closed.[98] Reagan also outlined that the US should be "taking a strategic—not just a tactical—view of terrorism" and that "[w]e must act together, or unilaterally if necessary, to ensure that terrorists have no sanctuary anywhere."[99] Between the summer of 1985 and the following spring, US officials debated the value of various policies and forms of military action in response to these attacks. The option of a full military response was first deployed following the April 5, 1986, bombing of a West Berlin disco popular with US servicemen, which killed one American and one Turkish woman. American officials viewed Libya as one of the major sponsors of recent attacks and had been closely following Libyan operatives in Europe. They quickly blamed the country for the disco bombing and began planning a large air raid against Libyan president Muammar Gaddafi and his forces, which was launched a week later.[100] Opposing the raid, France, Spain, and Italy forced the US to fly around their airspaces en route from bases in the UK.

At congressional hearings in 1986 to address the "impact of international terrorism on travel" in the wake of the attack on Libya, former State Department policy planning staffer Cord D. Hansen-Sturm represented a dissenting voice who challenged the militarization of the US's counterterrorism policy.[101] Hansen-Sturm, at the time working as an economist for a group of US tour operators, argued that "the effect" of this shift in US policy was "to reduce both travel flows and travelers' security."[102] Hansen-Sturm highlighted that US allies "refused to participate in America's counterproductive policies of military and economic force."[103] A strong advocate of the idea that expanded international travel serves US political and economic interests, Hansen-Sturm observed that "preserving US overseas travel flow simply was not considered a foreign policy objective," as US actions had only increased American travel fears.[104] In fact, he noted that American officials hoped that declining flows of American tourists would pressure European states into cooperating with

US counterterrorism policies. His conclusion highlighted the eclipse of the American Century, noting: "The extended overseas travel network is increasingly vulnerable to attack because US power is waning. The world's oceans no longer look like American lakes. The brief post–World War II *Pax Americana* is history. American overseas travelers are dependent on security provided by other governments rather than our own."[105]

The *9/11 Commission Report* observes that the US bombing of Libya "was seen at the time as a success. The lesson then taken from Libya was that terrorism could be stopped by the use of U.S. air power that inflicted pain on the authors or sponsors of terrorist acts."[106] A year and a half after the bombing, however, a Pan Am 747 would be blown up while flying over Scotland, killing all 243 passengers, 16 crew, and 11 people on the ground.[107] The *9/11 Commission Report* therefore also recognizes that "[e]vidence accumulated later, including the 1988 bombing of Pan Am 103, clearly showed that the [1986] operation did not curb Qadhafi's interest in terrorism."[108]

The quadruple airplane hijackings on the morning of September 11, 2001, resulted in almost three thousand fatalities and represented a new level of violence and media spectacle for Americans. Regardless of the scale, the aviation-related terrorist incidents of the 1970s and 1980s ensured that Americans were likely to view the hijackings as an "act of war" requiring a militarized response. Derek Gregory notes that, "Ironically one of the immediate consequences of September 11 was to contract the space of American tourism as flights were cancelled and aircraft flew half-empty."[109] Two weeks later, President George W. Bush would give a speech at Chicago's O'Hare airport, telling its employees that "one of our great goals of this war is to tell the traveling public: Get on board."[110] Declaring "we will not surrender our freedom to travel," Bush encouraged Americans to "[g]et down to Disney World in Florida. Take your families and enjoy life the way we want it to be enjoyed. . . . these are good things for our nation, because this nation will not live in fear."[111] Referring to President Bush's comments, Gregory notes: "This must count as one of the most bizarre reasons for waging war in human history, and yet it also speaks a powerful truth. Modern metropolitan cultures privilege their own mobility."[112] Ironically, as the US was mobilizing its military forces to occupy the Middle East, the cities of the Persian Gulf, including Dubai, Doha, and Abu Dhabi, were expanding their airports to serve as hubs for globe spanning "super-connecting" airlines that would do more to expand aeromobility for passengers and destinations across the globe than any US airline ever had.[113]

Meanwhile, in the ensuing "global war on terror," the US would deploy new forms of aerial warfare that include drones, seeking "command of the skies" across several continents.[114] Van Vleck writes that "even as the United States' commercial air empire has declined since its early jet-age apex, U.S. military infrastructure—which Pan Am and other commercial airlines played a crucial role in building and maintaining—remains more extensive and more expansive than ever and increasingly normalized as a permanent, inevitable aspect of American life."[115]

Endnotes

1. Mike Davis, *Dead Cities: And Other Tales* (New York: The New Press, 2002), 1.
2. Davis, *Dead Cities*, 1.
3. Davis, *Dead Cities*, 4, 13.
4. Michael Ignatieff, "The Burden," *New York Times*, January 3, 2003, 50.
5. National Commission on Terrorist Attacks upon the United States, *The 9/11 Commission Report* (New York: W. W. Norton, 2004), 362.
6. Davis, *Dead Cities*, 7.
7. Davis, *Dead Cities*, 8.
8. Ernst Bloch, "The Anxiety of the Engineer," in *Literary Essays*, trans. Andrew Joron et al. (Stanford, CA: Stanford University Press, 1998), 307.
9. Davis, *Dead Cities*, 8.
10. Davis, *Dead Cities*, 18.
11. Davis, *Dead Cities*, 18.
12. Mike Davis, *Buda's Wagon: A Brief History of the Car Bomb* (London: Verso, 2007), 5.
13. Peter Adey, Lucy Budd, and Phil Hubbard, "Flying Lessons: Exploring the Social and Cultural Geographies of Global Air Travel," *Progress in Human Geography* 31, no. 6 (2007): 774. See also Saulo Cwerner, Sven Kesselring, and John Urry, eds., *Aeromobilities* (London: Routledge, 2009); Peter Adey, "Aeromobilities: Geographies, Subjects and Vision," *Geography Compass* 2, no. 5 (2008): 1318–36.
14. Yoav Di-Capua, "Common Skies Divided Horizons: Aviation, Class and Modernity in Early Twentieth Century Egypt," *Journal of Social History* 41, no. 4 (2008): 917.
15. Alexander De Seversky, *Victory Through Air Power* (New York: Simon and Schuster, 1942), 125. The following year, Walt Disney Productions released a Technicolor film adaptation.
16. These efforts anticipate the development of supply chain security. See Deborah Cowen, *The Deadly Life of Logistics: Mapping Violence in Global Trade* (Minneapolis: University of Minnesota Press, 2014), 2–3.
17. Henry Luce, "The American Century," *Life*, February 7, 1941; reprinted in *Diplomatic History* 23, no. 2 (Spring 1999): 166.
18. Jenifer Van Vleck, *Empire of the Air: Aviation and the American Ascendancy* (Cambridge, MA: Harvard University Press, 2013).
19. Luce, "American Century," 159–71.
20. Luce, "American Century," 165.
21. See Van Vleck, *Empire of the Air*, 122–30.
22. See Van Vleck, *Empire of the Air*, 121.

23 Robert Strausz-Hupé, "Aviation and International Co-Operation," *The Annals of the American Academy of Political and Social Science* 299 (May 1955): 134.
24 Strausz-Hupé, "Aviation and International Co-Operation," 135.
25 "Memorandum by the Civil Air Attaché for the Middle East (Thayer)," May 14, 1953, in *Foreign Relations of The United States, 1952–1954, General: Economic and Political Matters, Volume I, Part 1* (Washington, DC: United States Government Printing Office, 1983), 408.
26 George A. Brownell, "American Aviation in the Middle East," *Middle East Journal* 1, no. 4 (October 1947): 402.
27 "American Interest in the Middle East: Future Traffic Volume," *Flight*, August 23, 1945, 198.
28 "American Interest in the Middle East," 198.
29 Keith Williams, "Commercial Aviation in Arab States: The Pattern of Control," *Middle East Journal* 11, no. 2 (Spring 1957): 128–29.
30 "Air Transport: The Urgent Need for an Imperial Policy," *The Round Table: The Commonwealth Journal of International Affairs*, 33, no. 131 (1943): 210–17.
31 Jeffrey A. Engel, *Cold War at 30,000 Feet: The Anglo-American Fight for Aviation Supremacy* (Cambridge, MA: Harvard University Press, 2007), 96.
32 "Memorandum from the Assistant Chief of the Aviation Division (Walstrom) to the Director of the Office of Near East and African Affairs (Henderson)," November 21, 1945, in *Foreign Relations of the United States: Diplomatic Papers, 1945, The Near East and Africa, vol. VIII* (Washington, DC: United States Government Printing Office, 1969), 77–80.
33 "Memorandum by the Civil Air Attaché for the Middle East (Thayer)."
34 Nathan J. Citino, *Envisioning the Arab Future: Modernization in US–Arab Relations, 1945–1967* (Cambridge: Cambridge University Press, 2017), 12.
35 George Horne, "Air Route Survey of the Middle East hailed as U.S. 'Master Stroke,"' *New York Times*, August 16, 1954, 33.
36 Hans Heymann Jr., "Air Transport and Economic Development: Some Comments on Foreign Aid," *The American Economic Review* 52, no. 2 (May 1962): 388.
37 Heymann, "Air Transport and Economic Development," 388.
38 Brownell, "American Aviation in the Middle East," 405.
39 Brownell, "American Aviation in the Middle East," 410.
40 "More Viscounts for Egypt," *Flight International*, August 9, 1957; "EGYPTAIR Holding Company," in *International Directory of Company Histories*, ed. Jay P. Pederson, vol. 130 (Detroit: St. James Press, 2012).
41 Gerald Butt, *History in the Arab Skies: Aviation's Impact on the Middle East* (Nicosia: Rimal Press, 2011), 176.
42 Irene L. Gendzier, *Notes from the Minefield: United States Intervention in Lebanon, 1945–1958* (New York: Columbia University Press, 1997), 101.
43 While Lebanon's president sought to invoke the 1957 Eisenhower Doctrine that pledged US support for governments facing "armed aggression from any nation controlled by international communism," US officials in Beirut were aware that the local insurrection was a product of internal political disputes, and thus, the US avoided engagement in the conflict and focused on assisting the election of a new president who would better promote stability and serve US strategic and economic interests. See Gendzier, *Notes from the Minefield*.
44 Najib Alamuddin, *The Flying Sheikh* (London: Quartet Books, 1987), 39.
45 Wassim Chemaitelli, "Middle East Airlines," *Cedar Jet Pages*; reposted as "Notes on the History of Air Travel in Lebanon," http://almashriq.hiof.no/lebanon/300/380/387/air-travel/.
46 Chemaitelli, "Middle East Airlines."
47 "Lebanon Flight Speeded: Pan American to Serve Beirut by Stratocruiser Friday," *New York Times*, October 25, 1950, 71.

48 C. B. Squire, "Levantine Air Links: Visiting the Arab States is Easy and Cheap," *New York Times*, May 15, 1955, X47.
49 Alamuddin, *Flying Sheikh*, 40.
50 Alamuddin, *Flying Sheikh*, 40.
51 Alamuddin, *Flying Sheikh*, 45.
52 Jesse Z. Lurie, "US-Middle East Air Fares Tumble," *Jerusalem Post*, May 24, 1965, 4.
53 Somerset R. Waters, "The American Tourist," *The Annals of the American Academy of Political and Social Science* 368 (1966): 109.
54 Waters, "American Tourist," 110.
55 Van Vleck, *Empire of the Air*, 241.
56 Christopher Endy, *Cold War Holidays: American Tourism in France* (Chapel Hill: University of North Carolina Press, 2004), 192.
57 Endy, *Cold War Holidays*, 197.
58 Brian M. Jenkins, *The Terrorist Threat to Commercial Aviation* (Santa Monica, CA: RAND Corporation, 1989), 1. https://www.rand.org/pubs/papers/P7540.html.
59 Brendan I. Koerner, *The Skies Belong to Us: Love and Terror in the Golden Age of Hijacking* (New York: Broadway Books, 2013), 46.
60 Bruce Hoffman, *Inside Terrorism* (New York: Columbia University Press, 2006), 63. See also Lisa Stampnitzky, *Disciplining Terror: How Experts Invented "Terrorism"* (Cambridge: Cambridge University Press, 2013).
61 Harold M. Cubert, *The PFLP's Changing Role in the Middle East* (London: Routledge, 1997), 133–4.
62 Ali Mazuri, "The Third World and International Terrorism," *Third World Quarterly* 7, no. 2 (April 1985): 350.
63 Davis, *Buda's Wagon*, 5, 11.
64 Paul T. Chamberlin, *The Global Offensive: The United States, the Palestine Liberation Organization, and the Making of the Post–Cold War Order* (New York: Oxford University Press, 2012), 72.
65 Leila Khaled, *My People Shall Live* (Toronto: NC Press, 1975), 141–2.
66 Sarah Irving, *Leila Khaled* (London: Pluto Press, 2012), 33.
67 Philip Baum, *Violence in the Skies: A History of Aircraft Hijackings and Bombings* (Chichester, UK: Summersdale, 2016), 58.
68 "4 Jets Hijacked; One, a 747, Is Blown Up," *New York Times*, September 7, 1970, 1.
69 *Flight International*, September 10, 1983, 695.
70 For a detailed account of the experience written by an Israeli-American held hostage, see David Raab, *Terror in Black September* (New York: Palgrave, 2007).
71 David Pascoe, *Airspaces* (London: Reaktion Books, 2001), 187–8.
72 Citino, *Envisioning the Arab Future*, 256. Wadie Haddad had conducted the hijackings in the absence of PFLP leader George Habash. The PFLP, which soon abandoned hijackings as a tactic, was temporarily suspended from the PLO Central Command while Haddad would go on to form his own breakaway PFLP faction.
73 Cited in James A. Arey, *The Sky Pirates* (New York: Charles Scribner's Sons, 1972), 307.
74 Stephen D. Krasner, *Structural Conflict: The Third World Against Global Liberalism* (Berkeley: University of California Press, 1985), 207.
75 Krasner, *Structural Conflict*, 207, 202–3.
76 Calculated from ICAO, *Annual Report of the Council* (Montréal: International Civil Aviation Organization, various years).
77 Anthony Sampson, *Empires of the Sky* (London: Hodder & Stoughton, 1984), 160.
78 Jenkins, "Terrorist Threat to Commercial Aviation," 8.
79 Alamuddin, *Flying Sheikh*, 171–8.
80 Butt, *History in the Arab Skies*, 191.
81 Reginald Turnill, *Lebanon's Crisis 1975–76 and Middle East Airlines' Battle for Survival* (London: Maxclif, 1977), 17.
82 Endy, *Cold War Holidays*, 41.

83 Van Vleck, *Empire of the Air*, 83.
84 Frank Mazza, "Air Boycotts Opposed by Chief of Pan Am," *New York Daily News*, September 10, 1970, 5.
85 Thomas M. Keesling, "Skyjacking" Hearing before the Committee on Finance, United States Senate, October 6, 1970 (Washington, DC: US Government Printing Office, 1970), 19–21.
86 Citied in Chamberlin, *Global Offensive*, 181.
87 Juan De Onis, "Lebanon Accuses Israel of Piracy in Jet Intercept," *New York Times*, August 12, 1973, 1; Miodrag Trajkovic, "Hi-Jacking: No Law to Outlaw," *Review of International Affairs* (Belgrade), November 20, 1973.
88 Melani McAlister, *Epic Encounters: Culture, Media, & U.S. Interests in the Middle East since 1945* (Berkeley: University of California Press, 2005), 183–87.
89 Testimony of Abraham Ribicoff, "International Terrorism" Hearings Before the Subcommittee on Aviation of the Committee on Public Works and Transportation House of Representatives, July 18, 19, 20, and 25, 1978 (Washington, DC: US Government Printing Office, 1978), 70.
90 McAlister, *Epic Encounters*, 201.
91 McAlister, *Epic Encounters*, 201.
92 Most of these events, such as the attacks at the Rome and Vienna airports, the hijacking of an EgyptAir flight, and the seizing of the Achille Lauro cruise ship, were carried out by operatives of fringe extremist groups. See "12 Months of Terror: The Middle East Connection," *New York Times*, April 8, 1986; reprinted in "Impact of International Terrorism on Travel," Joint Hearings before the Subcommittees on Arms Control, International Security, and Science, and on International Operations of the Committee on Foreign Affairs, and the Subcommittee on Aviation of the Committee on Public Works and Transportation, Ninety-Ninth Congress, second session, February 19, April 17, 22, and May 15, 1986 (Washington, DC: US Government Printing Office, 1986), 376.
93 William E. Smith, "Terror Aboard Flight 847," *Time*, June 24, 1985, 18–25; Robert Fisk, *Pity the Nation* (New York: Nation Books, 2002), 605–9.
94 Davis, *Buda's Wagon*, 80, 83.
95 Comments of Frank Lautenberg, "International Airport Security and Anti-Hijacking Measures," Hearing before the Subcommittee on Aviation of the Committee on Commerce, Science, and Transportation, United States Senate, June 27, 1985 (Washington, DC: US Government Printing Office, 1985), 34.
96 Sevil F. Sönmez, Yiorgos Apostolopoulos and Peter Tarlow, "Tourism in Crisis: Managing the Effects of Terrorism," *Journal of Travel Research*, 38, 1 (1999): 15.
97 Chris Ryan, *Tourism, Terrorism, and Violence: The Risks of Wider World Travel*, Conflict Studies No. 24 (London: Research Institute for the Study of Conflict and Terrorism, 1991), 1–2.
98 Ronald Reagan, "Remarks at the Annual Convention of the American Bar Association," July 8, 1985, https://www.reaganlibrary.gov/research/speeches/70885a.
99 Reagan, "Remarks at the Annual Convention of the American Bar Association."
100 David C. Wills, *The First War on Terrorism* (Lanham, MD: Rowman & Littlefield, 2003), 187–212.
101 "Impact of International Terrorism on Travel," 264–267.
102 "Impact of International Terrorism on Travel," 265.
103 "Impact of International Terrorism on Travel," 414.
104 Cord D. Hansen-Strum, "Terrorism: Why We Can't Shoot Our Way Out (Part II)," *The Travel Agent*, April 17, 1986; reprinted in "Impact of International Terrorism on Travel," 384.
105 Cord D. Hansen-Strum, "Terrorism: Why We Can't Shoot Our Way Out (Part I)," *The Travel Agent*, April 10, 1986, 24; reprinted in "Impact of International Terrorism on Travel," 383.
106 National Commission on Terrorist Attacks, *9/11 Commission Report*, 98.

AVIATION, HIJACKINGS, AND THE ECLIPSE

107 Van Vleck, *Empire of the Air*, 286. Compounding Pan Am's financial troubles, the bombing was the "final nail in its coffin" (287).
108 National Commission on Terrorist Attacks, *9/11 Commission Report*, 98.
109 Derek Gregory, *The Colonial Present: Afghanistan, Iraq, Palestine* (Malden, MA: Blackwell, 2004), 257.
110 Cited in Gregory, *Colonial Present*, 257.
111 "Excerpts from Bush Speech on Travel," *New York Times*, September 28, 2001, B6.
112 Gregory, *Colonial Present*, 257.
113 See Afshin Molavi, "The Arab Battle for U.S. Skies," *Foreign Policy*, May, 4, 2015, http://foreignpolicy.com/2015/05/04/dubai-qatar-etihad-emirates-fair-skies-open-skies-american-delta-united/.
114 Literary scholar Elaine Scarry, however, notes the impotence of US airpower in defending against the terrorist hijacking on September 11, 2001. She argues that the only effective defense against aerial terrorism that day was "the egalitarian model of defense," represented by the passengers on Flight 93 who brought down the plane headed to strike the US Capitol Building. See Elaine Scarry, *Who Will Defend the Country?* (Boston: Beacon Press, 2003).
115 Van Vleck, *Empire of the Air*, 292–3.

LINEAGES OF INFRASTRUCTURAL POWER

Los Angeles as a Logistical Nightmare

Charmaine Chua

When the *CMA CGM Benjamin Franklin* lumbered its way into harbor at the Port of Los Angeles in the predawn hours of Boxing Day 2015, the consonance of date and occasion could not have been better orchestrated. The *Benjamin Franklin* was and is to date the largest container ship ever to call at a North American seaport, bringing some 18,000 boxes (or twenty-foot equivalent units, TEUs) of global commodities to shore. If an image of commodity fetishism might have been epitomized in the proliferation of goods and throngs of post-Christmas shoppers in the hinterland that day, its shadowy and less visible other would have been this behemoth ship arriving, without much fanfare, into the walled-off mouth of the port, its monstrous scale hidden from the view of downtown urban cores.

At 1,300 feet long, 177 feet wide, and 197 feet tall, the *Benjamin Franklin* carries one third more in volume than previously seen in the Port of LA. Newspaper coverage registered awe at its size: "as wide as 14 freeway lanes"[1] and "longer than the Empire State Building is tall."[2] Yet the ship is not exceptional. It is part of an onslaught of megavessels seeking the title of "world's largest ship." Ninety-seven ships capable of carrying between 18,000 and 20,000 twenty-foot equivalent container units will be delivered to various companies by mid-2019. These ships signal an era of international trade in which state funding, public-private partnerships, and finance have poured investment into logistics-related growth as a key to city, state, and national development regimes. This is why Los Angeles Mayor Eric Garcetti saw the ship as a symbol of economic promise: "When I look up at this ship, I don't just see a 20-story building. I see a reminder of what is possible when we all come together in this town."[3] In LA, celebrations of the largest ship in town go beyond simple fascinations with monumentality. They also reflect an ideology of speculation that frames logistical distribution and the expansion of infrastructures of mobility as central to the future of the city. As shipping lines have sought to build larger vessels in order to capture economies of scale in fuel and crew costs, port cities have tried to keep pace with these infrastructural explosions, investing heavily in capital-intensive projects to enhance supply chain efficiencies so as to become part of global production networks deemed indispensable to the city's sustainability.

In this essay, I chart an image of the city and its growth, not by looking at its downtown core and the infrastructures of financialization that have crystallized in centralized commercial zones and business districts but by looking at capital's other underbelly: the logistics sector that manages the circulation of goods, materials, and information across the supply chain.[4] In interrogating how infrastructures of "supply chain capitalism" draw global economies of violence to the foreground, I draw particular insight from Mike Davis's work, which has often engaged these "power lines" as material structures that bifurcate and bypass collective structures in service of strategies of capital accumulation that centralize wealth and power.[5] In *Late Victorian Holocausts*, for example, Davis shows that public investments channeled toward the construction of railroads and deep-sea ports actively produced an imperial infrastructure that carried cash crops away to the metropole, tying grain to the world market and elevating food prices out of the poor's reach, leading to between thirty-two and sixty-one million deaths in Africa, China, Brazil, and South Asia.[6] As Davis illustrates, the "power lines" of global supply chains structure the displacement, exploitation, and death of poor and working people by reorganizing their relationship to economies of supply, from the Victorian era to the present.

Today, the expansion of transport infrastructure—originally driven by the demands of military control and export agriculture—has become shaped by the just-in-time logistics of flexible supply chains. As downtowns undergo what Davis has dubbed "centermania" and "disneyfication,"[7] the expansion of logistics systems meanwhile creates a hinterland of distribution, linking global production networks to feverish new emphases on just-in-time delivery and linking global outsourcing and subcontracting relationships to the US consumer through a built environment of logistical violence. What develops in the outer fields of Los Angeles and other megacities is an architecture of urban capitalism that has shifted away from "public works"—infrastructure as a public good—and toward remaking the globe as a logistical leviathan: an integrated network of roads, railways, and systems of algorithmic tracking that centers on an accumulation strategy based on widening the scale and speed of global commodity distribution. In the process, this strategy provisions not only needs and wants but also inequality and vulnerability to premature death.[8]

The Logistical City

In response to the challenges of deindustrialization that resulted in manufacturing job losses and global economic restructuring in the 1960s, Southern California's leaders pursued two interlinked strategies to revitalize cities by turning them into financial centers and major hubs of consumption. The first of these, traced in Mike Davis's pathbreaking work in the *City of Quartz* and *Dead Cities*, is the "infinite game" of downtown redevelopment and business district revitalization.[9] Foreign capital from the Pacific Rim countries that benefited from US losses in the global trade war came to be the chief source of real estate investment in the downtown economy, which was "illicitly dependent on the continuation of the structural imbalance that recycled US deficits as foreign speculation in American assets."[10]

As downtown revitalization became "a perverse monument to deindustrialization" in the city center, a second, quieter, though no less monumental shift was taking place in the revitalization of Southern California's sprawling transport infrastructure: investments in the massive network of highways, ports, and railways that tied the development of LA's regional economy to that of a growing global commodity trade.[11] Logistics—a supply chain management philosophy that sought to coordinate and manage the production and sale of goods, from raw materials to final products—became a viable antidote to deindustrialization. It offered the possibility of bringing jobs back to deindustrialized neighborhoods, while simultaneously enabling and facilitating the culture of retail consumption on the basis of which LA was pursuing a growth strategy in the suburbs.[12]

Between 1970 and 2010, North America lost approximately six million manufacturing jobs. Globally, the Chinese economy proved an alluring destination for investment because it offered access to a seemingly inexhaustible supply of surplus labor, while at the same time, state-backed capital enabled both foreign and Chinese producers to invest in new facilities that allowed them to achieve great economies of scale in a relatively short time span. By 2008, according to the US International Trade Commission, Chinese goods represented 16.1 percent of all US imports—compared to 6.5 percent in 1996—and are projected to increase by 5.5 percent every year between 2020 and 2030.[13] The projected expectation that US–Asia trade would grow—coupled with the recognition that manufacturing jobs would not return—placed the logistics industry at the center of an accumulation strategy premised on increasing the rate and mass of circulation. The logistics industry thereby expands the capacity for commercial capital to reproduce itself by accelerating the rate at which the value latent in commercial goods can be realized in their sale.

Logistical methods became prominent during the rise of twentieth-century industrial warfare as a military art concerned with ensuring the uninterrupted flow of fuel, food, and weapons to lubricate the war machinery.[14] In the 1960s and 1970s, these logistical techniques and interventions came to be applied to expanding realms of social life as the technical operations of military counterinsurgency doctrine became entangled with corporate experiments in supply chain efficiency. Thereafter, logistics management rose to prominence in business management schools and transnational corporations. By the late twentieth century, traditional mass manufacturing sectors in advanced industrialized countries had declined due to a combination of factors that included intensified international competition, accelerated technological change, and market saturation.[15] Firms turned to offshoring and subcontracting to optimize profits, moving low-cost production facilities to the Global South, where cheaper land and labor costs promised higher profit margins. Since moving manufacturing across the oceans widened the geographical divide between the production of value and its realization, firms in the North had to solve a transportation and connectivity problem: US firms could only benefit from China becoming the "factory of the world" if the cost savings that were gained through outsourcing were not lost in shipping those goods back to existing consumer markets in the Global North.

Marx himself foresaw the centrality of the transport industry in expanding capital's ability to reproduce the conditions for accumulation: in selling a change in location, he argued, the act of moving commodities through their "actual course in space" makes transportation an "independent branch of production, and hence a particular sphere for the investment of productive capital."[16] In this sense, logistical systems do not simply reduce the costs of transportation but also expand the capacity for capital to reproduce the relations of production. Therefore, logistics plays a key role in accumulation strategies, allowing firms to turn to a global strategy grounded in flexible production systems that depend on the seamless circulation of raw materials, final parts, and labor across a global just-in-time delivery system.

To reduce the interfaces and enhance the efficiency of delivery, logistical systems reorganize transportation environments in standardized ways to facilitate efficient movement: trains move on tracks with standardized gauges, trucks run on interstate highways, and so forth. The most important infrastructure in this regard, however, was the shipping container. The container sought to become a technological solution to the "problem" of labor-intensive circulation. By boxing everything up into packable and stackable forms, the container caused freight rates between North America and Asia to fall by 40 to 60 percent.[17] The Vietnam War was an early staging ground for these experiments: the container proved the most efficient solution to the problem of distributing war materiel from Oakland to Cam Ranh Bay, a region largely inaccessible to US troops. This success, coupled with the stocking of returning, US-bound containers with goods from East Asia, showed that high capacity containerization could be utilized to reduce costs and create profitability. In fact, one economist argues that the shipping container is twice as important in increasing international trade flows between industrialized countries as governments' efforts to eliminate formal trade barriers.[18]

Container ships such as the *CMA CGM Benjamin Franklin* are thus not isolated infrastructures but are part of a feverish expansion of container ship sizes aimed at extending and expanding containerized efficiency at larger economies of scale. Since 1956, when the world's first commercially successful container ship *Ideal X* set sail from Newark, New Jersey, container-carrying capacities have increased by 1,200 percent; in the last ten years alone, by 80 percent.[19] Because megaships depend on the global extension of infrastructure, the extent to which megaships can fulfill their projected economic outcomes is determined by the ability of port cities to adapt their infrastructure to support these behemoths of global trade. Terminals built to discharge cargo from an earlier era of ships are now struggling to handle cargo from megavessels with twice as much carrying capacity in 2005 and four times as much in 2019. Cities and states whose growth hinges on their role in distribution have thus poured private and public investment into supersized ports to match these volumes.

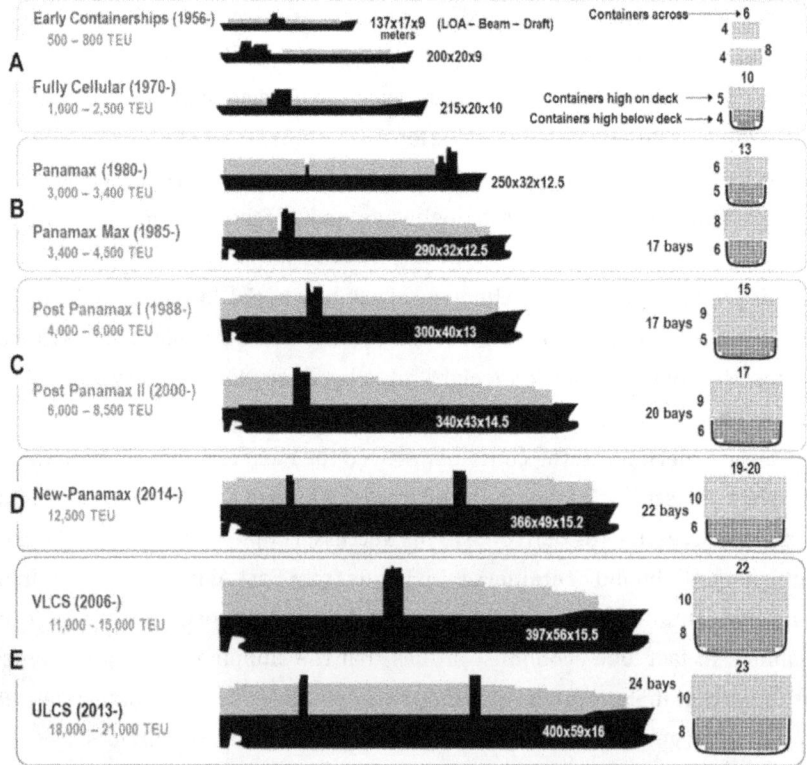

Figure 1: The Evolution of Containerships, 2020, in Jean-Paul Rodrigue, *The Geography of Transport Systems*, Fifth Edition, (New York: Routledge), https://transportgeography.org/?page_id=2232. Courtesy of Jean-Paul Rodrigue.

LINEAGES OF INFRASTRUCTURAL POWER

These developments in logistics are part of a broader, global move to promote megainfrastructural projects as a key antidote to sluggish growth. Worldwide, regions have been preparing pipelines of "bankable megaprojects" to implement master plans for infrastructure, arguing that transportation facilities provide "structural transformation" and create jobs, green economies, and increases in "value added" in production chains.[20] China's Belt and Road Initiative, for example, is one such massive state-led project that seeks to establish new trade routes from China to Europe and beyond, involving the construction of extensive networks of satellites, warehouses, ports, railroads, and highways across transnational territory.[21] In this respect, although the Port of Los Angeles is the focus of this essay, logistics-based development projects are situated within system-wide efforts to expand global trade infrastructure. Across the world, transportation networks struggle to expand at a rate commensurate with the needs of these vessels: harbors are dredged to make way for ships with greater depths, intermodal railways inscribe themselves under surface streets and through neighborhoods, distribution warehouses are constructed at regular intervals along major interstate freeways, trucks trundle back and forth across the continent for months at a time, and railroad lines crawl across the deindustrialized hinterland.

Port Dreams

Prior to the development of its port, LA was a city with no natural harbor and a city center twenty miles from the coast. In the 1850s and 1860s, businessmen seeking investment in LA saw the harbor as a crucial gateway through which growing transatlantic and Pacific trade could enter the US and positioned themselves to build the necessary infrastructure. Among them was financier and businessman Phineas Banning, the "Father of the Los Angeles Harbor," who poured profits from his trade networks into creating greater transport connections to LA. A number of successful developments by Banning—organizing the development of a port complex; creating roads, telegraphs, and other connections; and constructing Southern California's first railroad system—allowed early LA businessmen to see Wilmington and San Pedro as viable sites for seaport development. In the 1890s, such efforts came to a head in what became known as the "Free Harbor Fight." Southern Pacific Railway's Collis Huntington, seeking to monopolize local shipping, jockeyed to make Santa Monica the port of the City of Los Angeles instead. San Pedro boosters successfully swayed public opinion against a railroad monopoly and toward a "free harbor," winning the dispute when they attained US congressional approval and federal subsidies for the development of the port.

As Mike Davis traces, however, the eschewal of a railroad monopoly in favor of a "free" harbor did not make control over the port more publicly accountable or democratic. Rather, it prompted the emergence of a powerful political elite that would come to dominate the speculative interests of the Los Angeles latifundia.[22] Access to the San Pedro Bay ports unlocked resources for LA boosters that allowed them to see the region anew. As James Tejani argues, their absolute ownership of San Pedro Bay's coastal tidelands enabled the City of Los Angeles—not private interests or state government—to control the entirety of the harbor and thus determine the full course of its future development and use.[23] In 1911, Thomas Edward Gibbon, the then LA Harbor Commissioner, made a presentation to the city's Realty Board that framed Los Angeles's existence on a global scale. The city, he argued, was not just at the center of US expansion but would also connect the markets of Europe and the Orient to US states inland, drawing together networks of modern machine technology and transportation and linking deepwater shipping and industry in the US hinterland to the Pacific world.[24] Gibbon's protologistical imagery in the early twentieth century provided the seeds for LA's commitment throughout the twentieth century to constructing an immense artificial infrastructure. In the decades that followed, the City of LA stitched together bond and tax revenues, federal funding, and private investment to build a vast network of railroads, aqueducts, highways, and port infrastructure that positioned the ports of Los Angeles and Long Beach as the busiest gateway to North America's inscription into the world market.

Historians have interpreted LA's territorial expansion toward the harbor as a story of land-based expansion, centered on the acquisition of square miles to gain assessed property, establish new industries, and obtain revenue sources.[25] Such narratives, while valid, obscure the centrality of commercial transport expansion to the formation of the city and the power of the application of transport as an economic and spatial category. Transportation infrastructure became the terrain on which LA's southward expansion sought less to control land itself than to control the mechanisms by which local and regional interests could tap into and facilitate global circuits of capital.[26] More than a battle between public authority and private interests, the "Free Harbor Fight" was a battle to set the terms, ideas, and boundaries of city expansion, premised on building a material space for globalization to flourish in the American West.

Figure 2: San Pedro Bay, 2015. Courtesy of the Port of Los Angeles. https://www.portoflosangeles.org/about/news-and-media/photo.

By 1958, when the first shipment of twenty containers arrived by sea on the *Hawaiian Merchant*, the port of LA had secured the resources, bureaucratic authority, and revenue necessary to solidify its place as the busiest port in the US. To do so, LA's political elites sought to secure access to the growing Pacific Rim trade: In 1962, the famously race-baiting, anti-Communist LA Mayor Sam Yorty led a trade mission to East Asia where he inked trade provisions with Hong Kong, Japan, and the Taiwanese Evergreen Line Company—a pro-trade growth strategy oddly out of line with the growth control platform that had won Yorty the mayoral race by capitalizing on the antielite resentments of suburbanite homeowners just a year before.[27] The LA Chamber of Commerce used its control over the harbor to attract additional ocean lines to the port, embarking on the largest dredging and landfill project in America that created a 590 acre site from the ocean bottom. As a result of these efforts to turn LA into a transpacific gateway, the volume of containerized cargo coming into the ports of Los Angeles and Long Beach increased from 750,000 in 1992 to 10 million in the early 2000s and 17.5 million in 2017.[28] The success of the harbor integrated the city's commercial interests with those of the American West, the nation, and the world, providing the foundation for building a commercial empire that spanned land and sea.

Establishing a distribution gateway to global commerce has long been key to state developmental regimes. The latest iteration of these developments, however, reflects a particular intensification in port cities' battle to become logistics hubs. Major seaports, from Long Beach to Burma, have been investing in capital-intensive adaptations to compete for a share of the logistics pie, engendering what Fernando Coronil calls "dazzling development projects that engender collective fantasies of progress."[29] The "power lines" of infrastructure thus lie in the political and economic coordination that states pour into large-scale projects, because they are bets on the continued flourishing of global, national, and city economies. As Henri Lefebvre notes when characterizing the state as a logistical enterprise, a chief concern of states is to make space abstract and homogenous as a productive force for the reproduction of capital, since only the state has "at its disposal the appropriate resources, techniques, and 'conceptual' capacity" to take charge of the management of space "on a grand scale."[30] Along with these developments, a dramatic repackaging of state and urban development strategies has occurred. These strategies articulate the importance of logistics and infrastructure as so crucial to national and regional economies that they require the public funding of private infrastructure, considered necessary to tap into the future of logistical accumulation.[31]

Logistics as a Public Good

It was not until the 1980s that Los Angeles began to articulate its vision for economic growth through the language of logistics.[32] If the initial growth of the port was prompted by the growth of industrialization across the American West, in the 1980s—as US production of commodity goods declined—economists and planners argued that logistics was an antidote to deindustrialization.

LINEAGES OF INFRASTRUCTURAL POWER

As Juan De Lara argues, what really distinguished Southern California as a hub for logistics development was its prescient ability "to capture some of the post-1980s global capital flows while other regions suffered from economic restructuring."[33] Between 1980 and 2010, policymakers framed development aims in the language of logistics in order to orchestrate the transfer of private and public resources to the regional goods-movement economy.[34] The industrial plants and factories that had made the central manufacturing districts of LA flourish in the 1930s and 1940s were now being emptied as capital, enabled by the cheapened costs of transportation, moved its factories to the Pacific Rim. Between 1978 and 1982, more than 75,000 manufacturing jobs were lost in cities south of downtown Los Angeles at the same time as US consumer demand steered imported commodity shipments to record numbers. Unsurprisingly, the loss of jobs corresponded to white flight and changes in the demographic composition of the region: once white, working-class suburbs are today majority Black and Latinx working-class cities. In cities such as South Gate, the Latinx population increased from 4 percent in 1969 to 46 percent by 1980 and 83 percent in 1990.[35]

It was the land on which these communities of color settled as well as the infrastructure that was left in empty lots and warehouses that became the experimental ground for a logistics growth strategy. Seeking to transform the city into a transpacific trade gateway, port boosters argued that logistics was "the only route that the region has available to helping those workers achieve growing standards of living while simultaneously correcting the deep slide in Southern California's relative prosperity vis-à-vis other major parts of the country."[36] Boosters proposed that unlike manufacturing, logistics was a sector that could not be easily offshored. Goods, after all, had to reach a growing base of voracious consumers whose access to new forms of readily available credit helped consolidate a culture of retail consumption. The construction of an extensive distribution network would help ensure that blue-collar jobs could be brought back to the American economy at the tail end (or "last mile") of the supply chain. To this end, public funds were invested in a logistics infrastructure that could connect imports from the meteoric rise of the trade with China to consumers in the American hinterland.

A massive 2020 Master Ports Plan and the Alameda Corridor Project, devised in 1980 and 1982 respectively, sought to outline a cohesive organizational strategy to adapt port, rail, and freeway infrastructure to projected increases in cargo volume. The plan called for the construction of a vast inland distribution system. Helped by a mixture of public and private funding, it embarked on a litany of expansion projects that included dredging and landfill expansion, the completion of the 710 Freeway, and the establishment of the Alameda Corridor, a twenty-mile-long rail cargo expressway that links the ports to a transcontinental rail network. The rail corridor proposed that shippers would be able to meet their just-in-time delivery demands and use "cheap land" in the Inland Empire to build larger warehouses.

Figure 3: The Alameda Corridor Trench, by Thomas Brightbill, https://www.flickr.com/photos/8825143@N06/3995028610. Licensed under CC by 2.0.

The proposal to construct the $2.4 billion Alameda Corridor involved the creation of new institutional arrangements that enabled Alameda Corridor proponents to apply for funding from regional, state, and federal agencies. To give the logistical project access to funds normally reserved for freeway, light-rail, and other public transportation projects, proponents of the corridor formed governance institutions that included the Alameda Corridor Transportation Authority (ACTA), which lobbied for broad support from the

LINEAGES OF INFRASTRUCTURAL POWER

Los Angeles County Metropolitan Transport Authority (LACMTA) and the harbor commissions of the two San Pedro Bay ports. Transportation leaders from these institutions argued that distribution networks should be publicly funded on the basis that logistics spending was a public good. This argument would prove successful, as in 1996 President Bill Clinton signed a federal loan for $400 million—a decision based on regional, state, and federal actors successfully framing Southern California's logistics network as "a public good worthy of federal funding."[37]

The Alameda Corridor example suggests that—beyond its specific economic investments in railways, roads, and other physical conduits—the state's production of a space for circulation is also an investment in turning the development of logistics infrastructure into a new political field, which sees the reproduction of the relations of production as a public good. "In reality," testified the executive director of the Port of Los Angeles, "the beneficiary of the Alameda Corridor's successful completion and operation is the American public, to whom our domestic and global transportation efficiency is critical."[38] By flattening the interests of capital into the interests of an "American public," economic growth is framed in elite language as a proxy for public welfare, even as the construction of the Alameda Corridor soon proved to be detrimental to the communities living alongside it.

The Alameda Corridor was designed to take truck-hauled containers off the Long Beach freeway. However, because the corridor is run on the basis of expensive user fees, many shipping companies have found it cheaper to stick to single-can trucks on the freeway. Today, the corridor is used at only 40 percent of its total capacity, and its operating profit does not cover its annual interest expense, much less its outstanding debt of $2.2 billion. Yet plans are afoot to increase its footprint, moving it eastward into the Inland Empire. As states are pressured to make space safe for logistics flows, local actors produce governance systems and rationales that argue that the region's economic future depends on optimizing future port capacity, rationalizing various forms of dispossession and increased vulnerability by asserting the necessity of prioritizing market forces over social ones. In this sense, while logistical networks justify their expansive occupation of space by promising to distribute wealth and economic growth, they also distribute inequality, containment, and what Ruth Wilson Gilmore calls "vulnerability to premature death."[39]

Distributing Vulnerability

Indeed, logistics-related pollution in the lower-income port communities surrounding the harbor evince the literally necropolitical dimensions of Gilmore's definition. A Health Impact Assessment Report—conducted in 2010 for the Environmental Protection Agency to estimate the human costs of pollution at the ports of LA and Long Beach—found well-documented health inequities for communities near the ports, including "asthma and other respiratory diseases, cardiovascular disease, lung cancer, pre-term and low-weight births, and premature death."[40] Shipping-related emissions from the ports are estimated to contribute to a total of 59 percent of total city emissions,[41] while roughly one third of all goods movement emissions across the state of California are generated in the Los Angeles region.[42] Many of the vehicles associated with logistics complexes, including trucks, trains, and container ships, operate on diesel fuel or heavy fuel oil, which release cancer-causing toxins.

The State of California Air Resources Board estimates that by 2008, approximately 3,700 Californians had died annually from cancer caused by exposure to logistics-related traffic and diesel emissions. One hundred and twenty of those yearly deaths are associated with diesel particulate emissions generated exclusively by the port. For Southern Californian school children, living within seventy-five meters of a major road or railway was associated with an increased risk of lifetime asthma, wheeze, and noise-related developmental difficulties.[43] It also estimates that far more people—eighteen thousand—died annually from exposure to ambient levels of diesel particulate matter emissions.[44] Furthermore, port expansion disproportionately affects parts of the Southern California region with high concentrations of poor, Black, and Latinx residents. Data from the Los Angeles County Health Survey reveal that Long Beach communities in close proximity to the Port of Los Angeles experience higher rates of asthma, coronary heart disease, and depression than other communities in LA.[45] These effects are not limited to port cities. In the counties of the Inland Empire, which received 42 percent of all truck traffic that traveled through Southern California in 2003, the risks are likely to be much higher, since diesel particulate emissions account for 84 percent of pollution-related cancer risks.[46]

In response to the Health Assessment Impact report of 2010, the Los Angeles County Business Federation issued a letter to the Environmental

Protection Agency protesting the inclusion of health data into Environmental Impact Assessments. "Economic status," they argued, "is the strongest indicator of health."[47] The Business Federation proceeded to portray health assessments as unnecessary bureaucratic red tape that prevented the important work of logistics expansion; the latter, in turn, was seen as good for the very local communities they are poisoning: "The goods movement industries serving the Ports have invested billions of dollars over the years in local infrastructure, provided hundreds of thousands of jobs, and have generated income to local and state economies and the federal government." These important contributions, the Business Federation claimed, were hampered by "[c]onfusing, questionable, and unnecessary duplicative processes like the proposed HIA [Health Impact Assessment]" that "jeopardize these advances, particularly by adding to California's already existing, vast regulatory processes."[48]

On April 12, 2002, the Alameda Corridor opened with great fanfare. Private investors, members of the House of Representatives, and harbor commissioners gathered by the waterfront to celebrate it as a job creator, one of the first public-private partnerships in the region, and a key to the future success of the ports of Los Angeles and Long Beach. Assemblywoman Betty Karnette opined that the California Gold Rush would "pale in comparison to the lasting boom that would come by linking local ports directly to the national rail network."[49] At the opening ceremony of the corridor, Los Angeles Mayor James Hahn declared:

> I believe that as we sit here today, right behind us is the Silk Road of the third millennium, because California is the gateway to the Pacific Rim and Latin America. And our being here today also is a further demonstration that we're standing up to what took place on September 11. We're not looking inward; we're looking outward, and that's a very important thing for us to do. And our presence here demonstrates the freedom born when we are on the cutting edge of technology, in the greatest state in the United States of America.[50]

By understanding the Alameda Corridor as "the Silk Road of the third millennium," Hahn links the economic well-being of the state of California to a vision of global trade domination premised on the spatial unification of disparate sites and entities. In fact, by capitalizing on worries over the attacks on the Twin Towers on September 11, 2001, Hahn attaches an ideological fantasy of national development and freedom to the spatial unification of the world market and the technocratic production of systems enabling capital to unite the globe. In this way, logistical megaprojects seek to spatially unify the world market by subjecting diverse sites of human and environmental habitation to the dictates of "just-in-time" circulation, all while framing the slow violence of these encroachments and displacements in the language of public interest and social good.

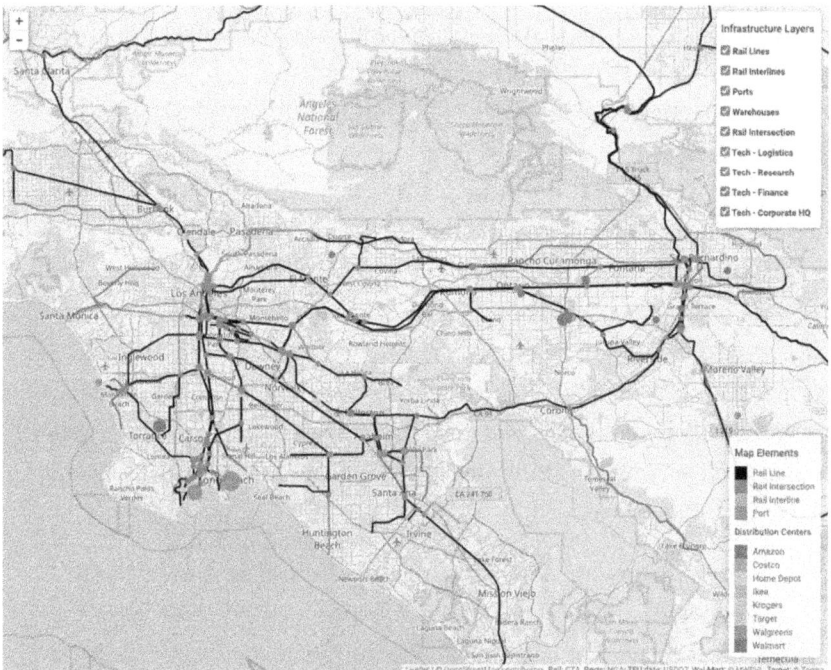

Figure 4: A map of LA's supply chain infrastructure, by The Empire Logistics Collective. http://www.empirelogistics.org/sci-map/. Courtesy of the Empire Logistics Collective

The politics surrounding the construction of the Alameda Corridor exemplify the complex relationships between corporate, city, and state interests that enmesh citizens and vulnerable populations in negotiations over how and where to build infrastructures of global circulation. As federal, state, and municipal governments identify infrastructure as a critical area of state intervention and investment, such projects become central not only to regional development strategies but also to the reproduction of capital across the system. These developments, often romanticized as job creators, are achieved through the production of an increasingly intensive and extensive system of spatial infrastructures through which the contradictions of capital are expressed in a turbulent flux of creative destruction and uneven geographical development.[51] Efforts to create and secure a "fast" world of just-in-time circulation in turn produce slow, material forms of violence in the landscapes they affect. They unevenly expand logistical violence across the city, shifting the costs of infrastructural expansion from the state–capital nexus to the people, socializing the risks by shifting them to the very communities and blue-collar workers left out of these promises of a prosperous future.

As Japhy Wilson and Manuel Bayón have argued in the case of the Manta–Manaus multimodal transport corridor in the Ecuadorian Amazon, the production of economic infrastructure does not only consist of "large-scale territorial planning strategies" or efforts to construct technocratic landscapes but is also "infused with idiosyncratic fantasies and hubristic ambitions . . . that exceed the instrumental rationalities of capitalist calculability."[52] Infrastructures of global circulation manifest the state's bet on the future of continued capital accumulation—a hope that materializes in physical transport projects. Even as supply chain infrastructure aims to make goods' movement through the city more fluid, the construction of such infrastructure fixes and freezes built environments in territorial space, placing disproportionate environmental, spatial, and social burdens on the public in the name of those for whose benefit such infrastructures are built.

In the process of coming to see aggregate economic growth as a proxy for the well-being of the people, infrastructural projects reflect "a contemporary world in which infrastructures allow the accumulation of capital to bypass the work of building durable or productive structures for collective life."[53] As capital has been drawn into large infrastructures, it flows into projects that weaken rather than enhance the possibilities for future collective life: into pipelines for oil exports, skyscraper condominiums, privatized airports, fracking fields, megaships, and railroad corridors. If we understand transport infrastructures to be the underlying material networks that regulate the mobility of capital at the expense of the mobility of people, then their function to both capital and the state goes beyond purely microeconomic concerns with transport efficiency or firm-level profits. They also gesture toward the state and capital's shared faith in the durability of economic well-being: heavy investments in transportation infrastructure are a speculative bet on the continued growth of trade volumes and thus the continued wealth of nations. Megaships, megaports, and rail corridors—whose expansion seems constant and indiscriminate—are monumental figurations and projects of capitalism's future more than they are utilitarian economic objects.[54]

Viewed in this way, the speculative investments made by states and capital privatize the ownership of the means of circulation, while they socialize risks by unevenly distributing the effects of these infrastructures across the population. As the act of clicking on a button for a two-day shipping delivery has become normalized in the industrialized Global North, it is perhaps more critical than ever that we are reminded that accelerated practices of just-in-time consumption, distribution, and production are not separate from political realities but instead contribute to the active precaritization and dispossession of vulnerable populations.

Endnotes

1. Rachel Uranga, "Why Port of Los Angeles Spent a Quarter-Million Dollars to Bring In a Megaship," *Daily Breeze,* August 6, 2016, https://www.dailybreeze.com/2016/08/06/why-port-of-los-angeles-spent-a-quarter-million-dollars-to-bring-in-a-megaship/.
2. Greg Yee, "New Era Dawns at Port of Los Angeles as Megaship Arrives," *Press Telegram,* December 26, 2015, https://www.presstelegram.com/2015/12/26/new-era-dawns-at-port-of-los-angeles-as-megaship-arrives/.
3. Yee, "New Era Dawns at Port of Los Angeles."
4. See Charmaine Chua et al., "Introduction: Turbulent Circulation: Towards a Critical Engagement with Logistics," *Environment and Planning D: Society and Space* 36, no. 4 (2018): 617–29; Deborah Cowen, *The Deadly Life of Logistics* (Minneapolis: University of Minnesota Press, 2014).
5. Mike Davis, *City of Quartz: Excavating the Future in Los Angeles* (London: Verso Press, 2006), 99–151.
6. Mike Davis, *Late Victorian Holocausts: El Niño Famines and the Making of the Third World* (London: Verso Press, 2001). On the role of railroads in famine, see 26–27, 142, and 332. As Davis writes, public works in India were driven first by the exigencies of military control and second by the demands of export agriculture. As the pro-irrigation lobby led by Sir Arthur Cotton and Florence Nightingale wrote during the 1876–77 famine: "Now we have before our eyes the sad and humiliating scene of magnificent Works [railroad] that have cost poor India 160 millions, which are so utterly worthless in the respect of the first want of India, that millions are dying by the side of them" (Davis 2001, 332).
7. Mike Davis, *Dead Cities: And Other Tales* (New York: The New Press, 2002), 161–2.
8. Ruth Wilson Gilmore, *Golden Gulag: Prisons, Surplus, Crisis, and Opposition in Globalizing California* (Berkeley: University of California Press, 2007), 27.
9. Davis, *Dead Cities,* 156.
10. Davis, *Dead Cities,* 156.

11 Davis, *Dead Cities*, 156.
12 For a detailed analysis of the rise of logistics, see Cowen, *Deadly Life of Logistics*, especially Chapters 1 and 2.
13 "Port Master Plan, Port of Los Angeles," 2014, accessed May 29, 2019, https://www.portoflosangeles.org/getmedia/2f2b99a8-f0c3-4e01-9bfe-ba34de05293d/amendment-28.
14 On the history of military logistics, see Manuel DeLanda, *War in the Age of Intelligent Machines* (New York: Zone Books, 1991); and Martin Van Creveld, *Supplying War: Logistics from Wallenstein to Patton*, 2nd ed. (Cambridge: Cambridge University Press, 2004).
15 Robert Brenner, *The Economics of Global Turbulence: The Advanced Capitalist Economies from Long Boom to Long Downturn, 1945–2005* (New York: Verso Press, 2005), 164.
16 Karl Marx, *Capital, Volume II*, trans. David Fernbach (London: Penguin books, 1978), 228–29.
17 Marc Levinson, *The Box: How the Shipping Container Made the World Smaller and the World Economy Bigger* (Princeton, NJ: Princeton University Press, 2006), 354.
18 Daniel Bernhofen, Zouheir El-Sahli, and Richard Kneller, "Estimating the Effects of the Container Revolution on World Trade," Lund University Working Paper 2013: 4 (Lund, Sweden: Department of Economics, School of Economics and Management, Lund University, 2013).
19 International Transport Forum, *The Impact of Mega-ships: Case-Specific Policy Analysis*, 2015, https://www.itf-oecd.org/sites/default/files/docs/15cspa_mega-ships.pdf.
20 See Antonio Tricario and Xavier Sol, "Mega-infrastructure as "Structural Adjustment 2.0," *Heinrich Böll Stiftung*, November 5, 2015, https://za.boell.org/2015/11/05/mega-infrastructure-structural-adjustment-20.
21 Brett Neilson, Ned Rossiter, and Ranabir Samaddar, eds. *Logistical Asia: The Labour of Making a World Region* (Singapore: Palgrave Macmillan, 2018).
22 Davis, *City of Quartz*, 112–3.
23 James Tejani, "Dredging the Future: The Destruction of Coastal Estuaries and the Creation of Metropolitan Los Angeles, 1858–1913," *Southern California Quarterly* 96, no. 1 (Spring 2014): 36.
24 Tejani, "Dredging the Future," 5–6.
25 See, for example, Steven P. Erie, *Globalizing L.A.: Trade, Infrastructure, and Regional Development* (Stanford, CA: Stanford University Press, 2004); William F. Deverell and Greg Hise, eds., *Land of Sunshine: An Environmental History of Metropolitan Los Angeles* (Pittsburgh, PA: University of Pittsburgh Press, 2005).
26 One good example of the mobilization of abstract space is LA's effort to annex the port, located well south of the city in Wilmington, to the jurisdiction of LA. Since this legislative maneuver required a territorial basis, Los Angeles boosters employed eminent domain to shoulder their way into establishing a "shoestring addition"—a contiguous land connection sixteen miles long and half a mile wide that was annexed in 1906 to connect the harbor and its resources to the city (see Figure 3).
27 See Davis, *City of Quartz*, 177–78 and 125–26.
28 "Port of Los Angeles Container Statistics," last accessed May 10, 2019, https://www.portoflosangeles.org/business/statistics/container-statistics.
29 Fernando Coronil, *The Magical State: Nature, Money and Modernity in Venezuela* (Chicago: University of Chicago Press, 1997).
30 Lefebvre, Henri, "Space and Mode of Production," in *State, Space, World: Selected Essays*, eds. Neil Brenner and Stuart Elden, trans. Gerald Moore, Neil Brenner, and Stuart Elden (Minneapolis: University of Minnesota Press, 2009), 90.
31 These measures have been crucial for maximizing the profits of large container lines such as Maersk: since their super-post-Panamax ships have launched, their freight costs have gone down from $3,108 per TEU in 2012 to $2,100 in 2017. "Maersk Strategy and Performance," *Maersk Investor Relations* Q1 2017, accessed May 10, 2019, https://investor.maersk.com/static-files/93f633a3-8235-4ed9-bac5-c1cfc6fcc2ae.

32 Edna Bonacich and Jake Wilson, *Getting the Goods: Ports, Labor, and the Logistics Revolution*. (Ithaca, NY: Cornell University Press, 2008).
33 Juan De Lara, *Inland Shift: Race, Space, and Capital in Southern California* (Berkeley: University of California Press, 2018), 42.
34 De Lara, *Inland Shift*, 39.
35 Will Recker, "Mitigating the Social and Environmental Impacts of Multimodal Freight Corridor Operations at Southern California Ports," *University of California Transportation Center Digital Library*, 2008, https://escholarship.org/uc/item/5dg5w4kp.
36 John Husing, 2004, quoted in De Lara, *Inland Shift*, 31.
37 De Lara, *Inland Shift*, 45.
38 Larry Keller, in *The Alameda Corridor Project: Its Successes and Challenges* (Washington, DC: US Government Printing Office, 2001).
39 Gilmore, *Golden Gulag*, 28.
40 Human Impact Partners, "Los Angeles and Long Beach Maritime Port HIA Scope," working draft prepared for the United States Environmental Protection Agency, May 17, 2010, 5, https://archive.epa.gov/region9/nepa/web/pdf/drafthiascope4portsoflalb.pdf.
41 Human Impact Partners, "Los Angeles and Long Beach Maritime Port HIA Scope."
42 See Recker, "Mitigating the Social and Environmental Impacts," 1. An OECD study of shipping emissions found that this number is similarly high in other major ports, with Hong Kong's port emissions contributing to 89 percent of total city emissions, and Rotterdam's port contributing 23–40 percent. OECD, "The Impact of Ports on Their Cities," in *The Competitiveness of Global Port-Cities* (Paris: OECD Publishing, 2014), 36, https://doi.org/10.1787/9789264205277-en.
43 Human Impact Partners, "Los Angeles and Long Beach Maritime Port HIA Scope," 27.
44 California Environmental Protection Agency, "Methodology for Estimating Premature Deaths Associated with Long-Term Exposure to Fine Airborne Particulate Matter in California," Air Resources Board, December 7, 2009, www.arb.ca.gov/research/health/pm-mort/pm-mortdraft.pdf.
45 Human Impact Partners, "Los Angeles and Long Beach Maritime Port HIA Scope," 16.
46 South Coast Air Quality Management District, quoted in De Lara, *Inland Shift*, 55.
47 Los Angeles County Business Federation to EPA, "Re: EPA's *Los Angeles and Long Beach Maritime Port HIA Scope: Working Draft*," September 22, 2010, US EPA Archive Document, https://archive.epa.gov/region9/nepa/web/pdf/bizfed.pdf.
48 Los Angeles County Business Federation, "Re: EPA."
49 Betty Karnette, "Alameda Corridor: Linking National Rail Network to Local Ports," *Los Angeles Times*, August 8, 1994, https://www.latimes.com/archives/la-xpm-1994-08-18-hl-28697-story.html.
50 James Hahn, in *The Forgotten Space*, directed by Allan Sekula and Noel Burch (New York: Icarus Films, 2012), 41:28–42:00.
51 See David Harvey, *Spaces of Neoliberalization: Towards a Theory of Uneven Geographical Development* (Stuttgart, Germany: Franz Steiner Verlag, 2005); and *The Limits to Capital* (London: Verso Press, 1999).
52 Japhy Wilson and Manuel Bayón, "Fantastical Materializations: Interoceanic Infrastructures in the Ecuadorian Amazon," *Environment and Planning D: Society and Space* 35, no. 5 (October 2017): 838.
53 Timothy Mitchell, "Introduction, Life of Infrastructure," *Comparative Studies of South Asia, Africa and the Middle East* 34, no. 3 (2014): 437.
54 For a different context in which such an argument is made, see the literature on hydroelectric dams as projects of modernity, for example James Kenny and Andrew Secord, "Engineering Modernity: Hydroelectric Development in New Brunswick, 1945–1970," *Acadiensis: Journal of the History of the Atlantic Region* 39, no. 1 (Winter/Spring 2010), https://journals.lib.unb.ca/index.php/Acadiensis/article/view/15382; Timothy Mitchell, *Rule of Experts: Egypt, Techno-Politics, Modernity* (Berkeley: University of California Press, 2002); and Erik Swyngedouw, *Liquid Power: Contested Hydro-Modernities in Twentieth-Century Spain* (Cambridge, MA: MIT Press, 2015).

DEATH CULTS OF EAST ANGLIA

China Miéville

Church ruins beyond a brutally hot field of dust. You took your pilgrimage route past exhausted pigs, a hollow way to the North Sea.

Once there were chambers hidden underground. As the shoreline erodes they are uncovered to jut from the cliffs. Whenever you come here there are changes to the seaside rubble, concrete rooms tumbled wrong-way-up onto the beach. This time a brick wall lay slanting down in the surf. You sat on it in the sun.

BETWEEN CATASTROPHE AND REVOLUTION

You drank the last of your water between desiccated tracts. The map was clear but the world so flat and arid, woodland so distant, your progress so slow you grew confused. You were specks in a stretched-out agribusiness sublime. There were no wrong turnings to take but you rechecked anyway. You grew thirstier and uneasy and wherever you were, it was a long walk back to where you'd started. Something was wrong with the landscape.

July 2018. It's as hot in Britain as anyone remembers. The temperatures peak in Suffolk.

Heat unmoors. You are vivid and smeared like a smudge of ink. Tethers deliquesce between things and their thingness: "[i]n the heat," L.P. Hartley had it of another remorseless East Anglian summer, "the commonest objects changed their nature." The air vibrates on the thresholds of horse exits in the Roman walls at Burgh. In these parts they said horses could see ghosts.

The rags of other heatwaves cling: you're in 2018 and 2006, too, 2003. And 1976, of course. Keeling and his colleagues put out their minatory and seminal piece "Atmospheric Carbon Dioxide Variation at Mauna Loa Observatory," and you're almost four years old and waiting for the water truck in a plague of ladybirds. Bishybarnybees, in local dialect, named for a heretic-hunting priest.

Now Malibu burns again. In Algeria, in Canada, in Japan, in South Korea, the heat kills. The jet stream's drifting north, and weak. There are all-time highs across the world. The arctic's in flames. "This is the moment," says Hans Joachim Schellnhuber, an author of "Trajectories of the Earth System in the Anthropocene," "when people start to realise that global warming is not a problem for future generations, but for us now." Nearly half of all Americans feel they have personal experience of climate change, according to a Yale study; 75 percent that it will harm future generations.

It's too hot to sleep. So the new nostrum is that this is the year when we wake up. The phrase reverberates in the reports of forest fires, mass extinctions, tipping points, and climate cascade, of ice-melt, warming seas, frost no-longer perma. A lifetime ago, Aldo Leopold wrote that "[o]ne of the penalties of an ecological education is that one lives alone in a world of wounds." Now millions of us labor toward such education, to live among those wounds. And still we're lonely.

DEATH CULTS OF EAST ANGLIA

The questions are not whether but how badly temperatures will rise, and what, if anything, "we"—that feint again—can do about it, and for how long. They come with a toll. More than 70 percent of Americans are worried, uncertain of their agency: more than half are "disgusted" or "helpless" or both. There can, notoriously, be *jouissance*, complex compensation, and investment in apocalypse thinking, but that does not countervail forthright and growing angst. In 2017, the American Psychological Association warned not only of "*acute* consequences of psychological well-being" given inevitable weather-pattern disasters, but of a longer-term existential impact; that the *longue durée* of climate change "will cause some of the most resounding *chronic* psychological consequences": depression, trauma, identity-loss, violence, helplessness, suicide.

Cautious data-crunching becomes a strange poetry of necessary imprecision: in a 2018 Yale/George Mason University study, "Climate Change in the American Mind," one chart is entitled "A Majority of Americans Who Think Global Warming Is Happening Feel a Range of Emotions." Global warming is the paradigmatic exemplar of what Timothy Morton calls a hyperobject, a diffuse thing of such enormous temporo-spatial scale that it evades traditional thingness, can be studied and considered but is, he writes, "something you cannot see or touch." It is "something on the tips of our tongues."

Language in and of this heat is evasive. "[T]here are hardly any intimate words" for what is happening, writes Zadie Smith in "Elegy for a Country's Seasons." This epoch is of the groping for utterance. What terms we coin for the sense of lamentation can only gesture at it—"ecoanxiety," Glenn Albrecht's "solastalgia," Renee Lertzmann's "environmental melancholia," Ashlee Cunsolo and Neville Ellis's "ecological grief," Deborah Bird Rose's "Anthropocene Noir." In December 2018, *Le Monde* reports that climatologists have "le blues."

(It is not long since you traveled a long way to the north, stood under the borealis, in polar night, and what you remember is that it was not cold enough. You think of it often. It seems the wrong verb for coldness but what cold there was *ebbed*. And with that memory always comes another, of the ebbing of heat from your mother's skin, under her head, when you held her, when she died.)

Whatever we call them, however much of them we can't articulate, these blues are real, growing, unfinished. "There is," as Cunsolo and Ellis put it, "much grief work to be done, and much of it will be hard."

DEATH CULTS OF EAST ANGLIA

Too hard for some. In the pages of the British tabloid the *Sun*—*nomen est omen*—Rod Liddle, thuggish jester-bully of the British commentariat, works anxiously to undermine such intuition and perspicacious grief.

"I remember the last few summers we've had—rainy and cool—and the climate change monkeys saying THAT was a consequence of global warming, too. You can't have it both ways." It's impossible to say how much of this is performance, whether Liddle is genuinely a fool. Weather systems are ultra-complex and overdetermined. No scientist thinks of them in monocausal or certain terms. The point, rather, as in the work of Friederike Otto, is to discern trends and the vastly increasing *likelihoods* of extreme events. On which basis one can, of course, have it both ways, the same systemic cascades being key determinants of contrasting phenomena.

"[T]his summer—a proper summer, at last—is something to be enjoyed, cherished and remembered," Liddle bangs on. His insistence is a cruel optimism of the Right. It exists not despite but because of those growing blues. Hence his deployment, alongside negation blatant enough to embarrass the most vulgar Freudian, of that standard reactionary trope, the demand for complicity. "[T]his hasn't been bad, has it?"

Has it? Has it?

Liddle, *en passant*, claims not to be a climate-change denier. Insofar as a coherent position beyond spite can be imputed to him, this is likely true, and symptomatic. Outright denialism remains a force, but for all the blare and bluster of its faithful, its season—its usefulness to the ruling class—is drawing slowly to a close. Now "residual doubts over global warming evaporate," the *Financial Times* reports. A Monmouth University poll tracks an increase in the number of Americans who "believe in" climate change of almost 10 percent in three years, to nearly eight in ten, including even close to two-thirds of Republicans, and 62 percent, Yale has it, see warming as mostly caused by human activity.

The Met Office "UK Climate Projections 2018" wargames temperature rises from one to five degrees for this place, already the driest part of the country. East Anglian summers will see more droughts. The region, says Charles Beardall of the Environmental Agency, is on the "front line of managing the impacts of climate change in the UK."

"Managing" is a verb with a lot of work to do.

BETWEEN CATASTROPHE AND REVOLUTION

As the ideological efficacy of denial decreases, climate hustlers try out other options. Simple Bad Hope can provide clickbait lists of Reasons for Optimism, faith that the adults in the room are bound to prevail. There is, too, more steely-eyed motivational management-think. "Like any disruptive force," writes Dimitris Tsitsiragos for the World Bank, as if of an exciting fintech startup, "climate change is creating opportunities for companies willing to innovate." These might range in the imaginary from Promethean geodreamwork of utopian technofix to more quotidian opportunism, a slavering at exciting markets of carbon capture, and so on. Sustainability is a "popular field that emerged to teach business how to become a force for ecological preservation," write Alan Bradshaw and Detlev Zwick, in "The Field of Business Sustainability and the Death Drive: A Radical Intervention"—and, they blithely add, it is "a project that *comes with its own guarantee of failure.*"

And what Naomi Klein has called the "monstrousness" of a certain supremacist antidenialism, a gloating that climate change is real, and will disproportionately affect the wretched of the earth, still largely subtextual in polite society, will grow. After all, mediated through the sociopathy of "entrepreneurialism," profiteering not only from supposed solutions to catastrophe, but from that catastrophe itself, is already celebrated.

"Take advantage of climate change business opportunities," enthuses nibusinessinfo.co.uk. "Climate change may increase demand for certain goods and services, such as water management products and equipment and clothing for extreme weather conditions." This is true, and depraved. With disaster does indeed come terrible need. These are not the sub-Ayn Randian ramblings of a marginal libertarian sadist, but the official business-guidance channel for Northern Ireland. The year 2018 "is likely to rank among the top 10 for the amount of sea ice melting in the Arctic Ocean," notes *Insurance Journal* of the opening waters. "While that's alarming to environmentalists concerned about global warming, ship owners carrying liquefied natural gas and other goods see it as an opportunity." In 2011, floods in Thailand killed hundreds, and affected over thirteen million. The country scrambled to develop flood-management systems—which the British Government's "national adaptation plan" two years later described as "a high-value business opportunity," preening that it "promotes and supports UK companies to access these opportunities."

"Your whole society," wrote Mike Davis in the voice of Plague, a decade and a half ago, "is suffering from acute apocalypse denial." Now both denial and its denial are commodified.

The stark heat seems magnified in this crumbling-edged selcouth landscape of clay and Pleistocene sand. A few cirrus do their best, as do dead trees and the eyelessly gazing water towers. But there's a drought of shadows too. The sunlight picks out roadside signs and rubble.

BETWEEN CATASTROPHE AND REVOLUTION

With effort and luck you might make anywhere do and mean anything, but there are prevailing semiotic tides, and their undertows (the Anglian moment, as Caitlín Doherty observes, is not uncorrelated with the place of Cambridge, UEA, and the Norwich Centre for Writing in the business of BritLit). This windblown place is dense with artistic glowerings, of Ruth Rendell, the Jameses P. D. and M. R., Sarah Perry, all the others in all the lists. Its big sky looms baleful above a certain existential crime noir; the recondite mooching of edgeland psychogeography; in spectral culture above all, ghosts, and the newly-fashionable bucolic uncanny of "Folk Horror."

Quis este site qui venit. Who is this who is coming?

Eeriness is fast catching up with its co-constitutive other, the weird, as an aesthetic to be noted. Robert MacFarlane has been a crucial skald, and the deeply mourned Mark Fisher its seminal theorist, his *The Weird and the Eerie* a fecund entry-point to the phenomenon.

For Fisher, the eerie "is constituted by a *failure of absence* or by a *failure of presence.*" Where the weird is a function of "the presence of *that which does not belong,*" the eerie arises where, and insofar as, "something [is] present where there should be nothing"—his example is of a bird's cry behind which is a sense of something beyond the animal—"or there is nothing present where there should be something"—a ruin, say, a place made strange by time, emptied of people. Which means "the central enigma" of the eerie "is the problem of agency": for the failure of absence, whether there is agency at all; for the failure of presence, what the nature is of that missing agency of which we feel a trace.

Unlike the radically unknowable of the Weird, the eerie is "merely" unknown—but constitutively so. Should it ever come to pass that the conundrum of agency be solved, "when knowledge is achieved," Fisher writes, "the eerie disappears."

There is to the Norfolk Broads "which lie in the midst of wide level marshes and tracts of sedgy fen," William Dutt writes in his 1906 book on the waterways, a "primeval, isolate beauty." Like the eco-anguish, it evades expression: "I had almost written sublimity." Almost but not quite: if the weird is the bad sublime, the eerie is sublime-proximate. For Thomas Hardy the "sublimity of a moor" was "chastened": in the flatland specificity of the broad is discernable a sublimity not chastened but *withheld.*

DEATH CULTS OF EAST ANGLIA

Fisher loved this eerie East Anglian landscape, this haunting land-sky configuration. His walks here were generative of his theories, political phenomenology. His strange heuristics of strangeness read aesthetics and their politics and the world that extrudes them. "Since the eerie turns crucially on the problem of agency, it is about the forces that govern our lives and the world," he wrote. "It should be especially clear to those of us in a globally tele-connected capitalist world that those forces are not fully available to our sensory apprehension." No wonder then that for him, "Capital is at every level an eerie entity."

Thus analysis, radical understanding. And what of the strategic resources, the lessons? What, to quote Matt Colquhoun (aka Xenogoth), in one example of the focus among many, are the "emancipatory potentials found within the *other-wordly*"?

For Colquhoun, with the "latent act of exit" from putative normality that Fisher terms "egress" in mind, the weird and eerie "resemble aesthetic tools for the creation of passageways between capitalism and its outside." He notes too, however, that "the political implications of egress, the weird and the eerie are not made as explicit as one might expect within the book itself."

BETWEEN CATASTROPHE AND REVOLUTION

What if those implications are not so much occult as absent, not even eerily so, and our hankering for their presence is a political problem?

The Left's fervid eagerness to derive politics and techniques from various fleeting and fleetingly succulent cultural morsels, from *the stuff we like*, is symptomatic of our terrible weakness.

Allow that not everything we enjoy or in which we find affective resonance can be effectively, politically, strategically, tactically, applied. Test everything that gets you up in the morning for whatever contingent inspiration you can find. But know that it comes from you, and traction for you is not traction *tout court*, still less some political Real. We are predisposed to such Procrustean activity, but we are not alone in that. In capitalism all signs are reversible. There are gothic fascisms as well as gothic Marxisms, and weird fascisms too, many of them, and if the Left decides it will "learn the lessons" of the Eerie, so too can our enemies. And it is not more eeriness that will defeat them, nor any placeness of the places in which we find it.

The admirable hate of #folkloreagainstfascism, of those invested in certain music and landscape, fables and hedge-magic—Yallery Brown, say, the Woolpit Green Children, Black Shuck, *Your preferred folktale here*—and who are aghast that they are snaffled by the Far Right for its murderous national kitsch, is righteous. Fascists should not, indeed, be allowed to own what they claim to own. What cannot follow though for such contested scobs is a Red essentialism—*something something subversive spirits of the land something something radical Albion*.

Yes, complicate and enrich what David Southwell calls the "ghost soil" with counterhistory and creative reading. Unwhite it: learn, say, from Wedaeli Chibelushi's "A Brief History of Blackness in East Anglia," of Thomas Parker, the "certayne dark mayne" of sixteenth-century Essex, Maria Sambo two centuries later, Allan Glaisyer Minns of Thetford, in 1904 the first Black mayor in Britain. Commemorate local histories of insurrection—Bury St Edmunds risings in 1264 and 1381, Kett's Rebellion of 1549, the riots of 1822, the Burston Rebellion of 1914. Keep them in mind, because they matter, wherever they take place, and because like Fisher you love *this* place, but not to find in them some ineffable intransigence intrinsic to this local earth. There is none, except to the extent that it is everywhere. In her celebration of "this uncanny land," Sarah Perry has it that "[t]he character of the East Anglian woman is radical, literate, rebellious, courageous, mystic and astute." Yes, but only to the extent that also No. This is no more *au fond* the nature of "the" East Anglian woman than is the nature of Aldeburgh locals, per George Crabbe's 1783 *The Village*, that of "a wild amphibious race, / With sullen wo display'd in every face." There are and were thoroughly mammalian and cheerful Aldeburghians, and actually existing East Anglian women, and men, include the reactionary, unread, conformist, cowardly, earthbound, and dim in usual proportions.

Is this too ungenerous? Too reductionist? Perry herself describes East Anglia as "ripe with myth." (As where is not?) Perhaps what such ruminations could call up, create, sustain is precisely a kind of myth. It will be a political myth, as all myths are.

Still, that literalist caution remains necessary: too many such invocations fail to distinguish essentialist truth-claims—a political ontology of place—and mythopoeic intervention. Adequately or at all. Which elision, whatever the intention and however conscious or not, inevitably serves reaction. And myth itself may be inevitable, but it is always ambiguous and polyvalent, never more so than when naturalized. The Far Right knows very well that myth is political. A key danger of mythopoesis of place is that it cleaves so very well with that agenda.

This is clear and troublesome to practitioners of art and thought within the melancholy field of "landscape punk" (Gary Budden), of "re-enchantment as resistance" (David Southwell). John Harrigan of the FoolishPeople collective, for example, insists "it's vital we don't permit racists/fascists to pervert the landscape of Britain." But even here is the sign of that essentialism, of a *genius loci*, a "truth" of place that has been "perverted." The danger is not merely of "technicized" in place of "genuine myth," in Károly Kerényi's terms, glossed by Andrea Cavaletti as the "instrumental distortion of ancient mythologemes for the purposes of political propaganda." The problem is of myth *tout court*, of the edifice that the great radical mythologist Furio Jesi, in his break with Kerényi, came bleakly to see as "the mythological machine."

The artist Paul Watson, in his own heartfelt straining to salvage landscape from the Right, calls "the oldest past version of a myth... the kernel, the most primal incarnation"; "Deep Myth." He is honest that he finds "[t]he desire to glimpse the deep myth... a strong one," and for him "in that glimpse of the primal comes a re-enchantment"—resistance. But Watson himself is clear of such deep myth that "[i]n realistic terms it's unknowable"—and, we should add, untrustworthy, if there was ever any such kernel at all. No matter how antique or otherwise are the lovingly deployed stories and tropes of locale, this is precisely *poiesis*, political myth-*making*, on one side or another. It is not spiritual archaeology of some ur-truth.

We may feel that "deep myth" can, as Watson avers, be "glimpsed as a partial reflection in the contemporary version." But, crucially, we cannot know what, if anything, it is that we actually glimpse, nor whence it comes; and what capacities we have for enchantment, radical and otherwise, inhere not in *what* we glimpse but in *that we yearn to glimpse it*, and in our sense that glimpse it we can.

These cautions must be explicit.

There is, though, a distinct and more productive conception of myth implicit in Watson's image of uncovering, in his mode of access to the putatively ancient: "[s]omewhere in the metaphorically dense language of the contemporary myth are echoes of the primal deep one." But any such echoes are not only relatively but absolutely autonomous of any originary sound. These echoes are not "within" but *are* in fact those very metaphors of which he speaks, drawing on Adrienne Rich on the "metaphoric density" of language—and, we can add, of any system of signs. There is no lonely hour of the last instance, no *grundnorm* of meaning at the metaphors' base.

"At the molten heart of things everything resembles everything else," writes Edward St Aubyn of metaphor and its annealing. That insight might be a source of gladness, rather than his protagonist's anguish. In metaphor, in the fire of the mind, everything does not so much resemble everything else, perhaps, as admix with it, become it. Even as it pours off soot and the slag of meaning, too, semiotic runoff, to set in fantastic opacities. It is by metaphors that we might, not recover, but construct, political myth. Mindful of political ambivalences, what we forge from place may—*may*—even be that radically inflected "denotative myth" of which the Marxist Bible scholar Roland Boer cautiously approves.

Our commitment is not to primality, to any imagined deep-time depth. Landscape must be something that we *do*, in fidelity to liberation.

The Island, they once called it, though it is not an island but a long strip of shingle and sand tethered to the coast. The military had a secret base. This place is notorious for bygone death rays and radar towers and UFOs, the moldering knoll-sided pagodas of an industry and statecraft of speculative apocalypse. Orford Ness is a litter of battle rubbish, engines and struts like the discards of invasion, now sculptures of themselves in rust. The holed and deserted shacks are overrun, wind, grass, birds. You pay a ferryman to cross the water—reality is not subtle—to trudge like mendicants in Hell.

The laboratories fell apart under the sun years ago. "[T]he closer I came to these ruins," W. G. Sebald wrote of his own, then-illicit, approach, "the more any notion of a mysterious isle of the dead receded, and the more I imagined myself amidst the ruins of our own civilisation after its extinction in some future catastrophe." As if that's a contradiction. The catastrophe is here, and these, like those of the church up the coast, are ruins by design. The policy is called "managed decline." A nationally sanctioned becoming-eerie.

In nineteenth-century Brazil, Mike Davis notes with cataclysm empathy, "millenarianism in the *sertão* was also a practical social framework for coping with environmental instability . . . sermonizing apocalypse but practicing energetic self-help." Why not? There are far worse strategies. Change that last conjunction, in fact, from "but" to "and" or "so," the sermons being inextricable from the struggle. For a new chiliasm of the Left. We could make sacred masks out of the military trash in the sand, if it helps, masks like those "burning at our gate" in the eleventh and harshest verse of Jini Fiennes's "Suffolk Song Cycle," masks that "glare" and that "[w]ith sightless sense interrupt."

Interruption could hardly be more urgent.

Lines of dead trees, lichened concrete in the bird sanctuary, drowned houses off the coast, everything means what it means and more than it means. Today everything is a metaphor for the end, for hope, and for hopelessness. On the other side of the world, bats are falling cooked alive out of the sky, and we don't pretend that doesn't matter or that everything will be alright. Against the yaysayers, undefeated despair is militancy. Richard Seymour: "[I]t is the catastrophists, the doom-mongers who believe in the future."

For the Catholic leftist Herbert McCabe, in the triumph of liberation, the post-ruptural Kingdom of God, so close to communism, "there will be no more Eucharist, no more sacramental religion, no more faith or hope." To hope against hope is not merely to contest all the dreg-like hope unearned: it is prefiguration. To live with an eye on the horizon where hope is no longer needed. In this baking flood-prone place the horizon is very clear.

Amid the stochastic specimens of collapse are more curated objects. They "do not come more chilling," writes Paddy Heazel in his history of Orford Ness, than the casing of a WE177 freefall bomb, ten times more powerful than the destroyers of Hiroshima and Nagasaki. There lies its husk.

This is a landscape of relics. Mummified roadkill hares. The local saints—Julian, Pega, Guthlac, Witburga, Tova. "[O]f St Gilbert two pieces," runs one ancient meticulous list of sanctified dead parts from a Norwich church, "of St. Euphemia the like, of the innocents the like, of St. Stephen four pieces, of St. Wulstan one piece, of St. Leger one piece," and so, grimly and lengthily, on.

It took strenuous propaganda by the twelfth-century monk Thomas of Monmouth for the cult of St. William of Norwich to flourish. The "poor ragged little lad," he retold the story, was tortured and murdered by Norwich Jews, in grotesque mockery of Christ's passion. The tale was obfuscation, defense of a down-at-heel knight for the murder of the banker to whom he owed money, by posthumously claiming his victim was ringleader of the child-killers. For the historian E. M. Rose, in indicting a whole community, the story was a key generative text of the blood libel, with all the antisemitic murder that followed. An ushering-in of mass death with a smearing of the dead, in the name of the honor of a dead boy, pornographically depicting his death-mocking death.

Monmouth's tract was lost for years. The repressed returns, of course. The man who unearthed it in "a small dank building in the churchyard" in 1890, who translated and introduced it, was the progenitor of the modern ghost story, that key eeritician, M. R. James himself.

"For James, who was both a horror writer and a conservative Christian," writes Fisher, "the fascination for the outside is always fateful."

If a Norfolk raven croaks above a house it portends death. As does a dog howling at night below a sickroom window. Bees swarming on a dead tree are death. Four crows in the road, an unmelted wick in a guttering candle, a candle burning at all in a shuttered room, the sound of a cuckoo heard from bed, a snake in the house, all mean death.

BETWEEN CATASTROPHE AND REVOLUTION

A cadaver that is not relic enough, that is too slow to enter rigor, is another presentiment of mortality to come. In this place death itself can be a sign for death. Death inadequately enacted invoking metadeath.

In 2013, the vicar Tony Higton—officiating chaplain for RAF Marham, erstwhile director of the Church's Ministry amongst Jewish People (CMJ), once called "Mary Whitehouse in a dog collar" for his traditionalist fervor during the Church's sexuality fights in the 1980s—started a new project. With his wife Patricia Higton, a reader in the church, the "high-profile West Norfolk clergyman," one Christian outlet enthused, inaugurated "a web campaign calling Christians to take Eschatology (the doctrine of the End Times) seriously." The site is regularly updated, navigating the traditional, much-mocked tea-and-biscuits moderation of Anglicanism with the urgency of doomsday augury: "There is an escalating fulfilment of the biblical signs of the end." Hence its assiduous evidence-parsing for impending Armageddon.

"You're living in a nihilistic death cult," writes Richard Seymour of the fetishized machinery of the border. That is not the cult's only mystery. It is not long since Corbyn's cordial refusal to pledge that he would enact pointless nuclear mass murder, like that imagined with the dead bomb, was a political scandal.

Capitalism oscillates between disavowal and death-avowal in these Higtonian end times. In the 2007 council climate-change strategy, "Tomorrow's Norfolk, Today's Challenge," the crises to come are itemized as if by some bureaucrat St. John—floods, destruction, sickness and death, the ruination of heritage, crop failure, pestilence. Then, immediately, come those familiar commercial opportunities.

"[H]otter, drier summers will help make Norfolk more favourable as a tourism destination."

Welcome to terminal beach.

Like those crows in the road, the guttering candles, like the unstraight sowing of seed in an East Anglian field, they say, #EFDS is a harbinger of death. "EcoFascist Death Squads," a dream of the online Deep Green Right.

The overt avowed hecatomb logic of genocide will increase in volume with the temperature. Brayers of a long-sedimented drive. "Long live death!" goes the fascist slogan—death of the enemy, the *untermenschen*, the unclean

DEATH CULTS OF EAST ANGLIA

and rootless, the weak and feminine, the snake in the garden, and of the world, and ultimately, even, perhaps, of the self. There will be supremacist suicide cults, embracing all doom, including their own. Already, Pentti Linkola, lugubrious doyen of fascist green thanatology, is clear: "If there were a button I could press, I would sacrifice myself without hesitating, if it meant millions of people would die."

It is not hard to imagine the semiotic bric-a-brac of these annihilationist myths to come. Such hothouse-Earth fascisms will festoon themselves of course in their pitiful solar symbols, maunder about Evola and solar civilisation, the sun wheel, the sun cross, the black sun, the sol invictus. They will be entranced by Albert Speer, the theory of "Ruin Value," of the central importance of bequeathing to deep time suitable Reich memorabilia, monumental and impressive ruins. They will pine, that is, as fascisms always have, to be a supremacist eerie. A crust like dried-up spittle. An absence proclaiming the triumph of death.

East Anglia is eroded by the sea. Out of "le blues," with fury and without surrender, must come a contestation, to bring to this moment of disaster capitalism and fascist eerie a ruin communism, hope against hope.

In the converted chapel at Westleton, among the piled-up books for sale a tattered old volume fell open in your hands. The ancient adverts in the back were for more lost volumes: *An Experiment with Time*; and *Nothing Dies*. You fanned yourself with the pages.

They call it Silly Suffolk, sometimes, then quickly stress that the adjective is a mutation of the old word "seely." That it means "holy," for all that hallowed ground. But seely has many meanings. "Pious" and "good" and "blessed," "holy," yes, "happy" and "lucky." But "deserving of sympathy," too, and "pitiable," the *OED* informs. "Worn-out" and "crazy." "Observant of due season." "In danger of divine judgement."

East Anglia in its due season, facing vastation.

They executed the ungodly so often in Norwich that one old map marks out "Ye place where ye Heretickes are custumably burned." In 1589, they put Francis Kett—grandson of he of the rebellion forty years before—to flame for denying the divinity of Jesus. One scandalized critic glossed his democratic theology of mortal flesh: "Christ Jesus is not God, but a good man, as others be." But as Dewey D. Wallace points out of Kett's heresies, "eschatological motifs are far more prominent than denial of the Trinity," and "[c]entral to his eschatology would seem to be the notion that redemption is future and imminent." Only when he ushers in the Kingdom will the son of man become God.

McCabe's beyond-hope draws near, in the hands of a self-actualizing humanity. Kett could hardly more clearly be, as Wallace says, a "link in that strange connection between bizarre religious notions and incipient rationalism," nor "further confirmation of the significance of the passage from specifically eschatological eccentricities to radicalism." Amen. Even his enemies marked his piety. At the stake, one allowed with grudging admiration, Kett "went leaping and dauncing . . . clapping his handes, he cried nothing, but blessed be God, blessed be God, blessed be God." There are new ways to die, to move, to be in the body.

In the broads, in the corridors of reeds, a shimmering split the surface and made it gleam. A snake swimming. Another strange, alternate animal motion. It crossed right before your prow, the most beautiful thing there's ever been. It thrust its head up out of the water as it went. It glared skyward, just as if it was staring down the sun.

All images courtesy of the author.

THE CALCULUS OF CLIMATE CHANGE

Andrew Ross

Feasting off exceptionally warm Atlantic waters, Harvey, Irma, and Maria, the hellcats of the 2017 hurricane season, racked and ruined islands and coastal cities in their path. The amped-up wind speed and rainfall brought record-breaking damage to metro areas like Houston, Jacksonville, and San Juan, and cut vital supports to rural Caribbean populations for months on end. As with other extreme weather events, the death toll was highly uneven. Poor communities with flimsy infrastructure were mercilessly exposed, while others with resources for resilience were much better insulated. Media coverage of the destruction and the response of government relief agencies were just as imbalanced, reflecting the hierarchy of value placed on different classes of human life. The plight of Houston suburbanites sucked up most of the attention, leaving a much skimpier ration for the humanitarian crisis on Puerto Rico's *campos*. There was little bandwidth left for outlying Caribbean islands. Gaston Browne, the prime minister of Antigua and Barbuda (population ninety-seven thousand before Maria) was reduced to petitioning the UN with the headline-grabbing plea: "For the first time in three hundred years, there is no permanent resident of Barbuda."

At roughly the same time, South Asian countries were deluged by the worst monsoon season in decades, but the devastating floods—which killed thousands and left tens of millions homeless—registered as a routine news item. Multitudinous loss of life in Bangladesh, Nepal, and India is regarded as almost customary, and it folds into a familiar pattern of expectation for spectators, never mind policymakers, in better-provisioned parts of the world. Climate watchers were more alert to the patterns of damage, noting the added impacts of permanent flooding from the steady rise of water levels in the Bay of Bengal. According to the Environmental Justice Foundation, the loss of landmass to the swelling ocean is displacing as many as 250,000 Bangladeshis each year, and by 2050, one in seven (or eighteen million) will be affected.[1] These audits of climate change impacts are now automatically tuned to the frequencies of the future, reflecting a different order of expectation about the catastrophic vulnerability of poor populations who reside near imperiled coastlines.

Such observations about the social asymmetry of extreme weather events call to mind *Late Victorian Holocausts*, Mike Davis's masterly dissection of a series of drought-famines that ravaged populations across the globe in the last quarter of the nineteenth century. Arguably the grimmest volume in Davis's oeuvre, it is also the most consequential. Published in 2000, and dwelling on events long before the signal of anthropogenic global warning emerged, the book is an indispensable model for responding to today's trifecta of meteorological extremity, ecosystem collapse, and economic royalism. Profiling the grisly "fate of tropical humanity" during the belle epoque of high imperialism, Davis added new material to the record of barbarism that accompanied capital's penetration of the peripheries in Africa, Asia, and South America. But the synchrony he detected between widespread and disparate floods and droughts (in 1877, 1888–91, and 1896–1902) also suggested a new role for climate in the toolkit of historical inquiry.

Attributing causality for these ruinous events to ENSO (El Niño-Southern Oscillation), the periodic variation in sea surface temperatures in the Indo-Pacific region, Davis introduced an underlying factor that would not be scientifically identified until the 1960s. But no matter how responsible ENSO was for the severe droughts and floods, it was not to blame for the calamitous hardship resulting from them. The culprit was the reigning laissez-faire economic philosophy, which allowed colonial authorities little leeway for famine relief, especially when the doctrine was bolstered by the presumption that the victims were going to perish in large numbers anyway—whether from malnutrition or from the disease epidemics that ravaged the refugee camps. Under the sway of Malthus's dismal theory of population, elites were inclined to see famine as a convenient, even "natural," solution to the problem of overpopulation.

THE CALCULUS OF CLIMATE CHANGE

Another factor was the collapse of traditional defenses against famine—in China, for example, the Qing's imperial granaries, flood control systems, and networks of emergency food distribution had all disintegrated in the face of foreign penetration. A third was the international emergence of a speculative commodity market that kept grain prices uniformly high when such staples were most urgently needed. Capitalism and colonialism did not originate the biblical-scale rainfalls or monsoon failures—the worst recorded in centuries—but, in Brecht's sardonic phrase, they "brilliantly organized" the mass starvation in the wake of the natural disasters.

In Davis's estimate, at least thirty million died overall. These numbers seem to have escaped the scrutiny of historians, even though they match, or surpass, the death toll registered in many of the twentieth century's centrally sourced massacres: the Shoah, Soviet gulags, Khmer Rouge's killing fields, Ukrainian Holodomor, and Armenian, East Timor, and Rwandan genocides. Yet the lessons Davis draws from the lethal cocktail of free-market religion and environmental insecurity are more serviceable to us as we confront a rapidly unfolding climate refugee crisis fed by the intransigence of fossil-fuel capitalists and intensified by the cruel vigilance of "armed lifeboat" proponents in the lineage of Garret Hardin.

Davis summons various sources of evidence in the course of his prosecution. Most predictable is the insouciance of colonial administrators. They view the emaciated famine victims through the saloon windows of their fast-moving vice-regal trains and see only the "laziness" of "relief cheats" and "shirkers," all the while protectively eying the mountains of grain that line the ports or railway sidings—just a stone's throw from the famine camps, and designated for export to the metropole. Frontline reports provide Davis with more graphic accounts, on page after page, of the walking skeletons, peasants reduced to eating their houses, mothers cooking their own children, orphanages turned into charnel houses, bleached skulls littering the landscape, and wild beasts exercising dominion, attacking humans in broad daylight. Last but not least, there are the stark mortality numbers, which Davis uses to punctuate every other visit to a disaster scene in the book. At times, he presents them in two forms: an official lowball assessment of deaths, followed by more capacious estimates offered by candid regional witnesses or demographers. The more inclusive numbers accounted for victims in the aftermath of a drought-famine, when the price gouging of grain profiteers, for example, took a heavy toll.

At the time, statistics like these carried a moral punch when wielded by critics of colonial policy. But mostly they ended up being placed on the (lesser) negative side of the "balance sheet" of empire, opposite the more weighty accounts of revenue streams extracted from colonial possessions. In the course of the twentieth century, the citation of colossal death tolls as a blunt indictment of an aggressor's conduct, or of "man's inhumanity to man," would become more routine, especially after human rights established its centrality in the realm of international relations. With the emergence of the environmental movement, the statistical profiling of ecological catastrophes would take on a new life as a weapon of advocacy. Activists used alarming facts and figures to stoke popular anxiety about overpopulation, species extinction, freshwater loss, glacier melt, sea level rise, and all manner of ecosystem collapse. Inevitably, efforts to check the runaway devastation coalesced around the shorthand of easily legible numbers. Scientists fixed on a *2°C rise* in global mean *temperature* as the threshold limit for averting drastic climate change, while grassroots movement groups targeted atmospheric CO_2 concentrations—such as 350.org (as measured in parts per million)—to publicize as a guardrail. These choices come with public warnings that breaching those limits will generate irreversible impacts on ecosystems, with consequences that are much more difficult to calculate as human and environmental costs.

Once again, a different form of accounting can be found on the other side of the balance sheet. The threat of climate change has given birth to a busy new world of financial speculation, in which disaster capitalism and a transformed insurance industry have emerged as voracious pacesetters. Predatory lenders have learned how to approach distressed communities with recovery loans in the wake of a catastrophe, while profiteers swoop down to bargain-pick public services on the auction block. Insurers play a different game. In January 2018, Munich Re, the world's leading reinsurer specializing in "complex global risk," estimated that overall losses from worldwide natural catastrophes in 2017 totaled $330 billion, up from $184 billion in 2016. The primary reason for the increase was the costly North Atlantic hurricane season. Hurricane Irma racked up $32 billion in insured losses in the United States and the Caribbean, while Hurricane Harvey and Hurricane Maria each resulted in $30 billion in insured damage. The company, which still managed to pay out €1.3 billion to shareholders, also estimated in its annual report, that ten thousand people lost their lives in 2017's natural disasters, slightly more than in 2016, but much fewer than the ten-year average of approximately sixty thousand and the thirty-year average of fifty-three thousand. The conclusion to the report noted "a long-term trend towards a reduction in the number of victims."

This decline accompanies a dramatic increase in the frequency of natural catastrophes, as recorded over the course of more than forty years by Munich Re's Geo Risks Research unit and logged in its NatCatSERVICE database. Company analysts are perfectly comfortable with attributing this increase to anthropogenic causes and naturally have sought to profit from the result. So while insured losses have risen accordingly, the landscape of heightened risk has opened up opportunities to develop new insurance products, many of them targeted at poor countries as investment strategies to offset losses from climate change. The NatCatSERVICE data show that, of the 861,000 people who lost their lives between 1980 and 2015 as a result of weather-related natural catastrophes worldwide, 61 percent (522,000) lived on less than $3 per day.

For firms offering "financial protection," such high mortality rates among the world's poorest people are viewed as a favorable misfortune. So while climate justice activists lobbied the climate policymakers of the *United Nations Framework Convention on Climate Change (*UNFCCC) to force the carbon-rich Northern beneficiaries of industrialization to pay their carbon debts to the Global South, insurers like Munich Re were pitching their products at the same international forums.[2] Their efforts paid off in 2015, when the G7 nations agreed to launch InsuResilience, a climate insurance initiative designed to provide coverage to the populations of emerging and developing nations, either for entire countries, or through direct policies for individuals. Under the InsuResilience scheme (rolled out at the 2017 UN Climate Conference in Bonn), claims payments are linked to clearly defined weather parameters, such as levels of rainfall or wind speed.

It is no surprise to find such profit-minded arithmetical alternatives to the number crunching of climate justice activists (whose pinnacle was the country-by-country breakdown of historical carbon debt researched by climatologist James Hansen and sent to Australian prime minister Kevin Rudd in 2008).[3] After all, the origins of the insurance industry lie in the mortality statistics compiled in seventeenth- and eighteenth-century life tables, and in the subsequent application of probabilities to life contingencies based on these numbers. The science of demography developed in tandem with insurance as a more "objective" endeavor. But, like many fields developed through putatively neutral methods, it has been hampered, especially from the time of Malthus onward, by persistently racialized assumptions about the relative worth of population segments. As we enter the fast-flowing mainstream of the era of climate refugees, the strongest countercurrents are being driven by the belief that there are just too many of the wrong kind of people.

A Debacle of Dependency

At the tail end of 2017, officials from Puerto Rico's Department of Public Safety announced that they were standing by their original finding that only sixty-four islanders had died as a result of Hurricane Maria. By then, there had been several estimates with much higher numbers (more than a thousand in one *New York Times* study) than the official count. In May 2018, a Harvard study, published in the *New England Journal of Medicine*, put the total number of deaths at 4,645. By then, the authorities responsible for relief—both in San Juan and Washington—had been pummeled for their inadequate efforts. Notwithstanding the difference between direct victims (from water and wind) and indirect fatalities (related to the storm's prolonged impact on the island's rickety infrastructure and public health resources), the discrepancy in death tolls suggested, at the very least, an institutional reluctance to acknowledge the scale of the disaster.

Under public pressure, the government of Puerto Rico contracted with George Washington University to review the official count. In August 2018, the Department of Public Safety sheepishly acknowledged that an overlooked government study had indeed suggested a death toll of 1,427, twenty times higher than the original figure. Later that month, the results of the George Washington University study were published, indicating that between 2,658 and 3,290 excess deaths occurred between September 2017 and February 2018, primarily driven by the effects and aftermath of Hurricane Maria. Governor Ricardo Rosselló acknowledged the results and revised the island's official death toll to 2,975 people.

THE CALCULUS OF CLIMATE CHANGE

But public anger over the government numbers fed off the prevailing perception that Puerto Ricans are themselves chronically undervalued by their own elected officials, never mind by federal lawmakers, whom they cannot elect. After all, Maria was just the final ingredient in the perfect neocolonial storm of debt and austerity that economic and political elites concocted in the years preceding the hurricane. Child poverty levels climbed past 60 percent, and public education and health systems were decimated as the fiscal affairs and debt restructuring of Puerto Rico were put under the control of the unelected, seven-member Financial Oversight and Management Board.[4] The anger accumulated over the next year, and massive protests were staged in the summer of 2019, resulting in the ouster of Rosselló.

The challenge to the death toll count in Puerto Rico was not the only contest over Maria's numbers. The mass exodus from the island took tens of thousands of climate refugees to the US mainland. By far the majority ended up in Florida, especially in the counties in the central part of the state—where Puerto Ricans had already established a strong presence, and where, coincidentally, the threat from coastal flooding and future hurricanes was less significant. The influx surprised many Americans, who were unaware that the incomers were US citizens. It also sparked predictable sentiment about services being overloaded by the migrants, and more toxic commentary about the "Puerto Rican Mariel," referencing the mass boatlift of 1980, which had emptied Cuba's prisons. For the refugees, Central Florida was not a soft choice. It already ranked among the top two metro areas nationally for unaffordable housing, and its low-wage tourist economy hardly needed a fresh supply of cheap labor.

Republican governor Rick Scott cited official estimates that the first wave had numbered 300,000 evacuees, a figure almost guaranteed to incite nativist prejudice about being "inundated." The figure also sharpened GOP fears that the newcomers, if they stayed, would swing the state's delicate electoral balance decisively to the Democrats in upcoming 2018 elections. Through their LIBRE initiative (a Latinx outreach arm), the Koch brothers rushed to bankroll outreach efforts ("Welcome to Florida") to the newcomers, in hopes that they would not hold Donald Trump's xenophobia against the party. But evidence of a blue wave proved elusive. In the four months after Maria, 60 percent of new Hispanic voters in Central Florida registered as independents, with less than 30 percent registering as Democrats and 8 percent as Republicans.[5] And, on Election Day itself, the Puerto Rican vote in Florida lagged behind that of other Hispanic populations. In Central Florida counties like Osceola—which absorbed the bulk of the climate refugees—those that voted may have put Scott over the top in his race for a Senate seat,[6] and, two years later, boosted Trump's Florida vote.

Scott's figure of 300,000 evacuees, based on the records of commercial airline departures from Puerto Rico, was quickly and effectively challenged. University of Florida economists issued an estimate of fifty thousand, drawing on new school enrolments and requests for state aid.[7] But many of the refugees were absorbed into the households of relatives and so did not stand out, as other classes of migrants would have done. Those without any such networks or resources were housed—with FEMA vouchers—in weekly rental hotels for several months, where their neighbors were Central Florida's homeless families. There was no need for refugee camps, and, unlike for other Caribbean climate refugees, there had been no barriers to their movement to the mainland. Their access to improved welfare benefits, Medicaid, and meaningful suffrage put them in a different league from sanctuary seekers in almost every other part of the world. Yet they shared the traumatic experience of being wrenched from their homes, radical uncertainty about any prospect of returning, and the bitter recognition of being powerless to alter their circumstances.

Significantly, the "climate refugee" label proved more persistent than in previous hurricanes, amplified by warming temperatures. The term was more widely used in press reporting about Maria than about Harvey, Katrina, or the Florida impacts of Irma. No doubt this was due to a widespread reluctance to view displacement within the US as akin to transborder migration. "Refugees" are supposed to come from poor countries and, since they migrate overwhelmingly to other poor countries, they tend to attract scrutiny only when they cross the borders of rich ones, and usually in significant numbers. The case of the Puerto Rican evacuees—both US and foreign—was more ambiguous. Yet they were in plentiful company in 2017, numbering among the more than one million Americans displaced by climate-driven events in the course of the year. Globally, the figures are steadily rising. In 2016, according to one UN estimate, more than twenty-four million people were displaced by sudden-onset, climate-driven hazards. Estimates of the impacts of slow-onset hazard events, such as drought or desertification, are more difficult to come by.[8] It is by no means easy to distinguish climate change as the primary motivating cause of many refugees' displacement. Nor is the label always welcomed. Given how badly refugees are treated in most parts of the world, people generally do not want to identify themselves in this way.

Climate Demography

The demography of disaster is a highly political art form. Statistical estimates of deaths, displacements, and damage have a direct bearing on decisions about the distribution of relief and blame. Disaster management is typically held up as a test case of governmental efficiency. Anarchists and other kinds of libertarians argue, often persuasively, that—in the short term at least—mutual aid is a more effective and resilient response to rapid-onset disasters than state-administered relief efforts.[9] Slow-moving, attritional catastrophes are another matter. For the most part, these are the domain of climate change, and the consequences show up in the unspectacular forms of species die-off, ice melt, aridification, biodiversity loss, soil erosion, ocean rise, and salinization. The direct impact on human mortality cannot be quantified with any accuracy, if only because climate change is typically only one of many factors. But this has not deterred the estimators. According to the Global Humanitarian Forum (2009), anthropogenic climate change is implicated in the annual deaths of over 300,000 people worldwide and significantly affects the lives of another 325 million people. The World Health Organization estimates that between 2030 and 2050, climate change will cause an additional 250,000 deaths per year, from malnutrition, malaria, diarrhea, and heat stress. A more alarming estimate, published in 2016 in *The Lancet*, predicted that by 2050, climate change will be claiming more than half a million lives worldwide due to reduced crop productivity.[10]

Nor has the demography of climate refugees been neglected. The UN Commission on Refugees does not keep numbers on climate refugees, but according to a 2015 report from the Internal Displacement Monitoring Centre, "since 2008, an average of 26.4 million people per year have been displaced from their homes by disasters brought on by natural hazards," at a rate that has doubled since 1970.[11]

A variety of sources, including the Intergovernmental Panel on Climate Change (IPCC) and the influential 2006 Stern Report, have issued various predictions that climate change will generate from as few as two hundred million to as many as one billion migrants by 2050. According to one Cornell University estimate, this figure will rise to two billion—or one-fifth of the world's projected population—by 2100.[12] Those forced to evacuate coastal cities alone could total 750 million. The Red Cross estimated that, by 2010, climate change migrants already outnumbered the volume of refugees from war and civic and state violence.[13]

Not surprisingly, the prospect of large numbers of desperate people on the move generates anxiety and even more extreme sentiments, in an era of xenophobic backlash and tightening borders. Some of these passions are fueled by the dismal legacy of Malthusianism—there is simply not enough to go around—which fueled the early, and lingering, environmentalist fears about overpopulation. Malthus's influence flares up at first mention of a demographic scare; the most recent example being the falling fertility rates of the white majority populations of Global North countries. Since the mid-1970s, when Garret Hardin promulgated "lifeboat ethics" (if the rich were to allow the poor on their boats, everyone will end up in the water), the spirit of Malthus has taken up residence in the anti-immigrant camp, adding a thin veneer of demographic rigor to the coarse texture of bigoted sentiment about undocumented border-crossing from the South.

Migration is the third of demography's chief domains, after fertility and mortality. It is the most difficult to track and the most destabilizing for any governing class's presentation of durable sovereignty. The current zeal—and not only in North America and Europe—for building walls and securing borders appears to echo Foucault's analysis of neoliberal rule, or governmentality, which takes population as its object, political economy as lead strategy, and security as its technical instrument. Far from being a perversion of bureaucracy, governmentality's preoccupation with statistics is a normal exercise of population management in the modern state, and any movement beyond the desired equilibrium of numbers—an optimal level of unemployment, debt, pay, GDP, public health, homelessness—must call forth a policy corrective. Few examples fit the bill more persuasively than the current refugee crisis.

By the end of 2017, the UN Refugee Agency reported that an unprecedented 68.5 million people—more than the population of the UK—were either refugees, asylum seekers, or internally displaced across the globe.

THE CALCULUS OF CLIMATE CHANGE

Among them were nearly 22.5 million cross-border *refugees*, over half of whom were under the age of eighteen, while more than 40 million were displaced within their own countries. By the time of the seventieth anniversary of the Universal Declaration of Human Rights in December 2018, most of the rich countries of the world were in full retreat from the spirit of the charter's Article 14: *"Everyone has the right to seek and to enjoy in other countries asylum from persecution."* Drafted in large part to respond to the postwar refugee crisis in Europe, that article became the basis for the United Nations Convention relating to the Status of Refugees, adopted in 1951, which remains the centerpiece of international refugee protection. At the time, protection was limited to persons displaced before 1951 within Europe, but in 1967, these geographic and temporal limits were removed. In contrast to earlier international refugee instruments, which applied to specific groups of refugees, the 1951 Convention endorsed a single definition of the term "refugee"—someone who is unable or unwilling to return to their country of origin owing to a well-founded fear of being persecuted for reasons of race, religion, nationality, membership of a particular social group, or political opinion.

Climate migrants may be the fastest growing class of refugees, but they are not protected under the 1951 Convention, nor is there any international legal recognition of their status. In a 2013 test case, a Kiribati man, Ioane Teitiota, unsuccessfully brought an asylum claim to the New Zealand Supreme Court based on his status as a "climate change refugee." The judges rejected the argument that historically high emitters of $CO2$ were his "persecutor" under the terms of the 1951 Convention and cleared the way for his and his family's deportation. Nor is it clear that legal recognition, typically based on recognition of rights rather than needs, is the most humane solution. Why create yet another level of second-class immigrant status to add to the maze of temporary visa categories? One study of residents from the low-lying Kiribati and Tuvalu islands, who are under threat of displacement from rising seas, found many of them resistant to the "refugee" label because of its association with desperation and helplessness and its neglect of their own skills or agency. They did not want to see themselves as victims, were apprehensive about being placed in camps, and were all too aware that the principle of international burden-sharing—which underpins the 1951 Convention—is not well respected or implemented. Millions of refugees who should enjoy protected status reside for long periods of time in the limbo of camps and detention centers. Why join them?

Nor, in a time of immigrant backlash, is there much of a political appetite for any new international agreements on refugee protection. In 2015, for the first time in the UNFCCC climate policymaking process, the COP21 Paris Agreement included language about protecting migrants in its preamble and authorized a task force on displacement and mobility.[14] But the nonbinding agreements of the UNFCCC process have produced few concrete gains, and the most vulnerable, least developed countries have had to fight tooth and nail for them. Besides, from the perspective of Global North elites, funding the relocation of populations affected by rising sea levels is a much more attractive solution than relinquishing their own high-carbon lifestyles. Like the UN's Reducing Emissions from Deforestation and Degradation program (REDD), which allows polluters to earn carbon-offset credits if they finance the conservation of Southern rainforests, the relocation option is a cost-effective way to *avoid* reducing greenhouse gas emissions.

In response, climate justice advocates have promoted alternative ways for Northern countries to pay back their historic carbon debts, through a combination of mitigation programs (decolonize the atmosphere via emission reductions), reparations (for centuries of plunder and ecological damage), and adaptation obligations (transfer and financing of sustainable technologies to the South). How do climate refugees qualify as carbon creditors? In much the same way as postwar immigrants from ex-colonies claimed their right to move to former metropoles like France and the UK and share in the wealth extracted from their communities during the colonial period. Confronted with hostility and hateful prejudice, the philosophical spirit of their response was: "We are here because you were there." So too, today's climate migrant might say, "I am here because the impact of your high-carbon lifestyle forced me off my land and deprived me of my livelihood."

The face-off between justice-driven remedies—which take their cue from inequalities, past and present—and the fiercely exercised right of powerful nations to "defend" their borders and forcibly limit population movement is on the verge of generating constitutional crises in the US, the UK, and a number of Northern democracies. In the meantime, the preferred middle path of green capitalism is to favor market solutions—which use carbon trading or "right pricing" as environmental tools, and position climate refugees as adaptive entrepreneurs seeking better livelihoods.[15]

Calculations on the Future

It is commonly observed that today's yawning wealth disparity more and more resembles the brutally uneven world of the Gilded Age, as portrayed in *Late Victorian Holocausts*. Three decades of wealth redistribution through free-market fundamentalism have deepened the pockets of "ultra-high net-worth individuals" and stagnated the incomes of mostly everyone else. So, too, the global traffic of migrant labor now echoes many aspects of the nineteenth-century coolie trade, which consigned tens of millions of contract laborers to overseas workplaces. Many of today's climate refugees travel the same routes as Davis's wretched famine sufferers who headed toward urban centers when their crops failed and their weakened rural support networks collapsed. Notably, the routine of blaming, criminalizing, and extorting the poor is once again a method of ruling.

Indeed, one of the more provocative arguments in Davis's book is that the origins of what came to be known as the "Third World" lie in the late Victorian colonial system's fatal confluence of laissez-faire economics and ecological adversity. The enclosing of commons, depleting of traditional agro-infrastructure, global market pricing, and ironfisted revenue extracting from debt and taxes left the populations of the periphery in a heavily exposed condition and especially vulnerable to natural disasters. Extractive capitalism marched to the tune of the Gatling gun into the interiors of these countries, securing their peasantry's structural dependency on faraway powers. The outcome was decades of underdevelopment; and then, after decolonization, the introduction of the "debt trap" and structural adjustment policies deepened the predicament of small rural producers all across the Global South.

In the twenty-first century, the concurrence of anthropogenic climate change and the rise of financialization have added new dimensions to this landscape of inequality. Both portend a future that is locked in or foreclosed for generations not yet born. We know that the impacts of atmospheric carbon concentrations will escalate, like compound interest, in the decades to come. No efforts to reduce emissions, not even the most heroic ones, will prevent the increase in global warming and radical alteration of ecosystems for untold centuries. The injustice visited on voiceless generations is the latest addition to the roster of present-day inequalities. Meanwhile, capital, having exhausted its capacity for profit-taking in the present, generates ever more paper claims on the future. Indeed, the primary source of accumulation for the 1 percent now comes in the form of economic rents (from debt-leveraging, capital gains, speculation through derivatives, and other forms of financial engineering)—a far cry from the vision of the "euthanasia of the rentier," which was Keynes's remedy for the dysfunctional capitalist system in 1936.[16]

In both instances, the mathematical calculation of risk has become the preferred mentality for determining the destiny of the world to come. In the alpha world of finance, the algorithms of Wall Street predict the future value of assets and commodities and direct the money flow accordingly; projected debt-to-GDP ratios bear heavily on decisions about which populations will be investment beneficiaries, while armies of actuaries work around the clock to quantify the degree of exposure, liability, and opportunity of any fiscal choice, far in advance of its execution. In keeping with the priorities of a creditocracy, the proliferation of debt instruments is now driven by the aim of capturing surplus income on a lifelong basis, so that each new surrender of a part of our lives to debt-financing further consumes the fruit of labor we have not yet performed in the form of compensation we have not yet earned.

Likewise, in the realm of the biosphere, the calculus of carbon accumulations commands most attention, shaping decisions about production, infrastructure, energy supply, urban policy, and population growth in accord with forecast risks from climate change. As Bill McKibben puts it: "The future of humanity depends on math." Reflecting on a 2016 study of fossil-fuel production by Oil Change International, a watchdog coalition, he observes: "Those numbers spell out, in simple arithmetic, how much of the fossil fuel in the world's existing coal mines and oil wells we can burn if we want to prevent global warming from cooking the planet. In other words, if our goal is to keep the Earth's temperature from rising more than two degrees Celsius—the upper limit identified by the nations of the world—how much more new digging and drilling can we do? Here's the answer: zero."[17] McKibben's apocalyptic math draws on macro data and takes aim at the root of the energy generation problem, but the habit of calculating future consequences of present-day choices has also gone molecular. In this vein, we are encouraged to gage the carbon footprint of our every action—Should I use the elevator or the stairs? Take a bus or a train? Buy imported organic food or local agro-industry products?—as part of a routine self-auditing our lifestyle. The goal of zero-carbon conduct is urged on us as a model of ascetic behavior, echoing the traditional commandments of many religions to practice some form of abstinence as a pathway to salvation. However important as a consciousness-changing exercise, the act of individualizing the responsibility for the climate crisis serves to deflect liability away from the fossil-fuel industry and the world's largest carbon-emitting corporations. Long used to externalizing the costs of their pollution, their owners will gladly offload the blame for anthropogenic global warming on the "human species," as long as guilt can be internalized in this way.

Arguably the most insidious kind of accounting is that which informs the triage mentality behind decisions about who is worth saving and who will be sacrificed in the event of ultimate ecological scarcity. This mindset of sizing up the odds of surviving harkens back to the calculated disinterest of the Utilitarians, who influenced British colonial policy in the late nineteenth century. Their Malthusian computations were informed by the belief that "surplus populations" were too costly to support, and, from a social Darwinist perspective, were not likely to pull through under straitened circumstances. Hence the notorious "Temple wage," instituted by Bengal's lieutenant governor Richard Temple during the great famine of 1877. In response to criticism that his administration had been excessive in its welfare expenditures and had created a dependency on government aid, Temple reduced the male wage for a day's work in the relief camps of Madras and Bombay to 450 grams (1 lb.) of grain, and less for women or laboring children. The moralism that prompted the Temple wage can be found lurking behind every contemporary effort at "welfare reform," but who could deny that a similar reasoning is also at work in the meager rations of climate aid promised (but not always delivered) to the vulnerable nations of the world? Or in the 2°C threshold for global warming set by policymakers under the Paris Agreement, which African nations, contributing a mere 4 percent of the world's greenhouse gases, have interpreted—quite justly—as a "death sentence."

Sanctuary Now

Most of the facts that Donald Trump cites in support of his "America first" policies are wildly inaccurate, but his statistical bestiary has helped inflame the chauvinist suspicion that the US is shouldering more than its fair share of contributions to global humanity, whether to international agencies or in the form of liberal immigration policies. The backlash he has fomented against refugees of all stripes is fueled by fallacious estimates of the acts of crime and terrorism perpetrated by foreigners entering the country, or of the net fiscal deficits from government expenditures on low-skilled migrants. These figures surely serve as a fig leaf for the barbarism of his administration's exclusion policies, but they are an indispensable prop nonetheless.

In response to Trump's abusive immigration policies, the New Sanctuary Movement (NSM) has inspired a human-rights crusade that owes nothing to the calculus of benefits and burdens routinely and cynically wielded by opinion makers. The NSM's rapid formation of support groups and mutual aid networks to shelter, defend, and assist undocumented immigrants and refugees has not been shaped by any analysis of community resources, let alone any assessment of the public interest. In true humanitarian style, NSM prioritizes needs over rights. Nor has the movement confined itself to the traditional sanctuary bailiwick of providing safe havens to those fleeing persecution. Operating in the ancient religious lineage of welcoming the stranger and sheltering the fugitive from earthly laws (most world religions have a version of sanctuary, including premonotheistic ones), the original Sanctuary organizers in the 1980s utilized churches and temples to harbor refugees from Reagan's dirty wars in Central America. Drawing on the US precedent of the Underground Railroad and popular resistance to the Fugitive Slaves Act, they eventually secured protections from Congress for many of the refugees. In the wake of post-9/11 xenophobia and immigrant scapegoating, the movement relaunched as NSM in 2006, expanding its scope far beyond the physical protection of individuals in places of worship. NSM's civil opposition to racist laws pushed out into the courts, City Halls, and state capitols and onto campuses and other institutional territories where a line of noncooperation was drawn against the persecutory activities of the federal immigration agencies.

As they gained moral ground, NSM activists tried to make common cause with other movements, like the Movement for Black Lives, in open resistance against state violence, criminalization of poverty, overpolicing, and mass incarceration. "Expanded Sanctuary" is the broad banner under which vulnerable populations (of nonimmigrant Muslims, LGBTQ people, Black and Indigenous communities, and political dissidents of all kinds) targeted by punitive policies uphold the need for protection from profiling, safety from surveillance and militarized enforcement, and support for inclusive alternatives to the "law and order" society.[18] It is only a matter of time before Sanctuary marches into the arena of environmental politics, where its broad, humanitarian spirit embraces the climate refugee and challenges the failure of states to honor their basic obligations.

The NSM ethos of care is nonjudgmental toward those it serves, and it can be nonintrusive about questioning the conditions from which refugees are fleeing. But just as the original Sanctuary activists called out US militarist interventions for displacing large numbers of Salvadorians and Guatemalans from their traditional homelands, so too should an NSM approach to climate refugees mount a clear-eyed critique of the reasons for migrant displacement from ecologically impoverished places. Unlike ENSO, the meteorological driver of so much mayhem in *Late Victorian Holocausts*, climate change is a product of human engineering and has its own roll call of villains and self-serving patrons. But the drama of migrant displacement is a more complex story, and many members of the cast—land grabbers, comprador monopolists, debt predators, labor profiteers, resource thieves, concession hunters, disinterested technocrats, and other wreckers of communal life—are familiar from the pages of Davis's book. As the twilight of European empires approached, their plunder only increased in intensity. Their contemporaries are no less grasping or desperate, though they are faced not with the prospect of flags being lowered but with final biophysical limits to growth.

Endnotes

1. *Environmental* Justice Foundation, *On the Frontlines: Climate Change in Bangladesh* (London: 2017), https://ejfoundation.org/reports/on-the-frontlines-climate-change-in-bangladesh.
2. Munich Re, "Climate Insurance – An Opportunity for Developing Countries," https://www.munichre.com/topics-online/en/2016/11/climate-insurance.

3   James Hansen, "Letter to Prime Minister Kevin Rudd," March 27, 2008, http://www.columbia.edu/~jeh1/mailings/2008/20080401_DearPrimeMinisterRudd.pdf.
4   In the meantime, and straight from the playbook of disaster capitalism, a predatory pack of bankers, real estate developers, cryptocurrency traders, and tax-averse entrepreneurs descended on the island to plan a fully deregulated Caribbean paradise in fulfilment of what Naomi Klein diagnosed as their "Randian secessionist fantasies." **Naomi Klein,** "The Battle for Paradise," *Intercept,* **March 20, 2018,** https://theintercept.com/2018/03/20/puerto-rico-hurricane-maria-recovery/.
5   Manuel Madrid, "Puerto Rican Refugees and the Elusive Blue Wave," *American Prospect,* March 10, 2018, http://prospect.org/article/puerto-rican-refugees-and-elusive-blue-wave.
6   Reid Wilson, "Puerto Ricans May Have Elected Rick Scott and Other Midterm Surprises," *Hill,* November 24, 2018, https://thehill.com/homenews/campaign/417918-puerto-ricans-may-have-elected-rick-scott-and-other-midterm-surprises.
7   Paul Brinkmann, "How Many Puerto Ricans Have Moved to Florida?" *Orlando Sentinel,* January 6, 2018, http://www.orlandosentinel.com/business/brinkmann-on-business/os-bz-puerto-rico-numbers-20180105-story.html.
8   Sarah Opitz Stapleton et al., "Climate Change, Migration and Displacement: The Need for a Risk-Informed and Coherent Approach," Overseas Development Institute/UN Development Programme, November 2017, https://www.odi.org/sites/odi.org.uk/files/resource-documents/11874.pdf.
9   See Rebecca Solnit, *A Paradise Built in Hell: The Extraordinary Communities That Arise in Disaster* (New York: Viking, 2009).
10 Marco Springmann et al., "Global and Regional Health Effects of Future Food Production under Climate Change: A Modelling Study," *Lancet* 387, no. 10031 (May 2016): 1937–46.
11 Internal Displacement Monitoring Centre, "Global Estimates 2015: People Displaced by Disasters," July 2015, http://www.internal-displacement.org/publications/2015/global-estimates-2015-people-displaced-by-disasters/.
12 Blaine Friedlander, "Rising Seas Could Result in 2 Billion Refugees by 2100," *Cornell Chronicle,* June 19, 2017, http://news.cornell.edu/stories/2017/06/rising-seas-could-result-2-billion-refugees-2100.
13 International Federation of Red Cross and Red Crescent Societies, *Climate Change and Human Mobility: A Humanitarian Point of View* (Hague: Red Cross and Red Crescent Climate Change Centre, 2009). https://www.ifrc.org/Global/Publications/disasters/climate%20change/climate_change_and_human_mobility-en.pdf,
14 "*Acknowledging that climate change is a common concern of humankind, parties should, when taking action to address climate change, respect, promote and consider their respective obligations on human rights, the right to health, the rights of indigenous peoples, local communities,* **migrants***, children, persons with disabilities and people in vulnerable situations and the right to development, as well as gender equality, empowerment of women and intergenerational equity.*" *COP21 Paris Agreement,* December 12, 2015, https://unfccc.int/sites/default/files/paris_agreement_english_.pdf.
15 See Daniel Faber and Christina Schlegel, "Give Me Shelter from the Storm: Framing the Climate Refugee Crisis in the Context of Neoliberal Capitalism," *Capitalism Nature Socialism* 28, no. 3 (2017): 1–17.
16 For the general framework, see Thomas Piketty, *Capital in the Twenty-First Century* (Cambridge, MA: Harvard University Press, 2014). For detailed data on how the 1 percent have captured income growth, see the reports by Emmanuel Saez, "Striking it Richer: The Evolution of Top Incomes in the United States." The first in the series was "Income Inequality in the United States, 1913–1998," *Quarterly Journal of Economics* 118, no. 1 (2003): 1–39. The most recent update (June 30, 2016) can be found at https://eml.berkeley.edu/~saez/saez-UStopincomes-2015.pdf.
17 Bill McKibben, "Recalculating the Climate Math," *New Republic,* September 22, 2016, https://newrepublic.com/article/136987/recalculating-climate-math. Chris Hayes

calculated the cost of walking away from that wealth at $10 trillion, comparable to the value of slave property lost by owners after Emancipation. "The New Abolitionism," *Nation*, April 22, 2014, https://www.thenation.com/article/new-abolitionism/.

18   Janae Bonsu, "Black People Need Sanctuary Cities, Too," *Essence*, March 10, 2017, https://www.essence.com/news/politics/sanctuary-cities-black-families-immigrants; Naomi Paik, "Abolitionist Futures and the US *Sanctuary* Movement," *Race & Class* 59, no. 2 (July 11, 2017): 3–25.

GATED ECOLOGIES

Rob Wallace, Kenichi Okamoto,
and Alex Liebman

Introduction

Houston, you are a problem. Fossil capitalism separates our economies from our ecologies, producing what political economist Karl Marx characterized as a series of *metabolic rifts*. Capital separates humanity into profit and the labor it commoditizes. It alienates nature from itself, breaking historically emergent ecological feedbacks and polluting soil, air, and water that only bacteria and other extremophiles can now survive. Human industry, in the general sense of how we appropriate nature, has been turned into a one-way ticket in expropriation the system cannot escape of its own accord. Capitalism can replicate itself only in such a way that the cooperative commons and regenerative biosystems on which it feeds struggle to reproduce.

Philosopher István Mészáros diagrammed these rifts (Figure 1).[1] A basal triangle represents what was humanity's mutual metabolism with nature, spotty as it was, up until global capitalism's emergence.[2] Humanity used nature, which shaped us in turn, changing how we used nature again.[3] As a result, human ecologies were robust in population. Outside noted wars and collapses, many societies the world over demographically cycled within resource boundaries co-constructed with nonhuman species, even in the course of transitioning from one mode of production to another. Limits protecting social reproduction emerged as both epiphenomenon and conscious ethos.[4]

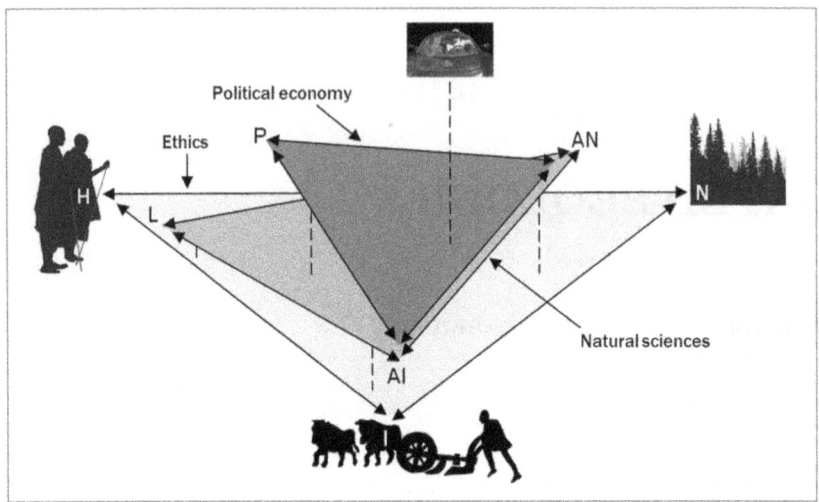

Figure 1: Capitalism atomized humanity (H) into profit (P) and the labor (L) it commoditizes, but also our industry (into alienated industry, AI) and nature from itself (alienated nature, AN). A second plane of interactions organized around producing (and privatizing) surplus value now operates divergent to the primary set. The basic and applied sciences central to the way the modern disciplines present themselves studying such systems are in actuality differentiated largely by how inquiry latches on the vector between alienated nature and alienated industry. We expect the applied natural sciences to cater to our now alienated industry, but the possibility that the basic sciences fail to address nature other than as it is filtered through capitalism's treatment might surprise scientist and civilian alike. Furthermore, the domains of ethics, political economy, and the natural sciences are decoupled from each other, each focusing on a different vertex in this fractured metaphysics. Graphic redrawn from Mészáros (1970).[5]

As Mészáros diagrams, a second plane of interactions around producing (and privatizing) surplus value now gashes off above, still necessarily dependent on the primary relationships between nonhuman nature and humanity, but first and foremost organized around capitalist dynamics. In effect, capitalism projects nature and people off Earth proper into a distinct space, where alienated nature and alienated people interact on commoditization's terms alone.[6]

It isn't all black and white, of course. "Mastery over nature" doesn't by definition preclude environmental conservation, nor does indigeneity bar overexploitation.[7] But neither is the resulting system a mush of gray. For capitalists themselves cast the operative distinctions here as a matter of celebrated principle. Industrialist Elon Musk's recent stunt, launching his Tesla Roadster into space, only marks what has already long passed. As a historically contingent system that, in the face of *all evidence to the contrary*, banks on infinite economic growth off a finite biosphere, capitalism has long left the planet.

Alienation

How might we analyze these dynamics, so central to our present crises? Alienation of nature and what was long our ecological appropriation has largely been treated in qualitative terms alone.[8] Terrific work and required reading, certainly. In the spirit of using natural science to open up science, reappropriating its mantle for more than just another iteration in capitalism, our team concluded that alienation in the Mészáros sense could be modeled in a statistically rigorous way. Moreover, we should be able to use it to help unpack the novel global epidemiologies that are now emerging out of alienated production. Those interested in the technical details of our program of study may find them online.[9] The aim of our chapter here is to offer a summary.

Our study system is an American one, as much a matter of access to data as of the US's role in driving industrial agriculture worldwide. The framework, however, can be applied anywhere. We define alienation in food production for the three axes presented in our introduction above: nature, human, and industry. Given the data sets available, *nature's alienation* in reference to agriculture was operationalized for US states for the period 1970–2000 as the complement percentage of a state's ratio of pasture cropland-to-crop cropland $(1 - p/c)$.[10] As much of the conversion from prairie and woodlands across the US Midwest was completed by the late 1800s, our initial thought for such a variable—wilderness-to-cropland—would have been anachronistic. Changes in pasture, however, should capture the state of system diversity, the scale of conversion to industrial fiber and grains, and the metabolic rift produced in removing livestock—sources of manure and promoters of carbon sequestration—from the open landscape. That is, markers of the latest effort to exit the "natural economy" of an agriculture still dependent on the sun and seasons.

Human alienation is represented here by the ratio of farmer wages-to-fertilizer expenditures $(1 - w/f)$.[11] The variable offers a proxy for the gap between investment in production and wage labor's capacity to reproduce itself, an agricultural analog to economist Thomas Piketty's capital-to-income ratio. Finally, *industry alienation* is measured by farm debt-to-equity.[12] This ratio represents the extent to which farm revenue is available to producers or passed onto paying off mortgages and/or buying corporate live feed, fertilizer, pesticide, seed, machinery, and other inputs and services that farmers once drew from nature and labor on-site.

For the twenty-five US states in the analysis, selected by a starting criterion of at least six million acres of cropland as of 1945, Figure 2 shows three major trends from 1970 onward.

First, we find variation across US states along all three axes. That variation is simultaneously holding steady—marking longue durée regionalism—and in flux. From somewhat different food regimes of origin, the Upper Midwest and the Corn Belt, along with outliers from the South/Appalachia and the Southern Plains/Delta, appear the bleeding edge of modern industrial agronomy. They move together into the front right corner of the graph where our composite alienation is greatest. Second, there appear crisis-driven dynamics, with all three variables going supernova during the farm crisis of the early and mid-1980s: less cropland pasture, more debt load, and comparatively less money spent on wages. But, third, that surge did not merely contract postcrisis. Commodity annuals gobbled up cropland pasture for good. States such as Oklahoma, Tennessee, and Texas that still hosted decent cropland pasture in 2000 lost nearly the rest by 2015. Even as the debt load lessened postcrisis, in part by virtue of economies of scale that drove consolidation and declines in farms in the hundreds of thousands, the wage-input gap never recovered in the Midwest, indicating a trade-off in industrial production's favor.

The states together embody an expanding if irregular cloud of alienation out from the origin of the graph. Certainly our study period was already a system in motion. By the first year in our study, 1970, the Livestock Revolution—marked by the accelerated growth in demand for meat and the expansion, vertical integration, and consolidation of the sector—is already in midswing for poultry. Crop production is on a parallel trajectory. But by 2000, almost all livestock are housed in sheds. Pastures that fed these animals have been almost all converted into commodity grain of just a few varieties (especially in the Midwest, where mechanization is most applied).

GATED ECOLOGIES

Figure 2: Agriculture alienation across twenty-five US states, 1970–2000. Study states in gray at top. We tracked the system every five years but in the interests of concision plot only three years here. The West (California, Colorado, and Montana) and the Northeast (New York, and Pennsylvania) largely group to themselves, while states of the Upper Midwest, the Corn Belt, the South/Appalachia, and the Southern Plains/Delta, above the US average and on the leading edge of industrial production, group toward the front right corner. A negative nature alienation marks a single case wherein pasture cropland slightly exceeded crop cropland (Tennessee, 1970), marking the end of an era on the Southern Plains. Negative human alienation, with wages exceeding fertilizer costs, marks no socialist turn, only that fertilizers had not been applied to the extent to which they came to dominate production by 2015 and/or that human labor still served as an important source of productive power onsite. California and Colorado, for instance, remained in the negative for human alienation as defined here for the entirety of the study period. From Okamoto, Liebman, and Wallace (2019).[13]

Our study period misses the alienation that continued across all three axes to the present day. Ostensibly, at some point such a system should breach a limit over which it or some of its parts are unable to socially reproduce themselves without external inputs replacing what local ecosystems and communities have lost to expropriation and the resulting environmental and social damage. The debt-to-equity ratio may rebound in farmers' favor, but only at the costs of increasing pesticide applications, polluting local waters, increasingly exploiting migrant labor, and running populations out of the rural counties they had lived in for generations.

Projection

We can learn much more about the dynamics underlying US agriculture's alienation beyond these general trends. As applied in the field, Marx's theory of alienation addresses a complex interplay across social and natural processes. How, for instance, do Minnesota, Iowa, and Wisconsin, bordering states at the heart of the genesis of industrial agriculture, move together (or apart or in some combination thereof) along the three axes of alienated agriculture? Understanding this causal web in such a high-dimensional space requires a method for capturing the essential structure of the complexity while accounting for its changes.

Developmental morphometrics offers a useful framework. In essence, the approach, using geometric morphometrics, deploys a statistical characterization of how the aggregate—the interrelationships among the data points in our agricultural alienation space—shifts over time (Figure 3). With the differences among the specimens in their rotation, scale, and position in their plots removed, the focus of the analysis is on the relative positions of the specimen *landmarks* or the *shape* of the configurations. Instead of on skeletons, we used the method on the specimen-years of our alienation space in Figure 2—the positions of the US states in the ag alienation space over time.

The approach offers three methodological payoffs. First, there is a rich body of mathematics for identifying the axes in the statistical distribution of our specimen shapes that highlight the greatest differences in our study samples. Such a principal components analysis reduces the total dimensions needed to describe the variation in shape across, in this case, our specimen-years for US states. We can then project each year's configuration of states onto these new axes to capture *how* the specimen shapes differ from each other in what are known as *relative warps*.

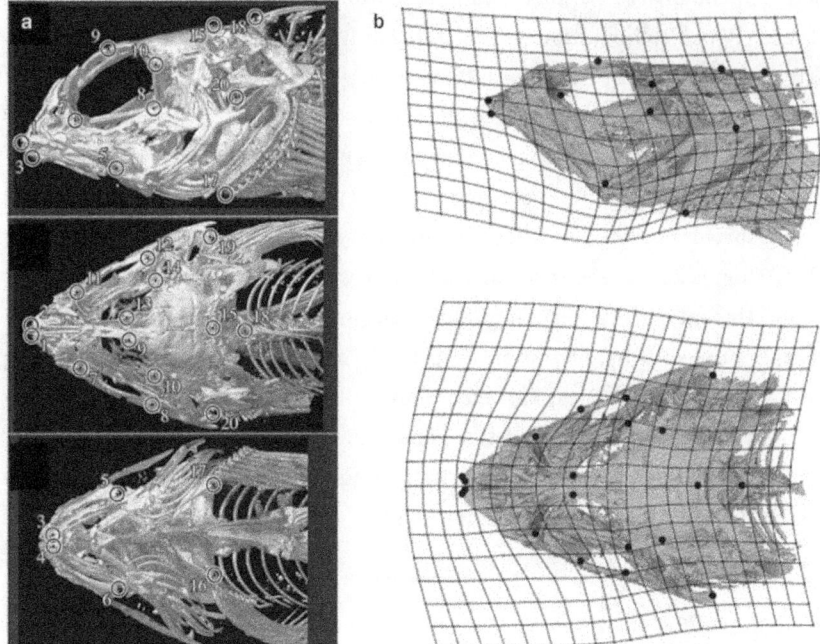

Figure 3: (a) Twenty landmarks across *Clinocottus (Clinocottus) analis* or woolly sculpin specimen for lateral (top), dorsal (middle), and ventral (bottom). (b) Thin-plate spline deformations of 3D *Clinocottus* landmarks from average skeleton shape across study taxa to an individual specimen for lateral (top) and dorsal (bottom) for most extreme positive values for principle component 1 of the data set. Adapted from Buser, Sidlauskas, and Summers (2018).[14]

In the second payoff, the popularity of geometric morphometrics derives in no small part from its capacity for visualizing these high-dimensional projections. We can *see* how our topologies differ systematically from each other. We can move each specimen's landmarks in such a way that we superimpose them atop a matching set from a reference configuration produced by averaging the data points across all the specimens, much as we might compare a baseball player's batting average with the league average. These superimpositions can be visualized as deformations in a Euclidean grid called *thin-plate splines*, as shown in Figure 3b.

Finally, the method around projecting these standardized coordinates allows us to statistically test for cofactors possibly related to the differences in shape. Are there, for instance, specific pathogens that are more fundamentally tied into the process of increasing alienation in American agriculture than others? *Which* combinations of US states at *which* spatial scales appear to be driving the emergence of these pathogens?

What did our geometric morphometrics find? First, Figure 4 shows the relative warps—the principal axes of differences in shape—for our ag alienation space of twenty-five US states, every five years, for the period 1970–2000. The first two relative warps account for 81 percent of the total variance in our plots' shapes across the three alienation axes and appear to recapitulate our qualitative interpretation of Figure 2 in the previous section. Relative warp 2 captures the shift in and out of the 1980s crisis. Relative warp 1, accounting for 70 percent of the total variance, shows that switchback left the US alienation space in a new configuration. The years 1970 and 2000 pre- and post-crisis may be in the same configuration along relative warp 2, but they are in widely different spots along relative warp 1.

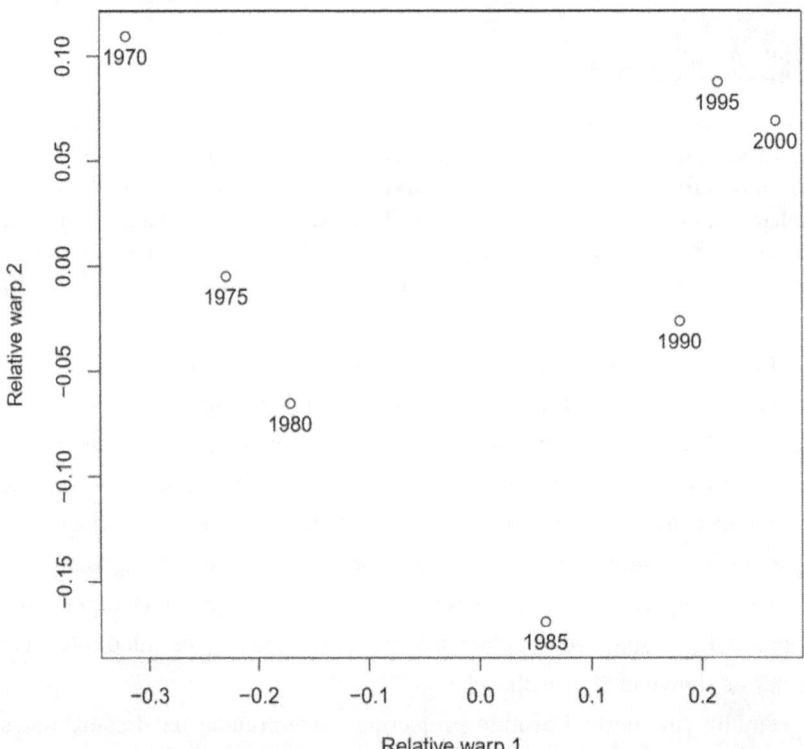

Figure 4: Biplot of relative warps 1 and 2 for twenty-five US agricultural states, every five years, 1970–2000. From Okamoto, Liebman, and Wallace (2019).[15]

By the thin-plate splines (TPS) shown in Figure 5, we can track such a turnover in US agriculture in much of its multilayered spatial detail.

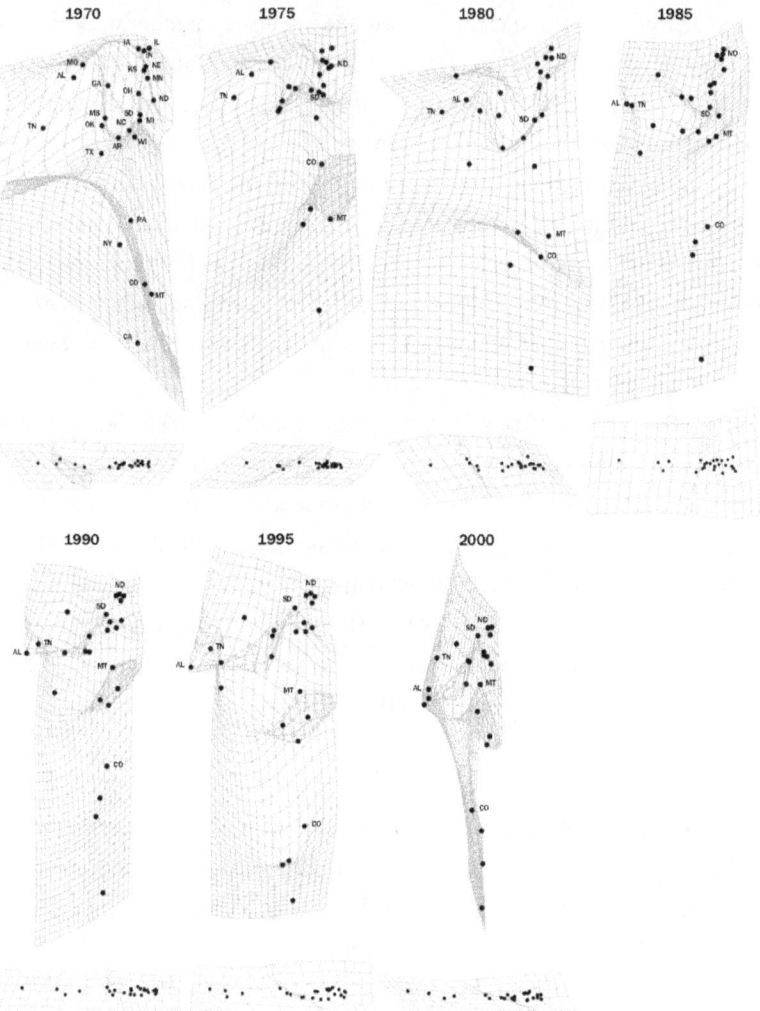

Figure 5: Thin-plate splines showing deformations from the consensus configuration for twenty-five US states across the agricultural alienation space of Figure 2 every five years, 1970–2000. For each year, the top spline shows deformations along the nature-human axis, the bottom for the human-industry axis. From Okamoto, Liebman, and Wallace (2019).[16]

The relative shifts among the states across the ag alienation space, in this case how each year's shape deviates from the average configuration, show an uneven regime shift in industrial production. For the top TPS for each year, showing the nature-human axes, we see membership in the cutting edge of industrial production in the upper-right of the splines change. By 1980, North Dakota, moving up along the human axis, has joined the Corn Belt states of Iowa, Illinois, and Indiana in its mix of commodity crops, a shift that economic geographers Meimei Lin and Qiping Huang recently tracked down to the county level.[17] Its neighbor South Dakota approaches this first tier but by a different trajectory. Other states take the long way toward such production. Colorado toward the bottom feints an exit out of labor-intensive, California-style production, but only Montana escapes into the heights of combine- and fertilizer-led production.

By 1985 on the nature axis, left-to-right for the top TPS, Tennessee—the last of true cropland pasture—surpasses Alabama in converting to commodity annuals, catching up to Texas and Oklahoma. By 2000, we see intimations of what would be the effective end of cropland pasture by 2015, for which the TPS would compress to a near vertical line. Along the industry axis in the bottom TPS, the relative positions across the states appear largely maintained, even in and out of the spike in industry alienation of the 1980s crisis, although there is more spread between the states for 1985.

Conclusion

What about disease? Do these shifts in agricultural alienation impact outbreaks in the US, as we initially proposed? Preliminary correlations indicate the two foodborne diseases we tested, shigellosis and salmonellosis in US cases per 100,000 in the period 1970–2000, are *not* generally associated with alienation shape at any scales of landmark interaction.[18] Only one relative warp on salmonella proved statistically significant, but the correlation, at one of the finer scales, appears largely dependent on a single year's projection and at a significance that would not stand up to a standard methodological correction. See our technical paper for details and possible explanations.[19]

Nevertheless, we have developed a modeling infrastructure that could be used to statistically test systemic alienation and its possible epidemiological aftermath. We have produced one of the first quantitative studies of alienation across nature, human, and industry, offering a hybrid of theory and, with our focus on a particular US moment, the kind of case study historian Mike Davis labeled as "Marx on the conjuncture."[20]

There is an irony found in our attempt here beyond conducting the kind of "quantoid" analysis some of Marxism's high theorists dismiss—a false dichotomy others have criticized in turn.[21] Our original intention was to pivot discussion off what is *lost* in the statistical machinery at the heart of most of these kinds of multivariate analyses. Much can be learned from rotating graph axes through a data cloud so as to better capture the greatest sources of variation in a system in a more compact way. As we discussed above, we can thereby reduce the dimensionality of the data set and capture the essence of the system more easily than out of the thatch of original data. We lose something along the way, however. The large table of multivariate coefficients produced show differences that may be unrelated to the true geometry of the original coordinates (in most analyses, an acceptable loss given what is captured in turn).

Mészáros's diagram with which we began, showing capitalism with its own metabolism, got us thinking that capitalists also rotate the axes of our socioecological systems. They do so not to make discoveries within virtual representations as scientists aim to, but to *impose* new orders of interactions in the world as it exists, including gating off the factory farm from community and environmental accountability. The resulting rotations turn the system from socioecological interactions that help produce what were once widely available bounties—Mészáros's base metabolism—to a nature geared to maximizing (and privatizing) capitalist profits. Today's riches rob the next generation of its capacity to reproduce itself. In other words, in capitalism we find a new social geometry—that secondary plane of Figure 1—that aims at short-circuiting the kind of social reproduction at the core of what *was* our once and future species-being but is now treated as old news. What we lose here is more than a matter of what any useful analytics trades off. We've lost our sense of our place in the ecosystems—and epidemiologies—on which even humanity's flexible wonders depend *as a matter of necessity*.

No matter how many an environmental poker hand civilizations misplayed before capitalism emerged—Sumeria, Ancient Egypt, the Roman and Mayan empires, Easter Island—it was always on the grounds of our primary metabolism with Earth. Capitalism, on the other hand, has indoctrinated much of humanity—including now neocolonial avatars and a techno-utopian left—against our long understanding that survival is ecological in basis.[22] We are now asked left-to-right to pretend that our social reproduction is *necessarily* alienated from the environment.[23] As if anything other than the barest of colonies could survive that way offworld, whether here already—hovering over an Earth approaching multiple environmental precipices—or on another planet orbiting some distant star.

Endnotes

1. István Mészáros, *Marx's Theory of Alienation* (London: Merlin Press, 1970); István Mészáros, *Beyond Capital: Toward a Theory of Transition* (1995; repr., New York: Monthly Review Press, 2010).
2. Eric J. Hobsbawm, "Introduction," in Karl Marx, *Pre-Capitalist Economic Formations* (1858; repr., New York: International Publishers, 1965); Maurice Godelier, *The Mental and the Material: Thought, Economy, and Society* (1986; repr., New York: Verso, 2011); Jason Moore, "'The Modern World-System' as Environmental History? Ecology and the Rise of Capitalism," *Theory and Society* 32 (2003): 307–77; Carolina Levis et al., "How People Domesticated Amazonian Forests," *Frontiers in Ecology and Evolution* (January 17, 2018): 171, https://doi.org/10.3389/fevo.2017.00171.
3. Erle C. Ellis et al., "Evolving the Human Niche," *PNAS*, 113, no. 31 (2016): E4436; Dolores R. Piperno et al., "Niche Construction and Optimal Foraging Theory in Neotropical Agricultural Origins: A Re-evaluation in Consideration of the Empirical Evidence, *Journal of Archaeological Science* 78 (2017): 214–20; Manuel Arroyo-Kalin et al., "Civilisation and Human Niche Construction," *Archaeology International* 20 (2017): 106–09.
4. Andrew E. Noble and William F. Fagan, "A Niche Remedy for the Dynamical Problems of Neutral Theory." *Theoretical Ecology* 8, no. 1 (2015):149–61; M. Jahi Chappell, *Beginning to End Hunger: Food and the Environment in Belo Horizonte, Brazil, and Beyond* (Berkeley: University of California Press, 2018); Giorgis Kallis, *Limits: Why Malthus Was Wrong and Why Environmentalists Should Care* (Stanford, CA: Stanford University Press, 2019).
5. Mészáros, *Marx's Theory of Alienation*.
6. Karl Marx, *Capital: Volume 1: A Critique of Political Economy* (1867; repr., London: Penguin Books, 1976); John B. Foster and Paul Burkett, *Marx and the Earth: An Anti-Critique* (Leiden: Brill, 2016).
7. Reiner Grundmann, "The Ecological Challenge to Marxism," *New Left Review* 187 (1991): 103–20; David Harvey, "The Nature of Environment: The Dialectics of Social and Environmental Change," in *The Ways of the World* (1993; repr., Oxford: Oxford University Press, 2016), 159–213.
8. Rebecca Clausen and Brett Clark, "The Metabolic Rift and Marine Ecology: An Analysis of the Ocean Crisis within Capitalist Production," *Organization & Environment* 18, no. 4 (2005): 422–44; Philip Mancus, "Nitrogen Fertilizer Dependency and Its Contradictions: A Theoretical Exploration of Social-Ecological Metabolism," *Rural Sociology* 72, no. 2 (2007): 269–88; Ryan Gunderson, "The Metabolic Rifts of Livestock Agribusiness," *Organization & Environment* 24, no. 4 (2011): 404–22; Rebecca Clausen, Brett Clark, and Stefano B. Longo, "Metabolic Rifts and Restoration: Agricultural Crises and the Potential of Cuba's Organic, Socialist Approach to Food Production," *World Review of Political Economy* 6, no. 1 (2015): 4–32; Mindi Schneider, "Wasting the Rural: Meat, Manure, and the Politics of Agro-Industrialization in Contemporary China," *Geoforum* 78 (2017): 89–97; Daniel Auerbach and Brett Clark, "Metabolic Rifts, Temporal Imperatives, and Geographical Shifts: Logging in the Adirondack Forest in the 1800s," *International Critical Thought* 8, no. 3 (2018): 468–86.

9   Kenichi Okamoto, Alex Liebman, and Robert G. Wallace, "At What Geographic Scale Does Agricultural Alienation Select for Foodborne Disease? A Statistical Test for 25 US States, 1970–2000," preprint, December 2019. https://www.medrxiv.org/content/10.1101/2019.12.13.19014910v1.full.pdf.
10 Data from the Economic Research Service of the US Department of Agriculture for years 1969 (assigned to 1970), 1974 (1975), 1978 (1980), 1987 (1985), 1992 (1990), 1997 (1995), and 2002 (2000). Negative percents indicate more pasture than cropland. The ERS notes, for these data, that cropland includes cropland harvested, crop failure, and summer fallow. The exact sources for the data, almost all from USDA sources, are listed in our technical paper: Okamoto, Liebman, and. Wallace, "At What Geographic Scale."
11 Data from the Bureau of Economic Analysis of the US Department of Commerce.
12 Data from the Economic Research Service of the US Department of Agriculture, and, for debt data prior to 1994, the Farmers Home Administration.
13 Okamoto, Liebman, and Wallace, "At What Geographic Scale."
14 Thaddaeus J. Buser, Brian L. Sidlauskas, and Adam P. Summers, "2D or Not 2D? Testing the Utility of 2D Vs. 3D Landmark Data in Geometric Morphometrics of the Sculpin Subfamily Oligocottinae (Pisces; Cottoidea)," *The Anatomical Record*, 301, no. 5 (2018), 806–818.
15 Okamoto, Liebman, and Wallace, "At What Geographic Scale."
16 Okamoto, Liebman, and Wallace, "At What Geographic Scale."
17 Meimei Lin and Qiping Huang, "Exploring the Relationship between Agricultural Intensification and Changes in Cropland Areas in the US," *Agriculture, Ecosystems & Environment* 274 (2019): 33–40.
18 Data from Samuel L. Groseclose et al., "Summary of Notifiable Diseases -- United States, 2001," *MMWR Weekly* 50, no. 53 (2003): 1–108.
19 Okamoto, Liebman, and Wallace, "At What Geographic Scale."
20 Matthew T. Clement, "A Basic Accounting of Variation in Municipal Solid-Waste Generation at the County Level in Texas, 2006: Groundwork for Applying Metabolic-Rift Theory to Waste Generation," *Rural Sociology* 74, no. 3 (2009): 412-429; Julius A. McGee and Camila Alvarez, "Sustaining Without Changing: The Metabolic Rift of Certified Organic Farming," *Sustainability* 8, no. 2 (2016):115; Mike Davis, *Old Gods, New Enigmas: Marx's Lost Theory* (New York: Verso, 2018).
21 David Harvey, "Revolutionary and Counter Revolutionary Theory in Geography and the Problem of Ghetto Formation," *Antipode* 4 (1972): 1–13; David Harvey, *Social Justice and the City* (1973; repr., Athens: University of Georgia Press, 2009); J. Amos Hatch, "The Quantoids versus the Smooshes: Struggling with Methodological Rapprochement," *Issues in Education* 3, no. 2 (1985): 158–67; Eric Sheppard, "Quantitative Geography: Representations, Practices, and Possibilities," *Environment and Planning D* 19, no. 5 (2001): 535–54; Luke Bergmann, Eric Sheppard, and Paul S. Plummer, "Capitalism beyond Harmonious Equilibrium."
22 István Mészáros, *Social Structure and Forms of Consciousness, Volume 1: The Social Determination of Method* (New York: Monthly Review Press, 2010); Amanda Armstrong "The Wooden Brain: Organizing Untimeliness in Marx's *Capital*," *Mediations* 31, no. 1 (2017): 3–26; Joseph Fracchia, "Organisms and Objectifications: A Historical-Materialist Inquiry into the 'Human and the Animal,'" Monthly Review 68, no. 10 (2017): 1–16; Marc A. Michael, "Biofinance: Biological Foundations of Capital Imaginaries," *Public Seminar*, March 13, 2018, http://www.publicseminar.org/2018/03/biofinance/.
23 Anthony Galluzzo, "Utopia as Method, Social Science Fiction, and the Flight from Reality (Review of Frase, *Four Futures*)," *b20*, 25 August (2017), https://www.boundary2.org/2017/08/anthony-galluzzo-utopia-as-method-social-science-fiction-and-the-flight-from-reality/; Rut E. Blomqvist, "Pulling the Magical Lever: A Critical Analysis of Techno-Utopian Imaginaries," *Uneven Earth*, September 2, 2018, http://unevenearth.org/2018/09/pulling-the-magical-lever/; Robert G. Wallace, "Redwashing Capital: Left Tech Bros are Honing Marx into a Capitalist Tool," *Uneven Earth,* July 11, 2019, http://unevenearth.org/2019/07/redwashing-capital/.

OTHERING THE MALL

Michael Sorkin

America's primal scene was enacted in the reciprocal gaze of the "first contact" between native Americans and Europeans. The need for instant classification that arose from mutual misrecognition founded a never-ending obsession with otherness that evolved into a complex national algorithm to reify, authorize, quantify, and valorize difference; to sort and manage degrees of citizenship and belonging and their relationship to an ever-increasing variety of others on "our" shores. This demanded a pricing mechanism to set new exchange rates for an old commodity: people. Situating subjects "in their place" between product and person, this process of comparative valuation and arbitrage launched the settler economy as well as centuries of pain for Native Americans, beginning with their mass extinction from imported diseases, including smallpox, measles, and influenza. As one English explorer, Thomas Harriot, wrote in 1585, "Within a few days after our departure from every such (Native American) town, the people began to die very fast, and many in short space; in some towns about twenty, in some forty, in some sixty, and in one six score, which in truth was very many in respect of their numbers...The disease was so strange that they neither knew what it was nor how to cure it."[1]

The commodification of Native Americans required monetization, which necessitated sorting degrees of humanity and, by extension, aptness for servitude and exchange. Indians rapidly joined the slave economy both as traders and captives. Beginning in the mid-seventeenth century they were held as chattel by the Spanish and, a little later, the British, and many were sold (in a triangular trade involving the Spanish, British, and the Indians themselves) and dispatched to the West Indies to harvest sugar along with Africans. In 1705, the Virginia General Assembly formalized the legality of this status, declaring that non-Christian servants "brought" into the colonies were to be considered slaves and "held to be real estate." The Indians eventually escaped this bondage by their value-stripping ability to slip away into familiar surroundings, by price wars over the cost of Africans, and by their own revolt against the colonizers.[2] All of this, however, helped to further assimilate the Indians into the protocols of private property—previously inscrutable to nomads and to the *collective* attachment to land by more stationary tribes, flimflammed into ceding "rights" they were completely unaware they had for a few trinkets or promises. The art of the deal had arrived.

For colonizer/colonized relations, this metaphysically based lack of a common economic language proved tractable only by submission, assimilation, or warfare. Obstinate Indians were winnowed by the "accidental" genocide of exotic disease, by displacement in the rush of someone else's manifest destiny, by "native" schools, and by the reservation system. Indigenous reluctance to privatize their own commons was finally—and decisively—sorted out in 1887 by the Dawes Act, which at once forcibly imposed a system of capitalist property relations via a system of limited allotment grants, which had the corollary benefit of allowing the appropriation of around two-thirds of the Indian domain at the time: a Native American Nakba.

The Dawes Act and its successors also forced the Indians to assimilate to the eugenic economy of otherness. White administrators parsed degrees of Indian-ness by bestowing automatic citizenship on mixed-blood (half-breed) people while offering allotment rights only to the full-blooded—a static prison of property. The overlord's need to sort this out resulted in the infamous "Blood Quantum" (BQ) laws, which derived from the "Indian Blood" statutes in the 1705 Virginia declaration, classifying those with one half or more native blood as genuine Indians in order to establish whom to deny rights to. Ultimately, the tribes themselves utilized such ancestry claims to determine who could consider themselves a member of a given tribe, and today the dispositive ratio ranges from zero to five-eighths. (This screening is applied not simply to verify lineage and connectedness but also to exclude false claimants to casino and tobacco profits from tribal lands.) These pregenetic calculations are certainly in the same family as the "one drop" rule for determining who was Black during Reconstruction (a standard which does make Elizabeth Warren an Indian). The Nuremberg Laws, which define a Jew as someone with three or four Jewish grandparents, seem almost benign by comparison.

This equivalence problem—with all its feudal precedents—arose almost immediately in the New World, normalized by the introduction of the "head-right" system of indentured servitude by the Virginia Company in 1618 and the first African slave sale in 1619. Such complex tiering of the moral and economic rights of othered subjects is now fully structural—our racialized immigration laws (bring on the Norwegians!) are a fine example—but is often accompanied by an elaborate apologetics for enduring discriminations. These range from the "they want to be with their own" explanation for ghettoes to the "we're all in the same boat" metaphor of the "melting pot" (or "smelting pot," per Ralph Waldo Emerson)[3], that brash teleology of egalitarian uniformity and solidarity that persists in never quite working out. In this fantasy—which substitutes universal rights for individual value—the other *willingly* surrenders their quotient of difference in exchange for a new and superior, *American* identity but conceals its undergirding elitism, racism, sexism, and other forms of privilege. This right is denominated in myopia by concealing these barriers to create the new subject-who-has-rights and enabling the dream of universal subjectivity enshrined in both the US Constitution and, concurrently, the Declaration of the Rights of Man. The latter's first article reads: "Men are born and remain free and equal in rights. Social distinctions can be founded only on the common utility."

Although the writers of the Constitution were not exactly *sans culottes* and the Declaration is more explicit about the redistributive (and retributive) side of governance, "patrimonial capitalism" quickly emerged from the aspirational fog of utopia and became the system in both France and the US, successfully papering over the facts of actually existing inequality: the gendering of these documents is not anachronistic diction. Our white male republic denied women the vote for a century and a half (and many of our finer universities kept them out for another half century). It was even worse in France, where the Jacobins demolished an emergent feminist movement, and French women didn't get the vote until *1944,* ironically a period *between* republics. In the US, the franchise also came late to other, overly other, others, and calculating the precise degree of difference of would-be democratic subjects became a vital operation for the state.

BETWEEN CATASTROPHE AND REVOLUTION

To keep the complicated imbalance of rights properly skewed, the state needed an accurate count to sort persons, mathematize their subjectivity, officialize difference, and reinforce key hierarchies. The first Article of the Constitution calls for a census every decade—conducted "in such a manner as (Congress) shall direct"—to enumerate the pool from which citizens could be drawn and accommodate continually shifting standards. This demanded exacting calculation: to keep the South in the confederation, the founders fixed an exchange rate to assay the quantum of humanity assigned to slaves. Their bodies were tabulated so their "self-evident" human rights could be transferred to their owners: the three-fifths clause in the Constitution established a fungible, arithmetic citizenship, enfranchising "free white men" and excluding "all other persons." This fiction of measurability is the Energizer Bunny of American racism; the operating system for eugenics, Tuskegee experiments, IQ and literacy tests, lynching, concentration camps, reservations, gerrymandering, border walls, Muslim bans, white privilege, Fox News, mass shootings, Trump.

Politics sets limits on rights—including the right to be different—defining the relationship between person and nation. One hundred thirty-seven years separate the Chinese Exclusion Act of 1882 (not repealed until 1943—the war required distinguishing good Asians from bad, much as the colonists had done with Indians, never mind the only good one is a dead one) from the lawsuit—now moving through the courts—against Harvard by Asian students over alleged discrimination, arising from what was perceived to be their *excessive* numbers on campus, their disproportionate achievement, and their refusal to follow the curve of diversity the university plots. Harvard pushes back with PR about looking at the "whole person," not just academic qualifications; an exact repetition of its reaction to a surfeit of Jews in the 1920s, who had done too well on the college's entrance exam. By use of a ranking and quota system (which included a metric, J1, J2, J3, to assess the likelihood that any given applicant was a bona fide Jew), Harvard successfully—and drastically—reduced the number of over-performing "Hebrews" on campus.[4] The university now argues that its approach is actually friendly to struggling strivers but—like the College Board's rollout of a numerical degree-of-disadvantage score as annex to the SATs—it utilizes a carefully vague standard for dodging, or exploiting, the unreliability of quantitative measurements for race sorting, clearing the way for legacies, gift givers (Jared's dad!), and football players.

Still, every list has an order and the ranking is ultimately numerical—a spurious exactitude of both excellence and deprivation camouflages the eternity of prejudice, providing plausible deniability. This is as American as apple pie, and the whole system thrives on a massive web of standards for admission and exclusion. Even as Harvard schemed to solve its "Jewish Problem," Congress was passing the 1924 Immigration Act, with draconian restrictions on the immigration of "other persons" from Eastern and Southern Europe, South Asia, the Arab world, and other "shithole" countries, in favor of Western and Northern Europeans. American identity demanded its subjects be identical. And as white as possible.

Other Space

The National Mall in Washington, the nation's totemic public space, has long served as our architectural clubhouse, choosing which applicant alterities can pass the velvet rope to the cultural mainstream. It is our pantheon of acceptable otherness, recording the sequencing of the definition, empowerment, and admission of other Americans and, ultimately, their clubbability. It has its own mathematics, derived from the continuous accumulation and cataloging of objects—butterflies to buildings—which continuously shifts its meaning-as-aggregation. The space and its institutions are difference collectors and their mission is a global panoptics, seeing—and grabbing—at least one of every (suitable) nonvirtual thing on earth. This accumulation requires systems of classification—whether phylogeny or connoisseurship—to push the boundaries of observation's compass and possess the planet. The Mall's collection of architectures and architects archives the irregular progress of American tolerance; a model melting pot that always lacks key ingredients.

The National Mall began as unbounded nothingness: a National Void, a wilderness. In the L'Enfant Plan of 1791—the new city set out in its all-at-once—the Mall is vaguely described but grandly dimensioned; an honorific, aspirational space (Dickens wrote about Washington in 1842 that "it is sometimes called the City of Magnificent Distances but it might with greater propriety be termed the City of Magnificent Intentions . . . Spacious avenues, that begin in nothing, and lead nowhere; streets, mile-long, that only want houses, roads, and inhabitants; public buildings that need but a public to be complete"[5]). It organizes the geometric and topographic relations of new civic institutions and has the juju to interrupt—stop in their tracks—the baroque axialities radiating from the major appliances of governance: the Capitol and the White House. It is the Dorian Gray version of Manifest Destiny: an empty spatial and ideological frontier awaiting domination.

As its collection grew, the Mall more precisely represented the values of the institutions, technologies, and mores undergirding the state. Until the eve of the Civil War, it housed slave pens and slave markets; a wetware emporium for the labor to construct both the Capitol and the White House. On leaving the presidency, George Washington built a town home on Capitol Hill, economizing on labor costs by using his own slaves. There were abattoirs, impassable landscapes, railroad tracks, brothels, army encampments, entertainment gardens, filthy streams, and pestilential swamps, all waiting to be subdued by the architectures of order.

At the beginning of the Second World War, my father moved to DC to work at the Navy Department, then housed in rather substantial "temporary" First World War buildings. These were bivouacked on the Mall with their backs to the Reflecting Pool, which lay between them and a parallel row of flimsier, wood-and-asbestos, Second World War "tempos" on the opposite bank. The bureaucracy of global conflict needed to be at the center of decision-making, and large areas of "empty" Mall space were removed from the public, recreational, green realm to house toiling war workers. My father's office was a small cog in the great wheel of death, but its hallways were fabulous and unalloyed to my boyhood self: a naval museum filled with big model ships of remarkable precision and detail. Naval *architecture*.

Expanding the workplace to encompass this gallery helped aestheticize the carnage and assimilate it into the larger project of the Mall, situating our never-ending violence in a museum-quality legacy of objects, like suits of armor at the Met. The beautiful model ships differed only in degree from the Enola Gay, buffed to a hyperreal mint condition and hangared forever in the National Air and Space Museum, surrounded by an exculpatory formation of less lethal flying objects: the Wright Flyer, Spirit of St. Louis, Apollo spacecraft, DC-3. Collection requires specialization, an idea of completeness, connoisseurship, rarity, and monetization, which supplement (and diminish) any founding functionality with a veneer of aesthetic appreciation. The class of objects makes no difference: whether Calders hanging from the ceiling at the National Gallery or buzz bombs suspended at Air and Space, the curation is the same. The Mall marries art and death and nurtures their spawn.

One summer, I interned in the ornithology department at the Natural History Museum. I had no special talent for taxidermy but was amazed at the endless, double-height cases of carcasses, arranged with taxonomic exactitude: ten thousand stuffed finches in mute Darwinian order, an astonishing act of curation. The bird collection deployed two key Mall media, an aesthetic of numbers (vast) and the need to explain (evolution). The same intersection of quantity and cause also appeared in the long tradition of *un-curated*, temporary, declamatory occupations: penned slaves, Union military encampments, the veterans' reunion of 1892, the Bonus Army in 1932, the Folklife Festival, fireworks (and tanks) on July 4, inaugural crowds, antiwar marches, the great 1963 civil rights march, Resurrection City in 1968, the Million Man March, the Women's March, the March For Our Lives, rock concerts, symphonic concerts, concerts by military bands, etc. Like the shacks of Resurrection City, the tents of the Bonus Army, or the vendors' kiosks at the folk festival, my father's Navy Department offices were provisional, simply of longer duration and more complex but single-minded in purpose. The acts of building and inhabiting give these extended encampments a special status, somewhere between the permanence of the museums and monuments and the evanescence of crowds. Many of these public assemblies worked as admissions interviews for excluded others and, eventually, produced a turn in the ethos of the Mall's institutional project, from collection to compensation. Large gatherings are like GRE scores: the higher the number, the more likely you are to get in. Trump had it right in his hyperventilation about the inaugural crowd: the Mall measures.

In the evolution of its hybridity—ground for parks, government buildings, memorials, and pools; demonstration and entertainment venue; museum complex—the Mall has gestated its own vetting principles, shadowing the body politic. By the mid-sixties, civil rights were entrenched in this discourse. An executive order issued by JFK in 1961 (E.O. 10925) called for the nation to "take affirmative action" to guarantee equal treatment for all. This ethic of expanded embrace came with its own styles of representation, and its progressivism radically transformed the Mall. Until the early sixties, neoclassicism had been the official style of the sacred space, controlled by the white mavens of the Fine Arts Commission and the jowly southern Senators who, looking at a classical column, wept for the Lost Cause. The Mall's defining, unadmitted, formal other was modernism.

Other Architecture

It seems no coincidence that the March on Washington, and its demand to liberate a long-oppressed other, coincided with the 1964 construction of the Mall's first toe-dipping modernist building, the deeply mediocre Museum of History and Technology (later the Museum of American History). The building was designed during the death throes of the legendary McKim, Mead, and White office, its remnant running on fumes. The firm tried to straddle the vexing divide: the building was "classical in definition, and the detailing is modern" (contemporaneous Pall Mall advertising syntax: "Outstanding, and they are mild"). For years, architects had been testing how many classical signifiers—fluted columns, entablatures, volutes, nymphs—could be shaved off without breaking the link to antiquity. "Stripped classicism" was the lingua franca of interwar works on and near the Mall, including Paul Cret's sumptuous—"the Banks Are Made of Marble"—Federal Reserve of 1937, John Russell Pope's graceful National Gallery of Art of 1941, and Pope's beautifully sited Jefferson Memorial of 1943. Asymptotes approaching the abscissa of modernity, all teetered at the threshold of minimalism. Like their architects, all these buildings are extremely white. And, there was a clear concordance between them and similar monumental projects in fascist Italy and Nazi Germany. They had weight.

The Technology Museum is a shaky bridge, fumbling with its own metaphor. Modernism's boyfriend is technology, and the mismatch of leading-edge science with faux-classical architecture was a no-go: not many steam locomotives in republican Rome. The most striking object on display, however, was Horatio Greenough's bare-chested, toga-draped, white marble, "classical" statue of George Washington, commemorating the centennial of his birth.[6] Its route had been circuitous: banished from the Capitol as pornographic, exiled to the Patent Office, then Smithsonian Castle, finally arriving at History and Technology. The statue effectively flipped convention, putting neoclassicism at the heart of the building and scrubbing any reminders from its skin, leaving naked mass. Washington's home among scientific objects both reinforced—and contradicted—Greenough's major intellectual construct: the "theory of inherent forms," a precocious functionalism. Greenough was critical of the appropriation of historical styles for American building and admired machine design, especially the sleek economy of ships.

When L'Enfant drew his plan for the city over a three-week charrette in 1791, he imagined the Mall as a combined boulevard and greensward; an enormous figural space, lined by embassies. He also sited three major, symbolic architectural elements. On an existing hill—spatial culmination to the east—was the Capitol, maternity ward of representative democracy. The Mall was to be semicruciform, with the White House on a lower hill at the northern end of the short arm of the cross. A tribute to Washington was planned for the intersection of the arms, figuring the symbolic center of town and nation. L'Enfant imagined that the monument would be—in the European manner—*equestrian*, with Washington, victorious, astride his frothing nag. Thomas Jefferson even wanted to move the prime meridian from Greenwich to mark the degree zero of a new civilization, and the monument's ultimate realization is as an *axis mundi*.

In 1833, a competition was held for the design. The winner, Robert Mills, proposed a 555-foot obelisk, its base surrounded by a scrotal temple on a high plinth. The entry to the great shaft was to be reached via a grand stair flanked by florid statuary: a mash-up of Doric, Egyptian, and Babylonian styles, confusion encircling—and encrusting—rectitude. Construction began in 1848 but was halted at the 156-foot level in 1854, when money ran out. Two decades later, Congress appropriated funds to complete it and work resumed in 1876. The seam between phases—the result of stone from two different quarries—remains visible.

This interregnum proved fortunate. Mills had died in 1865 and the project was remanded to the Army Corps of Engineers in the no-nonsense person of Lt. Colonel Thomas Lincoln Casey, who vacuumed the frou-frou and—after consulting with an expert on Pharaonic architecture—decided to finish the monument as a simple, if gigantic, pyramid-peaked obelisk with a stair and an elevator inside to take visitors to view a spectacular panorama of the city at the top. Finally completed in 1884, the Washington Monument was the world's tallest building until 1889, when it was superseded by the Eiffel Tower, another instant metonym for its hometown. The pair are skyscrapers avant la lettre: high enough by far to qualify but barely occupiable, their only non-symbolic function ascent and view (and at the Eiffel Tower, of course, dining). Strikingly, these towers lie at the roots of the two main expressive branches of modernism: minimalism and structural expressionism. It took another century for modernism-as-such to arrive.

The Capitol also grew in fits and starts. Its original design was mainly by Benjamin Latrobe: a simple structure crowned by a low dome by Charles Bulfinch. That building was burned by the British in 1814 and quickly rebuilt, but by 1850, it had become too small and Thomas U. Walter was hired to enlarge it. Realizing that the expansion made the original dome look puny, Walter designed—and built—one three times higher, channeling St. Peter's in Rome, St. Paul's in London, and Les Invalides in Paris. This structure was supported by a pioneering use of cast iron, the most up-to-date technology of the time, invisibly holding the classical dome in place. Engineering was modernism's covert stalking horse.

Wanting to top his new dome with a suitable finial, Walter invited the sculptor Thomas Crawford to design it. His first sketch depicted a woman holding a "liberty cap" at the end of a long rod, referencing a Roman tradition in which touching this symbol of freedom preceded a formal manumission ceremony. The actual Roman headgear—the *pileus*—was the ancestor of the familiar Phrygian cap, an eighteenth-century mistranslation that copied the wrong hat. Nonetheless, this droopier chapeau rapidly became liberty's logo, worn by Marianne on the barricades, by Britannia (who began carrying one atop her pole following Britain's 1807 ban on slave trade), and by our own Columbia, who sported one on US coins (including the Liberty half dollar) until 1947. By the mid-nineteenth century, the liberty cap was installed as a wearable symbol of republican values, declaratively worn by American freedmen in the streets of the antebellum north.

Realizing the massive scale of Walter's dome, Crawford created larger options, the first a female figure *wearing* a liberty cap and kitted with shield, wreath, and sword: "Armed Liberty." The design was sent for approval to the Secretary of War, who was responsible for overseeing all work on the Capitol. This turned out to be Jefferson Davis, who objected to the liberty cap, suggesting a helmet instead. Crawford compliantly substituted a Roman model, crested with a Carmen Miranda flourish; "a bold arrangement of feathers, suggested by the costume of our Indian tribes."[7] Armed Liberty—the first piece of public art on the Mall—represented an anthropomorphized *quality* rather than a personality, beginning what would become an ongoing dialectic of individuality, abstraction, appropriation, and invention.

If the Museum of Science and Technology brought the official architectural default to an almost-modernism, the Hirshhorn Museum (1974) was first to go all the way. A bunker-like, cylindrical donut clad by an opaque facade with a single gun-port-like aperture facing the Mall (looking much like the turret of the Union ironclad, Monitor), it is modernist through and through, designed to house the Mall's first dedicated collection of modern art, gifted by Joseph Hirshhorn, along with a relatively minor portion of the construction costs. This affirmative action for modernity was undertaken by a collector, Hirshhorn, and designed by an architect, Gordon Bunshaft of SOM, who were Jewish; another first. Sub-rosa controversy arose over naming the museum for its donor;[8] an obvious contrast to the Protestant discretion of Andrew Mellon, who had bequeathed the National Gallery and its old masters without insisting his name be chiseled in stone.

The Hirshhorn was quickly followed by the National Air and Space Museum (1976), a more successful version—alternating full-height stone and glass panels—of the push-pull façade of the American History Museum. Air and Space is lofty, and its huge windows background its collection of formerly flying objects against a real sky. The architect was Gyo Obata—lead designer of the uber-corporate firm HOK—an American of Japanese descent who had escaped internment in the Second World War by a timely transfer from Berkeley to Washington University. The rest of his family was not as lucky and was shipped to the camps for the duration of the war. Obata was *another* other—the first Asian American to build in the national space. The Mall's expanding unconscious of compensation chose an architect of Japanese heritage to neutralize the aura of the shiny genocide machine—the plane that dropped the A-bomb on Hiroshima—inside.

The modernist beachhead was firmly consolidated by the East Wing of the National Gallery (1978), built to house its own growing collection of modern art. The architect, I. M. Pei, was, like Bunshaft and Obata, a major player in the world of high corporate and institutional modernism and a master of weighty abstraction. The East Wing is rigorously geometrical, based on two interlocking triangles, one isosceles, one right. There is triangularity all over the Mall, perhaps springing from the Freemasonry of so many of the founders, including George Washington, Ben Franklin, James Monroe, Paul Revere, and John Hancock—or, perhaps, the triangle trade, which had allowed the North to profit from slavery without actually having to practice it. The Washington Monument's pyramidal peak (a three-dimensional combination of four identical triangles) recurs—topped by an eye of providence—as a secular seal of approval on that fundament of the American economy, the dollar bill. Like the Hirshhorn (as well as Pei's famous glass pyramid at the Louvre), this Euclidean palette fudged any lingering distinction between classicism with modern characteristics and modernism with classical characteristics. Pei was born in China. The other exclusion act had been repealed.

The architectural context for the Hirshhorn, the East Wing, and the Air and Space Museum included the three gleaming tributes to great white presidents and the growing institutions guarding our national swag: the Rembrandts, dinosaurs, and anthropological tableaux; the accumulating loot of a rising colonial power. Modernism's arrival recalls the originating alterity of the Smithsonian's first building. The "Castle"—by James Renwick Jr. (1855)—was a crenellated red sandstone confection, overlooking the rogue occupation of the Mall-as-frontier. It housed labs, offices, and a gallery displaying an eclectic collection of expeditionary specimens pilfered by explorers, surveyors, and naturalists; formaldehyde for the global other, including Pacific Islanders and Native Americans. Built just before the peak of the Victorian-era gothic revival (with its nostalgic whiff of feudalism), the building was a complete conceptual other to the Jeffersonian classical ideal. The gothic revival was, for its apologists, highly antimodern; a recuperation of a mythical origin point as antidote to modernity's driver—industrialization—and its urban miseries.

The National Museum Building (1881) was the Mall's first purpose-built museum, its architecture torn between available formal paradigms. Its overstuffed, grab-bag collection was typical of increasingly popular world's fairs and their cornucopian curation. The new Museum was a near copy of the Government Building at the Philadelphia Fair of 1876 (the first international exposition on US soil) and was crammed with much of the same stuff (Congress had accepted the contents as repayment of a loan). With polychrome brick for a chromatic match with the Castle, it's hard to parse; a vaguely Renaissance, vaguely Gothic, vaguely industrial pastiche; an overcooked meatball from the premodern melting pot.

By 1911, white stone classicism resumed full control of the Mall in the form of the National Museum of Natural History, modeled closely on Daniel Burnham's Palace of Fine Arts at the World's Columbian Exposition in Chicago, which celebrated the four hundredth anniversary of the continent's "discovery" by Columbus, bringing "the torch of civilization to the new world." The Exposition was *the summa* of the City Beautiful Movement, a fully realized architectural expression of America's imperial moment, and a model for a new urbanism that would subdue cities' disorder. The main attraction at the fair was the "White City" (The City Beautiful's primary color): spectacular neoclassical buildings ranged around a giant pool, illuminated by an astonishing hundred thousand light bulbs, and meant to be spectacularly uplifting. The missionary high-mindedness was inverted by its underside, the louche entertainment on the Midway (Little Egypt, a penned African "cannibal tribe," Buffalo Bill, beer)—a merger of world's fair and circus that prototyped the theme park. The City Beautiful was meant to be a global style: in 1905, Daniel Burnham—lead architect for the White City—drew up a canonical City Beautiful plan for colonized Manila.

The Chicago Fair and its legatees inspired a total reenvisioning of the Mall. The McMillan Plan of 1902 (named for the senator who sponsored it) sought to make the capital the most rigorously beautiful City Beautiful on earth. We had earned it. The Battles of San Juan Hill and Manila Bay were both won in 1898 and the Great White Fleet set sail in 1907. The new plan cleared the Mall's remaining funk, replacing it with the entire beaux-arts apparatus of allées, lawns, topiary, and parterres, flanked by its own Great White Fleet of civic buildings. The Mall's void was pushed westward into the Potomac on landfill, a site for Lincoln's memorial. L'Enfant's asymmetrical cruciform was completed by an extension to the south, for Jefferson. A vast neoclassical bureaucratic city—The Federal Triangle—was to rise between the Mall and Pennsylvania Avenue. The austere base of the Washington Monument was cloaked—as Mills originally intended—in thick decoration;

a baroque cock ring for the phallus of the great white father. The plan was enthusiastically received and eventually implemented in its entirety, initially during the irrational exuberance of the gilded age and later as part of the New Deal. Its final piece was not completed until 1998 and named for Ronald—"government is the problem"—Reagan. It now houses the Woodrow Wilson Center, established by Congress in 1968 to honor the racist-nationalist visionary and scholar who saw us through the First World War. A physical monument to Wilson is a few miles downstream on the Potomac in the form of a bridge on the interstate. The Reagan Building now finds itself behind the Trump Hotel, formerly the main post office.

The Freer Gallery, a mansion-scale, neoclassical work, was completed in 1923 by Charles Platt to house a distinguished collection that joined, in Freer's words, "modern work with masterpieces of certain periods of high civilization harmonious in spiritual suggestion." It included extensive holdings in Asian art and more than *thirteen hundred* Whistlers, among them the fabulous "Peacock Room." Actual peacocks strutted the grounds. The museum was the first on the Mall to treat the work of others as art, not simply evidence. In 1987, the Freer was joined by (and to) the twinned National Museum of African Art and the Sackler (the opioid folks) Gallery of Asian Art. Both these museums are *underground*: basements without buildings, entombments of these "periods of high civilization," suggesting a connection beyond mere otherness. The architect was French-born Jean Paul Carlhian of the white-shoe Boston firm of Shepley, Bulfinch, Richardson, and Abbott.[9] All that is visible on the ground are two small entry pavilions, decorated with primitive markers of cultural difference: Africa's entry is topped by little domes and has a round window; Asia's has little pyramids with a diamond window. What is radical is their penetration of the Mall's ground plane, which instigates equivalence between above and below and transforms the subterranean into valuable real estate, while reinforcing the invisibility of these others, now keeping what is already under the Mall company: a highway, train tracks, parking, and sewers; and the dead.

Other Malls

In April 1983, the Beach Boys—who had played Independence Day concerts on the Mall the previous three years—were banned from appearing as scheduled.

OTHERING THE MALL

The order came from James Watt, Reagan's Interior Secretary, a rabid antienvironmentalist and racist who had famously described the country as being divided between "liberals and Americans." Watt avowed that rock and roll authorized drinking and taking drugs and would attract a bad element and, with it, *crime*. This fit well with Nancy Reagan's "Just Say No" campaign and President Reagan's animus toward youth culture, especially hippies. In a stump speech, the Gipper, with blithe homophobia, described an imaginary one, who "had a haircut like Tarzan, walked like Jane, and smelled like Cheetah."[10] Unfortunately for Watt, vice president Poppy Bush was friendly with the Beach Boys, and Ron and Nancy were fans. Watt was forced to apologize and, soon, resign. By the time calm returned, the Beach Boys were booked elsewhere and Watt—in a genius move—replaced them with the easy-listening lounge lizard, Wayne Newton. He was booed when he took the stage.

Newton's appearance refigured the Mall as Vegas. Morphologically, both are based on a spine and event model: what Caesar's is to the Strip, the Air and Space Museum is to the Mall. It is an urban commonplace. JFK Airport uses a curving spine, like a necklace, to distribute the competing temples of the airlines. The Albany Mall is a ham-handed, grandiose, sterile version. Daniel Burnham's 1903 plan for the civic center of Cleveland ranged a phalanx of public buildings along a grand greensward. San Francisco: ditto. Saint Louis: check. The form does have a degenerate doppelganger, its own Midway—the "strip," a pioneering urbanism of the automobile, an American original, enabling the suburbs. The string of muffler shops and McDonald's restaurants along the busy roadway morphed into the shopping center and ultimately the shopping mall, bringing the spine indoors. The most honorific spots are reserved for the ends, where Macy's or The Limited stand in for the Capitol and Lincoln Memorial. Conceptually (and literally, given the importance of gift shops), the Mall has been malled.

Other Memories

The Vietnam Veterans Memorial was completed in 1982 to a chorus of veneration and vilification. It radically shifted the language of commemoration and finalized the thematic division of the Mall into its museal east and memorial west ends. It was also the first work to install tragedy in our memory palace; the first war memorial on the Mall. And, it's *black*. A polished granite retaining wall—a "V" shape at an angle too wide to suggest victory (but clearly triangular)—is inscribed with the names of more than fifty-eight thousand American dead in order of demise; a bar graph of the rate of slaughter. The Memorial is a work of subtraction, sunken into the ground, with open sky above. The mood is somber, funerary; a monument to futility. The tragedies it records are individual, one after another, the names of the needless dead. The "body count" was how we measured wartime success, and the Memorial establishes whose bodies count.

Rage at the Memorial did not just target its "defeatist" aesthetic but also its authorship. Maya Lin, the winning designer, was a highly overdetermined other: young, a student, a woman (the first—and only—to build on the Mall), and Asian American: an intolerable surplus. This excess of otherness encroached on a sacred space thought to be under control. To pacify its detractors, Lin's design was forcibly augmented by two vitiating additions, a bronze statue of three soldiers and an American flag. Frederick Hart's sculpture carefully presents the troopers as recognizably European American, African American, and Hispanic American: the first permanent desegregation of the Mall's memorial space and a recuperation of the human figure as antidote to Lin's abstraction. The statuary muddies the representational debate—and the meaning of all those names—by presenting "individuals" who are deliberately generic examples of racial difference; stereotypes, like the half-scale Navajo or Neanderthals around their campfires behind glass; natural history. These are *symbolic* people. Their direct ancestor—the Iwo Jima Memorial—depicts six heroic and identifiable individuals in a moment of American triumph, planting the flag on Mount Suribachi. It was sculpted by Felix de Weldon on the basis of Joe Rosenthal's famous photo of what was actually a reenactment of an earlier, unrecorded raising: a simulacrum of a semi-simulacrum.

Soon after came Korea, another land war in Asia ending in humiliation and a country resplit between communist and capitalist regimes. A 1986 competition had a winner, but the architects withdrew when too many changes, too contrary to their artistic intent, were demanded and their lawsuit failed. What emerged was committee work, cobbled by a group with no clear, shared visual or conceptual referent. At a loss, they recruited the ambient vibe, coming up with a black stone triangle (another one!) and statues of larger-than-life anonymous soldiers. Instead of identity, ornament appeared—sandblasted cartouches of generic war scenes. The triangle's apex punctures a circular pool like a pipette piercing an in vitro egg. Nineteen bronzes of weary GIs in helmets and ponchos slog through the shrubbery in the imaginary rain, their insignia in correct statistical proportion to the representation of their branches of service on the battlefield. Frank Gaylord's sad soldiers are exhausted by meaninglessness, out of action.

The Mall does have one memorial ensemble of soldiers in uniform that is successfully heroic: Henry Shrady's Grant Memorial at the base of Capitol Hill. The tableau surrounds the famously calm general—stillness at the heart of battle—with Union troops in action, charging cavalry, and careening artillerymen. Thrilling, kinetic, even scary, these imagined men represent energy well spent, victors in a righteous war to free the enslaved other. The anonymity does not disturb: "they" fought for a great cause and defer to their commander. Here is Armed Liberty. Korea mourns by numbers, a ledger of death by body count. Every fallen soldier becomes unknown—the null set evaporates difference. Metonymy and accountancy duke it out.

Two contemporaneous memorials are dedicated to Franklin D. Roosevelt and Martin Luther King. How to individuate them deferentially in light of the Mall's new mnemonics? Lin's work blurs the line between architecture and landscape, offering them equal rights in an expanding field. Both FDR and MLK memorials are likewise grounded in the fluidity of landscape, not the fixity of architecture. The 1974 design for Roosevelt's memorial (completed in 1997) is organized into four "outdoor rooms" (one for each term in office), covering seven and a half acres through which visitors are meant to wander freely, in no particular order. Like the Korean War Memorial, it is both narrative and encyclopedic, an *almost* museum. The design is by Lawrence Halprin—a Brooklyn-born Jew who served during the Second World War on a ship that was struck by a kamikaze, perhaps flying a Zero fighter like the one in the collection of the Air and Space Museum.

The one contentious issue was the representation of Roosevelt's own other: the man crippled by the polio he concealed from the public. The bronze for Room Three by Neil Estern depicts a president "at once vulnerable and strong" but conceals his wheelchair and leg braces under a voluminous cape. Attempting to finesse the controversy that arose, Estern added tiny bronze casters, peeking from the drapery and visible only from the rear. In response, a disability rights organization raised the funds to produce *another* statue of Roosevelt, seated in a faithful—and demonstrative—replica of his wheelchair, placed at the entry to the Memorial in 2001, eleven years after the passage of the Americans With Disabilities Act. This late addition of the wheelchair signaled acceptance—even admiration—of Roosevelt's relation to his illness but created a two-Roosevelt problem: infirmity separable from the man. The commemorative conundrum was further complicated by FDR's own wishes for a memorial that was a simple block of stone in a small green space in front of the National Archives. Such an object was placed there in 1965, fulfillment and a riposte to the overblown outcome of a failed 1959 competition. That winning design consisted of eight enormous concrete slabs engraved with quotations from the president's speeches. Nobody liked it, especially Roosevelt's daughter Anna, who led the resistance. Soubriquets included "instant Stonehenge" and a "collection of bookends The architects scaled down the glyphs and added a statue of Roosevelt. No dice. The Memorial Commission junked the design *and* the competition and gave the job to Marcel Breuer (born Hungarian, Bauhaus hero, refugee from the Nazis, and Jewish until he renounced the faith to marry his German girlfriend). A good choice, in theory. But Breuer also missed the boat, designing *another* arrangement of slabs, now horizontal: a spiral of sixty-foot triangular (!) granite blades with a mini-Kaaba at the center engraved with Roosevelt's image. Recordings of the Fireside Chats were to seep from speakers hidden in the bushes. The design was summarily rejected by the lordly Fine Arts Commission, which included two competitive architects of Breuer's generation: Gordon Bunshaft and John Carl Warnecke, a favorite of Jackie Kennedy.

The King Memorial, completed in 2011, finally invited the most reviled other to join the white people pantheon; the first memorial to honor a *specific* African American. Although the Mall has been an arena for Black struggles from the day it was surveyed, African American presence had been temporary, provisional, compelled, or displaced. There is that museum of *African* art but that culture is not "ours," however influential, making it safe for disinterested aesthetic appreciation.[11] The King Memorial's formal particulars come from an established honorific vocabulary, signaling its alignment with Lincoln, Jefferson, Washington, and FDR—at home on the Mall. The work is in stone and includes stirring quotations from one of our most eloquent sons on a

450-foot long "inscription wall." It is sited expansively near Roosevelt, on the banks of the Tidal Basin, in an ordered, calmly artistic landscape. The main focus is a thirty-foot statue of King carved in *white* granite by Chinese sculptor Lei Yixin, author of more than 150 public monuments in China, including dozens to Chairman Mao. His King was carved in his studio in China, from stone quarried in China by Chinese laborers, and assembled in DC by a (non-union) Chinese crew flown in for the job.

This other's perspective on the other's other may explain why the statue does not look (to my eyes, at least) like MLK. The unmissable implication of choosing a Chinese national was that African Americans (including many great artists) could not be entrusted with the commission to sculpt a memorial to one of their own. The selection of Lei got around the obvious impossibility of hiring a white artist by turning to the work of another subordinate other—one from the parent culture of our own, overperforming model minority. The decision reads forward to the Harvard lawsuit and to the crisis in admission to New York's selective high schools. The most prestigious of these is Stuyvesant, at which 74 percent of students (of a total of around 3,400) are Asian. The class entering in 2019 includes only *seven* Black people. This hyper-segregation is an outrage, but the zero-sum mentality of the resistance, suggesting that Asian Americans are taking the seats of African Americans, has now maneuvered the battles of affirmative action into a minority race war, which white folk can cheer from the sidelines.

The backward sequence of memorials finally arrived at the "good war." A Second World War memorial was authorized in 1996, half a century after V-J Day. Veterans were passing away in their thousands and the splintering national psyche was in urgent need of a unifying, unassailable, familiar, prideful nostalgia to reclaim the cultural high ground from hedonistic boomer culture, the ingrate spawn of the Greatest Generation. The world war was recruited as the unambiguous anti-Vietnam. In 1998, Steven Spielberg's "realistic" *Saving Private Ryan* was released. Its precursor *Schindler's List* premiered in 1993. A sequence anticipating the Holocaust Memorial's opening prior to the inauguration of the World War II Memorial on the Mall was rehearsed in Hollywood history. Tom Brokaw's *The Greatest Generation* was published the same year. Tom Hanks, the star of *Private Ryan*, became a key fundraiser and spokesperson for the effort. He did look the part: we all saw him struggling to get ashore through the mayhem on bloody Omaha beach. A home front hero. Reagan redux.

The competition was won by Friedrich St. Florian, an Austrian-born architect who continued, despite his whiteness, the uninterrupted fifteen-year streak of othered authorship of the Mall's museums and monuments. St. Florian was raised in Nazi Austria (his Tyrolian hometown was "liberated" by American troops in 1945 when St. Florian, né Gartler, was twelve years old). As built, the scheme is a diminished version of a more robust original. It references not only earlier plans from Mills and McMillan to reframe the Washington Monument but, more meaningfully, many memorials from the First World War, built on the killing fields of the Western Front.[12] The relatively short time between these monuments' design and their completion, together with the supervision of the British side by the Imperial (later Commonwealth) War Graves Commission—which engaged, as architectural directors, three renowned British architects of the day: Herbert Baker, Reginald Blomfield, and Edwin Lutyens (with Rudyard Kipling as literary advisor)—yielded a remarkable stylistic convergence. The *parti* was often an axial void, passing through a field of marked graves to a culminating memorial. Here, numbers tell the story. Like our civil war memorials in situ, these are a distributed commemoration at the sites where the interred died; greened-over scenes of the crimes. Under the crosses, remains. Among the architecturally strongest are the American Cemeteries at Meuse-Argonne by York and Sawyer (graduates of the McKim, Meade, and White office), the Chateau-Thiery Memorial by Paul Cret, and monuments to the Commonwealth dead by Edwin Lutyens, with his perfect sense of massing, proportion, and detail. Among the most moving of these is the Thiepval Memorial to 73,337 unknown British dead from the Battle of the Somme, recalled in horrifying anonymity.

The World War II Memorial is almost entirely emotionless Mall Math, pinched between commemoration and celebration. As there was no national consensus on the iconography of victory, St. Florian reverted to the style of the Great War tributes and to ornamental enumeration. Two triumphal arches, one for the Atlantic and the other for the Pacific, reinforce the axial symmetry. Fifty-six granite steles, one each for the forty-eight states of 1945, plus an extra eight for DC and our overseas territories. Then, 4,048 gold stars on a curving wall, each "equal" to one hundred American dead. Bronze laurel wreaths attached to everything. Metal eagles perched above. Twenty-four bas-reliefs ("inspired" by the Elgin Marbles) show scenes from factory, kitchen, and battlefield. Like the censored, sanitized images from the early months of the war (and from Hollywood until long after), everything is clean and orderly. The stage blood in the movies is our prurient contribution.

Other Ambiguities

The triumphalism of St. Florian's design (some catch a whiff of Hitler's cloddish architect Albert Speer) is a compensatory other to the *first* World War II Memorial on the Mall. In 1993, the United States Holocaust Memorial Museum opened just south of the Washington Monument, a scaled-up merger of memorial and museum that introduces a highly narrative approach to an experience economy already flirting with entertainment. The building is by I. M. Pei's firm—global go-to for gravitas—and designed by his partner James Ingo Freed, himself Jewish, who fled Germany with his family to escape the Nazis. If the Vietnam Memorial found a respectful, nonheroic register, the Holocaust Museum ups the ante, introducing genocide to the national commemorative space and setting the stage for two additional redress museums to come.

Theodore Adorno's epigram—"to write poetry after Auschwitz is barbaric"—is not an injunction against artistic practice, but a call for resituating the conditions of its production in the light of this eternally incomprehensible event. This taboo nevertheless dogs the prosody of an architecture that tries to directly represent the inexpressible. The interior of Freed's museum runs variations on the tectonics of the camps—a stage set for a mini-series—while its exterior is in standard limestone semiclassicism like the buildings around it. In form, it defers to context and does not stage its exceptionality; a reductive misdirection. Like Spielberg's film, the museum's scenography represents—if not the Disney version—our setting, our reconstitution of the story: an idealization edited to fit available screen time. The exhibition is a self-guided tour, a one-way ride culminating in a large, light-filled room, a caesura of spirituality, a rump heaven, and a reassurance that something positive—our embracing democracy and concrete reassurance that we won't forget—resulted.

In these passages of instructional nightmare, voids fill in—at all three major museums of compensation (the American Indian and the African American are the others)—for both the ineffable and the unthinkable: the empty boxcar, the empty hold of the slave ship on the Middle Passage, the empty coffin of Emmett Till, the graphically neutral map of the disappearing journey along the trail of tears, the descent into the voided earth at the Vietnam Memorial; temporary burial. The precision—and designer elegance—of the exhibition blends with the Aristotelean structure of not just the movies, but also of the world's fair pavilions, the Newseum, the presidential libraries, and other managed didactics. Isolating the objects within the museum-container gives perverse encouragement to the plausibility of denial. What is really the provenance of that pile of shoes? Narrative opens the space for counternarrative, and deniers and neo-Nazis are coming out of the woodwork. One murdered a guard on duty at the Holocaust Museum, a black man. Good people on both sides.

The Museum of the American Indian is arguably the most architecturally other of the Mall's modernisms, balancing its tragedies by focusing on what these holocausts were not, depicting Native American experiences as part of whole lives, and shifting the story from victimhood to creativity. However, the "Indian" label manufactures a single "people" from the multinationalism and cultural diversity that confronted the colonizer (and that largely stumps the museum's curators). The building itself was designed by an appropriately credentialed other, a Canadian architect of Blackfoot descent, Douglas Cardinal. The process was contentious. Cardinal was sacked, lawsuits ensued, same old, same old. The finished building is clad in a beautiful golden limestone, laminated, curvilinear, and anti-Euclidean (though not threatening the rectangular confines of its site), representing the weathered face of geological strata: a "natural" building for "natural" peoples and a modest affront to the white angles all around. Like the buried African and Asian museums, this container homogenizes the First Nations, whose individual and tribal identities must be expressed via mock stratigraphy rather than with more abstractly neutral modernities or reference to their own multitudinous architectures.

The Mall's final museum is the logical omega; a symbolic reparation for America's second original sin. The African American Museum has a striking silhouette, allusively African in its recollection of a Yoruban caryatid[13]—a *Corona*—respectfully serrated at the angle of the pyramidal crown of the Washington Monument. Like the Vietnam Memorial's pointing arms, it locates itself by offering new perspectives on the nearby obelisk and White House and the histories they materialize, walking a fine line between deference and difference. The building is not white, not stone, modernist in its strong shape and simple geometry, but clad in a tiered screen of filigreed aluminum of shade-shifting (copper, sepia, rust) tones, meant to evoke the metalwork of African American blacksmiths that ornamented the balconies and gables of white homes in the antebellum South. A building of color.

Lead designer was David Adjaye, a British-Ghanaian architect, who collaborated with two leading, socially engaged, African American architects: Philip Freelon and J. Max Bond Jr., the "dean" of African American architects, whose early career feats include exceptional buildings in Ghana. Their design was chosen in a competition among six big names, but only the Adjaye, Bond, and Freelon team was Black in both leadership and depth, and theirs was the only scheme with the iconicity the project demanded. That the lead designer was a non-American, African starchitect complicated the formula for fixing other authorship but was also deeply authenticating—a connection to an origin point, to roots—if again erasing diversity with the figure of a unitary "Africa." The building was stirringly inaugurated by President Obama, a moving historical conjunction, reinforcing the importance of African paternity. This same question of foreign fatherhood is at the heart of Obama's *Dreams from My Father*. Fathers still gender the Mall.

The museum is organized, like the Holocaust Museum, for a crowd walking a fixed route. Visitors progress along a narrative trail that begins with a descent to a dark space several levels into the earth, an underground railway to Africa and origins, simultaneously excavation and burial. The visitor journey literally follows the African American experience up from slavery, arriving at the main level, brightly lit by expansive windows and overlooking green fields—green pastures—the triumph of normality. This space of transition is a seam between the fixed storytelling below and the theaters, meeting places, and changing—and generally upbeat and "popular" (hip-hop, Oprah, contemporary art and art practices from Africa)—installations on the floors above, where modulations of sun and view are curated by the canted screens.

Other Ends

The final closing of the Mall's frontier will be the Eisenhower Memorial, under construction on its last vacant site, four acres across Independence Avenue from the Air and Space Museum. It is enclosed on one long side—like the African American Museum—by a metal scrim. Frank Gehry's design is a Rosetta stone of monumental intertextuality—serious bricolage. Gehry is best known for complex, gestural works of plastic abstraction and for a shape grammar that yielded the first signature style of the digital age. He began the trajectory of his formal reinvention by overturning standard outcomes via defamiliarizing recombination, inventing an idiosyncratic architecture and a radical departure from frustrating corporate practice. Gehry's *architectural* self-othering began with a literal superposition of architectures in the renovation of his own house, a found domestic object he wrapped and rejuvenated with cheap materials, including corrugated metal, plywood, and—famously—chain link fencing. In the first iteration of the memorial, the space was enclosed on one side by a 440-foot-long stainless steel mesh "tapestry" supported on giant cylindrical columns, depicting a pacific view of rural landscapes around Ike's Kansas home. This other architecture had an originary parallel in Gehry's *private* self-othering: he changed his name from Goldberg and moved from Toronto to LA. The US is where you start over, become another.

Gehry was impressed by a speech of Eisenhower's that evoked the "dreams of a barefoot boy," and his memorial is pastoral, antiheroic, lightly surreal. It honors the "modesty" of a man who made his mark as a general, leader of the largest invasion in history. The original scheme included a life-sized (i.e., child-sized)[14] statue of Eisenhower as a barefoot boy, seated on a wall, gazing at his unformed future. In the middle of the space was an irregular, enigmatic stack of massive stone blocks inscribed with apposite quotations and supporting bas-reliefs of two famous images of Ike: in Eisenhower jacket, sending off the troops on D-day, and in suit and tie, gazing at the presidential globe.

The outcry was immediate. The metal tapestry was a billboard and an iron curtain—an "Eisen Curtain." The fat columns were Coke cans, missile silos, fascist grandiosity. The rural mood and little boy in bronze came in for special opprobrium, especially from Eisenhower's granddaughters, outraged at seeing Ike's life distilled into "a Horatio Alger–like narrative," and insisting that "the man we celebrate is not a dreamy boy."[15] Congress withheld funds. Classicists held their own competition. Historians complained that Eisenhower's building the interstates, desegregating the schools, and warning against the military-industrial complex were slighted. Others found the design *nonmonumental*, even incomprehensible.

Negotiations ensued, changing little but saving face and making good on the handsome fees already paid. The image on the screen migrated from Kansas wheat fields to the cliffs of Pointe du Hoc at Normandy. The bas-reliefs became "heroic-sized" bronze statues of the same images. Several of the columns were eighty-sixed. Stone blocks were slightly adjusted. The little boy still sat in a corner. A hearty helping from the smorgasbord of precertified signifiers—abstraction, statuary, inscriptions, budding grove, stonework, pictures, pathways, soft green space, scrims—got it! It is hard to know how the outcome will feel as space, but I cannot help feeling a creepy transaction. Maybe a stretch, but Gehry's change of name and life and the Mall's increasingly dialogic, intertextual style somehow evokes a pairing with the Holocaust Museum, the suggestion of two paths for Jewry: assimilation or incineration.

The sculptor was born and educated in the Soviet Union, emigrated under *glasnost*. The tapestry is by a Pole.

Recently Received

A press release from the GWOT Memorial Foundation, a "congressionally-designated non-profit foundation tasked with organizing, fundraising and coordinating efforts to build a new memorial on the National Mall in Washington, D.C." It announced that an architect had been selected to help manage the "24-step process" required to secure approval to proceed. The acronym is for the Global War on Terror. The endless memorial.

Just In

In February 2020, Trump—our vaudeville Mussolini—issued an executive order entitled "Making Federal Buildings Beautiful Again," which commands that "the classical architectural style shall be the preferred and default style" for all future construction.

Endnotes

1. Quoted by John W. Kincheloe III, "Earliest American Explorers: Adventure and Survival," *Tar Heel Junior Historian* 47, no. 1 (Fall 2007): 6–8.
2. Alan Gallay, *The Indian Slave Trade: The Rise of the English Empire in the American South 1670–1717* (New Haven, CT: Yale University Press, 2002).
3. See, for example, Luthor Luedtke, "Ralph Waldo Emerson Envisions the 'Smelting Pot'," *Melus* 6, no. 2 (Summer 1979): 3–14.
4. Ian Shapira, "Before Asian Americans Sued Harvard, the School Once Tried Restricting Number of Jews," *Washington Post*, October 15, 2018, https://www.washingtonpost.com/news/retropolis/wp/2018/09/14/before-asian-americans-sued-harvard-the-school-tried-restricting-the-number-of-jews/.
5. Charles Dickens, *American Notes* (1842; repr., London: Penguin, 2000), 129–130. This account of Dickens's trip to the US is by turns hilarious, astute, and patronizing. He describes Washington as "the head-quarters of tobacco-tinctured saliva," of "those two odious practices of chewing and expectorating," habits which simultaneously revolt and fascinate him.
6. In "The Myth of Whiteness in Classical Sculpture" (*New Yorker*, October 22, 2018, https://www.newyorker.com/magazine/2018/10/29/the-myth-of-whiteness-in-classical-sculpture), Margaret Talbot points out that the idea of classical antiquity as glisteningly white is based on a fundamental misunderstanding. In fact, the sculpture and buildings of the Attic and Roman worlds were exuberantly, even garishly, painted. They *became* white.
7. "The Statue of Freedom | Architect of the Capitol," accessed July 16, 2020, https://www.aoc.gov/explore-capitol-campus/art/statue-freedom.
8. DeWayne Cuthbertson, "The Lady on the Dome," *Washington Post*, April 23, 1982, https://advance-lexis-com.exlibris.colgate.edu/api/document?collection=news&id=urn:-contentItem:3S8G-G1M0-0009-W3W0-00000-00&context=1516831.
9. Due to our long and cooperative relations (Lafayette, L'Enfant, de Toqueville, Rochambaud, et al.), the French get a pass on the othering sweeps.
10. Ronald Reagan, as cited in Martin A. Lee and Bruce Shlain, *Acid Dreams: The Complete Social History of LSD* (New York: Grove Weidenfeld, 1992), 163.
11. An anecdote was told during civil rights days about an African UN representative who unknowingly tried to order a meal at a segregated lunch counter. When refused, he showed his diplomatic credentials and demanded service. The proprietor replied: "Hell, I didn't know you was a diplomat, I thought you was just a n*****."
12. There is, as yet, no substantial commemoration of the Great War in the capital, and the Mall is full up. In 2014, a memorial was authorized by Congress for a site several blocks away on (appropriately enough) Pershing Square but decidedly not on the Mall. There was a competition, won by Joe Weishaar, a twenty-five-year-old architect, and Sabin Howard, a classical sculptor known for such works as "Hermes," "Apollo," and "Aphrodite." Their selection represents a reverse othering, a revanchist slap at modernist abstraction and at contemporary landscape design. This animus is dire, as Pershing Square is the site of a beautiful little park by M. Paul Friedberg, who has made his objections clear. The project is apparently being revised out of respect for its betters.

    The work itself—"The Weight of Sacrifice"—is a collage of regurgitated signifiers set in a Euclidean park, organized into three rectangular "rooms" (the FDR and MLK thing). Their geometry is informed by a connection to off-site markers (the Vietnam thing) in an attempt to garnish urbanity by association. The "interior" of the major room, enclosed by berms, is ringed by a "realistic" bronze frieze of life-sized doughboys leaving their families, battling the Boche, and returning home. Its expressive apparatus—sunkenness, representational sculpture, wall of text, park-like setting, zany arithmetic ("Each cubic foot of the memorial represents an American soldier lost in the war"; we are talking about air here)—is completely familiar. An entablature without a temple.

    The frieze is being fabricated at the Weta Workshop in New Zealand, which has expertise in a specialized technology: the use of 3-D computer modeling to create bronze statuary. The Workshop is mainly devoted to film work and has been involved in *Lord of* the Rings, *Planet of Apes*, and *Avatar*, among many others. One of their (highly germane) specialties is reproducing weapons and armor. There are two ways to computationally acquire an image that can be transformed into a physical object. The first is to create the thing from scratch in the computer, as an architect designs a building or Boeing an aircraft. The second is to precisely measure—using a sonar-like technology—an actual object (say, a medieval broadsword), creating a digital model that can be transmitted to the machinery that makes the mold for the bronze pour. Howard is using this technique to reproduce human models in First World War uniforms, thrusting their bayonets at nothing or otherwise soldiering on. This is another generic/specific romance, in which the computer guarantees the accuracy of the representation of individuals born almost a century after the war. Artists have always used models interpretatively, adding their own creative supplement. But the authority of Howard's work seems Warholian. Or Koonsian. What is on offer is the exactitude of the translation; the substitution of precision for personality.

13 It is, perhaps, of interest that Adjaye's skyscraper condo project in the Financial District has the same profile, with smaller serrations. And it is actually black.
14 Surprisingly, I have not found any evidence of conflict over the relative size of explicit representation. Lincoln, Jefferson, and King are very large. FDR is life-sized, as are—more or less—all those supernumerary troops.
15 Jeffrey Frank, "Rescuing the Eisenhower Memorial," *New Yorker*, March 25, 2013, https://www.newyorker.com/news/news-desk/rescuing-the-eisenhower-memorial.

CONTRIBUTORS

Mauro J. Caraccioli is assistant professor in the Department of Political Science and core faculty in the Alliance for Social, Political, Ethical, and Cultural Thought (ASPECT) at Virginia Tech. He writes on the interplay of faith, nature, and empire in the history of colonial Spanish America, as well as Latin American environmental politics. His current research considers the millenarian anxieties surrounding narratives of climate change and planetary collapse.

A Rio de Janeiro native, **Bruno Carvalho** approaches cities as lived and imagined spaces. His publications include *Porous City* (Liverpool University Press, 2013) and the co-edited *Occupy All Streets* (Terreform, 2016). He is writing a book on various ways in which people have imagined the future of cities since the 1700s. At Harvard, he is co-director of the Harvard Mellon Urban Initiative, professor in Romance Languages and Literatures and African and African American Studies, and affiliate professor at the Graduate School of Design.

Charmaine Chua is an assistant professor of Global Studies at the University of California, Santa Barbara. Her work explores the co-constitution of technologies of globalization, transpacific supply chains, and racialized dispossession in the context of US empire. Charmaine holds a PhD in Political Science from the University of Minnesota, Twin Cities. She is the review and open site editor for *Environment and Planning D: Society and Space* and a member of the *Abolition* journal collective.

William E. Connolly is Krieger-Eisenhower Professor at Johns Hopkins University, where he teaches political theory. His recent books include *Aspirational Fascism* (2017); *Facing the Planetary: Entangled Humanism and the Politics of Swarming* (2017); and *Climate Machines, Fascist Drives and Truth*

(2019). He is currently working on a political memoir that explores the intersections between memory, thinking, and events.

Mustafa Dikeç is professor of Urban Studies at the Ecole d'Urbanisme de Paris and visiting professor at Malmö University. He is the author of *Badlands of the Republic: Space, Politics and Urban Policy* (Blackwell, 2007); *Space, Politics and Aesthetics* (Edinburgh University Press, 2015); and *Urban Rage: The Revolt of the Excluded* (Yale University Press, 2017). He is currently working on a book project on the politics of time in nineteenth-century Paris.

Jairus Grove is the Director of the Hawai'i Research Center for Futures Studies and associate professor of International Relations at the University of Hawai'i at Manoa. His book *Savage Ecology: War and Geopolitics at the End of the World* is available via Duke University Press.

Waleed Hazbun is Richard L. Chambers Professor of Middle Eastern Studies in the Department of Political Science at the University of Alabama. He previously taught at the American University of Beirut. He is the author of *Beaches, Ruins, Resorts: The Politics of Tourism in the Arab World* (Minnesota, 2008), a coeditor of *New Conflict Dynamics* (Copenhagen, 2017), and a founding member of the "Critical Security Studies in the Arab World" working group supported by the Beirut-based Arab Council for the Social Sciences.

Andrew Herscher is a cofounding member of a series of militant research collaboratives including the *We the People of Detroit Community Research Collective*, *Detroit Resists*, and the *Settler Colonial City Project*. In his own writing, he works across a range of global sites to explore the architecture of political violence, displacement and migration, and self-determination and resistance. Among his books are *Violence Taking Place: The Architecture of the Kosovo Conflict* (Stanford University Press, 2010), *The Unreal Estate Guide to Detroit* (University of Michigan Press, 2012), *Displacements: Architecture and Refugee* (Sternberg Press, 2017), and *Spatial Violence*, coedited with Anooradha Iyer Siddiqi (Routledge, 2017). He is an associate professor in Architecture, Art History, and Slavic Languages and Literatures at the University of Michigan.

CONTRIBUTORS

Alex Liebman is a PhD student in human geography at Rutgers University. He is exploring how agricultural data science reproduces particular forms of standardization and homogeneity that constitute racialized and exclusionary forms of international development and environmental management across the Global South. His work is focused on agrarian frontier zones in Colombia. He has an MSc in agronomy from University of Minnesota and a BA from Macalester College.

China Miéville is the writer of various works of fiction and nonfiction, including *The City & The City* and *This Census-Taker*, and *October: The Story of the Russian Revolution*. He is a founding editor of the journal *Salvage*.

Don Mitchell is professor of Cultural Geography at Uppsala University and Distinguished Professor of Geography Emeritus at Syracuse University. His most recent books are *They Saved the Crops: Landscape, Labor and the Struggle Over Industrial Farming in Bracero Era California* (2012), *Revolting New York: How 400 Years of Riot, Rebellion, Uprising, and Revolution Shaped a City* (with the late Neil Smith, 2018), and *Mean Streets: Homelessness, Public Space, and the Limits of Capital* (2020).

Daniel Bertrand Monk holds the George R. and Myra T. Chair in Peace and Conflict Studies at Colgate University, where he is professor of Geography and Middle East Studies. He is the author of *An Aesthetic Occupation* as well as a number of other studies on the territorial and spatial practices of the Israel-Palestine conflict. He has written about Middle East Wars, the Geography of the Post-Conflict Environment, Refugees and Humanitarianism. Monk has been awarded a MacArthur Foundation Fellowship in International Peace and Security [SSRC-CIPS], as well as a Woodrow Wilson Fellowship [WWICS] for his research on contemporary conflict.

Jacob Mundy is an associate professor of Peace and Conflict Studies and Middle Eastern and Islamic Studies at Colgate University. His books include *Western Sahara: War, Nationalism, and Conflict Irresolution* (Syracuse University Press, 2015), coauthored with Stephen Zunes; *The Post-Conflict Environment* (University of Michigan Press, 2014), coedited with Daniel Bertrand Monk;

Imaginative Geographies of Algerian Violence (Stanford University Press, 2015); and *Libya* (Polity Press 2018). During the 2018–19 academic year, he taught courses at the Université de Tunis in political economy as a Fulbright Scholar.

Ana Muñiz is an assistant professor in the Department of Criminology, Law and Society at the University of California, Irvine. She is the author of *Police, Power, and the Production of Racial Boundaries* (Rutgers University Press, 2015) and the forthcoming book *Borderland Circuitry: Immigration Surveillance in the United States and Beyond* (University of California Press, 2022).

Kenichi Okamoto is an assistant professor in the Department of Biology at the University of Saint Thomas in Saint Paul, Minnesota.

Christian Parenti is associate professor of economics at John Jay College, City University of New York. His books include *Radical Hamilton: How Big Government Industrialized America* (Verso 2020); *Tropic of Chaos: Climate Change and the New Geography of Violence* (2011); *The Freedom: Shadows and Hallucinations in Occupied Iraq* (2004); *The Soft Cage: Surveillance in America from Slavery to the War on Terror* (2002); and *Lockdown America: Police and Prisons in the Age of Crisis* (2000/second edition 2008). He has reported extensively from Afghanistan, Iraq, and various parts of Africa, Asia, and Latin America for *The Nation*, *Fortune*, *The London Review of Books*, *The New York Times*, and other publications.

Andrew Ross is professor of Social and Cultural Analysis and director of the American Studies Program at NYU. A contributor to the *Guardian*, the *New York Times*, *The Nation*, and *Al Jazeera*, he is the author or editor of more than twenty books, including *Stone Men: The Palestinians Who Built Israel*, *Creditocracy and the Case for Debt Refusal*, *Bird On Fire*, *Nice Work if You Can Get It*, *Fast Boat to China*, *No-Collar*, and *The Celebration Chronicles*.

Michael Sorkin was Distinguished Professor of Architecture and Director of the Graduate Program in Urban Design at the City College of New York. He was the principal of Michael Sorkin Studio—a design practice with a particular interest in urbanism and sustainable building—and president of Terreform, a

CONTRIBUTORS

nonprofit urban research and advocacy center and the publisher of UR Books, for which Sorkin was editor-in-chief. Sorkin was also architecture critic for *The Nation* and the author of many books and projects. Sorkin passed away on 26 March 2020 from COVID-19.

Rob Wallace is an evolutionary biologist and public health phylogeographer with the Agroecology and Rural Economics Research Corps (ARERC). He is coauthor of *Neoliberal Ebola: Modeling Disease Emergence from Finance to Forest and Farm* (Springer, 2016) and *Clear-Cutting Disease Control: Capital-Led Deforestation, Public Health Austerity, and Vector-Borne Infection* (Springer, 2018). He has consulted for the Food and Agriculture Organization of the United Nations and the Centers for Disease Control and Prevention (CDC).

www.ingramcontent.com/pod-product-compliance
Lightning Source LLC
Chambersburg PA
CBHW020240030426

42336CB00010B/559